Migration in South Africa:
Conflicts and Identities

EDITED BY

Eddie M. Rakabe

&

Chris C. Nshimbi

MAPUNGUBWE
INSTITUTE FOR STRATEGIC REFLECTION (MISTRA)

First published by the Mapungubwe Institute for Strategic Reflection (MISTRA) in 2024

142 Western Service Road
Woodmead
Johannesburg

ISBN 978-1-991274-01-4

© MISTRA, 2024

Production and design by Jacana Media, 2024
Cover design: Hothouse
Text editor: Terry Shakinovsky
Copy editor: Lara Jacob
Proofreader: Megan Mance
Indexer: Ali Parry
Designer: Sam van Straaten
Set in Stempel Garamond 10.5/15pt

Please cite this publication as follows:
MISTRA. 2024. *Migration in South Africa: Conflicts and Identities.* **Eddie M. Rakabe and Chris C. Nshimbi (eds). Johannesburg: Mapungubwe Institute for Strategic Reflection**

Other books published by MISTRA

MAPUNGUBWE
INSTITUTE FOR STRATEGIC REFLECTION (MISTRA)

Why Innovations Live or Die (2024)

The Evolving Structure of South Africa's Economy: Faultlines and Futures (2023)

Protest in South Africa: Rejection, Reassertion, Reclamation (2023)

A Just Transition to a Low Carbon Future in South Africa (2022)

Youth in South Africa: Agency (In)visibility and National Development (2022)

Marriages of Inconvenience: The Politics of Coalitions in South Africa (2021)

Mintirho Ya Vulavula: Arts, National Identities and Democracy in South Africa (2021)

Land in South Africa: Contested Meanings and Nation Formation (2021)

LEAP 4.0: African Perspectives on the Fourth Industrial Revolution (2020)

Africa and the World: Navigating Shifting Geopolitics (2020)

Beyond Tenderpreneurship: Rethinking Black Business and Economic Empowerment (2020)

The Future of Mining in South Africa: Sunset or Sunrise? (2019)

Epidemics and the Health of African Nations (2019)

Traditional Leaders in a Democracy: Resources, Respect and Resistance (2019)

Beyond Imagination: The Ethics and Applications of Nanotechnology and Bio-Economics in South Africa (2018)

Whiteness, Afrikaans, Afrikaners: Addressing Post-Apartheid Legacies, Privileges and Burdens (2018)

The Pedagogy of Mathematics in South Africa: Is There a Unifying Logic? (2017)

Seeking the Ethical Foundations of the South African Nation (2017)

Reimagining Basic Education in South Africa: Lessons from the Eastern Cape (2017)

Changing Economic Balances and Integration in 'Africa Rising' (2017)

The Great Recession and its Implications for Human Values: Lessons for Africa (2016)

The Emergence of Systems of Innovation in South(ern) Africa: Long Histories and Contemporary Debates (2016)

The Role of Intellectuals in the State–Society Nexus (2016)

Resurgent Resource Nationalism? A Study into the Global Phenomenon (2016)

20 Years of South African Democracy: So Where to Now? (2015)

Earth, Wind and Fire: Unpacking the Political, Economic and Security Implications of Discourse on the Green Economy (2015)

Mapungubwe Reconsidered: A Living Legacy – Exploring Beyond the Rise and Decline of the Mapungubwe State (2015)

The Rise and Decline and Rise of China: Searching for an Organising Philosophy (2015)

Nation Formation and Social Cohesion: An Enquiry into the Hopes and Aspirations of South Africans (2014)

Essays on the Evolution of the Post-Apartheid State: Legacies, Reforms and Prospects (2013)

Patronage Politics Divides Us: A Study of Poverty, Patronage and Inequality in South Africa (2013)

South Africa and the Global Hydrogen Economy: The Strategic Role of Platinum Group Metals (2013)

The Concept and Application of Transdisciplinarity in Intellectual Discourse and Research (2013)

From Agriculture to Agricology: Towards a Glocal Circular Economy (2013)

The Art, Philosophy and Science of Football in South Africa (2013)

Visit the MISTRA website for more information:

Contents

Preface ix

Acknowledgements. xii

List of Contributors xiv

List of Abbreviations xix

Chapter 1:   Introduction: Deciphering international migration
               towards South Africa: Theoretical underpinnings,
               policy and practice
               – *Chris C. Nshimbi with Wandile M. Ngcaweni* 1

SECTION ONE:
SOCIAL COHESION, MIGRATION AND IDENTITY

Chapter 2:   Mobilities past and mobilities present in the Southern
               African Development Community (SADC) region:
               An epigrammatic overview
               – *Chris C. Nshimbi* 27

Chapter 3:   Native migrant animosity – aggrieved, not xenophobic:
               The case of South Africa
               – *Vusumuzi Gumbi* 54

Chapter 4:   Migrants, the politics of belonging and social cohesion
               in post-apartheid South Africa
               – *Sifiso Ndlovu* 79

Chapter 5:   Unlocking international migrant domestic workers'
             agency in claiming the right to compensation for
             occupational injuries and diseases in South Africa
             – *Janet Munakamwe* 101

SECTION TWO:
MIGRATION AND SOUTH AFRICA'S
POLITICAL ECONOMY

Chapter 6:   Gendered dimensions of migration in South Africa:
             Governance and implications for livelihoods
             – *David Fadiran and Hammed Amusa* 125

Chapter 7:   Migrants' lived experience of the nutrition transition in
             Johannesburg: Understanding dietary change through
             participatory research
             – *Brittany Kesselman* 164

Chapter 8:   Exploring the structural nexus between migration,
             retail conglomerates and township spaza shops
             – *Amuzweni Ngoma and Wandile M. Ngcaweni* . . . 191

Chapter 9:   Rethinking migrant human settlement as an advantage
             to township dwellers: The case of Soweto
             – *Malaika Lesego Samora Mahlatsi* 219

Chapter 10: Internal migration, spatial divisions and the
             redistribution dilemma in South Africa
             – *Eddie M. Rakabe* 240

SECTION THREE:
THE STATE AND MIGRATION GOVERNANCE

Chapter 11: Migration governance in South Africa
             – *Eddie M. Rakabe, Wandile M. Ngcaweni and Gabriel
             Lubale* 275

Chapter 12: Securitisation of borders and migration in the context

Contents

of uneven regional development in southern Africa
– *Innocent Moyo* 297

Chapter 13: The digital policy on asylum protection in South Africa
– *Lindokuhle Mdabe*......................... 313

Chapter 14: Conclusion: Whole-of-route approach to migration
– *Eddie M. Rakabe* 327

Preface

Mobility has been part of human ways for millennia. Many factors influence people's migration for settlement in areas perceived as providing better circumstances for individuals, families and communities. These include environmental, economic, political and other oscillations in natural and social phenomena. Fission and fusion have been both cause and effect of migration.

With the emergence of nation-states, the regulation of migration became a critical part of public policy, generating all manner of contestation within and among nations. Intra- and inter-state conflicts, rising inequality, increasing incidence of natural disasters and improved networks of communication and transport have added new impetus to this trend.

There have been growing campaigns within many host societies to stem what is perceived as a flood of aliens threatening both socioeconomic and cultural ways of life. Others have argued for a more holistic and humanitarian approach, citing both the push and pull factors that generate mass migration.

Regional and global conventions have sought to find sustainable approaches to the migration challenge, in addition to domestic attempts. The more securitised the approach, the more the human ingenuity of desperation comes into play, rendering such efforts largely ineffective. On the other hand, turning a blind eye to social concerns, especially those arising from irregular migration, has the effect of feeding xenophobic impulses.

African migration experiences are not much different from those in other regions of the world. But they are also informed by the unique history of a continent whose nation-states were carved artificially on the basis of colonial conquests. In the process, nationalities and even families were rent asunder, rendering borderlines virtually meaningless. The colonial political economies also fashioned economic centres and peripheries within countries and regions, with developmental path dependencies that have endured into the post-colonial era.

It is in this context that the South African experience of migration has evolved. Its modern roots are found in the emergence of the agricultural, mining and manufacturing complex, which generated the demand for cheap labour from internal and cross-border labour reserves. The post-apartheid period has also given rise to unique push-and-pull factors, with South Africa a leading destination of choice for regional and other migrants because of the country's relatively stable political, economic and social environment.

This book, *Migration in South Africa: Conflicts and Identities*, interrogates migration patterns and policy debates in the country, collocating these with experiences across the continent and further afield. The authors trace the historical evolution of migration to and within South Africa against the backdrop of an evolving regional political economy. They interrogate the resentment of marginalised 'native' communities struggling to access benefits that were meant to come with political freedom, issues of identity and prejudices that attach to the 'othering' of migrants. Some chapters also provide insights into the mutual co-existence and benefit accruing in areas where migrants have settled, as well as the joint struggles of citizens and migrants in specific occupations such as domestic work.

Generic trends prevalent in many countries such as variegated treatment of skilled and unskilled migrants, and relative preponderance of migrants in some trades and informal businesses, are also examined. So is the gendered perspective on the growing independent migration of women, which is redefining traditional gender roles, and the impact of nutritional transitions associated with dietary changes.

The discussion with the former Minister of Home Affairs on the evolution of South Africa's migration policies, including the treatment of refugees – which anchors one of the chapters – seeks to clarify the country's approach to various international conventions and how practical experience has led to proposed legislative changes.

This volume approaches the issue of migration from a transdisciplinary perspective, straddling social and economic factors as well as gender, race, culture and identity, and the elusive sense of belonging. What is clear is that a humanitarian approach needs to be combined with the effective application of laws – keeping in mind Africa's long-term objective of free movement of goods and people.

The Mapungubwe Institute for Strategic Reflection (MISTRA) is hugely indebted to the authors, peer reviewers and coordinators responsible for this volume. Our deep gratitude also goes to the funders, including the Department of Home Affairs, which have made this and other research endeavours possible.

Joel Netshitenzhe
Executive Director

Acknowledgements

The Mapungubwe Institute for Strategic Reflection (MISTRA) would like to express its sincere gratitude to the editors of this volume, Chris C. Nshimbi and Eddie M. Rakabe. Gratitude also goes to the project coordinator, Wandile M. Ngcaweni.

Thank you to the MISTRA staff who contributed to the successful outcome of this project: the Research Director, Susan Booysen, for her continuous efforts to ensure that the publication meets the highest standards; to Lorraine Pillay for fundraising and financial management activities with support from Magati Nindi-Galenge; to Terry Shakinovsky for editing and overseeing the publication process. Deepest gratitude also goes to Joel Netshitenzhe for his thorough reading of the manuscript.

MISTRA is honoured to have worked with the researchers who contributed to the work in this volume – our grateful thanks to you all. Thanks also go to the blind peer reviewers, whose suggestions and input were invaluable.

MISTRA extends its appreciation to Jacana Media, who was responsible for the editing and proofreading, design and layout, cover design and production of the publication.

MISTRA FUNDERS

Intellectual endeavours of this magnitude are not possible without financial resources. Special thanks go to the Department of Home Affairs for their support of this project. MISTRA also thanks the donors who support the Institute and make its work possible. They include:

Anglo American Platinum
Aspen Pharmacare
Batho Batho Trust
Department of Science and Innovation
Department of Home Affairs
Discovery Central Services
Friedrich-Ebert-Stiftung (FES)
Oppenheimer Memorial Trust (OMT)
Standard Bank
Transnet
Yellowwoods

List of Contributors

Amuzweni Ngoma is a director at the Gauteng Department of Education where she manages the conceptualisation and implementation of large-scale skills development projects. She holds a Master's degree and PhD in Sociology from the University of the Witwatersrand and Rhodes University respectively. She is the co-editor of a MISTRA book titled *The Evolving Structure of South Africa's Economy: Faultlines and Futures*. Amuzweni is a seasoned researcher, having managed multiple research projects. Her publications span a range of topics, from party political coalition practice to the influence of mega-churches on the black middle class. Amuzweni is an investment committee member of the National Treasury's Jobs Fund.

Brittany Kesselman is a postdoctoral research fellow with the Bioeconomy Chair at the University of Cape Town (UCT). Her work focuses on the relationship between agroecology (as science, practice and movement) and traditional/indigenous food and farming knowledge and practices, in order to better understand how they can be brought together to contribute to a more sustainable, decolonised food system in South Africa. Brittany's prior research as a postdoctoral research fellow at the Society, Work & Politics Institute (SWOP) examined pathways to urban food justice, dietary change and the impact of colonialism on food and health. Her PhD research, at the University of KwaZulu-Natal (UKZN), focused on the contribution of urban community food gardens to food sovereignty in Johannesburg.

Chris C. Nshimbi is Director of GovInn (Centre for the Study of Governance Innovation), SARChI Chair in the Political Economy of Migration in the SADC Region and Associate Professor in the Department of Political Sciences, University of Pretoria. He researches and teaches migration, borders, regional integration, the informal economy and water governance.

David Fadiran holds a PhD in Economics from the University of Cape Town (UCT), a Master's degree from Northern Illinois University (NIU), a Master's degree from the University of Wisconsin-Milwaukee (UWM) and a Bachelor's degree in Economics & Statistics from the University of eSwatini. He is an experienced economist, with a focus on institutional economics, natural resource economics and local government dynamics, with a keen interest in applying spatial econometric analysis to these topics. Other research interests include the intersections of institutions with international trade, illicit financial flows and economic performance. David is a Junior Research Fellow (JRF) of PRISM, in the School of Economics at UCT and has done work for the United Nations University (UNU-WIDER), the African Development Bank (AfDB) and Council for the Development of Social Science Research in Africa (CODESRIA).

Eddie M. Rakabe is a senior researcher for Political Economy at the Mapungubwe Institute for Strategic Reflection (MISTRA). Prior to joining MISTRA, he worked at the Financial and Fiscal Commission focusing on public education and health finance, housing, public expenditure management and intergovernmental fiscal relations. He has also worked as an economist at the National Treasury and for the South African Square Kilometre Array project.

Gabriel Lubale holds a PhD in Business Administration and a Master's degree in Business Administration. He has a background in human resources and extensive experience in leadership roles within the public service of Kenya. He is currently a Principal Immigration Officer, Head of the Kenya Institute for Migration Studies (KIMS) and deployed as an Adjunct Lecturer at the University of Nairobi in the Department of Geography, Population and Environmental Studies.

Hammed Amusa is currently a research economist in the Macroeconomic Policy, Debt Sustainability and Forecasting Division of the African Development Bank (AfDB), where he is tasked with leading and contributing to analytical and research work focusing on macroeconomic issues relevant for the Bank's regional member countries, the Bank's High 5 agenda, as well as the Bank's knowledge management activities. Prior to joining the AfDB, Amusa was with the Macroeconomic & Public Finance Unit of the Financial and Fiscal Commission in South Africa where his work dealt with research on macroeconomic aspects of the South African economy, public finance and the South Africa's intergovernmental fiscal relations system, as well as implications of exogenous macroeconomic factors, regional integration initiatives and global economic relations on the South African economy. An experienced economist of over 15 years, Amusa has also served as lecturer with the Department of Economics at the University of Pretoria and was a Visiting Research Fellow at the University of Johannesburg's School of Economics. As a Carter G. Woodson scholar, Amusa obtained his PhD and MA in Economics from Northern Illinois University. He also holds both a BA (Social Sciences) and an MA in Economics from the University of Botswana. Passionate about the application of programming languages and econometric software to analysing economic-related data, Amusa's research interests are in the fields of public finance, macroeconomic analysis, development economics, applied economics and public policy.

Innocent Moyo is an associate professor in the Department of Geography and Environmental Studies at the University of Zululand, South Africa. He researches borders and migration and the political economy of the informal economy in the southern African region.

Janet Munakamwe is a pan-African feminist scholar. Currently, she serves as a senior visiting lecturer at the Wits Mining Institute, University of the Witwatersrand. A labour migration policy specialist, she graduated with a Migration & Development PhD from the African Centre for Migration & Society, University of the Witwatersrand. She is the chairperson of the African Diaspora Workers Network (ADWN).

Lindokuhle Mdabe holds an LLB (Wits) and LLM (UKZN). He has been a human rights lawyer and activist for 10 years. He has written and litigated on several issues, including refugee law, housing and evictions, constitutional and administrative law. He is the co-founder of the LAIC Law Clinic and former head of the Johannesburg Law Clinic at Lawyers for Human Rights. He is currently the director at Mametja Attorneys.

Malaika Lesego Samora Mahlatsi is a geographer and researcher at the Institute for Pan African Thought and Conversation, University of Johannesburg. She is a research consultant at the Centre on African Public Spaces (CAPS) and the board secretary of the Mzwandile Masina Foundation for Education (MMF). She holds a Master's degree in Public Affairs (Food Security) from the Tshwane University of Technology, a Master's degree in Urban and Regional Planning from the University of Johannesburg and a Master's of Science (Water Resource Science) from Rhodes University. She is currently a PhD candidate and research fellow at the University of Bayreuth, Germany.

Sifiso Ndlovu holds a PhD from the University of the Witwatersrand. She is a political science lecturer at the University of Mpumalanga. She previously held a postdoctoral research fellowship at the Johannesburg Institute for Advanced Studies (JIAS)-University of Johannesburg and Public Affairs Research Institute (PARI). She has published journal articles and book chapters on the politics of belonging, nation-building and Ndebele ethnicity.

Vusumuzi Gumbi is a research assistant at the Institute for Pan African Thought and Conversation (IPATC) at the University of Johannesburg. He obtained his Master's in Politics – cum laude – where his dissertation explored the role of symbolism in voter choice and electoral outcome. He obtained a distinction for his BA (Honours) dissertation, which explored the accountability deficit in the South African parliament. His research interests in elections and political processes, democracy and governance institutions were reinforced through deployment as part of the EISA International Election Observation Missions to the

2017 elections in Lesotho and 2019 elections in Mozambique led by former presidents Rupiah Banda (Zambia) and John Dramani Mahama (Ghana) respectively. He is a published researcher and occasionally writes opinion editorials and gives political analysis. In 2020, he won South Africa's Youth Leadership Debate Show, One Day Leader, run by the public broadcaster, the SABC.

Wandile M. Ngcaweni is an associate researcher for Political Economy at the Mapungubwe Institute for Strategic Reflection (MISTRA). He has a Master's in Critical Diversity Studies from the University of the Witwatersrand.

List of Abbreviations

AfDB	African Development Bank
ANC	African National Congress
ATM	African Transformation Movement
AU	African Union
BASA	Banking Association South Africa
BMA	Border Management Authority
CBD	central business district
CCMA	Commission for Conciliation, Mediation and Arbitration
CEE	Commission for Employment Equity
COIDA	Compensation for Occupational Injuries and Diseases Act
CoJ	City of Johannesburg
COSATU	Congress of South African Trade Unions
CRDP	Comprehensive Rural Development Programme
DAC	Department of Arts and Culture
DEL	Department of Employment and Labour
DHA	Department of Home Affairs
DIRCO	Department of International Relations and Cooperation
DRC	Democratic Republic of the Congo
DSBD	Department of Small Business Development
DTIC	Department of Trade, Industry and Competition
EAC	East African Community
EU	European Union
FAO	Food and Agriculture Organization
FDI	foreign direct investment
FRONTEX	European Border and Coast Guard Agency
FTA	free trade agreement
GBV	gender-based violence
GCM	Global Compact for Safe, Orderly and Regular Migration

GDP	gross domestic product
GMDAC	Global Migration Data Analysis Centre
GRDP	gross regional domestic product
HSRC	Human Sciences Research Council
ICBTs	informal cross-border traders
ICC	International Criminal Court
ICESCR	International Covenant on Economic, Social and Cultural Rights
ICRMW	International Convention on the Protection of the Rights of All Migrants and Members of Their Families
ICT	information and communication technology
IDZs	industrial development zones
IGAD	Intergovernmental Authority on Development
IHRL	International Human Rights Law
ILO	International Labour Organization
IMF	International Monetary Fund
IOM	International Organization for Migration
ISS	international security studies
LDCs	least-developed countries
LGBTIQ+	lesbian, gay, bisexual, trans, intersex, queer, asexual +
MFLM	Multilateral Framework on Labour Migration
MGI	Migration Governance Indicators
MiGOF	Migration Governance Framework
MROs	migrant-rights organisations
NCDs	non-communicable diseases
NDP	National Development Plan
NDPG	Neighbourhood Development Partnership Grant
Nedlac	National Economic Development and Labour Council
NELM	new economies of labour migration
NGO	non-governmental organisation
NHI	National Health Insurance
NICC	National Intelligence Co-ordinating Committee
NIIS	National Immigration Information System
NNSSF	National Norms and Standards for School Funding
NRA	New Regionalism Approach
NSDP	National Spatial Development Perspective
OAU	Organisation of African Unity

OECD	Organisation for Economic Co-operation and Development
PA	Patriotic Alliance
PAIA	Promotion of Access to Information Act
PAJA	Promotion of Administrative Justice Act
PEPs	public employment programmes POPI ... Protection of Personal Information Act
PILOs	public interest law organisations
RDP	Reconstruction and Development Programme
REC	regional economic community
RIDMP	Regional Infrastructure Development Master Plan 2012–2017
RRO	Refugee Reception Office
RSDO	refugee status determination officer
SACN	South African Cities Network
SACU	Southern African Customs Union
SADC	Southern African Development Community
SADSAWU	South African Domestic Service and Allied Workers Union
SAHRC	South African Human Rights Commission
SAPS	South African Police Service
SDGs	Sustainable Development Goals
SDIs	spatial development initiatives
SETAs	Sector Education and Training Authorities
SEZs	special economic zones
SIBG	School Infrastructure Backlog Grant
SISR	SADC Industrialisation Strategy and Roadmap 2015–2063
SLF	Sustainable Livelihoods Foundation
SMMEs	small, medium and micro enterprises
SSA	sub-Saharan Africa
TBVC	Transkei, Bophuthatswana, Venda and Ciskei
THUSA	Transition and Health during Urbanisation of South Africans
UDHR	Universal Declaration of Human Rights
UDWOSA	United Domestic Workers of South Africa
UIF	Unemployment Insurance Fund
UK	United Kingdom
UN	United Nations

List of Abbreviations

UNDESA	United Nations Department of Economic and Social Affairs
UNDP	United Nations Development Programme
UNHCR	United Nations High Commissioner for Refugees
UNOCHA	United Nations Office for the Coordination of Humanitarian Affairs
UNSC	United Nations Security Council
USA	United States of America
USDG	Urban Settlements Development Grant
WDI	World Development Indicators
ZEP	Zimbabwe exemption permit

ONE

Introduction: Deciphering international migration towards South Africa: Theoretical underpinnings, policy and practice

CHRIS C. NSHIMBI
WITH WANDILE M. NGCAWENI

Migration has long shaped the political and socioeconomic history of South Africa and the southern African region. It is a significant factor in South Africa's historic development from pre-colonial times up to and beyond the apartheid and colonial eras. The focus on migration in the public domain is exemplified in debates and political contestations to regulate it. There are contrasting views on the effects of migration in South Africa and appropriate remedial and regulatory policy measures to deal with these realities. However, these public debates are constrained by insufficient data and research on post-apartheid migration, and how it impacts on politics, governance and socioeconomic conditions.

This book attempts to address this deficit and add to the work on migration in South Africa. The contributions in the volume explore various issues relating to international migration towards South Africa, including the intersection between socioeconomic rights, identity and social cohesion. Chapters also interrogate the changing nature of migrant livelihood strategies in South Africa in view of tense competition for limited economic opportunities and the changing spatial economic landscape. Further, contributing authors document emerging practices aimed at tightening immigration controls in the country. Authors explore debates in the public domain, policy circles and literature on migration towards South Africa from other African countries – especially Zimbabwe, Nigeria, eSwatini, Lesotho, Malawi and Mozambique.

Most of the debates in the relevant literature focus on the economic aspects of migration and depict migrants from the cited countries as seeking relief from dire conditions in their countries of origin (Mawadza, 2008; Kalitanyi and Visser, 2010; Crush and Tevera, 2010; Crush et al., 2012; Odok, 2019). Some of this literature also discusses violations of migrants' human rights; social cohesion and discord; the mistreatment of migrants; populism and the politicisation of migration; and government policy approaches to managing mixed migration (Segatti and Landau, 2011; Kwenge, 2020; Isike and Isike, 2022). 'Mixed' migration refers to the movement of people for varied reasons, e.g., for economic or education incentives or fear of prosecution.

The contributions in this volume also challenge a fixation on economic drivers at the cost of neglecting other equally important aspects of migration. Some of these economic drivers relate to debates that focus on gendered dependencies, insecurity and the vulnerability of migrants. These debates present migrants as desperately risking their lives to scale rough terrain and cross crocodile-infested rivers for a living in South Africa (Mawadza, 2008; Rutherford, 2020; Tshimpaka and Inaka, 2020). Further, they argue that the migrants are willing to live and work in precarious conditions in the host country, if only to escape difficult conditions in their countries of origin (Hlatshwayo, 2019; Jinnah, 2020). According to this narrative, migrants adopt economic and survivalist strategies, which entail willingly and readily accepting any jobs to support their own livelihoods in the host country and those of family and relatives back home. However, chapters 4 and 6 in this book challenge this notion and suggest that migrants increasingly display agency and can have a positive influence on their own migration trajectory and experience through various forms of protest and advocacy.

A few other debates on migration in southern Africa extend the discussion to historical and sociocultural factors and the significance of such factors in understanding migration in the region. Southern Africa boasts a long history of human interaction and migration that predates the Westphalian state and is defined by strong relationships between ethnic groups who transverse the nation-state borders of the countries of the region (Mlambo, 2010; Nshimbi, 2015, 2019; Moyo, 2016). Migration for people who belong to such groups can be seen as more about kinship ties and fulfilling sociocultural obligations and needs than economic drivers (Nshimbi, 2019). Further debates emphasise the importance of social capital within networks of migrants across nation-state borders in southern Africa (Nshimbi, 2015).

Some of the contributions in this volume engage with historical and sociocultural aspects of migration in southern Africa and towards South Africa. Chapter 2 of the book particularly expands on historical ties through the lens of accumulation by dispossession to show how migrants in southern Africa were inserted in a pattern of forced migration and intrinsically tied into an exploitative South African labour market.

It is worth reiterating and emphasising that economic drivers dominate explanations of migration towards South Africa. However, the interest in debates that privilege economic drivers is that they lead to questions of contest and competition for resources, social services and, even, social relationships, between migrants and their hosts. This is despite overwhelming evidence that fits migration realities into some of the underlying theoretical views briefly highlighted in the foregoing discussion.

Built into questions of competition for resources are accusations that migrants steal jobs and take away economic opportunities from their hosts (Crush and Ramachandran, 2016). Further, the hosts blame migrants for declining socioeconomic conditions and the poor

3

provision of services in the host country. Tensions between migrants and their hosts and within host communities are, therefore, attributed to the presence of migrants and the ways in which the hosts perceive the migrants. The hosts consider migrants a threat to their wellbeing. Politicians, policymakers and populists who exploit anti-immigration sentiments adopt this narrative and couch it in language that frames migrants as a threat to the security of host communities and the country, as the third section of this introductory chapter theorises. Chapter 3 of this book examines the depiction of migrants as a threat and discusses tensions between them and host communities further, arguing that 'indlala ibanga ulaka' (hunger causes anger). Chapter 8 explores the complex intersection between regional economies, local economies and migrants' livelihood strategies.

This introductory chapter presents some underlying theoretical debates and everyday migration practices and realities with a focus on southern Africa and particularly South Africa. The contributions in this book extend and apply some of these viewpoints (and others) to the South African context, as outlined at the end of this chapter.

The first section of this chapter presents an overview of recent trends and patterns of migration in the southern African region, particularly towards South Africa. This section highlights some of the key drivers of migration flows towards South Africa, as well as major post-apartheid immigration legislation and policy responses.

The second section of this introduction discusses some dominant theoretical and pragmatic approaches to understanding migration governance in southern Africa, namely, the so-called 'push-pull' approach; the new economics of labour migration (NELM); the migration–development nexus and the securitisation approach. Among these theoretical perspectives, the securitisation approach seems to dominate the lens through which South Africa and other southern African states and populist politicians seem to approach international migration in the region. This stance clearly contrasts with a commitment to harnessing migration for development at regional and continental levels (SADC, 2005; African Union, 1991, 2006, 2018a, 2018b).

The third section of this chapter explores the securitisation approach through a discussion of the South African government's policies and legislative positions on international migration. These are evident in, among other initiatives, the 2023 proposal to overhaul the country's immigration system and the 2017 White Paper on International Migration (DHA, 2017).

The fourth section recounts some migration realities in South Africa and the surrounding region and takes stock of the South African government's view. The last section of this chapter outlines the structure of the book.

OVERVIEW OF HISTORICAL TRENDS AND PATTERNS OF MIGRATION TOWARDS SOUTH AFRICA

The patterns and trends in migration in southern Africa and towards South Africa broadly mirror those globally. For instance, the immigrant population in South Africa is about 2.4 million or approximately 3 per cent of the country's total population (Statistics South Africa, 2022). This corresponds with figures at the global level, where approximately 96.4 per cent of the world's population lives in countries of birth (UNDESA, 2020; IOM, 2020).

The top five countries that contribute to the immigrant population in South Africa are Zimbabwe, Mozambique, Lesotho, Malawi and the United Kingdom (Moyo and Nshimbi, 2019; Statistics South Africa, 2022: 32). However, patterns and trends in migration in southern Africa are complex and historically unique, as detailed in some of the chapters in this book (see, for instance, chapters 2, 3 and 10). The history and patterns of migration in the region are somewhat different from the established global migration logic and follow entrenched colonial patterns involving capital accumulation.

White settler colonialism has notably had a significant and enduring role in migration towards South Africa and within the wider region. Some of the many Europeans who migrated and permanently settled in Africa in the 19th century engaged in large-scale agriculture in countries like post-colonial South Africa and Zimbabwe. They exploited local and immigrant labour from within the African continent and from places as far-flung as British colonial territories in the Indian subcontinent. With the discovery of gold and diamonds,

5

others ventured into mining in Johannesburg and Kimberley at the end of the 19th and beginning of the 20th centuries. This entailed large numbers of workers migrating from within what would become South Africa and neighbouring countries now known as eSwatini, Lesotho, Malawi, Mozambique and Zimbabwe to supply labour for the mines (Nshimbi and Fioramonti, 2013). Contract labour in the agriculture and mining sectors has thus constituted a major, enduring contributor to migration towards South Africa (and in the southern African region in general) since the early 20th century and before. Later, and more recently, the construction and service sectors also attracted migrant labour to South Africa, especially in the post-colonial era.

The colonial and post-colonial periods also witnessed flows of forcefully displaced persons fleeing conflict, war and economic turmoil in neighbouring countries. The people sought asylum or refuge in what is now South Africa, among other countries, in what has become the Southern African Development Community (SADC) region.

Although the post-apartheid regime in South Africa pursues a restrictive migration policy (Crush and Peberdy, 2003), it has granted amnesties to undocumented migrants, asylum seekers and refugees from neighbouring countries such as Mozambique and Zimbabwe (Nshimbi and Fioramonti, 2013).

In particular, undocumented Zimbabwean migrants have most recently had their amnesties extended to allow them to formalise their immigration status through special dispensation permits. According to Moyo (2018), these permits are granted on a humanitarian basis. Many undocumented immigrants from Lesotho benefit from a similar scheme. Despite this, formalised labour migration towards South Africa has declined since the early 1990s because of a deliberate government policy to reduce it, and to make South Africa less dependent on migrant labour (Crush and McDonald, 2003; Crush and Peberdy, 2003; Nshimbi and Fioramonti, 2014).

The decline in formal migration, however, hides the fact that undocumented migration towards South Africa continues. The persistence of this type of migration is exploited by some political leaders. However, it is also an actual cause of hostility towards migrants in their host communities and the general South African population.

This is because of the view that migrants are a threat and compete for jobs and services with their hosts. This perception of migrants essentially emphasises economic factors as the major drivers of migration towards South Africa. It therefore corroborates the theoretical approach that encompasses both the 'pull' of opportunity towards countries of destination and the 'push' of dire conditions in countries of origin. This 'push-pull' approach is one of the key theoretical perspectives on migration briefly elaborated on in the next section.

DOMINANT THEORETICAL PERSPECTIVES ON MIGRATION IN THE SOUTH(ERN) AFRICAN CONTEXT

The chapters in this volume offer unique insights and views, which add to the wide range of existing knowledge and theories of migration that they examine. The issues and themes they explore include security, human rights, social cohesion, populism, xenophobia, nation-building, gender, the feminisation of migration, local government and development, spatial divisions, redistribution, borders and the militarisation of borders and regional integration. This wide range of issues and themes can be examined from multiple dimensions and viewed through various theoretical perspectives. For the sake of brevity, this chapter highlights only the theoretical views on migration that are relevant to the contributions in this book.

Economic and trade theory posits that regional economic integration, such as the type that member states of SADC pursue, is beneficial to development. Integration makes economic sense for a region such as southern Africa and a continent such as Africa, where most economies are small. Meaningful integration in this context entails the unhindered movement of goods, services and persons. According to trade and customs union theory, integration of this sort enhances economies of scale for participating countries, expands markets and creates opportunities to increase productive capacities, leading to development (Balassa, 1961). This is the theoretical view that forms the basis of SADC integration. SADC's vision is to move through key stages that progress from a state of no free trade to complete integration, wherein all factors, including goods, services, capital and people, move freely across the nation-state borders of members within the region. The key stages through which the integration progresses include a free trade area (FTA), customs union, common market, economic and monetary union and complete integration. Considerable obstacles to the movement of goods and services exist at the initial stage(s) but member states will have eliminated them by the time the region becomes completely integrated.

SADC is on record as seeking to advance through these key milestones 'including the establishment of a Free Trade Area by 2008, Customs Union by 2010, Common Market by 2015, Monetary Union by 2016 and a Single Currency by 2018' (SADC Secretariat, 2019: vii). SADC attained FTA status in 2008. However, it discontinued the pursuit of integration through the linear stages cited in the short term in order to adopt a developmental approach focused on sectoral cooperation, infrastructure development and industrialisation (SADC Secretariat, 2019). With this revised approach, the free movement of persons in the region could be enhanced indirectly through infrastructure development, including transport and border processing. SADC crafted the 2005 Protocol on the Facilitation of Movement of Persons in SADC, which is, however, not yet in force for lack of ratification by the required number of member states. Some scholars point to the securitised approach to migration among some member states of SADC as the reason why the Facilitation of Movement Protocol remains unratified.

Migration and development

The African Union (AU) and SADC consider migration to be a tool for development. This is clearly stated in various declarations, programmes, policy documents, protocols and treaties of these organisations (see, for example, AU Agenda 2063; the African Common Position on Migration and Development; the Migration Policy Framework for Africa and Plan of Action (2018–2030); 1991 Treaty Establishing the African Economic Community; the SADC Declaration and Treaty; the SADC Regional Indicative Strategic Development Plan). This implies that even member states that seem to be opposed to intra-African migration subscribe to the long-term positions on migration of these organisations by virtue of membership. Migration is a source of foreign exchange and national savings from migrants sending remittances back to their countries of origin. Remittances contribute to increased income and improve social welfare even at the micro or household level (Moyo and Nicolau, 2016). Besides money, in-kind remittances – including goods, technical know-how, skills and abilities acquired abroad by returning migrants – can contribute to the development of origin countries. Migration further provides for the supply of skilled workers (within Africa, for instance) to countries that have a deficit of these (Fioramonti and Nshimbi, 2016). Even for receiving countries, chapter 9 in this book shows that migrants contribute to the development of local economies. This happens, among other ways, through tenant–landlord relationships where migrants pay for rental services to local landlords. However, chapter 10 of this book shows that unsystematic spatial transformation might raise distributional tensions. This shows the necessity of taking migration into consideration in development planning for spatial and structural transformation.

Migration and social cohesion

Migration and its relationship to social cohesion in countries such as South Africa is highly emotional and politicised. It constantly features in the media, public debates, academia and politicians' speeches. Newspaper headlines, for example, carry lurid 'headlines [that] speak of "floods", "tidal waves" and "swarms" of migrants "flattening the country's borders" while some politicians, activists, academicians and researchers "use ... unsubstantiated figures to make definitive statements" about the "cost" of migrants to the country' (Crush and Williams, 2001: 1). This exacerbates moral panic and tensions between immigrants and their hosts. In extreme cases it flares up into violent attacks on immigrants (Crush and Ramachandran, 2016). Negative attitudes towards migrants, sometimes extending to xenophobia, are a serious problem in any country because they undermine social cohesion, good governance, peaceful co-existence and human rights (Crush and Pendleton, 2004).

Some discussions of social cohesion in a country deem it necessary to deal with migration and its effects on employment and settlement patterns. As chapter 4 in this book argues, social cohesion and initiatives to integrate migrants in host countries are complex and play out in nuanced ways in relation to nation-building and the politics of belonging.

This complexity is reflected in this book in the difference between the arguments presented in chapters 8 and 9. While the former argues that migrant-owned spaza shops in South African townships are a source of social tension, the latter chapter presents evidence of the instrumental role migrants play in the development of the local communities in which they reside. Chapter 7 extends the notion of integration with an examination of how community gardens and traditional foods could both help address migrant nutrition challenges and provide bridges between immigrant and host communities

There are, however, national immigration policies and other policies that impact on such attempts at social cohesion. There are issues raised relating to migrants' rights that extend beyond the rejection of multiculturalism and assertions that migrants threaten local culture because they are foreign, different and do not belong. In view of limited resources, debates abound on whether the welfare state should support migrants identified as 'outsiders' and on whether they should even have access to social services such as health and education (particularly their children). Women migrants and children suffer the most from the violation of migrants' rights during migration and in host countries.

Women and migration

Globally, women are increasingly present in migration processes, as underscored in chapter 6 of this book. Furthermore, across the world women are increasingly migrating on their own. Women migrate for many reasons, including marriage, education, economic purposes, work and reunification with family.

In places such as Africa, many migrant women have social and cultural norms to contend with in their countries of origin, transit and destination. Beyond this, migrant women and children have particular needs and characteristics that the world fails to meet adequately, ignores or violates.

Migrant women and children in Africa tend to be unaware of their rights. They also tend to be unaware that the law provides various forms of protection for migrants and that officers of the law can protect them. Some women migrants believe that the law and law enforcement officers do not recognise immigrants because of the attitudes of law enforcement officials and ordinary people towards them. Consequently, these women prefer not to seek redress from the authorities when their rights are violated during migration and as immigrants in a host country. In South Africa, for instance, studies show that women migrants do not report crimes against them to the police because the officers threaten them with deportation and regularly refer them back to the communities where their rights were violated (Sigsworth et al., 2008; Matose et al., 2022). Migrant women also describe experiences of sexual harassment and abuse during migration from fellow migrant men and law enforcement officers (Matose et al., 2022).

This points to the many risks women face in migration and that they barely benefit from national legislation and international declarations, conventions and laws designed to protect them and their children. Despite the existence of protection measures, migrant women's and children's rights generally remain unprotected and they lack access to resources and services such as health, finance and legal protection. Even law enforcement and legal officials who should represent and protect migrant women's and children's rights tend to lack the training to carry out these functions. Although migration can empower women, it can also threaten their human security. However, this does not translate into a lack of agency for women migrants. Chapter 5 in this book shows that migrant women exercise agency and those in the domestic service sector in South Africa advocate for their human and labour rights and for social justice, notwithstanding their vulnerability.

SECURITISATION OF MIGRATION

Chapters 3 and 12 in this book suggest that South Africa's approach to migration is increasingly securitised. The country, and other migrant-receiving ones in the SADC region, increasingly perceive migration through the lens of it constituting a threat to national security. This lens has its origin in the application of a constructivist approach in security studies. In this approach, security threats are regarded as intersubjective social constructions and not objective realities. The Copenhagen School of Security Studies first formulated the securitisation approach in the early 1990s (Buzan et al., 1998). The starting point of the approach is the suggestion that security agendas are useful pawns in political battles. The parties who win security debates succeed in *securitising* the issue or cause for which they are campaigning. They do so by transforming or transferring the issue from the domain of normal politics into the sphere of the politics of urgency, threat and survival. A *securitising move*, according to the Copenhagen School, consists of portraying an issue as an existential threat and then raising the need to urgently counter that threat in all ways necessary. Securitisation succeeds when the threat is placed high on the political agenda, and it is found acceptable to deal with the threat through emergency and exceptional means. Such means involve the suspension of the normal rules and procedures that would ordinarily be used to deal with an issue.

According to the Copenhagen School, securitising moves involve 'speech acts' made by elites who have political influence. These elites are best able to succeed in using securitising speech acts because of their expertise, power, positions of authority and perceived legitimacy. This places actors such as defence bodies, cabinet ministers and heads of state in positions of advantage to speak on security. The words of these influential elites have an impact. This is because a successful securitising speech act creates a sense of urgency and crisis that allows for the implementation of emergency and exceptional measures to deal with a perceived threat.

This introductory chapter now traces the securitisation of migration in South Africa by analysing speech acts at the elite level. These are evident in the policy paper discussed below, which aims to overhaul the country's immigration system. The assumption underlying this tracking is that securitising moves should translate into changes in policy for a perceived threat to be addressed urgently and effectively. The proceeding discussion highlights that the government and the particular minister and department in charge of immigration will be significant actors in the securitisation of immigration in South Africa.

POLICY AND PRACTICES RELATING TO MIGRATION: VIEWS OF THE SOUTH AFRICAN GOVERNMENT ON IMMIGRATION

States' or governments' positions and views on issues relevant within their territorial jurisdiction are most aptly reflected in their policies, legislation and decisions of the courts (Nshimbi, 2022). South Africa is not exceptional in this respect. On 1 November 2023, the Cabinet of the government of South Africa approved the White Paper on Citizenship, Immigration and Refugee Protection: Towards a Complete Overhaul of the Migration System in South Africa (hereafter referred to as 'White Paper') for public comment.

The White Paper aims to overhaul South Africa's migration system and therefore to replace the 2017 White Paper on International Migration. The reform was prompted by a resolution of the 55th National Conference of the African National Congress (ANC) held from 16 to 20 December 2022. The resolution states that 'The ANC-led government must completely overhaul the Citizenship Act, Refugees Act and Immigration Act to meet the new challenges facing South Africa' (South Africa, 2023: para 9.1.7).

The challenges referred to relate to the simultaneous decline in demand for migrant labour in the mining and agriculture sectors and the ongoing irregular migration taking place when, according to government, it seeks to expand opportunities for previously marginalised South Africans. The closure of some mines and a combination of economic, political, environmental and climate-related factors in the SADC region have created conditions for mixed migration flows. These include both regular and irregular, displaced migrants who increasingly rely on channels for human smuggling to enter the country in the face of strict formal entry requirements (Tati, 2008). Concerns about irregular migration are accompanied by social intolerance often expressed through violent attacks, political rhetoric and the deportation of mainly African migrants (Crush and Ramachandran, 2016; Nshimbi and Fioramonti, 2013).

The White Paper proposes 'radical changes and new policy frameworks intended to lead to stability, economic development, valuable citizenship, immigration and protection measures for refugees in South Africa (South Africa, 2023). The White Paper covers three broad areas and makes several policy recommendations and proposals for new migration policy frameworks, legislation and regulations. The three areas are refugee protection and asylum, citizenship, and immigration. The White Paper considers the proposed overhaul of South Africa's migration system to be consistent with similar trends globally. However, it is clear that the reforms are equally animated by concerns over irregular (popularly referred to as 'illegal') migration. The White Paper (South Africa, 2023: paras 88, 91) categorically expresses concern over 'many foreign nationals [who] come to South Africa and stay in the country "illegally" and "illegal" foreigners entering the country illegally'.

In a newspaper article published in 2022, the Minister of Home Affairs, Aaron Motsoaledi, attributes the recurring violence against African migrants to competition for limited economic opportunities and suggests that it signals 'a migration crisis' in the country (Motsoaledi, 2022). Government acknowledges that the crises emanate in part from a failure to secure national borders, the need to comply with international conventions on migration and the attractiveness of South Africa to migrants searching for economic opportunities. However, Mr Motsoaledi says that, according to the United Nations High Commissioner for Refugees (UNHCR), 'South Africa has the most progressive immigration laws in the world' and argues that this has opened 'the doors for some migrants to abuse the country's refugee-friendly laws'. Mr Motsoaledi asserts that migrants who received exemptions from complying with all immigration requirements have gone on to abuse the system by demanding permanent residence through litigation. He says that others demand that children born in South Africa should be granted citizenship and those studying expect to be granted permanent residence and work permits (Motsoaledi, 2022).

The 'crisis' being referred to here, as chapter 2 argues, is interpreted by some as veiled reservations about allowing certain social actors to migrate within southern Africa because they belong to the lower levels of social hierarchies or are 'irregular' or 'undesirable'. The White Paper echoes the need for strict immigration laws to protect the rights and identities of South Africans in what chapters 3 and 12 describe as the growing securitisation of migration in the country. The securitisation approach, as theorised earlier and as chapter 3 argues, derives from contestation over South Africa's identity in the context of migrants coming into a country where black citizens have historically been deprived of citizenship and access to opportunities. This complicates the project of nation-building and social cohesion as homogenised notions of nationhood and belonging prevail over the need to accommodate appropriate transnationalism and construct a more inclusive collective identity.

STRUCTURE OF THE BOOK

The contributions in this book are organised into three broad themes. The chapters in Section One engage in a broad discussion of migration from a historical perspective, highlight past and present trends in migration, and explore the politics of migration. Section Two is titled 'Migration and South Africa's Political Economy'. The contributions in this section range from discussion of gender to migrants' lived experiences of nutrition; migration and the retail sector; migration and spatiality; and migration and human settlement. Section Three focuses on the state and migration governance. The chapters in this section zoom in on the SADC region and consider, among other things, the relationship between migration and the securitisation of borders, as well as how the digital policies of individual member states impact on asylum protection.

Chapter 2, by Chris C. Nshimbi, looks back to make the point that migration in southern Africa is historical and also that the past has an impact on contemporary migration practice in the region. The chapter traces the evolution of migration governance in the SADC region and underscores the complex and continuously evolving nature of this human reality the world over. Nshimbi argues that international migration interacts with various contextual and structural factors, and interactions of international migration are multidimensional and interdependent. The chapter also presents evidence to counter Eurocentric notions of homogeneity among African peoples across the continent. The author takes us through historical and current theoretical and conceptual approaches that have helped foster the governance aspect of migration. Nshimbi primarily contends that the migration governance systems established by colonial authorities to exploit cheap labour during the colonial era still persist in post-colonial southern Africa. He concludes that the social divisions and hierarchies established under colonial rule persist in 21st-century southern Africa.

Chapter 3 by Vusi Gumbi examines how migration patterns and movements relate to security, including national security, human security and societal stability. The chapter takes a nuanced position on how and why South Africans resist the influx of migrants into the country. Gumbi points out that discussions on migration reveal a narrow view that labels South Africans xenophobic. He concludes that the securitisation of migration is a complex and contested process and one subject to change over time, depending on political developments, economic conditions and social factors. Gumbi recommends that South Africa promotes social integration and peaceful coexistence, and underscores the need for a nuanced strategy that addresses the causes of migration and fosters social cohesiveness with a balance between security concerns and immigrant rights.

Chapter 4 by Sifiso Ndlovu examines social cohesion and the integration of migrants into society in South Africa, which constitutes a major migrant destination for many people from other parts of Africa and beyond. The chapter uses the notions of nation-building and social cohesion to show that migrants add a layer of complication to the politics of belonging and nation-building in the country. The author argues that perceiving migrants as outsiders is at odds with crafting and achieving social cohesion and exposes South Africa's national project as a continuation of apartheid logic. In this regard, the chapter resonates with the arguments put forward in chapter 2, although the concepts are expressed differently. Ndlovu concludes with the suggestion that because nation-building and social cohesion are long-standing challenges, which post-apartheid South Africa struggles to resolve, the majority of South Africans still feel themselves marginalised. The author argues that a consequence of this is that migrants and migrations will continue to be viewed as additional challenges.

Chapter 5 by Janet Munakamwe shows the ways in which international migrants in South Africa advocate for human and labour rights. With the help of a case study, the chapter highlights the agency of migrant domestic workers who advocate for social justice in the face of vulnerabilities. The chapter also shows that migrant domestic workers are exposed to various forms of discrimination based on gender, class, race, nationality and citizenship. Like chapter 1, chapter 5 considers these issues from the perspective of the history of South Africa's relationship with labour migration and concludes that migrants frequently mobilise around a spectrum of economic, social and political issues that impact on their lives.

Chapter 6 by David Fadiran and Hammed Amusa presents the gender dimension of migration in South Africa and its implications for livelihoods. The authors underscore the growing presence of women in international migration trends. Global patterns of migration indicate that the number of female migrants has tripled in the past 60 years, from 46 million to 135 million in 2020. Fadiran and Amusa argue that the feminisation of migration in Africa represents a move away from male-dominated, long-term, long-distance migration. Their conclusion supports Munakamwes' observation in chapter 5 that domestic work is a key driver of immigration for female migrants and that integration into the labour market does not allow for full utilisation of the skill sets that female migrants come with.

Chapter 7 by Brittany Kesselman argues that South Africa is going through a nutrition transition, which is pronounced in urban areas and especially affects migrants from rural areas who find themselves on Westernised diets from harmful food sources. Kesselman examines the lived experiences of this nutrition transition among internal and international migrants in Johannesburg. According to Kesselman, identity, status and the desire for communal eating are under-appreciated factors that influence migrants' food practices. She concludes with the observation that local-level, collective solutions – such as community gardens and a focus on traditional foods – might be effective approaches to dealing with migrant nutrition challenges.

Chapter 8 by Amuzweni Ngoma and Wandile M. Ngcaweni explores the structural nexus between migration, retail conglomerates and township spaza shops. The chapter considers the evolution of the political economy of southern Africa and its effects on the township economy, and on informal and formal township traders. The authors point to the need for a macro strategy to link the development of SADC's informal economies and township economies to the region's trading class. The authors conclude that for local enterprises to thrive, the country must review its national industrial, agricultural and competition policies.

Chapter 9 by Malaika Lesego Samora Mahlatsi analyses the relationship between migrant tenants and local landlords as a growing feature of the geographies in the Soweto townships of Braamfischerville, Meadowlands and Dobsonville. The chapter demonstrates how the migrant tenant community is instrumental in township economic development and social cohesion. This view differs from the argument in chapter 7, namely that foreign-owned spaza shops are a source of tension. Instead, Mahlatsi argues, the township economy is strengthened by the participation of migrant traders who respond to the demand for goods and services and create employment opportunities. The chapter highlights the positive aspects of the local landlord and migrant tenant relationship, such as the supplementing of income, transfers of skills, job creation and the provision of access to food and nutrition.

Chapter 10 by Eddie M. Rakabe examines internal migration, spatial division and redistribution dilemmas. The chapter highlights the distribution tensions that rise from an unsystematic spatial transformation agenda and argues that migration should not be considered a single action but rather an integral part of spatial and structural transformation processes. It is accompanied and inspired by technological changes and sectoral restructuring, from scattered rural agricultural activities to concentrated urban industry and labour migration from rural areas to cities. All this is made possible by advances in transport and communication linkages. Rakabe concludes that the slow pace of spatial transformation often leads to and reinforces sub-optimal organisation of economic geography or spatial mismatches, such as when industries concentrate with a misalignment between density and housing, amenities and skilled labour.

Chapter 11 by Eddie M. Rakabe, Wandile M. Ngcaweni and Gabriel Lubale delves into migration governance and acknowledges that it is complex and difficult for South African policymakers and government officials. The chapter provides an overview of the challenges and opportunities associated with migration governance in South Africa, including a discussion with the Minister of Home Affairs about difficulties encountered and proposed solutions. The authors discuss various international policy instruments and show how these impact on domestic migration laws and governance frameworks. They describe the steps taken by the government of South Africa to create a more effective migration governance system. Rakabe, Ngcaweni and Lubale conclude that migration governance in southern Africa requires a comprehensive, coordinated and integrated approach from government and other stakeholders.

Chapter 12 by Innocent Moyo discusses borders and migration in the context of uneven regional development in the southern African region. The chapter argues that, in a region like SADC, border militarisation and securitisation do not amount to the effective management and governance of borders; rather, they lead to and exacerbate cross-border security challenges by entrenching underground, sophisticated cross-border illegalities. Moyo argues that border militarisation and securitisation deal only ineffectively with a symptom, leaving the causes of the problems of people crossing borders illegally untouched and hidden. In conclusion, Moyo highlights that the SADC region is characterised by uneven development, which has led to an influx of immigrants from less economically developed countries. Moyo also finds that uneven development stands in the way of regional integration as it militates against a coordinated regional migration approach.

Chapter 13 by Lindokuhle Mdabe investigates digital policy in relation to the protection of asylum seekers in South Africa. The chapter puts forward the argument that while South Africa has progressive legislative and policy frameworks to support digitalised public administration, it has not established a coherent asylum digital policy. Mdabe argues for a context-specific, coherent digital policy, arising out of legislative and policy frameworks, to regulate digital practice in the asylum system, particularly the use of digital tools to manage asylum applications, issue and extend visas, and verify asylum status.

The chapters in this volume cover key debates on the social, economic and political drivers of migration in South Africa. The authors discuss various real-life migration and related issues in the country, including migration and populism; the securitisation of migration; the place of migration in development; the integration of migrants into host communities; the rights of migrants, migration and gender; migration and spatial division/distribution; migration and nation-state borders. Researchers and migration scholars from various scientific disciplines will find the perspectives on international migration presented in the book insightful.

REFERENCES

African Union. 1991. 'Abuja Treaty Establishing the African Economic Community', https://au.int/en/treaties/treaty-establishing-african-economic-community, accessed 30 November 2023.

African Union. 2006. 'African common position on migration and development'. Executive Council, Ninth Ordinary Session, Banjul, The Gambia, 25–29 June.

African Union. 2018a. 'Migration Policy Framework for Africa and Plan of Action (2018–2030)', https://au.int/sites/default/files/documents/35956-doc-au-mpfa-executive-summary-eng.pdf, accessed 30 November 2023.

African Union. 2018b. 'Protocol to the treaty establishing the African economic community relating to free movement of persons, right of residence and right of establishment', https://au.int/en/treaties/protocol-treaty-establishing-african-economic-community-relating-free-movement-persons, accessed 30 November 2023.

Balassa, B. 1961. *The Theory of Economic Integration*. Homewood, Il: Richard D. Irwin.

Buzan, B., Wæver, O. and De Wilde, J. 1998. *Security: A new framework for analysis*. Colorado: Lynne Rienner Publishers.

Crush, J., Chikanda, A. and Tawodzera, G. 2012. 'The Third Wave: Mixed migration from Zimbabwe to South Africa'. SAMP Migration Policy Series No. 59, https://scholars.wlu.ca/cgi/viewcontent.cgi?article=1037&context=samp, accessed 20 January 2023.

Crush, J. and McDonald, D. 2003. 'Understanding skilled migration in Southern Africa'. *Africa Insight*, 30, 3–9.

Crush, J. and Peberdy, S. 2003. 'Criminal tendencies: Immigrants and illegality in South Africa'. SAMP Migration Policy Brief No. 10, https://scholars.

wlu.ca/cgi/viewcontent.cgi?article=1067&context=samp, accessed on 20 January 2024.21 *Introduction*

Crush, J. and Pendleton, W. 2004. 'Regionalizing xenophobia?': Citizen attitudes to immigration and refugee policy in Southern Africa'. SAMP Migration Policy Series No. 30, https://scholars.wlu.ca/cgi/viewcontent.cgi?referer=&httpsredir=1&article=1126&context=samp, accessed 20 January 2024.

Crush, J. and Ramachandran, S. 2016. 'Xenophobic violence in South Africa: Denialism, minimalism, realism'. SAMP Migration Policy Series No. 66, https://scholars.wlu.ca/cgi/viewcontent.cgi?article=1030&context=samp, accessed 20 January 2023.

Crush, J. and Tevera, D. 2010. 'Exiting Zimbabwe', in Crush, J. and Tevera, D. (eds), *Zimbabwe's Exodus: Crisis, migration, survival.* Cape Town: SAMP.

Crush, J. and Williams, V. (eds). 2001. 'Making up the numbers: Measuring "illegal immigration" to South Africa'. SAMP Migration Policy Brief No. 3, https://scholars.wlu.ca/cgi/viewcontent.cgi?article=1060&context=samp, accessed 20 January 2023.

Department of Home Affairs. 2017. 'White Paper on International Migration For South Africa'. https://www.dha.gov.za/WhitePaperonInternationalMigration-20170602.pdf, accessed 18 November 2023.

Fioramonti, L. and Nshimbi, C. C. 2016. *Regional Migration Governance in the African Continent. Current state of affairs and the way forward.* Potsdam: SEF/Development and Peace Foundation.

Hlatshwayo, M. 2019. 'Precarious work and precarious resistance: A case study of Zimbabwean migrant women workers in Johannesburg, South Africa'. *Diaspora Studies*, 12(2), 160–178.

International Organisation for Migration (IOM). 2020. 'World Migration Report 2020', https://publications.iom.int/system/files/pdf/wmr_2020.pdf, accessed 1 July 2023.

Isike, C. and Isike, E. M. (eds). 2022. *Conflict and Concord: The ambivalence of African migrant/host relations in South Africa.* Singapore: Palgrave Macmillan.

Jinnah, Z. 2020. 'Negotiated precarity in the global south: A case study of migration and domestic work in South Africa'. *Studies in Social Justice*, 14(1), 210–227.

Kalitanyi, V. and Visser, K. 2010. 'African immigrants in South Africa: Job takers or job creators?'. *South African Journal of Economic and Management Sciences*, 13(4), 376–390.

Kwenge, M. 2020. 'Migration and the locality: Community peacebuilding as a deterrent to collective violence in South Africa', in Moyo, I., Nshimbi, C. and Laine, J. (eds), *Migration Conundrums, Regional Integration and Development – Africa's Global Engagement: Perspectives from emerging countries*. Singapore: Palgrave Macmillan.

Matose, T., Maviza, G. and Nunu, W. N. 2022. 'Pervasive irregular migration and the vulnerabilities of irregular female migrants at Plumtree border post in Zimbabwe'. *Journal of Migration and Health*, 5.

Mawadza, A. 2008. 'The nexus between migration and human security Zimbabwean migrants in South Africa'. Institute for Security Studies Papers, 162, 12.

Mlambo, A. 2010. 'A history of Zimbabwean migration to 1990', in Crush, J. and Tevera, D. (eds), *Zimbabwe's Exodus: Crisis, migration, survival*. Kingston and Cape Town: Southern African Migration Programme (SAMP), 52–78.

Motsoaledi, A. 13 March 2022. 'Violence driven by economic inequality'. *City Press*, https://www.news24.com/citypress/voices/aaron-motsoaledi-violence-driven-by-economic-inequality-20220313, accessed 23 December 2023.

Moyo, I. 2016. 'The Beitbridge–Mussina interface: Towards flexible citizenship, sovereignty and territoriality at the border'. *Journal of Borderlands Studies*, 31(4), 427–440.

Moyo, I. 2018. 'Zimbabwean dispensation, special and exemption permits in South Africa: On humanitarian logic, depoliticisation and invisibilisation of migrants'. *Journal of Asian and African Studies*, 53(8), 1141–1157.

Moyo, I. and Nicolau, M. D. 2016. 'Remittances and development: Zimbabwean migrant teachers in South Africa and their impact on their Zimbabwean families'. *African Population Studies*, 30(2), 2506–2519.

Moyo, I. and Nshimbi, C. C. 2019. 'Border practices at Beitbridge border and Johannesburg inner city: Implications for the SADC regional integration project'. *Journal of Asian and African Studies*, 54(3), 309–330.

Nshimbi, C. C. 2015. 'Networks of cross-border non-state actors: The role of social capital in regional integration'. *Journal of Borderlands Studies*, 30(4), 537–560.

Nshimbi, C. C. 2019. 'Life in the fringes: Economic and sociocultural practices in the Zambia–Malawi–Mozambique borderlands in comparative perspective'. *Journal of Borderlands Studies*, 34(1), 47–70.

Nshimbi, C. C. 2022. 'Parities and disparities in applying immigration legislation/policies from a world-class national constitution', in Isike, C. and Isike, E. M. (eds), *Conflict and Concord: The ambivalence of African migrant/host relations in South Africa*. Singapore: Palgrave Macmillan.

Nshimbi, C. C. and Fioramonti, L. 2013. *A Region Without Borders? Policy Frameworks for Regional Labour Migration Towards South Africa*. Johannesburg: African Centre for Migration & Society.

Nshimbi, C. C. and Fioramonti, L. 2014. 'The will to integrate: South Africa's responses to regional migration from the SADC region'. *African Development Review*, 26(S1), 52–63.

Odok, G. E. 2019. 'Economic or climate migrants? Human security experiences of Nigerian migrants in South Africa'. *Ubuntu: Journal of Conflict and Social Transformation*, 8(2), 241–254.

Rutherford, B. 2020. 'Nervous conditions on the Limpopo: Gendered insecurities, livelihoods, and Zimbabwean migrants in Northern South Africa'. *Studies in Social Justice*, 14(1), 169–187.

SADC Secretariat. 2019. 'Status of integration in the Southern African development community', https://www.sadc.int/sites/default/files/2021-08/Status_of_Integration_in_the_SADC_Region_Report.pdf, accessed 30 November 2023.

SADC (Southern African Development Community). 2005. 'Draft protocol on the facilitation of movement of persons', https://www.sadc.int/document/protocol-facilitation-movement-persons-2005, accessed 30 November 2023.

Segatti, A. and Landau, L. B. (eds). 2011. *Contemporary Migration to South Africa: A regional development issue*. Washington, DC: World Bank.

Sigsworth, R., Ngwane, C. and Pino, A. 2008. *The Gendered Nature of Xenophobia in South Africa*. Southern Africa Regional Office: Heinrich Böll Stiftung.

South Africa. 2023. Department of Home Affairs- Public Consultation Policy Paper, 'White Paper on Citizenship, Immigration and Refugee Protection: Towards a Complete Overhaul of the Migration System in South Africa'. *Government Gazette No. 49661*.

Statistics South Africa. 2022. 'Census 2022', https://census.statssa.gov.za/assets/documents/2022/P03014_Census_2022_Statistical_Release.pdf, accessed 25 November 2023.

Tati, G. 2008. 'The immigration issues in the post-apartheid South Africa: Discourses, policies and social repercussions'. *Geopolitiuqe et population*, 3, 423–440.

Tshimpaka, L. M. and Inaka, S. J. 2020. 'Long march to South Africa: The breaking of colonial borders through migrant smuggling of Congolese'. *Borders, Sociocultural Encounters and Contestations*. London: Routledge, 89–111.

UNDESA. 2020. 'International Migration 2020: Highlights', https://www.un.org/development/desa/pd/sites/www.un.org.development.desa.pd/files/undesa_pd_2020_international_migration_highlights.pdf, accessed 1 July 2023.

Section One

Social Cohesion, Migration and Identity

TWO

Mobilities past and mobilities present in the Southern African Development Community (SADC) region: An epigrammatic overview

CHRIS C. NSHIMBI

This chapter risks oversimplification by attempting a concise, pano-ramic discussion of the evolution of international migration governance in the geographical area that constitutes the Southern African Development Community (SADC),[1] with a bias on mobilities towards what is now the Republic of South Africa. The oversimplification takes cognisance of the complexity of international migration in the SADC region, and in general.

A broad understanding of international migration considers

---

1 SADC is a major African regional economic community of 16 member states comprising Angola, Botswana, Comoros, Democratic Republic of the Congo, eSwatini, Lesotho, Madagascar, Malawi, Mauritius, Mozambique, Namibia, Seychelles, South Africa, United Republic of Tanzania, Zambia and Zimbabwe.

it simply a change in a population's area of usual residence, or people moving to settle in an area other than their home. A precise conceptualisation insists on a population or community moving to a country other than that of 'usual residence for a period of at least a year (12 months) so that the country of destination effectively becomes ... [the] new country of usual residence' (UN, 1998: 36).

As a concept, international migration itself seems to be ontologically evolving – from generally connoting the movement of populations or entire communities, to defining the international or cross-border movement of a particular type or group of persons. Discourses on international migration in the early 21st century help to illustrate the point. Policy and public debates on the matter in this period seem focused on undocumented or so-called 'illegal' migrants. At the global level, for example, this culminated in the negotiation, formulation and signing of the Global Compact for Safe, Orderly and Regular Migration (GCM) in 2018, under the sponsorship of the United Nations (UN). As the instrument's name suggests, the GCM's primary objective reveals the world's and especially high-income countries' preoccupation with curbing undocumented or irregular migration. And as the last section of this chapter suggests, this preoccupation is driven by veiled reservations about the people who undertake this form of movement, rather than purported concern for their welfare and safety. The UN and member state signatories to the GCM are cascading the instrument's provisions and implementing it – down from the global to regional and nation-state levels (United Nations Network on Migration, 2023).

Besides the GCM, various regional blocs and nation-states around the world draw up and continually design, amend and implement local mechanisms for governing international migration within their respective jurisdictions (Nshimbi and Fioramonti, 2013). I present a broad but concise overview of how such mechanisms have evolved in the SADC region, from circa the 16th century to the early 21st century. I do so after briefly reiterating that international migration is complex and underscoring the point that the governance of migration in various parts of the world transcends the early 21st-century preoccupation with the undocumented or irregular aspects of this human reality.

International migration interacts with, shapes and is shaped by various contextual and structural factors. Such factors include, among others, (un)employment, health, poverty, (human) wellbeing, the environment, demographic increase and urbanisation. In this regard, the interactions that relate to international migration are multidirectional, involving various actors and institutional and organisational entities and structures. This adds to the complexity of migration. International migration, additionally, reflects a variety of interdependencies. These are manifested through trade and other forms of economic exchange between nation-states, corporations and individuals; culture and social mobility; and, at the barest minimum, the mobility-related decisions that people make either as individuals or as collectives.

Scholarly attempts to make sense of these complex social, economic, cultural, organisational and (even) environmental migration-related realities are dominated by neoclassical economics assumptions. The assumptions emphasise differences in incomes and wealth at the macro level while they emphasise human capital at the micro or individual level (De Haas, 2010; Abreu, 2012; Castles et al., 2020). The assumptions explain the rational decision-making behaviours of people who migrate. However, they fail to account for structural factors that reduce people's ability to migrate.

A body of literature that presents different views from the rational decision-making models distinguishes between migrants' capabilities to migrate and migrants' ambitions to migrate (Carling and Collins, 2018). Models within this literature underscore social ties and intra-network communication. Yet, it is puzzling how perfectly informed people still risk migrating, despite the massive campaigns on the dangers of irregular migration in the early 21st century, and the knowledge possessed about this (Carling and Hernández-Carretero, 2011; Heller, 2014; Oeppen, 2016; Watkins, 2020).

The objective of this chapter is to better understand the underlying historical shapers of international migration or the international mobility of people in the SADC region, in view of the region's socioeconomic and political history. The chapter grapples with the broader question of how international migration is governed. Neither the countries nor the peoples of the SADC region are as homogeneous as most Eurocentric literature in particular presents them. Rather, within the countries of the region there are great variations and heterogeneity in types of polity and economy, economic size, activity and vibrancy; responses to globalisation and globalising forces; the composition of populations, and their social and cultural traits. The chapter notes that nation-state governments in the region are not always in full control of who enters or leaves their territorial jurisdictions or the region. Although the literature and media commonly present Zimbabwe as a country that has experienced mass emigration since 2000 (Crush and Tevera, 2010; Hammar et al., 2010), a World Bank (2016) report presents data which shows that about 6.5 per cent or 973,200 people out of Zimbabwe's total population of 15.2 million people emigrated in 2016.

For its part, South Africa is considered the recipient of the largest number of Zimbabwean migrants in the SADC region and it struggles to stem both the influx of migrants and the exodus of South African professionals from South Africa. This is despite the general opposition to both immigration and emigration in the country (Ehlers et al., 2003; Kasiram, 2009; Chingwete, 2016; Dryding, 2020). Regarding the latter, for instance, South Africa experienced a net loss of 9,529 economically active people in 2003, including 703 accountants, 693 medical personnel, 547 industrial and production engineers and 542 natural scientists (Ellis and Segatti, 2011: 74). The chapter does not find entire national populations that migrate to neighbouring countries either. And among the people who migrate, the chapter does not conclude that all migrants completely disregard all nation-state and region-sanctioned laws in their countries of destination. Rather, the chapter examines mechanisms that are undergirded by dynamics within, and/or aspirations to navigate, a region that is, paradoxically, resource-abundant but burdened with human-made constraints. Examining international migration governance in such a region provides insights into mechanisms that regulate mobility but are otherwise too complex to understand.

METHODS

The chapter deploys a qualitative research design and uses historical and textual evidence from scholarly literature to inform the analysis that supports the argument herein. This approach is supported by the research methodology argument that textual data provides an 'attractive nuisance' that offers insights into observable facts (Miles, 1979). A qualitative approach also provides holistic perspectives and allows for the gathering of in-depth knowledge on particular subjects. And, as Maxwell (2009) argues, qualitative studies conveniently help to understand people's activities, situations and events. These methodological postulations are put forward to make the case that the approach deployed in the chapter is the most appropriate one for understanding the evolution of international migration governance in the SADC region.

After this introduction, the second section presents theoretical and conceptual lenses through which to examine the evolution of international migration governance in the SADC region. It presents an overview of the historical development of the perspectives that dominate the literature on international migration, emphasising two that are deployed in the chapter: the Marxist thesis of accumulation by dispossession; and the New Regionalism Approach (NRA). The second section also defines the main concept deployed for the analysis in this chapter. The third section presents historical and textual evidence in support of the argument in the chapter regarding the evolution of the governance of international migration in southern Africa from the 16th century to the early 21st century. The section implicitly underscores the view that SADC nation-states and governments are not the sole actors and architects of the frameworks that govern international migration in the region. The last section concludes by suggesting that popular reservations towards migration in the SADC region essentially constitute apprehensions with a certain class of people on the move.

THEORETICAL AND CONCEPTUAL APPROACH

Studies of international migration seldom engage in actual theoretical discussion of the *governance* aspect of this human reality. They tend to focus rather on either the process of migration or on migrants and their agency (or lack thereof) during migration processes. Theoretical discourses on the process of international migration attempt to explain why people migrate. Scholarly attempts to explain this age-old human reality are relatively new. The seminal work of Massey et al. (1993) is foundational to this scholarship, as it consolidates various migration theories. Ravenstein, however, wrote on migration about a century before Massey et al. (1993). Ravenstein (1885) used empirical data to propose 'Laws of Migration'. His laws demonstrated that most people only moved short distances from places of origin to their destinations when they migrated. Writing after Ravenstein (1885), the early theorist, Zipf (1946), on the other hand, developed gravity models that explained migration as a reality determined by the proximity between the areas from which migrants originated and their destinations. He suggested that an inverse relationship existed between this and the distance covered.

The 1950s saw a departure from the purely mechanical to more sophisticated theories of migration. Lewis's (1954) dual economy model, for example, theoretically proposed that migration flows were a consequence of differences in labour supply and the demand for labour between urban and rural economies. Harris and Todaro (1970) augmented Lewis's postulation through empirical observations that confirmed migration as a subject of mechanical models that aggregated empirical data and also as a process that unfolded towards equilibrium.

From the 1980s, more elaborate models examined individual motivations for migration in addition to the focus on structural factors at play in the communities from which migrants hailed. Hence, most postulations that attempt to explain the commencement and continuation of migration draw on differences in factors such as wealth and health in the migrants' places of origin and their destinations (Wegge, 1998; Van Hear, 2010; Bodvarsson et al., 2015; Van Hear et al., 2018).

Various studies add to debates on the initiation and the perpetuation of migration, including those that consider the integration of migrants in host communities and/or countries; those that engage with return migration; and the ones that deal with the reintegration of return migrants in their countries of origin. Some debates within this scholarship underscore factors that either push migrants out of their countries of origin or pull them towards countries of destination. The classical literature on push-pull models of migration argues that factors such as low incomes in countries of origin push migrants to move to countries where they are pulled by higher incomes, affluence and the promise of better economic prospects (Lee, 1966; Dorigo and Tobler, 1983). Some studies extend these debates beyond the push-pull factors and attempt to explain migration in terms of the 'drivers of migration'. Van Hear et al. (2018), for example, distinguish between various drivers, which they conceive as forces that lead to the initiation and perpetuation of migration. The distinction is 'between predisposing, proximate, precipitating and mediating drivers', the combination of which defines situations and contexts in which people choose to either migrate or not (Van Hear et al., 2018: 931). These 'driver complexes', according to Van Hear et al. (2018), build on push-pull factors to shape migration.

More recent literature focuses on less economic issues, including social, cultural, environmental and political factors, and links macro and micro levels in analysing migration (Bakewell, 2010; Castles, 2010; Portes, 2010; Van Hear, 2010; Carling and Collins, 2018). Other recent research not only distinguishes between the causes of migration and the perpetuation of migration but also advances the importance of understanding decision-making in analysing migration (Carling and Collins, 2018; Czaika et al., 2021).

Some explanations of the initiation and perpetuation of migration that focus on the micro level emphasise, for example, a variety of factors such as language, culture, household decision-making and geographical proximity, while those that focus on the meso and macro levels point to, among others, labour recruitment, social networks and even warfare (Castles et al., 2020; MacDonald and MacDonald, 1964). The latter argue that after migration is initiated, culture and networks are crucial to perpetuating it. The former, however, consider the importance of strategies devised at the household level, in addition to individual decisions, in determining the initiation of migration.

Notwithstanding the foregoing views, research exists which argues that migrants are passive victims in migration processes (Peisker and Tilbury, 2003; Ghorashi, 2005; Agustin, 2007). That research holds external factors beyond migrants' control as responsible for driving migration. However, research which questions this tradition adopts approaches that show the migrant as an active agent in the migration process (Peisker and Tilbury, 2003; McNamara and Gibson, 2009; Brun and Fábos, 2015; Nshimbi, 2021).

The scarce scholarship that focuses on the governance aspect of international migration tends to be state-centric, focusing on state-authored legislation, policies and regulations for managing the international movement of people (see, e.g., Betts, 2011; Czaika and De Haas, 2013). That scholarship assumes that the state is responsible for and a custodian of international migration – to the extent that it designs migration policies and legislation and even controls people's cross-border movements. But such assumptions are trapped in a Westphalian view that is subsequently imposed on African political and socioeconomic reality.

For, how should the organisation of human mobilities among social, economic and political actors in pre-colonial Africa be explained when no nation-states, or nation-state borders as they are known in the 21st century, existed? Even if one starts from the colonial period and goes up to the 21st century, how does one explain how economic and social agents who do not operate 'under the state's gaze', and especially those located in its outlying areas (Nshimbi, 2020a; Turner, 2013), organise their mobilities? Further, how does one explain the apparent failure of states such as South Africa and Zimbabwe to, respectively, completely stop the immigration and emigration of their skilled and unskilled citizens? With respect to mobilities and the southern African region's past, and especially in relation to labour migration, Van Der Walt (2007) categorically calls out the inadequacy of using the nation-state as a frame through which to understand the history of the region's labour. This is because besides avoiding 'methodological nationalism', international labour markets in southern Africa during the colonial period extended across the region, beyond disparate, demarcated colonial territories or nation-states and the British Empire, into networks of transnational working-class movements (Van Der Walt, 2007; Inaka et al., 2024).

This chapter adopts an approach that is distinct from most discourses on international migration in two ways. Firstly, it deploys an inclusive analytical framework that accommodates various actors and activities. These include states and their activities, non-state actors and actors who tend to not be 'under the state's gaze', at the peripheries of nation-states, and their activities (Nshimbi, 2020a; Turner, 2013). With this, the chapter escapes what I call the 'Westphalian trap' and makes better sense of the governance of migration within and beyond the confines of the Westphalian[2]-type state system. This makes it possible for the chapter to discern the governance of mobilities, not only in the pre-colonial epoch but also before the nation-state as it is known in the international system from the 17th century onwards, and during and after (the advent of) colonial rule.

Secondly, the approach converses with, but goes beyond, Marxist explanations of labour mobility that relate to notions of the African experience of being dispossessed of agricultural production by colonial capitalists. The explanations also expound on how similar types of African actors, who would be considered irregular in the 21st century, were forced into state-sanctioned migration systems orchestrated by private capital (Arrighi et al., 2010; Nshimbi, 2022).

Recall some early literature that critiques classical works on migration such as those by authors such as Harris and Todaro (1970), who demonstrated that low incomes pushed people to migrate from rural economies or their countries and pulled them towards urban economies or high-income countries for better incomes and economic prospects. The critics not only considered the push-pull model overly simplistic and inadequate to fully explain migration, but also rather attributed migration to the longstanding inequalities caused by centuries-long exploitation of low-income countries by high-income countries (Sassen, 1988; Skeldon, 1990; Garip, 2012; Pânzaru and Reisz, 2013). Those critical views, however, do not go far enough in exposing the factor that lies at the core of the governance mechanisms that regulate migration in the SADC region from the start of colonial rule up to the early 21st century. This chapter argues that colonial rule brought with it a global classification of human beings into hierarchies that divided them into superior and inferior beings on the basis of economic and socially constructed categories, and that this has had

---

2   This refers to a principle in international law, according to which all states should be guaranteed exclusive sovereignty over their territories.

enduring effects on international migration in the SADC region.

The New Regionalism Approach

A critical and reflectivist analytical framework provides the most appropriate lens for examining international migration or human mobility in the SADC region. This is because cross-border mobilities in the region defy nation-state borders (Moyo, 2016; Moyo and Nshimbi, 2020; Nshimbi, 2019, 2021). Besides that, mobilities in the SADC region have historically transcended nation-states (Nshimbi, 2019, 2020b) and are, chiefly, a historical human reality. In the 21st century, international migration further constitutes an essential component of state-led cooperative projects between the countries of the region, and tangible economic, social and cultural processes that occur at the grassroots between those countries (Nshimbi, 2015, 2020b, 2023). Whether by design or default, regionalism (the former) and regionalisation (the latter) interlink the nation-states of the area. And cross-border human mobilities are central to the ideals and processes that foster that cooperation. This makes the New Regionalism Approach (NRA) the most suitable theoretical perspective for looking at these mobilities, as well as the pitfall of 'methodological nationalism' or the limitation of using the nation-state as a unit of analysis to examine international migration in such a region (Van der Walt, 2007; Nshimbi, 2019; Inaka et al., 2024).

The NRA emphasises historical context and how states and non-state actors are organised in formal and informal processes of regionalisation. It gives a unique, multidimensional view of interactions between various actors in multilevel and multipolar configurations of regional integration (Tshimpaka et al., 2021). The NRA anticipates that social and cultural networks will develop in an area, in addition to patterns of trade, economic and state-led regionalism (Hettne et al., 2000). International migration is among the many various human activities that form some of the anticipated networks in NRA.

The NRA is also a robust analytical lens for assessing the ways in which various actors interact in multipolar settings. Because the interactions are multidimensional, the state is not the sole architect of mechanisms that govern behaviour within its territory and beyond, within a region. The populations within and outside the state's territory are not passive participants either in the mechanisms that explain their mobilities in the region. This view is unlike other theoretical approaches such as neofunctionalism, which posit views that are not only state-centric but also completely ignore/exclude certain actors in an analysis of regionalism.

The NRA, therefore, uniquely helps point to collective human action that shows that the frameworks that govern international migration in the SADC region are an outcome of the activities and multidimensional, dynamic interactions of various actors. These include states and non-state actors and their natural or physical environments. The approach permits the critical assessment of complex issues relating to the state–society interphase. For this reason, the NRA adopted in this chapter corresponds with the Marxist notion of accumulation by dispossession and is used to analyse the evolution of frameworks that govern migration in the SADC region from around the advent of colonial rule in the 16th century to the 21st century.

Accumulation by dispossession and 'Africa of the labour reserves'

Like Arrighi et al. (2010), the chapter uses Harvey's (2003: 144) concept of 'accumulation by dispossession' synonymously with the Marxist concept of primitive accumulation, where the 'predatory practices' of colonisers and capitalists in southern Africa played a central role in their accumulation of capital for themselves. For Harvey (2003: 144–145):

> [The] process of accumulation by dispossession involved the forceful eviction of black African peasant populations from their land and the subsequent commodification and privatisation of the land; the suppression of African indigenous systems of production and consumption; the commodification of labour; and the appropriation of assets through processes of colonialism, neo-colonialism and imperialism.

This is the context in which Amin (1972, 1976) considered eastern and southern Africa a third macro region of Africa, namely 'Africa of the labour reserves'. He argued that colonisers forcefully displaced rural Africans from so-called 'traditional' societies and forced them into being suppliers of labour (hence, Africa of the labour reserves) to overcome labour shortages in the colonisers' and capitalists' agricultural and mining ventures. The colonisers drove the Africans into geographical areas of rough terrain and then settled and practised agriculture on the fertile land they arrogated from the Africans. They accumulated wealth from agriculture and mining. Amin argues that the process of dispossession turned Africans into suppliers of cheap labour to European settlers' farms, mines and manufacturing industries.

This chapter uses the concept of accumulation by dispossession to not so much engage with either the accumulation or dispossession posited in the Marxist thesis but rather to point at the displacement of Africans that resulted from the dispossession. It builds on the thesis to advance the notion that the pattern of mobility into which Africans were forced, through coerced participation in the colonisers' and capitalists' system of economic production, constituted a governance mechanism for migration in southern Africa. Because they were dispossessed of land as the Marxist thesis posits, Africans effectively got pushed and had to move to dwell in marginal areas. This translated into migration or forced displacement.

The process did not end there, however. Rather, it would force Africans into a life of migration in two ways. Firstly, the rough topographical landscape of their new areas made it difficult for Africans to live off the land. Secondly, the colonisers schemed by coming up with policies such as imposing taxes on Africans, which could only be paid in the colonisers' currency. This forced Africans to participate in the colonisers' wage economy – to earn incomes to pay taxes. Because the colonisers had a great demand for labour and Africans had initially been unwilling to give the labour (Caldwell, 1985), they forcefully incorporated the Africans into the colonisers' capitalist system of production or wage economy through policy and raw violence to supply labour (Inaka et al., 2024). The system, as the textual evidence in the next section shows, extended far and wide across eastern and southern Africa.

The forced incorporation of Africans into the colonial/capitalist wage economy meant that they would have to live lives of migration – between the marginal geographical areas to which they had been displaced and the urban areas/colonial territories where they provided labour in colonisers' mines, farms and industries. In Amin's analysis, the labour mobility of Africans who dwelt in marginal areas was central to the patterns of colonialism established in the southern African region. In turn, those patterns established a regime wherein Africans oscillated between their new homelands and the farms, mines and urban centres where they were forced to sell their labour.

This mobility or migration regime imposed on Africans constitutes an example of a framework that, whether by design or default, structured Africans' movement between two areas: their poor, rural ones and European settlers'/colonisers' farms, mines and urban areas or colonial territories. Such a regime constitutes an example of a mechanism for migration governance. For this chapter, international migration governance relates to the frameworks or mechanisms that regulate human mobility across nation-state borders.

The mechanisms may be formal, as seen in the policies and legislation drawn up by many governments around the world. In this regard, the 2017 White Paper on International Migration for South Africa and Immigration Act of 2002 for South Africa serve as examples of instruments designed to govern human mobility in/to the nation-state borders of South Africa. The mechanisms may be informal too. Discussions of human trafficking and human smuggling, for example, tend to fall short of coming to terms with the fact that these activities, though vile, are carefully planned, orchestrated and executed. Notwithstanding the lack of ethics and illegality entailed, these constitute mechanisms through which those who are responsible for them govern human mobility.

A CONCISE HISTORICAL OVERVIEW OF INTERNATIONAL MIGRATION GOVERNANCE IN SOUTHERN AFRICA

Pre-colonial mobilities

Historians dismiss as a baseless stereotype the argument that pre-colonial African populations were perpetually mobile (Trevor-Roper, 1965; Hair, 1967). They argue that this depiction of Africa(ns) is based on preconceived European ideas of Africa as a violent continent of barbarians who persistently conquered and invaded each other, leading to forced displacements (Isaacman and Isaacman, 1977; Ivanov, 2002). Contrary to such racist views, the majority of Africans tended to be sedentary before colonialism (Ndeda, 2019). While people in pre-colonial Africa admittedly moved around the continent, not all of them were mobile. Mobile populations only constituted a fraction and co-existed with sedentary populations. Ndeda (2019) confirms this in her examination of the Luo people and their movement to, and establishment of society in, the area around Lake Victoria just before colonial rule began:

> Alliances were important because the Luo did not migrate into empty areas. They found people of Bantu origin already settled. These Bantu speakers were good farmers and led a sedentary life. They cultivated grain, rice and bananas. They used iron hoes and spears and made pottery for cooking and water storage. They had large herds of cattle, goats and sheep but they laid more emphasis on their crops than their animals. Before the arrival of the Luo, the Bantu speakers had major settlements in Yimbo and Samia.

Here, Ndeda shows the mobility of a group of Luo in a particular part of Africa and simultaneously indicates that other groups in the same area, including the Bantu Gusii, Luhya and Nilotic Luo, were sedentary. This historical reality can be extended to many other parts of Africa. Hair (1967), for example, examines linguistic continuity in the coastal area and immediate hinterland that stretches from Guinea on the western side of Africa to Cameroon in central Africa over a period spanning about five centuries up to the 1900s. His study demonstrates the sedentary nature of the peoples who live in this expansive north-west to east-central coastal area of Africa. A noteworthy concept here is how the speakers of the languages Hair examined were steadily domiciled in the region and how this clearly contradicts the idea that Africans were perpetually mobile. Hair (1967: 247) conveys this revelation thus:

> We can thus prepare an inventory of present-day ethnolinguistic units along the coast and in the immediate hinterland.

Investigation has shown that a similar inventory, almost as full, can be drawn from the early written sources on the Guinea coast, that is, from Portuguese and other European records between 1440 and 1700. If we now compare the ethnolinguistic inventory of today with that of the period before 1700, we find a striking continuity. In the particulars compared, the ethnolinguistic units of the Guinea coast have remained very much the same for three, four or five centuries (the period depending on the date of the earliest documentation). This continuity is striking because it contrasts with the impression of wholesale disturbance, and hence discontinuity, given in the standard history texts (under such headings as 'Slave Trade' and 'Imperialism') or in the oral traditions (where sagas of unrelenting migration are relieved only by lists of rival units exterminated *en route*) [emphasis in original].

Still, some sections of pre-colonial African populations were mobile. Cases in point are farmers, hunter-gatherers, herdsmen and fishers. Farmers in pre-colonial Africa were not as sedentary as they generally are in the 21st century. This is because they practised shifting agriculture (Rösler, 1997). They farmed large swathes of land but moved because they could not farm the same land every year. Delius et al. (2012), however, argue that it is important to be wary of making this practice the default mode for reconstructing pre-colonial agriculture. They do not dispute the prevalence of shifting agriculture and settlement mobility in many parts of pre-colonial Africa, but they posit that even where evidence of shifting agriculture exists, blanket assumptions cannot be made that settlements had to be moved frequently. Sheriff (1974) argues that historical evidence of agricultural intensification in places like pre-colonial East Africa questions the universality of shifting agriculture.

Various herdsmen pastoralists and nomads in several parts of Africa still practice transhumance in the 21st century. Where transhumance was (and is still is) practised in Africa, it involved pastoralists regularly moving flocks between fixed locations for their animals to access seasonally available pastures (Morris, 2017). However, the practice has reduced and faces many challenges. Conditions for pastoral societies are more difficult because of, among other things, nation-state borders imposed on Africa and accompanying national economic, social and political systems, and climate-related changes.

Transhumant pastoralists tend to engage in one or all of three forms of movement. First, within a country: to search for water and forage for themselves and their livestock. These movements tend to be seasonal and occur especially with the onset of rains that stimulate the growth of good forage. Second, movements may be towards water bodies during dry seasons and may involve crossing nation-state borders. Third, the pastoralists may equally return to arid areas at the onset of rain and the prospect of rising waters in the terrain around the water bodies.

As migration expresses a change in the relationship between people, time and space, it is clear that pre-colonial African mobilities occurred when farmers or herdsmen reorganised their spaces and the resources within those spaces. Such movements boil(ed) down to the quest for livelihoods. This would have precipitated regular population movements, which depended on the exploitation of the natural environment. The movements were thus associated with human activities, including hunter-gathering, pastoralism, agriculture and fishing.

Hunter-gatherers followed game and camped where they found sufficient plants to feed on. Their movements were thus seasonal. Pastoralists had to graze and have water for their animals to drink. Therefore, they had to seasonally engage in transhumance. In some cases, this occurred over long distances, but the movements were seasonal, happened from year to year and often followed the same routes. Though herdsmen were sometimes susceptible to variations in climate, it clearly can be posited that their movements – just like those practised by farmers – were actually regular, having occurred seasonally. In the case of farmers, for instance, the practice of shifting agriculture saw them move in order to leave land that had been cultivated to fallow. When the distance between a settlement and newly cultivated land became considerably long, villagers shifted to be closer to their fields. Populations settled on fertile land and because they did not have sufficient technology to keep the land fertile, permanent cultivation was rare.

Though fishers were generally sedentary, they sometimes moved and camped on riverbanks in places distant from their villages. They did this for months on end because of variations in the water levels of the rivers from which they fished.

That said, it is worth noting that the population groups discussed here were not exclusive. This, again, is contrary to stereotypes which suggest that African ethnic groups had no contact with other population groups or the outside world. For example, the communities around Lake Victoria that Ndeda (2019) examines included ethnic groups whose origins were different and yet they 'interacted with each other and borrowed extensively from each other'. Furthermore, Ndeda (2019) points out that:

> The Luyia subgroups practised trade among themselves in the precolonial era. Iron hoes, spear points, and ivory, for example, could be traded for grains or animals. Precolonial trade covered a distance of no more than 72 kilometres, but there were three precolonial markets where Luo, Nandi, and Abaluyia came together to trade baskets, wooden tools, quail, and various foodstuffs for cattle, fish, tobacco, and so forth. Hence despite their sometimes conflictual relations they interacted amicably.

At the micro level, various other factors drove individuals to move. For example, marriage or the desire to live with kin. Some historians also cite the example of the pre-colonial city of Zimbabwe and its population of approximately 10,000 around the beginning of the 14th century; they suggest that earlier migration had occurred to the city. This indicates that urbanisation contributed to population movements in pre-colonial Africa.

In summary, some pre-colonial African mobilities, population movements or migrations were organised, among other things, around livelihoods or livelihood strategies. Of course, there was more to the movements than economic factors. Some individuals or groups moved because of conflict or mortality. The types of mobility discussed in this section, however, were dictated by the need to hunt or gather food, feed livestock, secure arable land and fish. These mobilities were centred on systems or modes of food production. In other words, the need to produce for consumption and survival determined when and where populations moved. The people of Africa became trapped and their mobilities were curtailed with the advent of colonialism, territorialisation, and the imposition of nation-state borders and the Westphalian state system on Africa.

Colonial mobilities

Nation-state borders are an enduring legacy of colonialism in Africa. A fundamental consequence of these socially and politically constructed institutions relates to their functions as markers of territory. Borders fulfil exclusionary and inclusionary functions and, thereby, regulate the movement of people into and out of a nation-state's territory (Anderson and O'Dowd, 1999; Wilson and Donnan, 1998, 2012). This is what came to define new African realities with the advent of colonialism. African populations could not move as freely as they previously did before European countries partitioned the continent for colonial domination at the Berlin Conference of 1884.

Colonial administrations and capitalist ventures established wage economies within the territories they colonised and established. They subsequently forced the Africans they subjugated within those territories to supply labour for the administrations and economic activities of the colonies (Amin, 1972, 1976; Inaka et al., 2024). Through a combination of policies (such as the hut tax) and brutal force, colonisers thus incorporated the African peasants they had dispossessed of land into the new capitalist economy (Inaka et al., 2024). In effect, this made migrants out of the African peasants. This is because the peasants had to take up work in the farms, mines, and administrative and commercial centres established by the colonisers. Amin (1972) says of this process that the colonial powers orchestrated political and economic procedures that created structures needed for large-scale production of agricultural and mineral products. These were produced for export and to attract investment while exploiting cheap labour. Amin writes that one such procedure consisted of

> ... political support to the social strata and classes which were allowed to appropriate de facto some of the tribal lands, and

44

the organization of internal migration from the regions which were deliberately left in their poverty so as to be used as labour reserves' (Amin, 1972: 115).

With time and increased investments, the organisation of labour migration extended beyond the borders of individual colonial territories into established, regional structures and networks. Added to this were discoveries of mineral deposits and resultant mining ventures in a number of countries/territories in the southern African region. Zambia (then Northern Rhodesia), for instance, and later Botswana, attracted labour from neighbouring countries in the region to their copper and diamond belts. Zimbabwe (then Southern Rhodesia) was known for agriculture and was a hub for migrant labour from neighbouring countries to farms and plantations there (Van Onselen, 1976). The discovery of gold and diamonds in the South African towns of Johannesburg and Kimberley in the 1880s extended and further established the regional labour migration system. Amin (1972: 114–115) writes:

In the region which we have called *Africa of the labour reserves* [emphasis in original] (Afrique des reserves), capital at the centre needed to have a large proletariat immediately available. This was because there was great mineral wealth to be exploited (gold and diamonds in South Africa, copper in Northern Rhodesia) or an untypical settler agriculture in tropical Africa (old Boer colonization in South Africa, new British settlement of Southern Rhodesia and, in the extreme north of the region, of Kenya which until 1919 was separated from the southern part of 'labour reserve Africa' by German Tanganyika). To obtain this proletariat quickly, the colonizers dispossessed the African rural communities by violence and drove them back deliberately into small regions. Furthermore, they kept them in these poor regions with no means of modernizing and intensifying their farming. Thereby they forced the 'traditional' society to be a supplier of temporary or permanent migrants on a vast scale, thus providing a cheap proletariat for the mines, the European farms, and later for the manufacturing industries of South Africa, Rhodesia and Kenya. Henceforth we can no longer speak of a traditional society in that region of the continent, since the labour reserve society had a function which had nothing to do with 'tradition': that of supplying a migrant proletariat. The African social formations of this region distorted and impoverished, lost even, the semblance of autonomy: the unhappy Africa of the Bantustans and apartheid was born: it was to supply the greatest return to central capital.

It is worth emphasising that the *'Africa of the labour reserves'* stretched from South Africa northeast as far as Kenya and included all territories in between. Thus Amin (1976: 318) writes:

> The eastern and southern parts of the continent (Kenya, Uganda, Tanzania, Rwanda, Burundi, Zambia, Malawi, Angola, Mozambique, Zimbabwe, Botswana, Lesotho, Swaziland, and South Africa) constitute the third microregion, 'the Africa of the labor reserves'.

The colonial authorities and private capital tapped into the labour reserves for their labour needs and, in so doing, established a mechanism for governing the steady flow of workers they were ensured.

Post-colonial mobilities

The labour migration governance system that the colonial authorities established to exploit 'the Africa of the labour reserves' in the colonial era persists in post-colonial southern Africa. Simultaneously, the region's economy remains predominantly based on extractives and agricultural industries. The ownership of the industries also seems to mirror this reality and exhibit continuities with the past. This implies that owners' motive to drive down costs of production persists. Labour tends to be the first casualty when industries restructure to cut costs. Where labour is vital, however, this further translates into the (quest for and) exploitation of cheap(er) labour. The liberalisation of many economies in southern Africa in the late 1980s and early 1990s is worth underscoring in relation to this. Many firms and governments downsized and opted to casualise labour. A few countries in the region also experienced economic and political difficulties in the same period. These 21st-century realities have consequences for human mobility, including irregular and forced migration, across the SADC region and within individual member states. The region, therefore, continues to experience migration despite nation-state borders.

The migration might vary and have slightly different nuances from those that occurred in the past, but it is certainly historical. Thus, the SADC region is characterised by notable historical patterns and processes of migration. Hubs of economic activity in the region, for example, have always attracted labour migrants. Examples include mining activities in countries like Botswana, South Africa and Zambia, and agricultural and farming activities in countries like South Africa and Zimbabwe. The forces behind this migration in the colonial era were clearly the colonisers and capitalist interests. These forces orchestrated networks and mechanisms through which they had a guaranteed supply of migrants to meet their labour needs. The fundamental structures, networks and mechanisms that govern these flows seem to have survived the mode of political governance experienced in the region. The extractive and agricultural industries continue to attract migrants from across the SADC region to countries where these economic activities occur.

MOBILITIES PAST AND PRESENT IN THE SADC REGION: CONCLUDING REMARKS

The history of migration in the SADC region consists of human mobilities that were dictated by the need for human survival before the advent of colonialism. The mobilities drastically changed with colonialism and the imposition of nation-state borders and a capitalist mode of production and economy on African territories.

To satisfy their labour needs, colonisers and capital created an 'Africa of the labour reserves'. This consisted of Africans who were both forcefully displaced from their traditional means of production and incorporated into the capitalist mode of production and wage economy. The system established essentially made Africans second-class individuals in terms of the social division of people. In other words, a primary intersectional factor was deployed that made the African less equal than the coloniser. Of this, the scholarship suggests that colonialism was part of a global campaign to hierarchise human beings into groups of inferior and superior beings based on economic, cultural and political contexts and that this originated from the Western-centric capitalist world system (De Sousa Santos, 2007; Grosfoguel et al., 2015).

In conclusion, this chapter suggests that, despite the end of colonialism, the social division of people and the hierarchisation of human beings established under colonial rule persists in 21st-century southern Africa. The divisions persist even if a shift seems to have occurred. The certain group of migrants described in the introduction to this chapter seems to be the social actors newly constructed as belonging to the 'Africa of the labour reserves'. With this, they are considered less desirable than the rest. The preoccupation with addressing so-called migration crises boils down to veiled reservations about allowing this type of social actor to engage in international mobility. They are irregular and undesirable because they belong to a lower level in a social hierarchy of beings.

REFERENCES

Abreu, A. 2012. 'The new economics of labor migration: Beware of neoclassicals bearing gifts'. *Forum for Social Economics*, 41(1), 46–67.

Agustin, L. M. 2007. *Sex at the Margins: Migration, labour markets, and the rescue industry*. London: Zed Books Ltd.

Amin, S. 1972. 'Underdevelopment and dependence in Black Africa – Origins and contemporary forms'. *The Journal of Modern African Studies*, 10(4), 503–524.

Amin, S. 1976. *Unequal Development: An essay on the social formations of peripheral capitalism*. New York: Monthly Review Press.

Anderson, J. and O'Dowd, L. 1999. 'Borders, border regions and territoriality: contradictory meanings, changing significance'. *Regional Studies*, 33(7), 593–604.

Arrighi, G., Aschoff, N. and Scully, B. 2010. 'Accumulation by dispossession and its limits: The southern Africa paradigm revisited'. *Studies in*

Comparative International Development, 45(4), 410–438.

Bakewell, O. 2010. 'Some reflections on structure and agency in migration theory'. *Journal of Ethnic and Migration Studies*, 36(10), 1689–1708.

Betts, A. 2011. 'Introduction: Global migration governance', in Betts, A. (ed.), *Global Migration Governance*. Oxford: Oxford University Press, 133.

Bodvarsson, Ö. B., Simpson, N. B. and Sparber, C. 2015. 'Migration Theory', in Chiswick, B. R. and Miller, P. W. (eds), *Handbook of the Economics of International Migration*. North Holland, 3–51.

Brun, C. and Fábos, A. 2015. 'Making homes in limbo? A conceptual framework'. *Refuge: Canada's Journal on Refugees*, 31(1), 5–17.

Caldwell, J. C. 1985. 'The social repercussions of colonial rule: Demographic aspects', in Boahen, A. A. (ed.), *General History of Africa, VII: Africa under colonial domination, 1880–1935*. Portsmouth: United Nations Educational, Scientific and Cultural Organization & Heinemann Educational Books Ltd, 458–486.

Carling, J. and Collins, F. 2018. 'Aspiration, desire and drivers of migration'. *Journal of Ethnic and Migration Studies*, 44(6), 909–926.

Carling, J. and Hernández-Carretero, M. 2011. 'Protecting Europe and protecting migrants? Strategies for managing unauthorised migration from Africa'. *The British Journal of Politics and International Relations*, 13(1), 42–58.

Castles, S. 2010. 'Understanding global migration: A social transformation perspective'. *Journal of Ethnic and Migration Studies*, 36(10), 1565–1586.

Castles, S., De Haas, H. and Miller, M. J. 2020. *The Age of Migration: International population movements in the modern world* (Sixth edition). New York: Guilford Publications Inc.

Chingwete, A. 9 February 2016. 'Immigration remains a challenge for South Africa's government and citizens'. *Afrobarometer Dispatch,* https://www.afrobarometer.org/publication/ad72-immigration-remains-challenge-for-south-africas-government-and-citizens/, accessed 1 August 2023.

Crush, J. and Tevera, D. S. (eds). 2010. *Zimbabwe's Exodus: Crisis, migration, survival*. Ottawa: International Development Research Center and Southern African Migration Programme.

Czaika, M., Bijak, J. and Prike, T. 2021. 'Migration decision-making and its key dimensions'. *The ANNALS of the American Academy of Political and Social Science*, 697(1), 15–31.

Czaika, M. and De Haas, H. 2013. 'The effectiveness of immigration policies'. *Population and Development Review*, 39(3), 487–508.

De Haas, H. 2010. 'Migration and development: A theoretical perspective'. *International Migration Review*, 44(1), 227–264.

Delius, P., Maggs, T. and Schoeman, M. 2012. 'Bokoni: Old structures, new paradigms? Rethinking pre-colonial society from the perspective of the stone-walled sites in Mpumalanga'. *Journal of Southern African Studies*,

38(2), 399–414.

Dorigo, G. and Tobler, W. 1983. 'Push-pull migration laws'. *Annals of the Association of American Geographers*, 73(1), 1–17.

Dryding, D. 2020. 'Half of South Africans would refuse asylum, bar foreign workers, place refugees in camps'. *Afrobarometer Dispatch*, 360, 1–12.

Ehlers, V. J., Oosthuizen, M. J., Bezuidenhout, M. C., Monareng, L. V. and Jooste, K. 2003. 'Post-basic nursing students' perceptions of the emigration of nurses from the Republic of South Africa: Research'. *Health SA Gesondheid*, 8(4), 24–37.

Ellis, S., and Segatti, A. 2011. 'The role of skilled labor', in Segatti, A. and Landau, L. B. (eds), *Contemporary Migration to South Africa: A regional development issue*. New York: The International Bank for Reconstruction and Development/The World Bank, 67–79.

Garip, F. 2012. 'Discovering diverse mechanisms of migration: The Mexico-US stream 1970–2000'. *Population and Development Review*, 38(3), 393–433.

Ghorashi, H. 2005. 'Agents of change or passive victims: The impact of welfare states (the case of the Netherlands) on refugees'. *Journal of Refugee Studies*, 18(2), 181–198.

Hair, P. E. H. 1967. 'Ethnolinguistic continuity on the Guinea coast'. *The Journal of African History*, 8(2), 247–268.

Hammar, A., McGregor, J. and Landau, L. 2010. 'Introduction – Displacing Zimbabwe: Crisis and construction in Southern Africa'. *Journal of Southern African Studies*, 36(2), 263–283.

Harris, J. and Todaro, M. 1970. 'Migration, unemployment and development: A two-sector analysis'. *The American Economic Review*, 60(1), 126–142.

Harvey, D. 2003. *The New Imperialism*. Oxford: Oxford University Press.

Heller, C. 2014. 'Perception management – Deterring potential migrants through information campaigns'. *Global Media and Communication*, 10(3), 303–318.

Hettne, B., Inotai, A. and Sunkel, O. (eds). 2000. *The New Regionalism and the Future of Security and Development*. United Kingdom: Palgrave Macmillan.

Inaka, S. J., Nshimbi, C. C. and Tshimpaka, L. M. 2024. *The Reconstruction of Post-War Labour Markets in the Southern African Development Community. Insights from the Democratic Republic of The Congo* (First edition). United Kingdom: Palgrave Macmillan.

Isaacman, A. and Isaacman, B. 1977. 'Resistance and collaboration in Southern and Central Africa, c. 1850–1920'. *The International Journal of African Historical Studies*, 10(1), 31.

Ivanov, P. 2002. 'Cannibals, warriors, conquerors, and colonizers: Western perceptions and Azande historiography'. *History in Africa*, 29, 89–217.

Kasiram, M. 2009. 'The emigration of South African social workers: Using social work education to address gaps in provision'. *Social Work Education*,

28(6), 646–654.

Lee, E. S. 1966. 'A theory of migration'. *Demography*, 3(1), 47–57.

Lewis, W. A. 1954. 'Economic development with unlimited supplies of labour'. *The Manchester School*, 22(2), 139–191.

MacDonald, J. S. and MacDonald, L. D. 1964. 'Chain migration ethnic neighborhood formation and social networks'. *The Milbank Memorial Fund Quarterly*, 42(1), 82–97.

Massey, D. S., Arango, J., Hugo, G., Kouaouci, A., Pellegrino, A. and Taylor, J. E. 1993. 'Theories of international migration: A review and appraisal'. *Population & Development Review*, 19(3), 431–466.

Maxwell, J. A. 2009. 'Designing a qualitative study', in Bickman, L. and Rog, D. J. (eds), *The SAGE Handbook of Applied Social Research Methods* (Second edition). California: SAGE Publications, 214–253.

McNamara, K. E. and Gibson, C. 2009. '"We do not want to leave our land": Pacific ambassadors at the United Nations resist the category of "climate refugees"'. *Geoforum*, 40(3), 475–483.

Miles, M. B. 1979. 'Qualitative data as an attractive nuisance: The problem of analysis'. *Administrative Science Quarterly*, 24(4), 590–601.

Morris, S. T. 2017. 'Overview of sheep production systems', in Ferguson, D. M., Lee, C. and Fisher, A. (eds), *Advances in Sheep Welfare*. Sawston: Woodhead Publishing, 19–35.

Moyo, I. 2016. 'The Beitbridge–Mussina interface: Towards flexible citizenship, sovereignty and territoriality at the border'. *Journal of Borderlands Studies*, 31(4), 427–440.

Moyo, I. and Nshimbi, C. C. 2020. 'Borders, mobility and integration in Africa revisited: Towards a new understanding of African realities', in Nshimbi, C. C. and Moyo, I. (eds), *Borders, Mobility, Regional Integration and Development: Issues, dynamics and perspectives in West, Eastern and Southern Africa*. New York: Springer Cham, 179–187.

Ndeda, M. A. J. 2019. 'Population movement, settlement and the construction of society to the east of Lake Victoria in precolonial times: The western Kenyan case'. *Les Cahiers d'Afrique de L'Est*, 52, 83–108.

Nshimbi, C. C. 2015. 'Networks of cross-border non-state actors: The role of social capital in regional integration'. *Journal of Borderlands Studies*, 30(4), 537–560.

Nshimbi, C. C. 2019. 'Life in the fringes: Economic and sociocultural practices in the Zambia–Malawi–Mozambique borderlands in comparative perspective'. *Journal of Borderlands Studies*, 34(1), 47–70.

Nshimbi, C. C. 2020a. 'Resilience nodes: Grassroots-state encounter and interactions in COMESA-EAC-SADC tripartite free trade area border spaces', in Nshimbi, C. C. Moyo, I. and Laine, J. P. (eds), *Borders, Sociocultural Encounters and Contestations*. England: Routledge, 37–59.

Nshimbi, C. C. 2020b. 'The human side of regions: Informal cross-border traders in the Zambia–Malawi–Mozambique growth triangle and prospects for integrating Southern Africa'. *Journal of Borderlands Studies*, 35(1), 75–97.

Nshimbi, C. C. 2021. 'Rational actors, passive and helpless victims, neither, both: EU borders and the drive to migrate in the horn of Africa'. *Social Inclusion*, 9(1), 257–267.

Nshimbi, C. C. 2022. '(Ir)relevant doctrines and African realities: Neoliberal and Marxist influences on labour migration governance in Southern Africa'. *Third World Quarterly*, 43(7), 1724–1743.

Nshimbi, C. C. 2023. 'Of "pieces of cake" and "elephants in the room"', in Oloruntoba, S. O., Nshimbi, C. C. and Tshimpaka, L. M. (eds), *Africa-EU Relations and the African Continental Free Trade Area*. England: Routledge, 162–178.

Nshimbi, C. C. and Fioramonti, L. 2013. *A Region Without Borders?: Policy frameworks for regional labour migration towards South Africa*. University of the Witwatersrand: African Centre for Migration & Society.

Oeppen, C. 2016. '"Leaving Afghanistan! Are you sure?" European efforts to deter potential migrants through information campaigns'. *Human Geography*, 9(2), 57–68.

Pânzaru, C. and Reisz, R. D. 2013. 'Validity of the push and pull hypothesis for the explanation of Romanian migration flows'. *Journal of Social Research & Policy*, 4(1), 93–108.

Peisker, V. C. and Tilbury, F. 2003. '"Active" and "passive" resettlement: The influence of support services and refugees' own resources on resettlement style'. *International Migration*, 41(5), 61–91.

Portes, A. 2010. 'Migration and social change: Some conceptual reflections'. *Journal of Ethnic and Migration Studies*, 36(10), 1537–1563.

Ravenstein, E. G. 1885. 'The laws of migration'. *Journal of the Statistical Society of London*, 48(2), 167–235.

Rösler, M. 1997. 'Shifting cultivation in the Ituri Forest [Haut-Zaïre]. Colonial intervention, present situation, economic and ecological prospects'. *Civilisations*, 44(1/2), 44–61.

Sassen, S. 1988. *The Mobility of Labor and Capital*. Cambridge: Cambridge University Press.

Sheriff, A. H. 1974. 'The dynamics of change in pre-colonial East African societies'. *African Economic History Review*, 1(2), 7–14.

Skeldon, R. 1990. *Population Mobility in Developing Countries: A reinterpretation*. Belhaven: Belhaven University Press.

Trevor-Roper, H. R. 1965. *The Rise of Christian Europe*. California: Harcourt, Brace & World.

Tshimpaka, L. M., Nshimbi, C. C. and Moyo, I. 2021. *Regional Economic Communities and Integration in Southern Africa*. Singapore: Springer.

Turner, S. 2013. 'Under the state's gaze: Upland trading-scapes on the Sino-

Vietnamese border'. *Singapore Journal of Tropical Geography*, 34(1), 9–24.

United Nations. 1998. *Recommendations on Statistics of International Migration.* Statistical Papers Series, 58(1).

United Nations Network on Migration. 2023. *GCM National Implementation Plans.* Implementing the GCM: Guidance for Governments and All Relevant Stakeholders.

Van Der Walt, L. 2007. 'The first globalisation and transnational labour activism in Southern Africa: White labourism, the IWW, and the ICU, 1904–1934'. *African Studies*, 66(2–3), 223–251.

Van Hear, N. 2010. 'Theories of migration and social change'. *Journal of Ethnic and Migration Studies*, 36(10), 1531–1536.

Van Hear, N., Bakewell, O. and Long, K. 2018. 'Push-pull plus: Reconsidering the drivers of migration'. *Journal of Ethnic and Migration Studies*, 44(6), 927–944.

Van Onselen, C. 1976. *Chibaro: African mine labour in Southern Rhodesia 1900–1933.* London: Pluto Press.

Watkins, J. 2020. 'Irregular migration, borders, and the moral geographies of migration management'. *Environment and Planning C: Politics and Space*, 38(6), 1108–1127.

Wegge, S. A. 1998. 'Chain migration and information networks: Evidence from nineteenth-century hesse-cassel'. *The Journal of Economic History*, 58(4), 957–986.

Wilson, T. M. and Donnan, H. 1998. 'Nation, state and identity at international borders', in Wilson, T. M. and Donnan, H. (eds), *Border Identities: Nation and state at international frontiers.* Cambridge: Cambridge University Press, 1–30.

Wilson, T. M. and Donnan, H. 2012. 'Borders and border studies', in Wilson, T. M. and Donnan, H. (eds), *A Companion to Border Studies.* New Jersey: Blackwell Publishing Ltd, 1–25.

World Bank. 2016. *Migration and Remittances Factbook 2016: Third Edition.* New York: World Bank.

Zipf, G. K. 1946. 'The P1 P2/D hypothesis: On the intercity movement of persons'. *American Sociological Review*, 11(6), 677–686.

THREE

Native migrant animosity – aggrieved, not xenophobic: The case of South Africa

VUSUMUZI GUMBI

INTRODUCTION

The relationship between migration and security in social sciences is a complex and multifaceted one that has been extensively debated and studied by scholars, policymakers and international organisations. It involves examining how migration patterns and movements impact on various aspects of security, including national security, human security and societal stability. Since the 2008 global financial crisis, South Africa has experienced a great influx of immigrants from the Southern African Development Community (SADC) region and from far-flung regions like West Africa and Asia – all seeking economic and political refuge. With the influx of foreign immigrants, however, also came a greater resistance from the locals. This chapter seeks to discuss and bring academic debate on the securitisation of migration in South Africa into perspective by drawing on the conceptualisation of the migration-security nexus to highlight other countries' experiences. This will be done to show that this growing phenomenon is not exclusive to South Africa, thus highlighting the emergence of a securitised approach to migration from other parts of the world.

The securitisation of migration, according to Charrett (2009), is based on establishing an agenda that would endeavour to safeguard the nation-state from identifiable threats to protect the state and, in the case of South Africa, change the status quo. Albert and Buzan (2011) from the Copenhagen School of Security Studies argue that securitisation extends beyond traditional militarisation to include economic, social and political sectors as well. The securitisation of migration will ordinarily find expression in South Africa because the post-apartheid economic reform programme has not adequately brought about the 'better life for all' promised at the beginning of democracy. This weakness is a result of the long-standing flaws in the programme, which prevent it from fully facilitating economic justice and improved prosperity for the majority of the population. Immigrants seem to not be aware that even South Africa is also susceptible to a fluctuation of stability as a social welfare state. Post-apartheid South Africa is characterised by a tense situation in which citizens are increasingly aware, through their participation in the political environment, that the country's constitution is slow in bringing about justice, equality or material benefits of citizenship (Gumede, 2020). The South African government is struggling to adequately cater for its own citizens' social and economic needs, with the documented unemployment rate sitting just above 32 per cent of the country's total working population (Statistics South Africa, 2023). This is an alarming statistic and it partly explains why local citizens feel threatened by foreign immigrants in the country. South Africans feel vulnerable, believing that the immigrants come to compete with them for the little that they have to make a living.

Methodologically, this chapter was developed through qualitative and investigative assessments into animosity towards local (South African) migrants: this involved a consideration of existing literature on securitisation of migration and on data drawn from both primary and secondary sources. The former included interviews with Vuyo

Zungula (South African politician) and Faith Mabusela (South African activist), both of whom have been at the forefront of advocating against porous borders and irregular migration. The chapter highlights how securitisation of migration is not exclusive to South Africa, providing examples of how it has taken place in other parts of the world. A qualitative approach enabled the study to investigate the question of whether South Africans are not xenophobic but rather aggrieved at their lack of human and societal security, an unequal system and deteriorating welfare in areas such as health.

BACKGROUND

South Africa has one of the largest immigrant populations in Africa due to its stable democracy and relatively well-developed economy in comparison with others in the region. Between 2.9 million and 3.9 million documented immigrants reside in the country, which equates to 5–6 per cent of the total population of roughly 60 million (UNOCHA, 2021; Africa Check, 2023). This figure is likely an underestimate given the widely recorded presence of undocumented immigrants, particularly those from neighbouring countries.

Figure 3.1: Recorded migration to South Africa

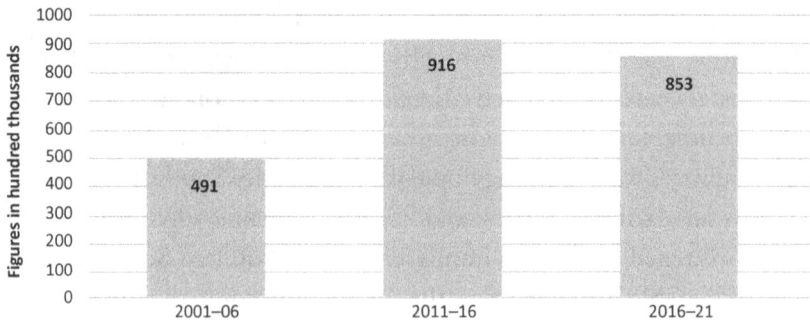

Source: UNOCHA (2021), adapted by the author

Figure 3.1 above demonstrates how immigration has tended to rise over the past few decades since the end of apartheid in 1994. According to the United Nations Office for the Coordination of Humanitarian Affairs (UNOCHA), a net estimate of 853,000 people migrated to the country over the 2016–21 period, a significant increase from 491,700 people in the 2001–06 period but a slight decline from the net immigration of 916,300 over the 2011–16 period (UNOCHA, 2021). In the years since, the profile of immigrants to South Africa has included low-skilled migrants from elsewhere in the region (many of whom are unauthorised), skilled African professionals, and refugees and asylum seekers (UNOCHA, 2021).

Despite the country's long history of immigration and sporadic attempts at legalisation (Migration Act of 2002; Refugees Act of 1998), many segments of South African society have shown intolerance towards immigrants, including workers and asylum seekers legally present in South Africa. The county has endured significant continuities in economic and social inequality since the apartheid regime ended in 1994. Black South Africans make up the bulk of those who are below the poverty line. Academics (Morris, 1999; Tshitereke, 1999) highlight the link between animosity towards migrants and inadequate progress in the post-apartheid era to fulfil the promises of a better life for previously disadvantaged citizens. Foreigners in general, and those from African countries in particular, have indeed been scapegoated for South African problems by some politicians manipulating the material conditions of the poor for their own electoral gains. It is also true that groups of citizens anywhere in the world would be inclined to protect themselves against perceived social and economic threats. These two points are not mutually exclusive; two truths can co-exist. This is important because the discussion of migration in South Africa usually falls short of nuances that explain the changing nature of South African society. Such debate usually reveals a bias that narrows the discussion to South Africans as xenophobic, sidestepping the broader complexities of immigration dynamics in South African black communities.

THEORETICAL CONCEPTUALISATION OF
THE MIGRATION–SECURITY NEXUS

The evolution of the security theory that contributed to the Copenhagen School of Security Studies involves a progression of ideas and paradigms that have shaped our understanding of security in international relations. Salter (2008) is of the view that this evolution encompasses the realist perspective, the emergence of broader security concepts, and ultimately finds expression in the Copenhagen School's unique approach to security. There are many diverse perspectives on what constitutes a security threat and who or what is vulnerable in the sphere of international relations. While this chapter does not attempt to list all the various theoretical approaches, a brief account is offered of the historical development of the field and the major theories to emerge from it. Discussion then moves on to an examination of the Copenhagen School securitisation theory.

Positions differ based on their ontological and epistemo-logical stances.

The broadening of the security field
The area of international security studies (ISS), a subfield of international relations, drew heavily on the works of older fields of political theory, incorporating both classical realism and liberalist texts such as those of classical Greece, Machiavelli, Hobbes, Mill and Montesquieu (Guler, 2019). Realism has been the pre-eminent paradigm in security studies due to the centrality of the concepts of the state and military power (Stepka, 2022a). Realist assumptions were put to the test by the demise of the Soviet Union, sparking a significant ideological shift. Both Buzan and Hansen (2009) and Stepka (2022a) argue that, in the Cold War period, securitisation focused on traditional militarisation in areas like nuclear and bipolar deterrence. The result was that securitisation in less traditional areas like migration was overlooked.

The concept of human security, which emphasises the security and wellbeing of individuals rather than just state interests, gained prominence during the 1990s. Human security considers factors such as poverty, health, education and human rights as essential components of security. Similarly, societal security recognises that threats can emerge from within societies, including from issues like ethnic tensions, social inequalities and cultural conflicts. These perspectives underscored the need to address not only external military threats but also internal societal vulnerabilities to achieve comprehensive security. In 1994, the United Nations Development Programme (UNDP) highlighted two major concerns relating to human security and one of these was 'freedom from fear'. The UNDP (1994) further outlined that for too long the concept of national security has been shaped by the potential for conflict between two states and equated with the threats to a country's borders, and argued that the requirements of national security have come to embrace the protection of communities and individuals from internal violence.

In the context of South Africa, this is particularly important for anti-migrant sentiments, where black South Africans have been hit hardest with economic downturns. In support of this claim, Pillay (2008a) rejects the simplistic notion that animosity to migrants is a result of identity problems and instead adopts a sociological perspective that provides a more nuanced approach to examining how socioeconomic status, power and access to resources interact to play a role in the discontent. The Copenhagen School's securitisation theory also offers an insightful lens through which to analyse how migration is transformed into a security issue. It highlights the importance of language, discourse and political actors in shaping perceptions of threats. However, it is crucial to complement this perspective with a broader understanding of structural factors, considerations about human rights, and the multiplicity of voices involved in the migration discourse.

Migration and securitisation

The term 'securitisation of migration' describes the framing of migration as a security threat to a state or society. Governments then respond by restricting conventional migration avenues or enacting more restrictive policies against migrants, such as greater monitoring, imprisonment and deportation. The personal security of migrants is severely impacted as a result. This insecurity motivates them to take riskier detours and to pay extortionate sums to migrant smugglers and human traffickers to reach their final destinations.

The Copenhagen School of Security Studies developed the idea of securitisation, which has changed how security concerns are perceived. It contends that in addition to military threats to national security, there are risks posed by societal, environmental, economic and political dimensions (Buzan et al., 1998; Stepka, 2022b; Farny, 2016).

How migration securitisation manifests

It is well documented that the main ways that the securitisation of migration is displayed are through tightening visa regulations in countries of origin or transit and strengthening border controls. Migrants also encounter detention and deportation, as well as hostile environments that undermine integration and acceptance into their final destinations (Horwood et al., 2019). As a result, the process of securitising migration involves four distinct dimensions: socioeconomic, political, security and identity (Estevens, 2018). The socioeconomic dimension entails potential loads on the welfare system; rivalry for jobs with South Africans and the health risks associated with access to facilities and any new and resurrected germs that immigrants may bring with them. Securitisation also covers threats to national security, borders and both internal and external safety.

According to Abebe (2019), the national identity and demographic stability of the host society are threatened by immigration, which results in distinctions being drawn between migrants and nationals. Political narratives of animosity towards migrants act to reinforce migrant hostility being generated in other spheres, namely socioeconomics, identity and security. The political element in this case is the most important since it serves as the foundation for policymaking. Abebe (2019) argues that although the military and security sectors have traditionally made substantial contributions to the formation of securitised viewpoints on migration, a larger range of players are involved in the securitisation of the landscape, as per the scholars who have broadened traditional security as we know it.

In the discipline of political science, the author Myron Weiner (1993) is recognised as having been among the first to foresee the potential of migration-related dangers to nation-states. Weiner divides risks or vulnerabilities resulting from migration-related issues into the following groupings (Weiner, 1993: 10):

- Threat or risk to the home regime
- Threat or risk to the host country
- Threat or risk to cultural identity
- Threat or risk to the economy
- Threat or risk to society
- Threat or risk to the sending countries if they are held hostages in the host countries.

A consideration of the facilitating factors suggested by the securitisation theory may extend our understanding of how the relationship between migration and security arises in some social and historical contexts but is absent from others. This can assist us in identifying the underlying issues that led to the creation of the migration–security nexus.

Indlala ibanga ulaka (Hunger causes anger)

These are insights from an interview with African Transformation Movement (ATM) president, Vuyo Zungula in 2023.

In 1994, South Africa's government changed but the social structure remained the same. Africa's most industrialised nation continues to be characterised by the juxtaposition of 'First World' and 'Third World' realities, the latter illustrated by the fact that 75 per cent of the population (mostly black) still suffer the effects of colonialism, racism and segregation. It has been 30 years since the 'end' of apartheid, yet its legacy continues unabated. Poverty and inequality continue to reach new heights, as a result of a history of exclusion and an economy that does not encourage any meaningful participation of the poor and fails to create enough jobs. Income inequality is much larger, and because there is no intergenerational mobility, inequalities are passed down from one generation to the next with little change over time. The gap between the rich and the poor remains high. Abahlali baseMjondolo, an organisation of shack-dwellers located principally in Durban, gave one of the most nuanced statements about native migrant animosity to date in 2008. An excerpt from a press release (Abahlali baseMjondolo, 2008) condemning violent anti-migrant attacks reads thus:

> We hear that the political analysts are saying that the poor must be educated about xenophobia. Always the solution is to 'educate the poor'. When we get cholera, we must be educated about washing our hands when in fact we need clean water. When we get burnt, we must be educated about fire when in fact we need electricity. This is just a way of blaming the poor for our suffering. We want land and housing in the cities, we want to go to university, we want water and electricity – we don't want to be educated to be good at surviving poverty on our own. The solution is not to educate the poor about xenophobia. The solution is to give the poor what they need to survive so that it becomes easier to be welcoming and generous. The solution is to stop the xenophobia at all levels of our society. Arrest the poor man who has become a murderer. But also arrest the corrupt policeman and the corrupt officials in Home Affairs. Close down Lindela and apologise for the suffering it has caused. Give papers to all the people sheltering in the police stations in Johannesburg.

With South Africa's population being just over 60 million people, approximately 55.5 per cent (30.3 million people) of the population are living in poverty and 18.2 million of that 30.3 million live below the poverty line of US$1.9 per day, defined by the World Bank in 2002 as the international threshold for absolute poverty. This is coupled with an extremely high rate of unemployment, which has been hovering between 30 and 35 per cent for the last five years (with over 50 per cent of young people unemployed, despite constituting the largest demographic group). South Africa's poverty and inequality manifest in two aspects: income inequality and spatial injustice.

Income inequality

The International Monetary Fund (IMF, 2020) shows that in South Africa over 68 per cent of the national income is held by the richest 20 per cent of the population (as opposed to an average of 47 per cent for comparable emerging markets). The bottom 40 per cent of the population earn only 7 per cent of the national income (as opposed to 16 per cent for other emerging markets). This represents a nation with an extremely high level of income and wealth inequality – an inequality largely determined by race and gender. Moreover, the richest 10 per cent of the population own more than 85 per cent of household wealth, while over half the population have more liabilities than assets (IMF, 2020). The impact of this opportunity gap more than doubles when factors like race, gender and age are considered. Low intergenerational economic mobility is a result of high wealth inequality, which keeps inequality from changing over time (World Bank, 2022). According to the World Bank (2022), the transition to fairer wealth distribution is being slowed down by a lack of access to important economic assets like land and skills.

Spatial injustice

The transformation of the apartheid legacy of separate development – under which townships and informal settlements functioned primarily as large labour reserves for African labourers and spaces for the consumption of commercial goods and services – has unquestionably not been achieved. Successive governments of the democratic dispensation have failed to address spatial injustice, which physically separates black people from productive and economic activity, condemning them to a life where accessing work and opportunities is both difficult and expensive. The gulf between where many people live (black women in particular) and where resources are concentrated aggravates poverty, inequality and unemployment. The nation's land distribution still reflects levels of inequality from the apartheid era. According to Fröhlich and Lopez-Granados (2019), more than half of South Africa's population, including African immigrants, continue to reside in townships and other informal settlements. These current residential patterns – a form of violence in itself – contribute to the nation's extraordinarily high rates of violent crime in general and of migrant animosity in particular. After South Africa's democratic transition, state priorities were improving infrastructure, land reform, providing public housing and acknowledging the role that geographical marginalisation plays in inequality. Implementation, however, has been limited at best: general land reform is still a contentious and unresolved political endeavour.

Additionally, wages are declining in real terms, the public health sector is severely strained, crime rates are increasing and municipalities are failing in areas of service delivery, which has a larger impact on previously disadvantaged individuals (Parliament of South Africa, 2023; Indlulamithi, 2023). The relationship between anti-migrant animosity and socioeconomic factors is widely acknowledged (Pillay, 2008a). The best way to understand the relationship between economic conditions and this animosity is to take account of how poverty, inequality and lack of access to opportunities exacerbate this animosity and other social attitudes. In a 2008 study by the Human Sciences Research Council (HSRC), Pillay (2008b) says that 'relative deprivation' can be defined as being deprived of something to which a person or group feels entitled.

This then causes sentiments of bitterness and a desire for retaliation. In a nation where more than 50 per cent of the people live in poverty, there is fierce competition among the poor for resources, and access to jobs and housing. This has been reflected in a UNDP report by Crush and Ramachandran (2009) in which it is argued that the 1994 democratic dispensation in South Africa has been characterised by 'insiders' and 'outsiders', which points to the ongoing battle for socioeconomic freedom for previously disadvantaged groups in the country.

Therefore, the majority have to make do with social grants while the strategic sectors of the economy remain largely in the hands of a minority group. South African politician Vuyo Zungula, president of the African Transformation Movement (ATM), which has been one of the most prominent voices on stricter migration laws, argued that (Interview, 21 August 2023):

If you go to the township economy, you find that South Africans do not even own one spaza. Most of the economic activities, whether it's a spaza, it's a tavern, it's a general dealer, it's a hardware store, it is all foreign nationals. The lack of economic opportunities leads to what we say in Xhosa, indlala ibanga ulaka (hunger causes anger).

This is important to highlight considering that, prior to 1994, the aforementioned businesses were run by black South Africans since there were restrictions on the types of business ventures they could undertake. This was to ensure that the minority continued to monopolise major economic sectors with no competition from black South Africans. Now, with the advent of democracy, strategic sectors remain monopolised while the businesses that were previously run by South African citizens are increasingly taken over by foreign nationals (World Bank, 2018). Zungula (Interview, 21 August 2023) said:

> Since 1994, you find that South Africans still could not be able to enter into some of these industries because of the barriers to entry. There's no transformation that is happening there in the sense that if you look at the banking industry, it's all these white companies that we know. If you look at the financial services company, it's the same thing. Construction industry, still the same thing. Now, what is difficult is that South Africans now are unable to enter into some of these spaces, at the same time, the spaces that they were previously in, the spaces I mentioned, your general dealers, etc., now have been taken away from them.

This has placed black South Africans in a very vulnerable position because they can't get into some of these white-owned spaces. At the same time, the economic spaces that previously 'belonged' to them, have now been taken over by foreign nationals. Therefore, the lack of transformation has had dire effects in the sense that native South Africans are excluded from any meaningful participation in the economy. Neocosmos (2010: 141) calls this the 'politics of fear', what he argues is a justifiable notion that the majority has been cheated of the promises of liberation.

Along similar lines, the leader of the Patriotic Alliance (PA), Gayton McKenzie, was quoted as saying, 'we are not going to sit back while the violence of hunger, violence of joblessness visit South Africans' (eNCA, 2022). He adds that the job market in South Africa must be reserved for South Africans, with the exception of jobs requiring critical skills that only legal foreigners can offer. This was in the context of a 2019/2020 report from the Commission for Employment Equity (CEE) (2020), which revealed that foreign nationals are being preferentially hired for entry-level jobs at an increasing rate. According to the report, foreign workers are increasingly filling job openings ahead of their South African counterparts. The commission cited this as one of the difficulties it has encountered in achieving the objectives it set out in 2015 to ensure employment equity. This was reflected in an interview with Zungula (21 August 2023) in which he says that 'companies even state that they're looking for certain types of workers, and they'll be specific to say, we're looking for Zimbabweans or Malawians. And you find that those are the jobs that South Africans can do'. Along similar lines, Pillay (2008a) revealed that tensions have previously existed in Imizamo Yethu informal settlement in the Western Cape as a result of locals losing their jobs to foreign workers. The local leadership claimed that this was brought about by the hiring of Namibians as fishermen and the firing of local fishermen, who were primarily based in Imizamo Yethu. In Gauteng, in areas such as Tembisa, residents expressed similar concerns about foreign nationals being preferred for jobs at their expense (HSRC, 2008). This is a consequence of foreign nationals constituting a pool of cheap labour in South Africa, which results in many of these foreigners being widely employed in various sectors throughout South Africa, which fans local migrant animosity (Nyar, 2011). In this situation, immigrants offer companies cheap labour and, as a result, frequently compete more successfully for jobs than underprivileged black South Africans (Everatt, 2011).

The Commission for Employment Equity report (2020) gave credence to the HSRC 2008 report, namely that when hiring foreign nationals over natives, businesses can evade paying required contributions to the Unemployment Insurance Fund (UIF) and tax. In addition, the foreign nationals are not unionised. Similarly, Zungula (Interview, 21 August 2023) complains: 'instead of paying a South African a minimum wage and having to comply with the basic conditions of employment, you can employ a non-South African.' The consistent situation of South Africans in a battle for jobs with foreigners was also laid bare in a focus group for the HSRC (2008: 38) report on Economy and Service Delivery. According to the report,

'Competition for jobs appears to be a critical trigger for tensions, xenophobia and violence'.

And as a result, a group of natives started an organisation called Put South Africans First in 2019, which was officially registered in 2020. National Chairperson, Faith Mabusela (Interview, 17 August 2023) is of the view that South Africans are viewed as xenophobic, when they might be making legitimate calls on behalf of aggrieved members of society who believe that South Africa is becoming a lawless country, and the security of the country is being compromised. On the morning of 31 August 2023, South Africa woke up to the horrifying news that over 70 people had died in a fire that broke out at one of the so-called 'hijacked' buildings in the Johannesburg CBD. A building was turned into a squatter camp, with shacks erected inside. According to Mzangwe (1 September 2023), tenants were mostly illegal foreign nationals who paid R1600 to rent single rooms divided by curtains, cardboard and bed sheets. 'We are not xenophobic!' said Mabusela. 'In fact, the word xenophobia for us, it feels like it's a word that was given to us to silence us, but it's a legitimate cause. We are saying our country is in dire need of control and there seems to be no political will to intervene in the situation like this' (Interview, 17 August 2023). Mabusela (Interview, 17 August 2023) further believes that, with regard to traditional security, porous borders make South Africa vulnerable to terrorist groups operating within the country. A 2022 United Nations Security Council (UNSC) (2022) report highlighted how ISIS has used South Africa-based members to transfer funds from ISIS leadership to ISIS affiliates across Africa. The report by the UNSC (2022) reflects how South Africa has become fertile ground for foreign nationals seeking to commit acts of crime.

The term 'xenophobia' does not tell the full story. It fuels the narrative of South Africans being prejudicial against foreign nationals and mistreating them on that basis. This chapter argues that this is not the case. Social media reflects the growing sentiment that foreign nationals do in South Africa what South Africans would not do in their countries (Bhengu, 2022). Migrants, like any population group, may not always be fully aware of the complexities and challenges that a host country like South Africa faces, including fluctuations in stability. Both migrants and host communities need to have a nuanced understanding of the sociopolitical and economic dynamics that can impact on the stability of a country.

However, the securitisation of migration is not exclusive to South Africa. It is part of the changing global dynamics as the world becomes more interdependent and interconnected. From a South African perspective, migration ought to be viewed through those lenses. This chapter highlights below how the securitisation of migration has taken place around the world, including on the African continent.

Rest of the world

Farny (2016) and Bigo (1994) argue that Europe has undergone significant changes since the 1980s, brought on by the growth of globalisation; the breakup of significant states like the former Soviet Union and Yugoslavia; and the establishment of the European Union (EU) and the Schengen region. Huysmans (2000: 755) calls it the 'Europeanization of migration policy'. Within the EU, immigration has grown more and more politicised as the geopolitical landscape has evolved (Karolewski and Benedikter, 2018). The security rationale for EU immigration and asylum policies, which have expanded border security, deportations and surveillance of immigrants, has been the subject of numerous studies (Ugur, 1995; Huysmans, 2000; Kostakopoulou, 2000). Therefore, one can argue that the securitisation of migration emerged first and foremost within the context of the European Union. However, we have witnessed the creation of similar discourses, and the framing of migration as a part of security policy, in the United States (Colome-Menendez et al., 2021). Although some authors (Huysmans, 2000; Karyotis, 2007) emphasise the role of the European Union in the process of securitising migrants, other authors (Ceyhan and Tsoukala, 2002; Tirman, 2006) analyse the securitisation of migration as a phenomenon of Western societies or as a global phenomenon.

Farny (2016) argues that as the United States (USA) has consistently been seen as a nation of immigrants, unlike the European Union, the issue of migration has never been construed as a danger to national identity. However, Farny (2016) and Karyotis (2007) suggest that with the terrorist attacks of 9/11 in 2001, the idea that migration poses a threat to American security took hold. Along similar lines, Abebe (2019) states that the election of Donald Trump in the United States and the vote for Brexit in Britain were significantly shaped by the global political rhetoric surrounding the securitisation of migration. In both instances, migration dominated the political conversation and was portrayed as the biggest threat to the survival and wellbeing of those countries – to the extent that building a wall between the USA and Mexico became the signature of the presidential campaign that took Donald Trump to the White House.

Europe has also experienced similar election trends over the last few decades. Migration dominated political discourse and anti-immigration parties made major election gains. This was expressively illustrated in 2018 in Italy where Matteo Salvini, who is the head of the right-wing League Party, won an election by portraying immigrants as a threat (*The Guardian*, 2018; Abebe, 2019). Despite Italy's history of embracing immigrants, the administration then passed a law in September of 2018 that made it simpler for immigrants to be expelled. Viktor Orbán, the prime minister of Hungary, is yet another instance of a politician who, in order to win a resounding victory for his third consecutive term in office in 2018, portrayed immigration as Hungary's main existential threat and stoked feelings of nationalist protectionism (Guler, 2019; Abebe, 2019). The BBC (2018) quoted him as saying that his victory provided Hungarians with 'the opportunity to defend themselves and to defend Hungary'. The anti-immigration party, Sweden Democrats, in 2018 also received 18 per cent of the votes in the national election in Sweden, which had been seen as a stronghold of diversity, up from 12.9 per cent in the previous election (BBC, 2018). As recently as March 2023, United Kingdom (UK) Home Secretary, Suella Braverman, tabled tougher anti-immigration legislation to parliament. Her initial address, posted on official social media platforms, was titled, 'Enough is enough. We must stop the boats.'

African countries and migration securitisation
Abebe (2019), in providing a holistic view of the securitisation of migration, argues that it is not only a global North phenomenon.

Many African nations have adopted securitised migration policies in response to worries about social cohesiveness, economic stability and national security. Upper-middle-income nations in Africa like Algeria, Morocco, Egypt and Botswana typically have more stringent visa policies for African travellers (Abebe, 2019). Some of the justifications stated for these harsher rules include the worry of a significant influx of individuals from low-income nations, protecting competitiveness in the employment market and security concerns.

Tanzania in 2019 asserted its intention to send Burundian refugee migrants back home (Al Jazeera, 2019). The idea that refugees pose a security concern has also been related to Kenya's repeated declarations that the Dadaab refugee camp will be closed (Abebe et al., 2019). An argument for the securitisation of migration can be made by pointing to well-documented threats to Africa's precarious peace and security situation and the variety of challenges it faces (Aslan, 2022). In 1983, following the global crisis of the previous year, Nigeria's economy was severely affected: as citizens scrambled to secure their livelihoods Nigeria deported an estimated two million illegal foreigners, one million of whom were from Ghana (Lawal, 2019; Daly, 2023). Similarly, in 2021, following the death of Chad's leader, Idriss Derby, Nigeria moved swiftly to reinforce its border security to avoid an influx of Chadians into the county (Reuters, 2021). This was after Derby was killed by rebels who had plunged the country into turmoil; Abuja feared that a ripple effect would lead to an influx of migrants. It can thus be seen that securitisation of migration is not a new phenomenon or one isolated to South Africa. Rather, it has been a recurring theme among nation-states throughout history.

EVOLVING LEGISLATION FOR SOUTH AFRICA'S SECURITISATION OF MIGRATION

Many countries around the world have implemented measures related to migration and security. These measures can include policies, laws, regulations and practices aimed at addressing security concerns associated with migration. It is important to note that the specific measures taken and the severity of them can vary widely depending on the country's geopolitical context, historical experiences and current security challenges. Some examples follow of how South Africa has implemented measures related to migration and security.

The securitisation of immigration is one of the anchors of South Africa's immigration policy. The 1991 Aliens Control Act was replaced by the Immigration Act of 2002. This law maintains an emphasis on facilitating skilled labour migration while simultaneously fighting irregular migration (UNOCHA, 2021). The law was later revised in 2007 and 2011 to reflect the altered character of South Africa's political terrain, but some aspects remain of earlier emphasis on allowing admission to certain kinds of immigrants while barring access to others (UNOCHA, 2021). Notably, the Immigration Act makes no provision for low-skilled workers from the SADC region. Owing to the significant challenges caused by irregular migrants, some would-be economic migrants have also turned to the nation's asylum system as a method of obtaining status.

Under the Refugees Act of 1998, asylum applicants were permitted to travel freely, work and attend school throughout the protracted adjudication process. However, subsequent changes to the legislation in 2008, 2011 and 2017 aimed to restrict these rights, in part in reaction to worries that the asylum system was being abused by those without a genuine fear of persecution to get work status. This was laid bare when a 39-year-old Ethiopian with refugee status in the country was arrested for being the kingpin of a house in the east of Johannesburg that housed over one hundred illegal foreign nationals (SABC, 2023). According to UNOCHA (2021) and Mfubu (2018), legislative steps have been taken to make South Africa less appealing to asylum seekers, in an effort to reduce asylum claims. The asylum system, Mfubu (2018) argues, is plagued by bureaucratic incompetence, with years-long backlogs and drawn-out appeals. And this finds credence in the fact that in 2019, 96 per cent of all asylum requests were turned down, as per UNOCHA (2021). The South African government is in the process of introducing tightened security measures on the grounds that it has come to see irregular migrants as risks to its security. For example, the government expressed concern about irregular immigration in its 2017 White Paper on International Migration (DHA, 2017: v), stating that it 'leads to unacceptable levels of corruption, human rights abuse, and national security risks' (Motsoaledi, 2024). It goes on to criticise the refugee system, contending that the country is exposed to security dangers as a result of excessively liberal laws and rights to humanitarian protection (DHA, 2017). This was reflected when the Gauteng High Court nullified the Department of Home Affairs' (DHA) refusal to grant 22 Afghan nationals asylum permits. Additionally, the 2017 government report expressed special concern about the unauthorised movement of low-skilled or unskilled migrants from elsewhere in the SADC area, which it claimed jeopardise the nation's economic stability and national sovereignty.

As a result of these sentiments, the government has recently implemented additional measures to restrict and track migrant movements, such as the Border Management Authority Bill (2020), which intends to centralise and consolidate border control duties. In order to prioritise securitisation, the government has moved the Department of Home Affairs from the Governance and Administrative Cluster to the Justice, Crime Prevention, and Security Cluster (UNOCHA, 2021). There it sits next to other departments that deal with law enforcement, defence and state security, among other departments concerned with criminal and security issues.

RECOMMENDATIONS

The securitisation of migration in South Africa reflects broader global debates about immigration and security. However, the country must deal with corruption at Home Affairs, in local municipalities and within the South African Police Service, in addition to tightening border controls and implementing programmes that promote social integration and peaceful coexistence for foreign nationals and immigrants. A comprehensive and nuanced strategy that addresses the reasons for migration and fosters social cohesiveness is needed to strike a balance between security concerns and immigrants' rights and wellbeing.

CONCLUSION

It is important to note that the securitisation of migration is a complex and contested process, and different actors within South Africa may have varying perspectives on the issue. Additionally, the dynamics of migration and its securitisation are subject to change over time based on political developments, economic conditions and social factors. South Africa, like many other countries, has undertaken debates and policy responses framed around security concerns related to migration. This chapter sought to highlight the nuances and broader complexities of immigration dynamics in South African black communities. It explored how South Africa, despite its relatively well-developed economy, struggles to meet the demands of its sizable unemployed population, which includes both native-born citizens and foreign-born nationals. The links between these challenges and anti-immigrant sentiment were outlined. This hostile sentiment was also viewed in a geopolitical context. The chapter highlighted how migration has been securitised in other parts of the world, thus providing a more nuanced approach to securitisation of migration within South Africa.

REFERENCES

Abahlali baseMjondolo. 12 May 2008. 'Abahlali baseMjondolo statement on the xenophobic attacks in Johannesburg', https://abahlali.org/node/3582/, accessed 8 October 2023.

Abebe, T. T. 2019. 'Securitisation of migration in Africa: The case of Agadez in Niger'. Institute for Security Studies, https://issafrica.s3.amazonaws.com/site/uploads/ar20.pdf, accessed 8 October 2023.

Abebe, T. T. Abebe, A. and Sharpe, M. 2019. 'The 1969 OAU refugee convention at 50'. Institute for Security Studies, https://issafrica.s3.amazonaws.com/site/uploads/ar19.pdf, accessed 8 October 2023.

Africa Check. 7 July 2023. 'Are there 15 million undocumented immigrants living in South Africa? No, another ActionSA party member repeats old, incorrect claim', https://africacheck.org/fact-checks/spotchecks/are-there-15-million-undocumented-immigrants-living-south-africa-no-another, accessed 19 August 2023.

Albert, M. and Buzan, B. 2011. 'Securitisation, sectors and functional differentiation'. *Security Dialogue,* 42(4/5), 413–425.

Al Jazeera. 27 August 2019. 'Tanzania to send back all Burundian refugees from October', https://www.aljazeera.com/news/2019/8/27/tanzania-to-send-back-all-burundian-refugees-from-october, accessed 24 August 2023.

Aslan, S. Y. 2022. 'Securitisation of migration in the EU and Africa'. *Insight Turkey*, 24(10), 153–172.

Bhengu, C. 19 January 2022. '"Hire locals": Malema visiting restaurants to check how many workers are foreign nationals'. *TimesLive*, https://www.timeslive.co.za/news/south-africa/2022-01-19-hire-locals-malema-visiting-restaurants-to-check-how-many-workers-are-foreign-nationals/, accessed 5 January 2024.

Bigo, D. 1994. 'The European internal security field: Stakes and rivalries in a newly developing area of police intervention', in Anderson, M. and Den Boer, M. (eds), *Policing Across National Boundaries*. London: Pinter.

British Broadcasting Corporation (BBC). 10 September 2018. 'Swedish election: Main blocs neck and neck as nationalists gain', https://www.bbc.com/news/world-europe-45466174, accessed 22 August 2023.

Buzan, B. and Hansen, L. 2009. *The Evolution of International Security Studies*. Cambridge: Cambridge University Press.

Buzan, B., Waever, O. and De Wilde, J. 1998. *Security: A new framework for analysis*. Colorado: Lynne Rienner Pub.

Ceyhan, A. and Tsoukala, A. 2002. 'The securitisation of migration in western societies: Ambivalent discourses and policies'. *Alternatives*. 27(1), 21–39.

Charrett, C. 2009. 'A critical application of securitisation theory: Overcoming the normative dilemma of writing security'. International Catalan Institute for Peace Working Paper No. 2009/7, https://papers.ssrn.com/sol3/papers.cfm?abstract_id=1884149, accessed 22 August 2023.

Colome-Menendez, D., Koops, A. J. and Weggemans, D. 2021. 'A country of immigrants no more? The securitization of immigration in the National Security Strategies of the United States of America'. *Global Affairs*, 7(1), 1–26.

Commission for Employment Equity. 2020. '20th commission for employment equity annual report 2019–20'. *Department of Labour*, https://www.labour.gov.za/DocumentCenter/Reports/Annual%20Reports/Employment%20Equity/2019%20-2020/20thCEE_Report_.pdf, accessed 22 August 2023.

Crush, J. and Ramachandran, S. 2009. 'Xenophobia, international migration and human development'. Human development research paper 2009/47, United Nations Development Programme, https://hdr.undp.org/system/files/documents/hdrp200947pdf.pdf, accessed 22 August 2023.

Daly, S. F. C. 2023. 'Ghana must go: Nativism and the politics of expulsion in west Africa, 1969–1985'. *Past and Present*, 259(1), 229–261.

Department of Home Affairs (DHA). 2017. 'White paper on international migration', https://www.gov.za/sites/default/files/gcis_document/201707/41009gon750.pdf, accessed 20 August 2023.

eNCA. 19 January 2022. 'Patriotic Alliance put South Africans first', https://www.youtube.com/watch?v=_65iryuJP-Q, accessed 21 August 2023.

Estevens, J. 2018. 'Migration crisis in the EU: Developing a framework for analysis of national security and defense strategies'. *Comparative Migration Studies*, 6(28), 1–21.

Everatt, D. 2011. 'Xenophobia, state and society in South Africa, 2008–2010'. *Politikon,* 38(1), 7–36.

Farny, E. 2016. 'Implications of the securitisation of migration'. *E-international Relations,* https://www.e-ir.info/2016/01/29/implications-of-the-securitisation-of-migration/, accessed 19 August 2023.

Fröhlich, M. and Lopez-Granados, E. 8 October 2019. 'Xenophobic violence and spatial inequality in South Africa'. PRIF Blog, https://blog.prif.org/2019/10/08/xenophobic-violence-and-spatial-inequality-in-south-africa/#:~:text=Spatial%20inequalities%20as%20violence,of%20services%2C%20employment%20and%20housing, accessed 8 October 2023.

Government Gazette. 2 December 1998. 'Refugees Act, No. 130', https://www.gov.za/sites/default/files/gcis_document/201409/a130-980.pdf, accessed 15 August 2023.

Government Gazette. 31 May 2002. 'Immigration Act, No. 13', https://www.gov.za/sites/default/files/gcis_document/201409/a13-020.pdf, accessed 15 August 2023.

Government Gazette. 21 July 2020. 'Border Management Authority Act, No. 2', https://www.gov.za/sites/default/files/gcis_document/202007/43536gon799.pdf, accessed 22 August 2023.

Guler, F. 2019. 'The securitisation of migration: A case study of discursive threat construction in Hungary during the European migration crisis'. Faculty of Culture and Society, Malmo University, https://www.diva-portal.org/smash/get/diva2:1481809/FULLTEXT01.pdf, accessed 1 July 2023.

Gumede, V. 2020. 'Elusive pursuit of reconciliation and development in post-apartheid South Africa'. *Strategic Review for Southern Africa,* 42(2), 129–152.

Horwood, C., Frouws, B. and Forin, R. 2019. 'The ever-rising securitisation off mixed migration', in Horwood, C., Frouws, B. and Forin, R. (eds), *Mixed Migration Review 2019,* http://www.mixedmigration.org/, accessed 20 August 2023.

Human Sciences Research Council (HSRC). 2008. 'Violence and xenophobia in South Africa: Developing consensus, moving to action'. A partnership between the Human Sciences Research Council (HSRC) and the High Commission of the United Kingdom.

Huysmans, J. 2000. 'The European Union and the securitisation of migration'. *Journal of Common Market Studies,* 38(5), 751–777.

Indlulamithi. 2023. 'Indlulamithi South Africa Scenarios 2035', Indlulamithi-SA-2035-Scenarios-Presentation-202311092.pdf, accessed 5 January 2024.

International Monetary Fund. 30 January 2020. 'Six charts explain South Africa's inequality', https://www.imf.org/en/News/Articles/2020/01/29/na012820six-charts-on-south-africas-persistent-and-multi-faceted-inequality, accessed 21 August 2023.

Karolewski, I. R. and Benedikter, R. 2018. 'Europe's refugee and migrant crisis: Political responses to asymmetrical pressures', *Politique Europenne*, 60, 98–132.

Karyotis, G. 2007. 'European migration policy in the aftermath of September 11'. *Innovation: The European Journal of Social Science Research*, 20(1), 1–17.

Kostakopoulou, D. 2000. 'The protective union: Change and continuity in migration law and policy in post-Amsterdam Europe'. *Journal of Common Market Studies*, 38(3), 497–518.

Lawal, S. 11 August 2019. 'Ghana must go: The ugly history of Africa's most famous bag'. *Mail & Guardian*, https://atavist.mg.co.za/ghana-must-go-the-ugly-history-of-africas-most-famous-bag/, accessed 22 August 2023.

Mfubu, P. 2018. 'What does the 2017 Refugee Amendment Act mean for asylum seekers and refugees living in South Africa?'. *Safe Spaces*, https://www.saferspaces.org.za/blog/entry/what-does-the-2017-refugee-amendment-act-mean-for-asylum-seekers-and-refuge, accessed 22 August 2023.

Morris, A. 1999. 'Race relations and racism in a racially diverse inner-city neighbourhood: A case study of Hillbrow, Johannesburg'. *Journal of Southern African Studies*, 25(4), 667–694.

Motsoaledi, A. 17 April 2024. 'Cabinet approves final white paper on citizenship, immigration and refugee protection'. *SA News*, https://www.sanews.gov.za/south-africa/cabinet-approves-final-white-paper-citizenship-immigration-and-refugee-protection, accessed 2 May 2024.

Neocosmos, M. 2010. *From 'Foreign Natives' to 'Native Foreigners': Explaining xenophobia in post-apartheid South Africa citizenship and nationalism, identity and politics*. Dakar: Council for the Development of Social Science Research in Africa

Nyar, A. 2011. *What Happened? A Narrative of the May 2008 Xenophobic Violence*. Gauteng City Region Observatory (GCRO). The Atlantic Philanthropies.

Parliament of South Africa. 2023. '2023 Budget and division revenue brief', https://www.parliament.gov.za/storage/app/media/PBO/Budget_Analysis/2023/2-may/02-05-2023/April_2023_PBO_Budget_and_Division_of_Revenue_Brief_-_04_April.pdf, accessed 5 January 2024.

Pillay, D. 2008a. 'Relative deprivation, social instability and cultures of entitlement', in Hassim, S., Worby, E. and Kupe, T. (eds), *Go Home or Die Here: Violence, xenophobia and the reinvention of difference in South*

Africa. Johannesburg: Wits University Press.

Pillay, S. 2008b. 'Xenophobia, violence and citizenship', in Hadland, A. (ed.), *Violence and Xenophobia in South Africa: Developing consensus, moving to action.* Pretoria: Human Sciences Research Council.

Reuters. 22 April 2021. 'Nigeria beefs up border to avoid Chadian influx – Defence minister', https://www.reuters.com/world/africa/nigeria-beefs-up-border-avoid-chadian-influx-defence-minister-2021-04-22/, accessed 18 August 2023.

South African Broadcasting Corporation (SABC). 1 September 2023. 'House where undocumented foreign nationals were arrested run by Ethiopian refugee: Motsoaledi', https://www.sabcnews.com/sabcnews/house-where-undocumented-foreign-nationals-were-arrested-run-by-ethiopian-refugee-motsoaledi/, accessed 2 September 2023.

Salter, M. B. 2008. 'Securitisation and desecuritisation: A dramaturgical analysis of the Canadian air transport security authority'. *Journal of International Relations and Development*, 11(4), 321–349.

Statistics South Africa. 2015. 'Census 2011: Migration dynamics in South Africa', https://www.statssa.gov.za/publications/Report-03-01-79/Report-03-01-792011.pdf, accessed 16 August 2023.

Statistics South Africa. 2023. 'Beyond unemployment – time-related underemployment in the SA labour market', https://www.statssa.gov.za/?p=16312#:~:text=South%20Africa's%20unemployment%20rate%20in,the%20fourth%20quarter%20of%202022, accessed 15 August 2023.

Stepka, M. 2022a. 'The Copenhagen School and beyond: A closer look at securitisation theory', in Skepta, M. (ed.), *Identifying Security Logics in the EU Policy Discourse.* New York: Springer, 19–31.

Stepka, M. 2022b. 'Analysing the conceptualisation of remedial actions towards the "migration crisis" at the EU level', in Stepka, M. (ed.), *Identifying Security Logics in the EU Policy Discourse.* New York: Springer, 93–119.

The Guardian. 9 August 2018. 'How Matteo Salvini pulled Italy to the far right', https://www.theguardian.com/news/2018/aug/09/how-matteo-salvini-pulled-italy-to-the-far-right, accessed 17 August 2023.

Tirman, J. 2006. 'Immigration and insecurity: Post-9/11 fear in the United States'. Audit of Conventional Wisdom series, MIT Center for International Studies, https://www.files.ethz.ch/isn/20631/Immigration_insecurity-09.pdf, accessed 22 August 2023.

Tshitereke, C. 1999. 'Xenophobia and relative deprivation'. *Crossings,* 3(2), 4–5.

Ugur, M. 1995. 'Freedom of movement vs. exclusion: A reinterpretation of the "insider"–"outsider" divide in the European Union'. *International Migration Review,* 29(4), 964–999.

United Nations Human Development Report. 1994. 'New dimensions of human security', https://hdr.undp.org/content/human-development-report-1994, accessed 16 August 2023.

United Nations Office for the Coordination of Humanitarian Affairs (UNOCHA). 2021. 'South Africa reckons with its status as a top immigration destination, apartheid history, and economic challenges', https://reliefweb.int/report/south-africa/south-africa-reckons-its-status-top-immigration-destination-apartheid-history, accessed 16 August 2023.

Weiner, M. 1993. *International Migration and Security*. Colorado: Westview Press.

World Bank. 2018. 'Republic of South Africa: Systemic country diagnostic', https://documents1.worldbank.org/curated/en/815401525706928690/pdf/WBG-South-Africa-Systematic-Country-Diagnostic-FINAL-for-board-SECPO-Edit-05032018.pdf, accessed 5 January 2024.

World Bank. 2022. 'Inequality In Southern Africa: An assessment of the Southern African customs union', https://documents.worldbank.org/en/publication/documents-reports/documentdetail/099125303072236903/p1649270c02a1f06b0a3ae02e57eadd7a82, accessed: 07 October 2023.

Interviews

Zungula, V. 21 August 2023. Interview by V. Gumbi.

Mabusela, F. 17 August 2023. Interview by V. Gumbi.

FOUR

Migrants, the politics of belonging and social cohesion in post-apartheid South Africa

Sifiso Ndlovu

INTRODUCTION

Migration is a global phenomenon that has received attention in policy circles and rapidly expanding scholarship spanning various academic disciplines. In this scholarship, there is great convergence on the idea that migration patterns change and are becoming more complex in ways that have led many countries to frame migration as a security issue (Landau and Bakewell, 2018; Wee et al., 2018; Misago, 2019; Vanyoro, 2019; Musoni, 2020; Bello, 2022; Vanyoro, 2023, to mention just a few). Increasingly changing patterns of migration have also complicated nation-building, politics of belonging and social cohesion in ways that warrant more scholarly reflections. This chapter is positioned within this context. It examines social cohesion and the integration of migrants into society in South Africa, which has been one of the major destinations for many migrants from the African continent and beyond.

Existing literature on migration has demonstrated that South Africa has historically been the destination most preferred by many migrants, especially from Africa, dating back to the mid-19th century, and will always be (Nshimbi and Lorenzo, 2014, 2016; Nyandoro, 2016; Moyo, 2017; Moyo et al., 2021). However, even though migrants constitute a significant feature of South African society, it is striking that existing literature offers as yet few reflections on the implications of this reality for the larger context. This context includes social cohesion initiatives and discourses around belonging, which are framed in terms of reversing the exclusionary legacies of the apartheid past. Broadly, the flow of migrant populations to South Africa has sparked numerous debates on subjects ranging from policy implications, health, security, human rights, attitudes of South African citizens and experiences of migrants in host communities (Peberdy, 2009; Nshimbi and Fioramonti, 2013; Mbembe, 2017; Moyo, 2017; Landau and Bakewell, 2018; Moyo et al., 2021). While the debates are interesting in their own right, this chapter explores what they reveal about the complicated place of migrants in nation-building and social cohesion initiatives. It will examine and interpret post-apartheid South Africa's project of nation-building and social cohesion as mediated by competing logics of inclusion and exclusion, which constitute a yawning gap in migration scholarship. This chapter will bring into sharp focus the politics of belonging in post-apartheid South Africa, as part of a broader discursive terrain which is tied to social cohesion initiatives. I will use this terrain as a rubric of analysis, and in so doing will make the case that migrants add a layer of complexity to this area of debate. I argue that their integration needs to be thought of beyond the confines of the foundational principles of nation-building.

The chapter utilises insights derived from scholarly works on migration, nation-building and policy documents as vantage points for an analysis of the complicated place of migrants in the politics of belonging in post-apartheid South Africa. As its point of departure, the chapter begins with an outline of the conceptual/theoretical frameworks that integrate key definitions, followed by a brief historical context of migration flows into South Africa. This section is crucial in laying a base to examine the phenomenon under investigation, migration and social cohesion in post-apartheid South Africa. This is followed by an analysis of the policing and exclusion of migrants in post-apartheid South Africa as a way of illuminating the argument that migrants add a layer that complicates the politics of belonging. The chapter concludes by pushing to the fore the observation that in the context of post-apartheid South Africa – which battles with crafting belonging in ways that will transcend the exclusionary articulations of the past – the continued presence of migrants is an added layer of complexity. It is argued that their integration into social cohesion initiatives requires a paradigm shift towards the micro-social settings in which migrants interact with South African citizens.

DEFINITION OF KEY TERMS: NATION-BUILDING AND SOCIAL COHESION

In what was once a discriminatory and racist country, social cohesion has been an appealing idea in post-apartheid South Africa. It is a slippery and complex concept that resists easy definitions but it has been raised in democratic South Africa as a way of changing the political order and reversing apartheid's exclusionary articulations of belonging. Scholars and policymakers have diverse understandings of what social cohesion means but one common denominator is apparent in definitions, namely the articulation of belonging in ways that tolerate diversity: this underlies debates about the inclusion of diverse groups in the imagined community in a shared space, political and social participation and social trust. The flexibility of the concept has led scholars like Novy et al. (2012) to argue that where there is social cohesion, diverse people can live together without necessarily belonging to a homogeneous group. It appears that much of the literature on social cohesion highlights the observation that debate about it in post-apartheid South Africa assumes a nationalistic approach that is intertwined with forging 'unity in diversity' in the nation-building project. There are scanty reflections on the integration of diverse groups of people at local levels where migrants with various dynamics – such as class, gender, age and general socioeconomic status – share spaces with South African citizens. The lack of consideration of these local-level spaces and dynamics is especially evident in policy circles, public debate and analysis. Yet, an approach that takes cognisance of these spaces holds important implications for the management of diversity in South African society and the integration of migrants into South Africa.

In this chapter, my conceptual understanding and analysis of social cohesion is guided by a definition from the Department of Arts and Culture (DAC) (2012: 1), which denotes social cohesion as the '... degree of social integration and inclusion in communities and society at large and the extent to which mutual solidarity finds expression among individuals and communities'. The Department of Arts and Culture further elaborates that (DAC, 2012: 11):

> a community or society is cohesive to the extent that the inequalities, exclusions and disparities based on ethnicity, gender, class, nationality, age, disability or any other distinctions which engender divisions, distrust and conflict are reduced and/ or eliminated in a planned and sustained manner [that enables] community members and citizens to work together for the attainment of shared goals, designed and agreed upon to improve living conditions for all.

From the DAC's definition, one can note that social cohesion is deployed as a tool in the nation-building project in post-apartheid South Africa and in constructing future community that advances social harmony, inclusivity and non-racialism. The overarching goal becomes the cultivation of inter-personal and inter-group social relationships at micro and macro levels of society (Cloete and Kotze, 2009). This therefore renders the imagined rainbow nation a normative concept that confirms the observation of Jensen (1998: 17), that it can mean 'the capacity to construct a collective identity, a sense of belonging or society's willingness and ability to assure equality of opportunity or its capacity to retain the legitimacy of political institutions'.

Related to social cohesion is the concept of nation-building, which has been a key project in transcending apartheid's discriminatory and exclusionary articulations of belonging. The DAC (2012: 30) defines nation-building as:

[T]he process whereby a society with diverse origins, histories, languages, cultures and religions come together within boundaries of a sovereign state with a unified constitutional and legal dispensation, a national public education system, an integrated national economy, shared symbols and values, as equals, to work towards eradicating the divisions and injustices of the past; to foster unity; and promote a countrywide conscious sense of being proudly South African, committed to the country and open to the continent and the world.

It is pertinent to note that in the above definition, social cohesion has been considered in constructing and imagining a post-apartheid South Africa. This can lead to making a case for the idea that social cohesion and nation-building are inherently linked in imagining a South African society in which the divisions of the past have been overcome, in part by unity in diversity. Palmary (2015) has some valuable insights into the conceptualisation of social cohesion and nation-building in the South African context, pointing out that 'social cohesion in South Africa is uniquely understood as a project of nation-building'. She says further that '... social cohesion is conceptualised as centrally about the making of citizens and the invention of a citizen identity' (Palmary, 2015).

The interlinkage between social cohesion and nation-building is well articulated in a MISTRA (2014) publication titled *Nation Formation and Social Cohesion in South Africa*. Authors in that edited volume argue that:

... social cohesion ... is generally conceived as a post-nationalist project in established nation states, where either sections of the national majority or historical and new immigrant minorities find themselves excluded and marginalised. In a certain sense, while social cohesion signifies a *process* related to nation formation based on optimal inclusion and solidarity, it is in fact more concerned with addressing the *negative effects* of economic, social, cultural and other forms of exclusion which develop in highly unequal and stratified societies or in ones where sections of the population, local or immigrant, are subject to systemic exclusions in different spheres of social life. Theories of social cohesion take their bearings from problems and experiences in recent developments in western European and North American societies but are applicable to all nation-states, where class, gender, generational, disability, cultural and social exclusions are prevalent.

MIGRATION AND THE POLITICS OF BELONGING IN SOUTH AFRICA: A HISTORICAL CONTEXT

I adopt the United Nations' (UN) definition of 'migrant' in this chapter. According to the UN, a migrant is 'an individual who has resided in a foreign country for more than one year irrespective of the causes, voluntary or involuntary, and the means, regular or irregular, used to migrate' (IOM, 2011: 62). Migration of black Africans from the rest of Africa to South Africa has a long history. Through the works of scholars such as Oliver and Oliver (2017), we learn of the long history of migration that dates back to 1652; they point out that colonisers – including individuals from countries like Italy, Netherlands, France, Great Britain, Portugal, Spain, Belgium – who eventually settled in what is present-day South Africa had travelled across the African continent. These imperialist settlers later attracted Indian migrants who came as indentured labourers to work in Natal colonies. This was the beginning of labour migration. Asian and Chinese migrants were later brought in by Dutch settlers who occupied the Cape Colony (Crush, 2001). Bilateral agreements for cheap labour propelled this kind of labour migration that subsequently had a bearing on the integration of whites and blacks into the South African labour system with whites granted citizenship, which was denied to black migrants.

South Africa continued to attract migrants, but it is important to note that the migration trajectory of black Africans differed from that of whites. South Africa's dependence on cheap labour attracted black migration, especially in sectors such as agriculture and mining when diamond and gold mines were established in Kimberley and the Witwatersrand areas in the 19th century (Peberdy and Crush, 1998).

These migrants mainly came from southern African areas such as the territories that are now Zimbabwe, Lesotho, Zambia, eSwatini and Mozambique. Crush (2001) noted that migration labour conventions dating back to 1909 were used to organise the migration of black labour and a resulting supply of cheap labour to mines. However, black migrants were denied citizenship rights. The contract labour system was designed to exclude black men and women from citizenship and to create conditions conducive to these migrants returning to their home countries at the termination of their contracts. This was despite the fact that they constituted the backbone of the economy through the cheap labour they provided. This was not the case with white migrants who were given permanent residence and citizenship.

Migration trends underwent some changes towards the end of apartheid as immigration to South Africa increased considerably and skilled labour from the rest of Africa began to enter the country. In addition, Crush and William's (2005: 4) work shows that migration from other SADC countries increased considerably in complex and multifaceted ways, ranging from asylum seekers to refugees and economic migrants. The dawn of democracy was ushering in a sense of hope for belonging to a new nation that would transcend discriminatory and racist patterns of citizenship. We shall return to this later as we continue to examine how migrants have been integrated into the crafting of social cohesion in South Africa.

Setting the scene of migration flows into South Africa through a historically grounded approach establishes a crucial vantage point for examining the key question of how migrants, as a significant feature of South African society, have been accommodated in South Africa.

POLICING OF MIGRANTS IN POST-APARTHEID SOUTH AFRICA

With the advent of democracy in 1994, the ruling African National Congress's (ANC) idea of a post-apartheid South Africa emphasised inclusivity and democracy as an antidote to the exclusion and inequality that had haunted South Africa since colonial encounters. Political leaders promoted the 'rainbow' metaphor to incorporate various identities cutting across race, ethnicity, class, age and other factors. The Nobel Peace laureate, Archbishop Desmond Tutu, popularised the idea of a rainbow nation in a speech he made a day before the Presidential Inauguration of 10 May 1994, which ended with these words: 'We of many cultures, languages and races have become one nation; we are the Rainbow People of God'. Nelson Mandela added credence to Tutu's speech in his inaugural address by proffering the vision of 'one nation, many cultures' (Villa-Vicenco, 2001: 24). F. W. de Klerk, the last head of the apartheid state, also proposed the construction of a rainbow nation in post-apartheid South Africa by saying: 'The "New South Africa" would recognise the reality of the need for people and communities to remain themselves and be able to preserve the values that are precious to them – so that the Zulus, the Sothos and the whites can feel secure in their distinctiveness' (Sparks, 1994: 128).

The imaginations of a post-apartheid South Africa under the ANC gestured towards reversing notions of nationhood in which prejudice, discrimination and exclusion were legitimised, and instead engineering social cohesion as a key priority. But fostering social cohesion has proceeded by imagining belonging to South Africa in ways that do not resonate with the realities of migration patterns or managing diversity as it cuts across dynamics such as gender, race, class, ethnicity, age and migrant flows. The hostile attitude to the immigrant community is rendered visible when one takes a closer look at institutions like the Department of Home Affairs (DHA) and the South African Police Service (SAPS). These are state institutions that have treated migrants as 'others' who do not belong to the imagined post-apartheid South African nation and consequently fall outside the law (Misago and Landau, 2022). Misago and Landau's (2022) work suggests that South Africa's national project has mirrored a continuation of the apartheid logic of dealing with immigration. For instance, in 1998, the then Minister of Home Affairs, Mangosuthu Buthelezi, is quoted in Landau's (2004) as having told parliament:

> If South Africans are going to compete for scarce resources with the millions of 'aliens' that are pouring into South Africa, then we can bid goodbye to our Reconstruction and Development Programme.

Buthelezi's utterances can be read as an exclusionary perception of migrants as 'outsiders' who do not belong to the South African nation; it follows then that the mechanisms employed to imagine this nation are at odds with crafting social cohesion. Such exclusionary perceptions of migrants as the 'other', who fall outside the imaginations of a cohesive post-apartheid society, have manifested in border controls and inland policing, as has been described by scholars like Peberdy (2010: 11):

> [U]sing skills developed in the apartheid years black Africans from the rest of the continent are subject to stop and search operations run by the South African Police Service (SAPS) sometimes in conjunction with the army. These are sometimes anti-crime operations but at other times they take place to specifically locate undocumented migrants and have been given names like 'Operation Passport'. Irregular migrants are identified by a range of superficial physical features such as skin colour (Africans from further north are held to be darker than South Africans); TB vaccination marks (many other African countries vaccinate children on their forearm whereas South Africans are usually vaccinated on their upper arm); by traditional scarification marks; and by accent, language, and dress...

We see the rhetorical categorisations that dovetail with discriminatory perceptions of differences in the physical appearances of South African citizens and migrants, particularly African migrants. These are framed in extra-legal forms of social profiling, based on physical stereotypes, to exclude migrants using parochial stereotyping and stigmatisation. According to Mathers and Landau (2007: 530), 'being black and foreign in South Africa, whether legal or illegal, worker or leisure tourist, marks one out for harassment, inconvenience and even violence, both psychological and physical', and this feeds into the anti-immigrant narratives. This social profiling of African immigrants has often been deployed to deny them access to rights and social services and to discriminate more generally against them.

The Department of Home Affairs has launched various operations in collaboration with the South African Police Service (SAPS), such as

Operation Crackdown in 2000 and Operation Fiela in 2015, as part of internal measures to control migration. These operations can be read as a way of policing migrants and viewing them as a threat to a sense of belonging in post-apartheid South Africa, in ways that hinder migrants' integration into a socially cohesive society. On the perceived threat of migrants, Kanayo et al. (2019: 73) argue that '[e]ven though migrants can provide substantial support in developing the host country, there are still doubts if immigrants are adding to South Africa's economic vitality'. Duncan (2015) writes that 'underpinning this logic seems to be an exclusive "us and them" nationalism, premised on sealing South African identity up from influences from the rest of the region'. This positioning of migrants as a threat has implications for the integration of migrants into the societies they live in.

AN ANALYSIS OF MIGRATION POLICY AND PRACTICE

The approach to human mobility draws heavily on securitisation, as discussed in previous chapters. Such securitisation of human mobility is largely a global phenomenon as indicated in the work of scholars like Bello (2022), who have identified the social construction of migration as a security threat. South Africa's case, however, is an intriguing one because the state's restrictive approach to migration works against efforts at achieving social cohesion, which has been articulated as part of an inclusive nation-building process in the post-apartheid period. Scholars like Lamb (2021), Adebayo (2019), Misago (2017) and Neocosmos (2008) offer analyses that highlight South Africa's perceived exclusionary and hostile immigration policy towards migrants. Some argue that the ways in which the Department of Home Affairs filters and regulates migrants alienate non-citizens and deny undocumented migrants any possibility of legal status. From 2002 to the present, there have been shifts in policies regulating the patterns of migrant flows to South Africa, ranging from welcoming skilled migrants on temporary residence permits to shutting out semi-skilled and unskilled migrants (Peberdy, 2009). However, these shifts have remained anchored in the stringent logic of exclusion based on a negative sentiment towards so-called 'illegal immigrants', which impedes attempts to build social cohesion, particularly between migrants and South African citizens. Anti-immigrant exclusion is reinforced through multi-faceted politics of belonging that shape the precarity of migrants. This is well articulated by Nyamnjoh (2022: 31), who noted that:

The violence of precarity is simultaneously produced through the political construction of outsiders evident in slogans like 'South Africans First' and sustained by xenophobic violence, bouts of police and civilian harassment and the ceaseless bureaucratic hurdles faced to secure the right to live and work in South Africa...

An analysis of South Africa's immigration policy provides a context for unpacking the integration of migrants and social cohesion. This analysis looks at the ways in which the country's immigration policy is embedded in complex articulations of belonging that establish grounds for the inclusion of 'deserving' South African citizenry, and the concomitant exclusion of irregular migrants. The failure of South Africa's immigration policy to facilitate belonging and social cohesion is emphasised by scholars like Khan (2007: 2), who then argued that 'South Africa's legislation falls short of covering the complex spectrum of migrants and presently it had only two instruments of law dealing with immigration; the Immigration Act of 2002 and the Refugees Act of 1998...'. One can argue that the immigration framework has reinforced the exclusion of immigrants in ways that have a bearing on the place of migrants in any crafting of social cohesion. Most recently, the Refugees Amendment Bill, which was passed in 2015, pushes to visibility the exclusionary articulations of belonging in South Africa. These exclusions have a bearing on the integration of migrants – asylum seekers in particular. The Bill was anchored on an exclusionary framework which means that asylum seekers' right to work or study can be revoked for failure to provide proof of employment or study within a stipulated period (DHA, 2015).

The current South African nation-building and social cohesion project is problematic in the sense that it highlights what are perceived to be authentic/indigenous linguistic and cultural symbols of being South African in ways that are anachronistic given the realities of global, transnational migration. Vertovec (2010: 86) describes this as 'more people are now moving from more places, through more places, to more places'. Contemporary human population movements have meant that reified and reductionist imaginings of social cohesion and nation-building, premised on modernist, state-centric understandings of belonging, are no longer tenable.

Nation-building and social cohesion have not fully accommodated the diverse identities of immigrants. A paradigm shift is needed such that nation-building and social cohesion are conceptualised in much broader terms that transcend notions of homogenised nationhood and belonging. Moodley and Adam (2000) observed that a single homogeneous claim often reflects and represents the ideals of a dominant social class and in the process subsumes diverse identities. One might then argue that the limited viability of the social cohesion and nation-building ideals propagated by South Africa's Department of Arts and Culture is the result of a uniform national identity based on elitist, state-centric notions. Claims of single, homogeneous versions of nationhood and social cohesion ignore and denigrate the social and economic aspirations of the sociopolitically weak or marginal polities.

Politicians, bureaucrats, academic practitioners and civic organisations involved in social cohesion and nation-building activities must reach out to people, ask and listen to them, document their stories and integrate them into the agenda of building a cohesive South African society. There is a compelling need to recognise and fully integrate the non-institutional voices of ordinary South Africans, including their attitudes to migration, into the social cohesion agenda. Scholars of migration studies have argued that South African state institutions like the Department of Home Affairs and the South African Police Service have played a key role in the hostility towards, and the nurturing of exclusionary discourses about, migrants. These exclusionary discourses have profound effects on communities in that they discursively reinforce and reproduce imaginations of belonging to South Africa that threaten social cohesion, even though one should not discount pockets of social cohesion in some communities. These pockets of social cohesion can best be understood by exploring why some areas of South Africa have witnessed low levels of xenophobia and xenophobic violence.[1] For instance, research by the Institute for Security Studies (ISS) (2015) has it that there are low levels of integration of migrants into some South African communities, but the levels of integration differ according to dynamics such as age, sex and country of origin (Chikohomero, 2023).

THE NEW SOUTH AFRICAN POLITICAL COMMUNITY AND THE EXCLUSION OF IMMIGRANTS

The integration of migrants into the process of building a cohesive South African society cannot be understood in isolation from debates on nation-building projects. Scholars like Neocosmos (2010) argue that anti-immigrant sentiments are evoked by the way the new South African political community is crafted. I build on these ideas to argue that the state's nationalist language places immigrants outside the political community. This has the effect of making immigrants 'soft' and immediate targets of ordinary black South Africans. It becomes clear that migrants are perceived as posing a threat to the very existence of ordinary black South Africans when the analytic gaze is directed to claims that migrants have squeezed the South African population out of the labour market and have choked the country's infrastructure and social services. Even though such claims do not stack up against hard facts on the ground, they get popularised and translated into exclusionary politics of belonging that sometimes manifest in violence against the undesirable other. The significant point here is that the post-apartheid political establishment has failed to empower black South Africans in meaningful ways. This explains why when anti-immigrant

---

1 Xenophobia is generally a highly contested term in terms of its meaning and usage, and its manifestations in the South African context. This is attested by the fact that it is sometimes used interchangeably with words such as anti-immigrant prejudice, immigrant phobia, autochthony and nativism, for example. Some simply use it to mean hatred or dislike of 'other'. In this chapter the term xenophobia is used to mean manifestations, attitudes and exclusion of persons or groups of people perceived to be outsiders or non-nationals in the South African context.

attitudes flare up the targets are mostly unskilled and semi-skilled black migrants from Africa who share impoverished township spaces with unskilled and poor black South Africans. Skilled migrants who reside in gated communities and affluent suburbs are usually spared from anti-immigrant attitudes and violence. These class dynamics speak to the complexities of crafting meaningful social cohesion initiatives in the context of contested meaning and belonging in post-apartheid South Africa, which is the focus of the section that follows below.

The reality remains that, three decades after 1994, the hope of an inclusive 'rainbow' South Africa is highly contested. The ANC's once-celebrated idea of an inclusive South Africa based on 'unity in diversity' is increasingly being questioned and challenged and has been one of the most fertile terrains of academic analysis (see, for example, Chipkin, 2007, 2016; Bundy, 2007; Dubow, 2007; Hassim et al., 2008; Neocosmos, 2010; Ndlovu-Gatsheni, 2010, 2012; Terreblanche, 2012; Habib, 2013; Mbembe, 2014). The literature on the current state of the imagination and meaning of belonging in post-apartheid South Africa reflects diverse views but these mainly converge on the perspective that the foundational myth of rainbowism has failed to include everyone. The idea of an inclusive South Africa is proving hard to achieve and unfulfilled promises threaten the once-celebrated imagination of a 'rainbow' nation.

Scholars like Moodley and Adam (2000: 54) warned about the political construction of national identity through evoking the Freedom Charter. They argue that this form of '… romanticised "rainbowism" …' negates a deeply embedded ethno-racial consciousness where 'the legacy of apartheid lives on [and] South Africa is still a deeply divided society in which racialised competition is likely to increase'. Post-apartheid South Africa has not yet succeeded in crystallising into a 'rainbow nation-state' that has delivered on the vision of South African society captured in the Freedom Charter, mainly because of the continuation of apartheid patterns of belonging in the post-apartheid era. This is a view shared by many scholars, and it warrants further unpacking. There is a need to explore how the legacies of this complicated past remain in ways that feed into consciousness that resonates with post-apartheid nationalism, articulated through rainbowism.

Historians like Dubow (2007: 72) remind us that '... the struggle for South Africa has long been, and continues to be, a struggle to become South African'. Dubow argues that what is supposed to constitute South Africa remains a puzzle. He poses the following questions (Dubow, 2007: 79):

> In the political catechism of the New South Africa, the primary enquiry remains the National Question. What is the post-apartheid nation? Who belongs or is excluded and on what basis? How does a 'national identity' gain its salience and power to transcend the particularities of ethnicity and race...?

Dubow highlighted the complexities surrounding identity in South Africa in the same year that Ivor Chipkin's (2007) ground-breaking study *Do South Africans Exist?* was published, in which he argues that the difference between ethnic groups and the nation lies in their relation to state power. He argued that when ethnic groups pursue state power, their ethnicity becomes nationalism. Chipkin's book reflected the complexities and paradoxes inherent in post-apartheid South Africa's crafting of a national identity out of diverse identities. A careful reading of Chipkin's work reveals how the question of what constitutes South African-ness was at the centre of his analysis. From his perspective, one understands the identity of the South African people in the post-apartheid era by examining the ANC-led nationalist struggle. There is a compelling need to continue tracing the evolution of the idea of South Africa through a historically grounded approach. This approach allows us to understand that migrants come into a context where there are long-standing challenges, namely harnessing complex identities into a normatively constructed, post-apartheid identity of a rainbow nation. These complex identities emerged along fault lines well captured by scholars such as Neocosmos (2010) entailing the construction of 'foreign natives' out of black, indigenous people and 'native foreigners' out of white settlers. Neocosmos's intervention is instructive in understanding that the idea of South Africa exists as a perennial question of identity and a contested work in progress. Construction of this identity has been a daunting task across time and space, thus eliciting comments from scholars such as Theron and Swart (2009: 153) that 'nowhere on the continent has this politics of identity been more prominent than in South Africa, during the pre- and post-apartheid eras'.

The main proposition of this chapter is that thinking about the increased numbers of migrants, and how they further complicate nation-building and social-cohesion initiatives, from the vantage point of a historical analysis enables us to see the challenges of homogenised notions of nationhood that are glaringly disconnected from the non-institutional voices of ordinary South Africans. The broader discursive terrain within which the politics of belonging and the idea of South Africa developed remains a contentious issue: it shapes patterns of belonging that do not accommodate multi-layered identities and frustrate social cohesion initiatives. As late as 1941, Calpin wrote a book entitled *There Are No South Africans* and could posit that 'The worst of South Africa is that you never come across a South African'. This intervention spoke of the daunting task of searching for belonging in South Africa, and the problematic nature of the question of who constitutes a subject and citizen of the nation.

Multi-layered identities inherited from a colonial past have been reproduced in ways that pose a challenge to the 'rainbow' nation and continue to throw up contentious questions about the politics of belonging. According to Hassim et al. (2008), patterns of marginalisation and exclusion still persist within South Africa, creating distinct citizenship experiences:

> Now in the view of many South Africans, it seems that the rainbow has been displaced by the onion, a way of imagining degrees of national belonging, layered around an authentic core. In this view, the fragile outer skin is made up of black African immigrants: Somalians, Congolese, Zimbabweans. Beneath that fragile exterior – so easily exfoliated and discarded – lie the Tsonga, Shangaan, Venda and Pedi people with a firmer claim to inclusion, but on the periphery of the political heartland and therefore of dubious loyalty to the national project... (Hassim et al., 2008: 16).

Their work reveals that the politics of 'othering' and the search for belonging in post-apartheid South Africa is a continuum that extends to certain South African ethnic groups whose autochthony is questioned. This chapter therefore proposes that issues about migrants are just one dimension of the broader complexities of how belonging and social cohesion initiatives in South Africa are forged.

CONCLUSION

In examining the social integration of migrants in South African society, this chapter used the context of competing logics of inclusion and exclusion in the nation-building project in post-apartheid South Africa. This rubric of analysis gives us the opportunity to see the dynamics at play in shaping the politics of belonging and the challenges of social cohesion. Presently, South Africa is struggling to transcend various forms of identity. These cover a wide range: historical and culture-based identities, commonly referred to as ethnic identities, which were re-invented and reified under colonialism and apartheid; market-based identities commonly known as classes; colonially invented political identities such as black versus white, citizens versus subjects, natives versus non-natives, and civilised versus primitive. Migrants then bring an added layer of complexity into this post-apartheid context in which nation-building and social cohesion are long-standing challenges, and the idea of being South African remains an illusion for the majority of the formerly marginalised. In attempting to offer an inflexion on the established literature on migrants and their integration in South Africa, the chapter argues that rather than viewing migrants/migration in isolation, it is valuable to bring a deeper understanding of the arduous task of creating an inclusive South Africa. It is important also to take cognisance of the persistence of the political and economic challenges that the majority of black South Africans face every day, and how this hinders the integration of migrants. Taking this perspective enabled an analysis of how South Africa has been conceived and imagined, and how new struggles 'for South Africa' and 'to become South African' today are inextricably intertwined with the challenges of transcending the patterns of belonging constructed by apartheid. Migrants then become an added layer of challenges and part of larger, more complex processes and politics of belonging waged against injustices of inequality and redistribution. The idea of an inclusive South Africa is still in the making and is proving hard to realise. This has created distinct experiences of belonging for the majority of formerly marginalised black South Africans who perceive migrants as posing a threat to their very existence and search for belonging. In a nutshell, a paradigm shift that embraces micro-level social cohesion initiatives might be helpful in efforts to integrate regular migrants who constitute an overlooked category in nationalistic-focused cohesion efforts.

REFERENCES

Adebayo, B. 8 August 2019. 'Police in South Africa arrest 560 "undocumented" foreigners in raid'. *CNN,* https://www.cnn.com/2019/08/08/africa/foreigners-arrest-south-africa-intl /index.html, accessed 5 May 2023.

Bello, V. 2022. 'The spiralling of the securitisation of migration in the EU: From the management of a "crisis" to a governance of human mobility?'. *Journal of Ethnic and Migration Studies,* 48(6), 1327–1344.

Bundy, C. 2007. 'New nation, new history? Constructing the past in post-Apartheid South Africa', in Stolten, S. (ed.), *History Making and Present-Day Politics: The meaning of collective memory in South Africa.* Uppsala: Nordic Africa Institute, 73–97.

Chikohomero, R. 2023. 'Understanding conflict between locals and migrants in South Africa: Case studies in Atteridgeville and Diepsloot'. *Institute for Security Studies (ISS) Southern Africa Report No. 55,* https://issafrica.s3.amazonaws.com/site/uploads/sar-55-rev.pdf, accessed 18 September 2023.

Chipkin, I. 2007. *Do South Africans Exist? Nationalism, democracy, and the identity of 'the people'.* Johannesburg: Wits University Press.

Chipkin, I. 2016. 'The decline of African nationalism and the state of South Africa'. *Journal of Southern African Studies,* 42(2), 215–227.

Cloete, P. and Kotze, F. 2009. 'Concept paper on social cohesion/inclusion in local integrated development plans'. Commissioned by Department of Social Development, Republic of South Africa, http://www.presidentsaward.co.za/wp-content/uploads/2013/04/Social-Cohesion-Final-Draftcorrect-IDP-DSD.pdf, accessed 15 February 2023.

Crush, J. 2001. 'The dark side of democracy: Migration, xenophobia and human rights in South Africa'. *International Migration,* 38(6), 103–133.

Crush, J. and Williams, V. 2005. 'International migration and development: Dynamics and challenges in South and Southern Africa'. UNDESA, https://www.un.org/en/development/desa/population/events/pdf/expert/8/P05_Crush&Williams.pdf, accessed 5 May 2023.

Department of Arts and Culture (DAC). 2012. 'A national strategy for developing an inclusive and cohesive South African society', https://www.gov.za/sites/default/files/gcis_document/201409/social-cohesion-strategy-1.pdf, accessed 15 February 2023.

Department of Home Affairs (DHA). 2015. *Strategy For Integration, Repatriation and Re-Settlement for Refugees*. Pretoria: Department of Home Affairs.

Dubow, S. 2007. 'Thoughts on South Africa: Some preliminary ideas', in Stolten, H. E. (ed.), *History Making and Present-Day Politics: The meaning of collective memory in South Africa*. Uppsala: Nordic Africa Institute, 51–72.

Duncan, J. 8 May 2015. 'Fortress South Africa'. South African Civil Society Information Service, https://sacsis.org.za/site/article/2369, accessed 5 October 2023.

Habib, A. 2013. *South Africa's Suspended Revolution: Hopes and prospects*. Johannesburg: Wits University Press.

Hassim, S. 2008. 'Introduction', in Hassim, S., Kupe, T. and Worby, E. (eds), *Go Home or Die Here: Violence and reinvention of difference in South Africa*. Johannesburg: Wits University Press.

IOM. 2011. 'World migration report 2021: Communicating effectively about migration', https://publications.iom.int/books/world-migration-report-2011, accessed 5 September 2023.

Institute for Security Studies (ISS). 2015. 'Understanding the conflict between locals and migrants in South Africa'. Case studies in Atteridgeville and Diepsloot.

Jensen, J. 1998. 'Mapping social cohesion: The state of Canadian research'. *Ottawa, Canadian Policy Research Networks*, Inc., CPRN Study No. 5/03.

Kanayo, O., Anjofuyi, P. and Stiegler, N. 2019. 'Analysis of ramifications of migration and xenophobia in Africa: Review of economic potentials, skills of migrants and related policies in South Africa'. *Journal of Foreign Affairs*, 6(2), 65–85.

Khan, F. 2007. 'Patterns and policies of migration in South Africa: Changing patterns and the need for a comprehensive approach'. University of Cape Town Refugee Rights Project, www.refugeerights.uct.ac.za/.../patterns_policies_ migration_FKhan.doc, accessed 5 May 2023.

Lamb, G. 2021. 'Safeguarding the republic? The South African police service, legitimacy and the tribulations of policing a violent democracy'. *Journal of Asian and African Studies,* 56(1), 92–108.

Landau, L. B. 2004. 'Myth and decision in South African management and research'. Paper prepared for African Migration Alliance Workshop, Forced Migration Working Paper Series, No. 11.

Landau, L. B. and Bakewell, O. 2018. 'Introduction: Forging a study of mobility, integration and belonging in Africa', in Landau, L. B. and Bakewell, O. (eds), *Forging African Communities: Mobility, integration and belonging*. London: Palgrave Macmillan.

Mathers, K. and Landau, L. B. 2007. 'Natives, tourists, and makwerekwere: Ethical concerns with "Proudly South African" tourism'. *Development Southern Africa*, 24(3), 523–537.

Mbembe, A. 2014. 'Difference and repetition: Reflections on South Africa now'. Presentation Delivered at the Research and Innovation Week, University of South Africa, 4 March 2014.

Mbembe, A. 24 March 2017. 'Africa needs free movement'. *Mail & Guardian*, https://mg.co.za/article/2017-03-24-00-africa-needs-free-movement/, accessed 8 August 2023.

Misago, J. P. 2017. 'Politics by other means? the political economy of xenophobic violence in post-apartheid South Africa'. *The Black Scholar,* 47(2), 40–53.

Misago, J. P. 2019. 'Political mobilisation as the trigger of xenophobic violence in post-apartheid South Africa'. *International Journal of Conflict and Violence,* 13, 1–10.

Misago, J. P. and Landau, L. B. 2022. '"Running them out of time": Xenophobia, violence, and co-authoring spatiotemporal exclusion in South Africa'. *Geopolitics*, 28(4), 1611–1631.

MISTRA. 2014. *Nation Formation and Social Cohesion*. Johannesburg: Real African Publishers (RAP).

Moodley, K. and Adam, H. 2000. 'Race and nation in post-apartheid South Africa'. *Current Sociology*, 48(3), 51–69.

Moyo, I. 2017. 'Changing migration status and shifting vulnerabilities: A research note on Zimbabwean migrants in South Africa'. *Journal of Trafficking, Organised Crime and Security*, 2, 108–112.

Moyo, I., Laine, J. and Nshimbi, C. C. (eds). 2021. *Intra-Africa Migrations: Reimagining borders and migration management*. London: Routledge.

Musoni, F. 2020. *Border Jumping and Migration Control in Southern Africa*. Bloomington: University of Indiana Press.

Ndlovu-Gatsheni, S. J. 2010. 'Do Africans exist? Genealogies and paradoxes of African identities and the discourses of nativism and xenophobia'. *African Identities*, 8(3), 281–295.

Ndlovu-Gatsheni, S. J. 2012. 'Racialised ethnicities and ethnicised races: Reflections on the making of South Africanism'. *African Identities*, 10(4), 1–16.

Neocosmos, M. 2008. 'The politics of fear and fear of politics: Reflections on xenophobic violence in South Africa'. *Journal of Asian and African Studies*, 43(6), 586–594.

Neocosmos, M. 2010. *From 'Foreign Natives' to 'Native foreigners': Explaining* xenophobia in post-apartheid South Africa: Citizenship and nationalism, identity and politics. Dakar: CODESRIA.

Novy, A., Swiatek, C. D. and Frank Moulaert, F. 2012. 'Social cohesion: A conceptual and political elucidation'. *Urban Studies,* 49(9), 1873–1889.

Nshimbi, C. C. and Fioramonti, L. 2013. 'A region without borders? Policy frameworks for regional labour migration towards South Africa'. Johannesburg Centre for Migration and Society, University of the Witwatersrand.

Nshimbi C. C. and Lorenzo F. 2014. 'The will to integrate: South Africa's responses to regional migration from the SADC region'. *African Development Review,* 26(1), 52–63.

Nshimbi, C. C. and Lorenzo. F. 2016. 'Regional migration governance in the African continent current state of affairs and the way forward'. Stiftung Entwicklung und Frieden (sef:)/ Development and Peace Foundation, Bonn.

Nyamnjoh, F. B. 30 June 2022. 'Uncontaining mobility: Lessons from Covid-19'. 2nd AMMODI (African Migration, Mobility and Displacement) Annual Keynote Lecture, https://ammodi.com/wp-content/uploads/2022/09/Uncontaining-Mobility-Nyamnjoh-2022.pdf, accessed 12 November 2023.

Nyandoro, M. 2016. 'Implications for policy discourse: The influx of Zimbabwean migrants into South Africa', in Guild, E. and Mantu, S. (eds), *Constructing and Imagining Labour Migration: Perspectives of control from five continents.* London: Routledge, 109–36.

Oliver, E. and Oliver, W. H. 2017. 'The colonisation of South Africa: A unique case'. *HTS Teologiese Studies/Theological Studies,* 73(3), 1–8.

Palmary, I. 2015. 'Reflections on social cohesion in contemporary South Africa'. *Psychology in Society,* 49, 62–69.

Peberdy, S. 2009. *Selecting Immigrants: National identity and South Africa's immigration policies 1910–2008.* Johannesburg: Wits University Press.

Peberdy, S. 2010. 'Setting the scene: Migration and urbanization in South Africa'. *The Atlantic Philanthropies,* https://www.atlanticphilanthropies.org/wp-content/uploads/2010/07/3_Setting_the_scene_c.pdf, accessed 5 October 2023.

Peberdy, S. and Crush, J. 1998. 'Trading places: Cross border traders and the South African informal sector'. Migration Series No. 6, South African Immigration Project, Cape Town and Kingston.

Sparks, A. 1994. *Tomorrow is Another Country: The inside story of South Africa's negotiated settlement.* Johannesburg: Struik.

Terreblanche, S. 2012. *Lost in Transformation: South Africa's search for a new future since 1986.* Sandton: KMM Review Publishing Company.

Theron, M. and Swart, G. 2009. 'South Africa and the new Africa: Chasing African rainbows', in Adibe, J. (ed.), *Who is an African?.* London: Adonis and Abbey, 153–177.

Vanyoro, K. P. 2019. '"Bringing time" into migration and critical border studies: Theoretical and methodological implications for African research'. Migrating out poverty research programme consortium Working paper 60, http://www.migratingoutofpoverty.org/files/file.php?name=wp60-vanyoro-2019-bringing-time-into-migration-and-border-studies.pdf&site=354, accessed 15 September 2023.

Vanyoro, K. 2023. 'The political work of migration governance binaries: Responses to Zimbabwean "survival migration" at the Zimbabwe South Africa border'. *Refugee Survey Quarterly*, 42(3), 286–312.

Vertovec, S. 2010. 'Diversity, cosmopolitans and locals'. *Max Planck Institute for the Study of Religious and Ethnic Diversity*, https://www.mmg.mpg.de/43991/blog-vertovec-diversity, accessed 4 September 2023.

Villa-Vicencio, C. 14 December 2001. 'The one and the many'. *The Star*. Advertising feature.

Wee, K., Vanyoro, K. P. and Jinna, Z. 2018. 'Repoliticising international migration narratives? Critical reflections on the civil society days of the global forum on migration and development'. *Globalizations*, 15(2), 1–14.

FIVE

Unlocking international migrant domestic workers' agency in claiming the right to compensation for occupational injuries and diseases in South Africa

JANET MUNAKAMWE

The chapter draws from the cases of domestic workers seeking recognition under the Compensation for Occupational Injuries and Diseases Act (COIDA) of 1993 in South Africa. Through a campaign that took place from 2018 to 2019, it illustrates how international migrants unlock their agency by collaborating with local counterparts to advocate for dignity and human and labour rights. Theoretically, it aligns with Antonio Gramsci's theory of hegemony. The chapter delves into international migration and reveals a dearth of literature on migrants' agency and the role of civil society in advocating for human and labour rights. Migrants are often seen as vulnerable (Ochs, 2006), thus overshadowing their capacity to stand up for social justice.

Furthermore, the chapter accentuates the significance of examining migrants' political subjectivities and participation within host countries through a human rights lens. Locating migrants' agency within the human rights discourse underscores the universality of rights embedded in the national constitution of South Africa. Contrary to constitutional precepts, over the years the country has been the site of acts of violence targeted at international migrants. The securitisation of migration, as evident in high rates of arrests and unlawful detentions, makes it difficult for migrants to effectively claim their rights. This situation is further exacerbated by the disjuncture between restrictive migration laws and protective labour laws (Munakamwe, 2018). Simultaneously, migrants at times distance themselves from the country's constitutional rights, viewing them as available only to protect citizens. Yet, research has demonstrated that when migrants are unable to represent themselves effectively, civil society often steps in to fill the gaps by amplifying the voices of migrants and upholding their constitutional rights (see Jinnah and Holladay, 2010).

INTRODUCTION

The chapter offers a panoramic view of the ways in which international migrants advocate for human and labour rights, using the domestic work sector as a case study. In 2018, I was commissioned by the Solidarity Center to conduct national research to inform strategic litigation that resulted in the inclusion of domestic workers under the Compensation for Occupational Injuries and Diseases Act (COIDA). Through the case of COIDA, this chapter aims to contribute to theoretical debates and highlight novel features of migrant workers' agency in advocating for labour rights.

The chapter focuses on the post-1994 era in South Africa, coinciding with the ideal of a 'Rainbow Nation'. Paradoxically, episodic and sporadic anti-immigrant tensions, as well as workplace discrimination, have persisted over the years (Munakamwe, 2022a). These actions are often partly prompted by a shrinking labour market and systemic unemployment. Some politicians frequently scapegoat migrants, blaming them for high levels of crime in the country. Attacks against international migrants have exposed human rights deficits while raising questions about inequality and discrimination based on nationality or migration status. It is worth noting, however, that the issue of negative attitudes towards migrants plays a central role in mobilisation, or the lack thereof, by international migrants and civil society. In other words, various factors determine the political subjectivities of workers in general. In this case, it is the issue of lack of recognition (Ally, 2011) and blatant exclusion from the COIDA that forged unity and solidarity among local and migrant domestic workers to unlock their agency and mobilise for social justice.

This chapter aims to contribute to a deeper theoretical under-standing of the complexities surrounding migrant workers' political subjectivities through the case of COIDA. It also sheds light on the critical role of traditional unions and civil society in advancing human and labour rights for all, irrespective of migration status. Despite a substantial body of literature on international migration and its impacts, there is a notable gap in research concerning migrants' agency and the role of civil society in advancing their rights. Migrants are often perceived as vulnerable, overshadowing their capacity to advocate for themselves. This chapter seeks to cover this research gap by examining, from a human rights perspective, the factors that shape political subjectivities and participation among migrants.

COIDA constitutes an integral component of workers' health benefits in the event of injuries or occupational diseases. Historically, the compensation fund was male-biased and structured along masculinities, as men would migrate to the mines through the contract migrant labour system, while women were excluded from formal labour markets (Wolpe, 1972; Arrighi, 1973; Burawoy, 1976; Allen, 1992; Fakier, 2012).Thus, this challenge by domestic workers in post-colonial South Africa was unprecedented as labour demands are often centred on wages and working conditions. At this point, a critical analysis of the role of trade unions, civic society or other worker organisations in representing the interests of workers becomes crucial. It is also important to note the feminist approach to organising aimed at challenging not only wage disparities but also gender discrimination as a subaltern of the working class. In a way, the domestic workers' challenge to COIDA represents a turning point in which migrant workers have openly fought for their rights in South Africa. This is consistent with Milkman (2006) who contends that migrants are organisable, based on the case of Latino janitors who self-organised beyond 'bread and butter' issues.

METHODOLOGY

This chapter employs a qualitative research approach while leveraging my extensive involvement in scientific studies and civil society advocacy, particularly focusing on vulnerable workers such as migrants, casual and domestic. The chapter draws on participant observation (see Munakamwe and Gwenyaya, 2019) and the case study of domestic workers' advocacy for COIDA to provide insights into migrant agency and political subjectivities.

OUTLINE OF THE CHAPTER

The introduction is followed by an outline of the context for the case study, namely the historical and contemporary backdrop for analysing international migration, paying particular focus on South Africa. The subsequent section explores Antonio Gramsci's theoretical framework and its relevance to understanding migrant agency. The literature section examines existing literature, drawn from global and local perspectives, which highlights human rights issues and initiatives for organising migrants. Furthermore, the vulnerabilities associated with the domestic work sector, irrespective of nationality, are highlighted. Domestic workers are exposed to various forms of discrimination, including gender, class and race and, for migrants, the additional layer of nationality or citizenship discrimination.

The section in this chapter on laws and policies underscores the significance of regular documentation, or lack thereof, in hindering migrant workers' mobilisation and their participation in advocating for social, economic and labour rights. The focus extends to migrants' agency in regularising their stay. The chapter also explores the institutionalised prejudice inherent in the work visa regime and the right to live and work. This has a huge impact on migrant domestic workers' capacity to claim their labour rights, in addition to their exclusion from COIDA.

CONTEXT

South Africa has a rich history of labour migration (Crush et al., 1991; Crush and James, 1995). According to Sachikonye (1998), it has been a longstanding phenomenon in southern African countries, predating the establishment of colonial boundaries. Since the late 18th century, countries in the southern Africa region have played dual roles as host and sending countries for labour migration (Sachikonye, 1998). Zambia, Zimbabwe, Botswana and South Africa historically served as primary hosts, while Malawi, Lesotho, Mozambique and eSwatini supplied workers to mines and commercial farms (Munakamwe, 2018). South Africa, particularly after the discovery of precious minerals like gold in 1886 (Callinicos, 2014), has remained the primary destination for migrants from the southern African region (Chirwa, 1996; Munakamwe, 2018). The male-dominated migrant labour workforce in mines and commercial farms has significantly influenced the evolution of social security benefits such as COIDA, which was originally crafted to benefit males until the Constitutional Court's landmark ruling in November 2019 (see Munakamwe and Gwenyaya, 2019).

Data from the International Labour Organization (ILO) in 2021 indicates a global count of 169 million international migrant workers, marking a five million increase from 2017 to 2019. Labour migration presents opportunities: the World Bank emphasises the benefits that countries of origin can gain from migrant workers (World Bank, n.d.). These include remittances, investments, trade, skills and technology transfers, which all contribute to poverty reduction and alleviation of unemployment rates. The World Bank's May 2022 report projected that remittances to low- and middle-income nations would exceed US$630 billion in 2022, surpassing the combined total of development aid by over three times.

In the post-apartheid era, South Africa has become a primary destination for immigrants, asylum seekers and refugees from various parts of the world, particularly from within the southern African region, notably Zimbabwe (Crush et al., 2017). However, after the contract migrant labour system, migration has become increasingly individualistic and often clandestine, leading to irregular migration and widespread human rights violations.

In recent years, South Africa has witnessed a surge in violations of the human rights of international migrants and attacks against them (Amnesty International, 2019). This is further exacerbated by institutionalised prejudice resulting from restrictive state-crafted migration laws and policies (Munakamwe, 2018, 2022). Prejudice against granting the right to work in the country – which is skewed towards highly skilled migrants – leaves low-skilled workers and those outside standard employment arrangements vulnerable and in desperate need of labour rights protection. Over the years, civil society has mobilised to address human rights violations against international migrants, including pursuing public litigation actions to secure the right to regularisation as well as the right to work.[1] Clandestine and irregular migration has become prevalent in the post-apartheid democratic epoch, in contrast with the regulated and contractual migrant labour system under apartheid. The Immigration Act of 2002, in some ways, categorises migrants as either desirable or undesirable and thus has the effect of disenfranchising the latter from enjoying constitutional rights.

AN OVERVIEW OF THE DOMESTIC WORKER SECTOR

In South Africa, approximately one million people, predominantly black women from marginalised backgrounds, are employed by middle-class families (Munakamwe and Gwenyaya, 2019) to work in private homes. Some work as full-time domestic workers and live on their employers' premises, often in backyard rooms, while others live off-site. A significant proportion of domestic workers are employed part-time

---

1   See *Minister of Home Affairs and Others v Watchenuka and Others* (010/2003) [2003] ZASCA 142; [2004] 1 All SA 21 (SCA) (28 November 2003). http://www.saflii.org/za/cases/ZASCA/2003/142.html, accessed 12 September 2023.

or on a temporary basis, working varied hours, wages and schedules for different employers. These employment practices not only result in a representation gap but also contribute to economic insecurity and impede mobilisation for labour rights. The absence of employment contracts, low wages and limited access to social security further exacerbate race, class and gender inequalities within the sector. In essence, the personal and unequal nature of the relationship between employers and domestic workers adds to the exploitative conditions of domestic work.

One of the prime challenges in the domestic work sector is the inherently personal and unequal relationship between employers and domestic workers. When domestic workers are considered 'part of the family', employers wield significant power to provide or withdraw support as they see fit (Munakamwe, 2022b). Employers may offer gifts, kindness and care to elicit greater labour and 'favours' from domestic workers, which would then create a hostile employment relationship when expectations are not met (Munakamwe and Gwenyaya, 2019). All these distressing conditions are further compounded by the precarious status of migrant domestic workers. Unions organising domestic workers have long called for the inclusion of migrant domestic workers to join their ranks and build solidarity against unfair labour practices, as employers often prefer hiring migrants with the aim of exploiting them and undercutting the national minimum wage.

POWER, POLITICAL MOBILISATION AND SOLIDARITY

Central to the discourse on human and labour rights advocacy is the fundamental question of power. In his concept of power, Gramsci argues that hegemony perpetuates domination, potentially dividing the proletarian class. Effectively, he elevates the conversation beyond mere class conflict by incorporating the concepts of power and hegemony as essential to understanding workers' struggles. He also posits that fundamentally civil society serves as an alternative voice for workers outside organised labour.

As mentioned earlier, the domestic sector occupies the periphery of the working class and of the global care economy (Parreñas, 2005; Fraser,

2016). The patronising power dynamics within this sector raise the question of who will advocate for the subaltern. Gramsci acknowledges the role of employers in fostering passivity among workers, a reflection evident in the domestic sector and further compounded by the authority vested in the Immigration Act of 2002. According to this Act, the sole responsibility for monitoring migrant workers in the country rests with employers (Munakamwe, 2018). This piece of legislation diminishes the agency of migrant domestic workers while promoting patronage. Consequently, migrant domestic workers often hesitate to join unions or engage in human rights advocacy for fear of reprisals or deportation (Vanyoro, 2019). Migrants are exposed to attacks in the communities they reside in and consequently avoid participating in protests aimed at asserting their constitutional, social and economic rights.

In his theory of hegemony, Antonio Gramsci appreciates that economic and material needs are not the sole catalysts for worker mobilisation. Various other factors such as ideology, politics, social dynamics, gender, culture and race also play significant roles. The issue of regular documentation can therefore be considered as one of the factors to be taken into account in an analysis of the agency of migrant domestic workers and their advocacy for the right to protection under the labour laws of South Africa, including compensation for injuries and occupational diseases.

In the absence of institutional power, international migrants rely on civil society as a unifying force and a vehicle for promoting solidarity with regard to human rights. Central to Gramsci's theory of domination is an emphasis on the need for solidarity among the subalterns (Brown, 2009). Therefore, it is crucial to assess the extent to which local and migrant domestic workers have been able to articulate common grievances. Gramsci's theory, an extension of Marxist theory, aims to broaden the analysis of working-class solidarity. It considers not only a class perspective and a universalist approach, as popularised by unions, but also multiple stakeholders such as civil society and its role in the balance of power and forces. This framework is essential for understanding social mobilisation based on everyday particularistic issues such as documentation and prejudice, which affect migrant domestic workers and impede their participation in human rights advocacy.

Gramsci argues that divisions within the working class jeopardise alliances of workers and contribute to factionalism. Based on my research experience and observations in the domestic sector, I have witnessed a transformation in attitudes within both groups. For example, a decade ago, it was challenging for migrant domestic workers to participate in labour rights workshops offered by the Commission for Conciliation, Mediation and Arbitration (CCMA) and championed by the largest union in the sector, the South African Domestic Service and Allied Workers Union (SADSAWU). However, following solidarity workshops conducted by organisations like the ILO, Rosa Luxemburg Foundation, Chris Hani Institute, Solidarity Center, Ditsela, and the Congress of South African Trade Unions (COSATU), the situation has significantly improved. Migrant domestic workers who have become more conscious are now able to exercise their agency as witnessed in the case of COIDA. One migrant domestic worker even secured a national organiser role during the advocacy campaign for COIDA, a campaign that enjoyed the support of traditional unions and civil society organisations. This campaign brought local and migrant domestic workers together in a unified front grounded in the principles of Marxist working-class solidarity.

At this juncture, it is important to point out that progress has been made in some areas, such as the adoption of ILO Conventions 189 and 190 to protect domestic workers from unfair labour practices and gender-based violence (GBV) in the workplace. The struggle for a shorter workday and political recognition for the working class dates back to the 1800s. The largest union organising domestic workers in South Africa, SADSAWU (Ally, 2008), led negotiations for the adoption of the ILO Convention 189 during the 100th General Conference of the ILO session on 16 June 2011. Furthermore, in 2019, domestic workers in South Africa fought for the right to recognition and inclusion in the COIDA.

However, it is concerning that some of these gains have been eroded in the wake of the Covid-19 pandemic. According to Statistics South Africa's Quarterly Labour Force Survey (Statistics SA, 2023), a significant number of domestic workers lost their jobs, including 67,000 in the first quarter of 2023.

VICTIMHOOD, ACQUIESCENCE OR AGENCY?

In the field of migration studies, a prevailing perspective often portrays migrants as passive victims instead of agents of change. This discourse of victimhood, as noted by Ochs (2006: 357), tends to obscure the agency of those classified as victims. However, research by European scholars such as Martiniello (2005) and Ireland (1994) challenges this notion by highlighting that migrants are not inherently docile. Martiniello, in particular, rejects the reductionist view inherent in classical Marxist analyses that suggest migrant apathy. Instead, Martiniello asserts that migrants actively contribute to political processes in their host countries (Martiniello, 2005).

Webster's (1985) study on internal migrant iron smiths on the East Rand of Johannesburg during the apartheid era further challenges conventional stereotypes of 'victimhood', 'quiescence' and 'dormancy' associated with migrant workers. Examining the context of the United States and the mobilisation of international migrants, Milkman (2006) dismisses the notion of dormancy among immigrants. She argues that immigrant workers are not passive but rather 'ripe' and capable of organisation. These examples underscore the agency of international migrants, which can be harnessed with the support of local unions, civil society and migrant-rights organisations (MROs).

Between 2008 and 2009, Polzer and Segatti conducted a study focused on various forms of collective mobilisation among immigrants in Gauteng province in South Africa, with a particular emphasis on their everyday political and social struggles. Their analysis also explored immigrants' representation, including the repositioning of migrant organisations before and after the 'crisis' of xenophobic attacks in May 2008 (Polzer and Segatti, 2012). The research yielded valuable insights into the concepts of mobilisation and representation among international migrants. Polzer and Segatti's study pointed to a degree of agency, active participation and representation among certain groups of nationals living in South Africa, notably among communities from the Democratic Republic of the Congo (DRC), Somalia and Zimbabwe. However, this participation tended to be more reactive than proactive, with immigrants becoming more visible when responding to crises, such as the xenophobic attacks that occurred in South Africa in May 2008 (Polzer and Segatti, 2012). These findings raise a critical question: When is the optimal time to mobilise or represent immigrant workers? Should this primarily be in response to crises, or should it be an ongoing and proactive process?

INSTITUTIONALISED XENOPHOBIA AND HUMAN RIGHTS VIOLATIONS IN CONTEMPORARY SOUTH AFRICA

Negative attitudes to irregular migration often serve to demobilise migrants, leading irregular migrants to elect to remain 'invisible' (Segatti and Munakamwe, 2014). In this context, 'invisibility' becomes a survival strategy to avoid reprisals and evade the attention of law enforcement agents, thereby reducing the risk of deportation. Supporting this notion, a study conducted by Jinnah and Holladay (2010: 139) revealed that:

> Migrants generally do not mobilize for rights, citing lack of documentation, discrimination, and language barriers as key obstacles to claiming rights. Migrants also have minimal interaction with state institutions, NGOs, and migrant-led organisations, minimal trust and reliance on institutions and organisations.

While there are undoubtedly challenges hampering the mobilisation of international migrants, it is crucial to appreciate that opportunities exist alongside these obstacles. For instance, migrants from labour-sending countries such as Malawi, Lesotho and Zimbabwe often mobilise around work visas, while those from Ethiopia, Pakistan, Nigeria and Somalia agitate for the right to operate small businesses. Migrants from refugee-producing countries, such as the DRC and Cameroon, engage in advocacy aimed at reforming asylum and refugee laws and policies. In contrast, migrant communities from Botswana, Ghana, Mozambique, Uganda and Zambia tend to be less conspicuous, while those from Cameroon, DRC and eSwatini are actively involved in political mobilisation against predatory regimes. Notably, the migrant community from Uganda engaged in political mobilisation, for the first time, against President Museveni's state visit to South Africa on 28 February 2023, accusing him of tyranny and human rights abuses against political activists and the LGBTQI+ community. Additionally, in response to violent attacks, some foreign nationals have mobilised against South African companies that have invested in their home countries, such as MTN in Nigeria (Adebayo, 2019).

A BRIEF SYNOPSIS OF LAWS AND POLICIES PROTECTING INTERNATIONAL MIGRANTS IN SOUTH AFRICA

The discourse on human rights encompasses a wide array of issues, with this section focusing primarily on migration, labour and health rights – central to COIDA – for migrant domestic workers. It is important to note that this section does not attempt to provide an exhaustive analysis of all legislative and policy frameworks but rather concentrates on the major statutory instruments relevant to the primary objective of this chapter. South Africa is a constitutional democracy and a signatory to multiple international and regional protocols and conventions aimed at upholding the rights of international migrants. In the absence of national policies and laws safeguarding the rights of international migrants, affected parties often invoke international legal instruments to advocate for their rights. Moreover, the national constitution guarantees universal rights to all individuals residing in the country.

Key international statutes central to this conversation include the International Human Rights Law (IHRL); the 1951 UN Convention Relating to the Status of Refugees; the 1967 Protocol to the Convention; the 1969 Organisation of African Unity (OAU) Refugee Convention governing aspects of refugee problems in Africa; and the ILO Convention 143, which is the International Convention on the Protection of the Rights of All Migrant Workers (C143). It is worth noting that only a few member states have ratified C143, partly due to the voluntary nature of international conventions (Munakamwe,

2018). For example, Article 9 of the International Covenant on Economic, Social and Cultural Rights (ICESCR) recognises the right of everyone to social security, including social insurance, as being of central importance in guaranteeing human dignity when individuals face circumstances that deprive them of their capacity to fully realise their Covenant rights (Tanzer and Gwenyaya, 2019).

These international human rights, combined with the rights enshrined in Chapter 2 of the Constitution of South Africa, are rights enjoyed by all individuals, not only citizens (Handmaker et al., 2001: 5). Consequently, the absence of citizenship does not imply a lack of state-guaranteed rights. However, international migrants in South Africa continue to face human rights violations despite the protection guarantees enshrined in the national constitution (Kabwe-Segatti, 2008: 58; Munakamwe, 2018). These violations occur at multiple levels, involving various state and non-state actors. Many of the violations happen under the guise of state-crafted migration laws, leading to institutionalised prejudice that makes it challenging for migrants to enter the country through formal channels (Munakamwe, 2018). At the same time, the push factors that lead to desperate acts of migration are hardly addressed in countries of origin or in interactions among the political leaders in the region and beyond.

Migrants, especially women, are exposed to sexual violations while using clandestine routes to enter the country. Subsequently, they are often hired to work under the category of the 'undocumented', subjecting them to super-exploitation. Women are particularly vulnerable and are more likely to be employed as casual or seasonal workers in vulnerable sectors such as domestic work, hospitality and agriculture (Coplan and Thoahlane, 1995; Munakamwe and Jinnah, 2015; Cazarin and Jinnah, 2016). However, it is important to point out that the government of South Africa has made efforts to regularise undocumented migrants (Nyakabawu, 2021).

CONSTITUTIONAL RIGHT TO HEALTH
FOR ALL IN SOUTH AFRICA?

The right to access healthcare services is a fundamental constitutional precept for both citizens and all residents of South Africa, as outlined in Section 27 of the Constitution and emphasised by Sustainable Development Goal 3 (SDG 3). The constitutional right to healthcare services is further elaborated upon by the National Health Act of 2003. According to the National Health Act, government clinics and community health centres funded by the state are obligated to provide free primary healthcare services to all individuals, except members of medical aid schemes and their dependants, as well as individuals receiving compensation for occupational diseases, subject to any conditions prescribed by the Minister of Health. Furthermore, it stipulates that pregnant and lactating women, as well as all children below the age of six, regardless of nationality, are entitled to free healthcare services based on their needs. This includes access to district, regional, tertiary and primary health facilities. A court order of 2023 has upheld this principle in response to a fee policy enforced by the Gauteng Department of Health on migrants.

In line with South Africa's commitment as a signatory of the Refugees Act, refugees and permanent residents have been included in the population eligible to receive basic healthcare services under the National Health Insurance (NHI). It is important to note that the number of internal migrants in South Africa is higher than cross-border migrants (Ginsburg et al., 2021). However, there is often a gap between policy and practice, and currently, there is no mechanism in place to collect disaggregated data on the movement of people – both internal and international migration – which impacts budgeting. Despite the existing laws and policies that ensure equal access to healthcare services for all, migrants often encounter unfair discriminatory practices within the healthcare system. It is also important to point out that the discrimination against domestic workers is widespread, as demonstrated in the fight for the rights enshrined in COIDA. The subsequent section provides a brief overview of this campaign, a pivotal moment in the sector's history.

MIGRANT DOMESTIC WORKERS AND THE STRUGGLE FOR THE COMPENSATION FOR OCCUPATIONAL INJURIES AND DISEASES ACT (COIDA)

This section draws extensively from empirical data gathered through participant observation. The author served as the lead researcher for the strategic study that informed the Covid-19 litigation. An official report of this study was published by the Solidarity Center, a philanthropic organisation that provided both material and technical support for the constitutional challenge resulting in this victory for human and labour rights (Munakamwe and Gwenyaya, 2019).

Beyond 'bread and butter' issues: Advocacy for COIDA

For over twenty years after the advent of democracy in South Africa, domestic workers were explicitly excluded from the COIDA, as noted by Munakamwe and Gwenyaya (2019). Through robust awareness-raising campaigns and advocacy for social justice led by trade unions, migrant-rights organisations and civil society organisations, domestic workers, regardless of nationality, came together in solidarity as an exploited working class to fight for their inclusion. On 19 November 2020, the Constitutional Court of South Africa declared COIDA unconstitutional and ordered its retrospective application for compensation. Importantly, this campaign for victory managed to unite local and migrant domestic workers. Feminist solidarity among domestic workers, centred on their shared experiences of super-exploitation rather than nationality, led to positive outcomes in securing human and labour rights for all workers in the sector. Local domestic workers, including migrants from Lesotho, eSwatini, Malawi and Zimbabwe, mobilised and established a coalition that continues to function beyond the Constitutional Court victory.

The WhatsApp platform created for national leaders in the domestic work sector during the COIDA campaign serves as a way of keeping domestic workers connected to other struggles and provides a platform for education about rights (Ueno and Bélanger, 2019). Trade union leaders in this sector realised that a nationalist approach to protecting workers' rights would undermine labour rights in general and result in wage undercutting. Guided by the principle that 'An injury to one is an injury to all', union leaders recognised that xenophobia would undermine the ethos of worker-to-worker solidarity. Hence, trade unions in the sector, SADSAWU and the United Domestic Workers of South Africa (UDWOSA), represent migrant workers who approach them for advice on labour disputes or GBV in the workplace. In August 2023, UDWOSA led a protest at one of the embassies in South Africa against one of their employees. They were demanding justice in the case involving a migrant domestic worker from Zimbabwe who was sexually harassed by her employer (embassy employee) and his family while she worked and lived with them.

While the domestic sector's case stands out in terms of human rights advocacy and mobilisation for migrant domestic workers, inconveniently, according to Munakamwe (2022a), the trade unions involved are not formally registered to represent workers at the National Economic Development and Labour Council (Nedlac). This presents hurdles to influencing the crafting of more inclusive migration laws and policies, despite the fact that regularising migrant domestic workers would help guarantee rights for all who live and work in South Africa, regardless of their origin and nationality, in line with the Bill of Rights in the Constitution (Coplan, 1995: 34). This victory was made possible through the support of local trade unions, migrant-rights organisations (MROs), public-interest law organisations (PILOs) and other civil society partners in the coalition. Antonio Gramsci's emphasis on civil society's role in workers' struggles is evident here. Moreover, solidarity is essential, as migrants cannot achieve this alone, even when self-organising. Successful mobilisation, as Agustin and Jorgensen (2022) argue, requires strong partnerships with progressive local civil society organisations and activists to find common ground for the equal enjoyment of constitutional rights.

CONCLUSION

This chapter explored the agency of international migrants, shedding light on how they navigate the intricate landscape of claiming their human and labour rights under restrictive migration laws and with the protection of the national constitution. Migrants frequently mobilise around a spectrum of economic, social and political issues directly impacting their lives. However, their participation in broader national issues is a less-explored area, hence the dearth of literature. When constitutional rights are violated, civil society emerges as a spirited transformative agent, employing various strategies such as public-interest litigation, direct confrontations, rights education programmes and awareness campaigns related to solidarity and xenophobia.

In this context, power dynamics have significant impact, particularly taking into account the working-class poor who are very often located at the lowest echelon of global care in the case of domestic work. Antonio Gramsci underscores that collective class resistance and full participation in advocating for labour and human rights, rooted in class solidarity, are imperative for challenging capitalism and class hegemony. It is noteworthy that insufficient attention to the regularisation of migrants as a fundamental right can adversely affect the entire working class (Munakamwe, 2018). Employers may exploit cheap migrant labour, potentially undermining collective bargaining agreements, leading to the undercutting of wages and labour rights violations. Promoting the regularisation of international domestic workers is a pivotal step in enabling them to fully unlock their agency and assert their human and labour rights (Vanyoro, 2019).

The case of COIDA epitomises the multifaceted nature of the agency of international migrants in claiming their rights, involving litigation, civil society mobilisation and solidarity transcending colonial borders. Acknowledging and addressing the challenges migrants face in affirming their rights is not only a matter of justice but also a means to advance the rights and wellbeing of all workers and marginalised communities.

REFERENCES

Adebayo, M. 2019. 'Xenophobic attacks: Angry Nigerians burn down MTN office, stage protest at Shoprite, Stanbic Bank over killing of citizens in South Africa'. *Daily Post*, https://dailypost.ng/2019/09/04/xenophobic-attacks-angry-nigerians-burn-mtn-office-stage-protest-shoprite-stanbic-bank-killing-citizens-south-africa-photos-video/, accessed 5 May 2024.

Agustin, O. G. and Jorgensen, M. B. 2022. 'On transversal solidarity: An approach to migration and multi-scalar solidarities', in Jorgensen, M. B. and Schierup, C. U. (eds), *Contending Global Apartheid: Transversal solidarities and politics of possibility*. Netherlands: Brill Publishers.

Allen, V. 1992. *History of Black Mineworkers in South Africa: The techniques of resistance, 1871–1948*. Keighley: Moor Press.

Ally, S. 2008. 'Domestic worker unionisation in post-apartheid South Africa: Demobilisation and depoliticisation by the democratic state'. *Politikon*, 35(1), 1–21.

Ally, S. 2011. *From Servants to Workers: South African domestic workers and the democratic state*. New York: Cornell University Press.

Amnesty International. 2019. *South Africa: Living in limbo: Rights of asylum seekers denied*. Johannesburg: Amnesty International.

Arrighi, G. 1973. 'Labour supplies in historical perspectives: A study of the proletarianisation of the African peasantry in Rhodesia', in Arrighi, G. and Soul, J. S. (eds), *Essays on the Political Economy of Africa. Journal of Development Studies*, 6, 197–234.

Brown, T. 2009. 'Gramsci and hegemony'. *Links International Journal of Socialist Renewal*, https://links.org.au/gramsci-and-hegemony, accessed 2 October 2023.

Burawoy, M. 1976. 'The functions and reproduction of migrant labour: Comparative material from Southern Africa and the United States'. *American Journal of Sociology*, 81(5), 1050–1087.

Callinicos, L. 2014. *Gold and Workers 1886–1924*. Johannesburg: Ravan Press.

Cazarin, R. and Jinnah, Z. 2016. 'Making guests feel comfortable: Migrancy and labour in the hospitality sector in South Africa'. MiWORC Report No 11, African Centre for Migration and Society (ACMS), University of the Witwatersrand.

Chirwa, W. C. 1996. 'The Malawi government and South African labour recruiters, 1974–92'. *The Journal of Modern African Studies*, 34(4), 623–642.

Coplan, D. B. 1995. *In the Time of Cannibals: The word music of South Africa's Basotho*. Chicago: University of Chicago Press.

Coplan, D. and Thoahlane, T. 1995. 'Motherless households, landless farms: Employment patterns among Lesotho migrants', in Crush, J. and James, W. (eds), *Crossing Boundaries: Mine migrancy in a democratic South Africa*. Cape Town: Institute for Democracy in South Africa (IDASA) and Canada: The International Development Research Centre.

Crush, J., Jeeves, A. H. and Yudelman, D. 1991. *South Africa's Labour Empire: A history of black migrancy to the gold mines*. Boulder: Westview Press and Cape Town: David Philip.

Crush, J., Tawodzera, G., Chikanda, A., Ramachandran, S. and Tevera, D. 2017. *South Africa Case Study: The double crisis–mass migration from*

Zimbabwe and xenophobic violence in South Africa. Vienna: International Centre for Migration Policy Development/Waterloo and Ontario: Southern African Migration Programme.

Fakier, K. 2012. 'Mobile care: Subverting traditional notions of motherhood in a precarious society'. Paper presented at colloquium on 'Politics of Precarious Society', Society, Work and Politics Institute, University of the Witwatersrand, 4–6 September.

Fraser, N. 2016. 'Capitalism's crisis of care'. *Issue 100 of New Left Review*, (July/August), 99–114.

Ginsburg, C., Collinson, M. A., Gómez-Olivé, F. X., Gross, M. and Harawa, S. 2021. 'Internal migration and health in South Africa: Determinants of healthcare utilisation in a young adult cohort'. *BMC Public Health*, 21, 554.

Handmaker, J., De la Hunt, L. A. and Klaaren, J. (eds), 2001. *Perspectives on Refugee Protection in South Africa*. Pretoria: Lawyers for Human Rights.

International Labour Organization (ILO). 2021. *Global Estimates on International Migrant Workers: Results and methodology*. Geneva: International Labour Organization.

Ireland, P. R. 1994. *The Policy Challenge of Ethnic Diversity: Immigrant politics in France and Switzerland*. Cambridge, MA: Harvard University Press.

Jinnah, Z. and Holaday, R. 2010. 'Migrant mobilisation: Structure and strategies for claiming rights in South Africa and Kenya', in Handmaker, J. and Berkhout, R. (eds), *Mobilising Social Justice in South Africa: Perspectives from researchers and practitioners*. Pretoria: Pretoria University Law Press (PULP), 137–176.

Kabwe-Segatti, A. 2008. 'Reforming South African immigration policy in the post-apartheid period (1990–2006): What it means and what it takes', in Kabwe-Sagatti, A. and Landau, L. (eds), *Migration in Post-Apartheid South Africa: Challenges and questions to policy-makers*. Johannesburg: Wits University Press.

Martiniello, M. 2005. 'Political participation, mobilisation and representation of immigrants and their offspring in Europe'. Willy Brandt Series of Working Papers in International Migration and Ethnic Relations, Malmö University.

Milkman, R. 2006. *L.A. Story: Immigrant workers and the future of the U.S. labour movement*. New York: Russell Sage Foundation Publications.

Munakamwe, J. 2018. 'Emerging political subjectivities in a post migrant labour regime: Mobilisation, participation and representation of foreign workers in South Africa (1980–2013)'. PhD Thesis, University of the Witwatersrand.

Munakamwe, J. 2022a. 'Social security exclusions in the wake of a deadly Covid pandemic: Experiences of migrant domestic workers in South Africa', in Munck, R., Kleibl, T. and Daňková, P. (eds), *Migration and Social Transformation: Engaged perspectives*. Dublin: Glasnevin Publishing.

Munakamwe, J. 2022b. 'Rethinking solidarity in a "post-migrant labour regime": The case of hospitality work in Johannesburg, South Africa', in Jorgensen, M. B. and Schierup, C. U. (eds), *Contending Global Apartheid: Transversal solidarities and politics of possibility*. Netherlands: Brill Publishers.

Munakamwe, J. and Gwenyaya, T. 2019. 'When the job hurts: Workplace injuries and diseases among South Africa's domestic workers'. *Solidarity Center*, https://www.solidaritycenter.org/wp-content/uploads/2020/01/Rule-of-Law.When-the-Job-Hurts-Workplace-Injury-and-Disease-among-South-Africas-Domestic-Workers.1.20.pdf, accessed 17 September 2023.

Munakamwe, J. and Jinnah, Z. 2015. 'A bitter harvest: Migrant workers and the commercial agricultural sector'. A report prepared and presented on behalf of the MIWORC Research Consortium at the African Centre for Migration & Society, University of the Witwatersrand.

Nyakabawu, S. 2021. 'Legal violence: Waiting for Zimbabwe exemption permit in South Africa'. *Journal of Law, Society and Development*, 8, 21.

Ochs, J. 2006. 'The politics of victimhood and its internal exegetes: Terror victims in Israel'. *History and Anthropology*, 17(4), 355–368.

Parreñas, R. S. 2005. *Servants of Globalization: Women, migration, and domestic work*. Stanford, CA: Stanford University Press.

Polzer, T. and Segatti, A. 2012. 'From defending migrant rights to new political subjectivities: Gauteng migrants' organisations after May 2008', in Landau, L. (ed.), *Exorcising the Demons Within*. Johannesburg: Wits University Press.

Sachikonye, L. 1998. (ed.). *Labour Migration in Southern Africa*. Harare: SAPES Books.

Segatti, A. and Munakamwe, J. 2014. 'Mobilising migrant workers in the South African post-migrant labour regime: Precariousness, invisibility and xenophobia'. Paper presented at the International Sociological Association (ISA) Congress, XVIII ISA World Congress, Yokohama, Japan.

Statistics SA. 2023. 'Quarterly Labour Force Survey, Quarter 1: 2023', https://www.statssa.gov.za/publications/P0211/P02111stQuarter2023.pdf, accessed 12 November 2023.

Tanzer, Z. and Gwenyaya, T. 2019. *Shadow Report: South Africa's Compliance with Labour Obligations under the International Covenant on Economic, Social and Cultural Rights*. Washington D.C: Solidarity Center.

Ueno, K. and Belanger, D. 2019. 'Facebook activism among foreign domestic workers in Singapore'. Conference Paper, International Sociological Association (ISA), Yokohama, Japan.

Vanyoro, K. P. 2019. 'Regularising labour migration of Zimbabwean domestic workers in South Africa'. African Centre for Migration and Society Policy Brief, http://www.migration.org.za/wp-content/uploads/2017/08/

Regularising-labour-migration-of-Zim-domestic-workers-in-SA-Issue-Brief-15-July-2019.pdf, accessed 17 September 2023.

Webster, E. 1985. *Cast in a Racial Mould: Labour process and trade unionism in the foundries*. Randburg: Ravan Press.

Wolpe, H. 1972. 'Capitalism and cheap labour-power in South Africa: From segregation to apartheid'. *Economy and Society*, 1(4), 425–456.

World Bank. (n.d.). 'Migration and remittances', https://www.worldbank.org/en/topic/migration/overview, accessed 12 September 2023.

World Bank. 12 May 2022. 'Officially recorded remittance flows to low- and middle-income countries (LMICs) are expected to increase by 4.2 per cent this year to reach $630 billion', https://www.worldbank.org>news, accessed 12 September 2023.

Section Two

Migration and South Africa's Political Economy

SIX

Gendered dimensions of migration in South Africa: Governance and implications for livelihoods

DAVID FADIRAN AND HAMMED AMUSA

INTRODUCTION

As an enduring feature of human existence, migration is a social and complex phenomenon that continues to influence human life. This influence stems largely from its impact on the environment in which it occurs and the factors that drive it. As a key element of an increasingly globalised world, international migration has increased considerably over the past five decades. According to the International Organization for Migration, in 2020, almost 281 million people or 3.6 per cent of the global population, lived in a country other than their country of birth. This number was about 128 million more than the 1990 figure of 153 million (or 2.9 per cent of the global population), and over three times the estimated 84 million in 1970.

The social and political dynamics of migration in Africa have mirrored the global trend, with a steady upward trajectory of migration flows since 2000 and, alongside mortality and fertility rates, manifested as one of the basic components or drivers of population growth across the continent (Pew Research Center, 2015). Through migration, an estimated 21 million Africans resided in another African country in 2021. This figure represents a considerable increase from 2015 when an estimated 18 million Africans were classified as living in African states that were not their country of citizenship or birth. A key feature of Africa's migration is that it is largely intracontinental, with the 21 million migrants living within the continent accounting for around 53.2 per cent of the 39.4 million African-born migrants in 2020.

In 2020, the largest share of all international migrants in Africa – 55.7 per cent – was hosted in East Africa (29.6 per cent) and West Africa (26 per cent) (see Figure 6.1). Uniquely, despite accounting for the smallest share of Africa's migrants, South Africa, the largest economy in the sub-region – remains the most attractive destination country in Africa with 2.9 million international migrants living in the country (McAuliffe and Triandafyllidou, 2021). The observed increase in migration is driven by a varied combination of push-pull factors largely linked to five key areas identified by Virupaksha et al. (2014: 233–239) and Diop and D'Aloisio (2007):

- personal or familiar (when people contemplate an intentional project of emancipation and improvement of conditions and prospects, particularly aimed at children);
- political (flight from wars, regimes, instability, persecution);
- economic (unemployment, poverty, absolute or relative deprivation, backwardness);
- social (terrorism, crime, violence, banditry, low security, inequalities and discrimination, religious conflicts); and
- cultural (fascination with different/external cultures when local practices and traditions are deemed archaic and restrictive).

Figure 6.1: Migrants: Africa and its regions, 2020

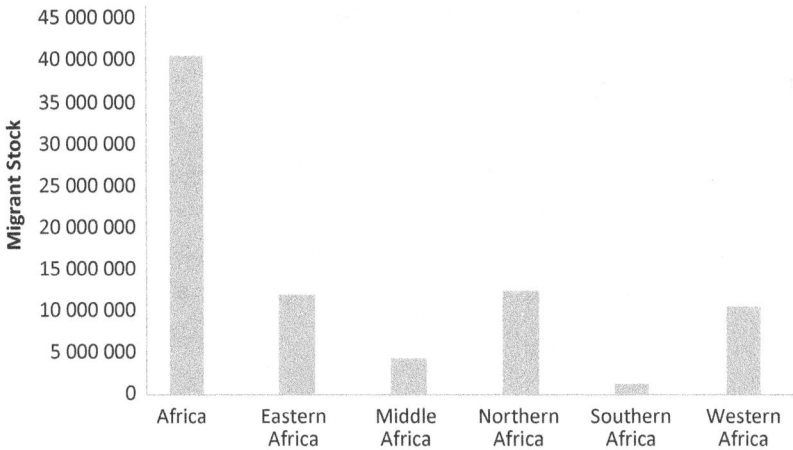

Source: UNDESA (2020)

An emerging feature of the rising trend in international migration is the increasing presence of women, especially in least-developed countries (LDCs). Analysis of global patterns of migration indicates that the number of female migrants has risen dramatically and almost tripled in the past 60 years, rising from 46 million in 1960 to 135 million in 2020 (Abel and Cohen 2022: 173). The African continent has not been immune from this global trend, dubbed the 'feminisation of migration'. In Africa, female migration is largely a new phenomenon that is increasingly changing the traditional pattern of migration within sub-Saharan Africa from one that was male-dominated, long-term and long-distance towards mobility that is increasingly feminised (Masanja, 2012). In 2020, over 46 per cent of migrants on the continent were female, but was closer to 50 per cent in central, northern and southern African regions during the same period (UNDESA, 2020).

Anecdotal evidence suggests that the increased migration of women, who had traditionally remained at home while men moved around in search of paid work, is driven by a desire to fulfil their own economic needs and not simply join a husband or other family member. The increased independent female migration is not confined by national borders. Driven by urbanisation and struggles for survival, women – both single and married – are now migrating independently in search of secure jobs in richer countries or regions, thus redefining traditional gender roles within families and societies (Adepoju, 2006).

There is a scholarly view (see for example, Beauchemin and Bocquier, 2004; Collinson et al., 2006; Collinson, 2009; Beguy et al., 2010; Reed et al., 2010) of feminisation as a core dimension of the new age of international migration and globalisation. Despite this, research and debates about drivers of migration and associated demographic and economic impacts have focused almost exclusively on men. While there are growing numbers of studies, in the context of African migration, that include women, the focus remains largely inadequate given the often-utilised approach of merely extending the frameworks developed to understand men's employment outcomes to women (Souza, 2020).

The remainder of the chapter is organised as follows: the next section gives a brief overview of some of the theories and frameworks that guide our analysis, including a comparative summary of livelihood strategies for migrant women in Africa and South Africa, followed by an empirical discussion of the determinants of female migration. Some insights into related aspects of migrant productivity and employment follow. Drawing on insights into the economic dimensions of female migration, the chapter analyses the institutional and governance dynamics that impact gendered migration. The chapter concludes with recommendations and conclusions.

A FEMINIST PERSPECTIVE OF IMMIGRANT WOMEN IN THE AFRICAN DIASPORA: THE SEARCH FOR RECOGNITION IN THE FORMAL AND INFORMAL SECTOR

The intersections of gender, immigration and labour policies strongly influence the migratory experiences of female migrants in ways different from those experienced by African men. Given this, and the need to ensure that migration fosters inclusive development and contributes to reducing inequalities and poverty, it is imperative to establish an understanding of the gendered dimensions of migration. It is also important to understand the associated implications for labour markets, productivity and social and economic opportunities both for migrants themselves and for their destination regions. This chapter aims to develop this understanding by building on extant literature (see, for example, Camlin et al., 2014; Popoola et al., 2021; Sharp, 2021), to analyse the drivers and implications of female migration in the African and South African context and examine – from the perspective of gendered migration – the drivers of migration, its institutional dynamics, and its implications for lives and livelihoods.

Several different frameworks for exploring migration are adopted in this chapter. These range from pure economic theory, such as neoclassical economic theory, to frameworks targeted at the migration of women, such as the feminisation of migration, intersectional approaches and gendered geographies of power. Neoclassical economic theory posits that labour relocates from areas of low productivity (typically poorer, less stable economies) to relatively more productive locations. This migration can be driven by wage differentials and would, by definition, augment productivity in the recipient country (Kurekova, 2011: 6–9). This is evidenced in the section discussing immigration and productivity. With regard to the varied frameworks for exploring the gendered aspect of migration, intersectional approaches recognise that other identities such as race, age, etc., also influence migratory patterns and experiences. And this encapsulates some of the issues we explore, such as governance, that may drive the South–South migration of women. This intersectional approach was first introduced by Crenshaw in 1989 but has been adopted and influential in the critical assessment of health outcomes for migrants (Viruell-Fuentes et al., 2012: 2099–2106), particularly women migrants in Asia (Chun et al., 2013: 917–940). This approach is also guided by the framework of the feminisation of migration, which focuses on the increasingly gendered nature of migration, and the potential push–pull factors accounting for it (Chammartin, 2002; Donato and Gabaccia, 2016). Further, the gendered geographies of power posit that the dynamics of power, along different hierarchies and scopes, have significant influence on the drivers of female migration and their lived experiences.

LIVELIHOOD STRATEGIES FOR MIGRANT WOMEN: THE AFRICAN CASE AND SOUTH AFRICAN CONTEXT

The world is increasingly confronted with instability of various kinds: climatic, political, geopolitical and economic. Developing countries are on the front line of the economic and social consequences of these multiple shocks. Women are particularly vulnerable to these disturbances and, like men, more and more of them are turning to emigration to escape from vulnerability. For Africa, the spotlight is often placed on emigration to northern countries because of the millions of women, men and children who take reckless risks to reach Europe via the Mediterranean in search of better living conditions (De Haas, 2010; Flahaux and De Haas, 2016; Gnimassoun and Anyanwu, 2019). African migration also concerns the emigration of talents, commonly known as the brain drain. However, this South–North migratory dynamic should not hide the reality of South–South migration, in particular migration between African countries, and its gender component. Indeed, contrary to collective belief, the majority of African men and women who leave their country remain in Africa. According to United Nations data on global migration (UN, 2023) in 2020 a majority of worldwide African migrants (51.5 per cent) lived in Africa, although the trend has been declining since the 1990s (UNDESA, 2020). Female migrants are more likely to stay in Africa than their male counterparts, as the majority of African female migrants (53 per cent) lived in Africa in 2020 compared to half of male ones. Historically in southern Africa, men from countries such as Malawi, Mozambique and Zimbabwe were prioritised to work in gold mines, while women worked in the informal sector as domestic workers, among other roles (Tati, 2008: 423–440).

Across the African continent, the flow and movement of immigrants between countries has increased considerably in recent decades, from 12.75 million in 2000 to nearly 21 million in 2020, an increase of 64 per cent in 20 years as shown in Table 6.1. The same dynamic is observed for intra-African female migration, which increased by 66 per cent over the same period, going from 6 million in 2000 to 10 million in

2020. However, the ratio of female immigrants has remained generally constant, around 47 per cent.

Table 6.1: Dynamics of immigration by gender (millions)

	Africa				South Africa			
	Total	Female	Male	Female ratio (%)	Total	Female	Male	Female ratio (%)
1990	13.43	6.31	7.12	46.99	0.75	0.22	0.53	29.30
1995	14.18	6.73	7.45	47.44	0.70	0.24	0.46	33.82
2000	12.75	6.02	6.73	47.24	0.70	0.26	0.44	36.90
2005	13.41	6.19	7.22	46.18	0.94	0.37	0.58	38.94
2010	14.57	6.82	7.75	46.83	1.54	0.61	0.93	39.80
2015	18.20	8.66	9.54	47.59	1.83	0.81	1.02	43.99
2020	20.92	10.01	10.91	47.85	1.85	0.78	1.07	41.96

Source: UN (2023)

For South Africa's part, UN data shows that the number of African immigrants increased 2.6 times over the same period, going from 0.7 million in 2000 to 1.85 million in 2020 with a notable increase in the ratio of female to male immigrants. However, the ratio of female immigrants in the country remains 6 percentage points below the African average. Several countries of origin are involved in immigration to South Africa: Figure 6.2 shows the top 10. The neighbourhood effect comes into full play, with South African migration dominated by migrants from Zimbabwe, Mozambique and Lesotho with 690,000, 350,000 and 192,000 people respectively, including 45 per cent, 33 per cent and 55.6 per cent women respectively. South African migration from predominantly Lesotho and eSwatini has the particularity of being dominated by women seeking employment in the informal sector.

Figure 6.2: Origin of migrants in South Africa in 2023 (thousands)

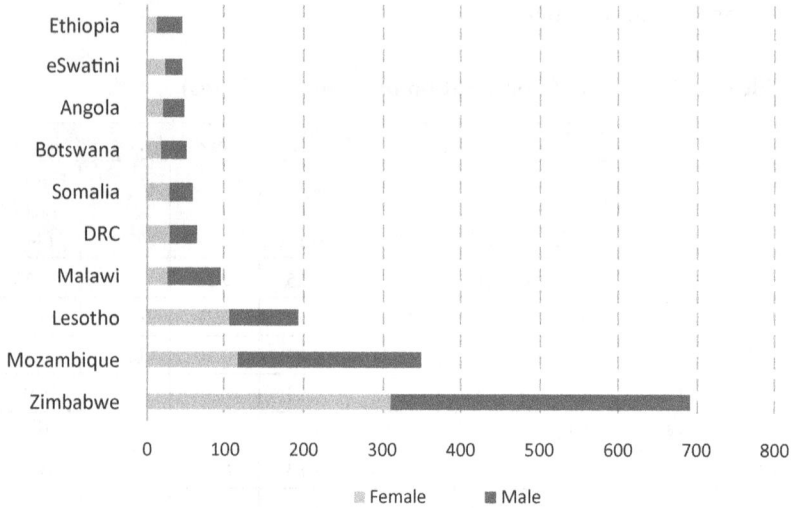

Source: UN (2023)

Although the flow of African immigrants is increasing significantly, the rate of intra-African[1] immigration remains very low with strong heterogeneity between countries. Table 6.2 presents the total and intra-African immigration rates in 2020 by country and gender. It appears that the immigration rate in Africa – stock of immigrants proportional to population – is 1.6 per cent (1.5 per cent for intra-African immigration) with a female ratio of 47.2 per cent. South Africa has a total immigration rate of 3.7 per cent and an intra-African immigration rate of 3.1 per cent with a female ratio of around 42 per cent. The country thus appears in 11th position among African countries with the highest rates of intra-African immigration. The five African countries with the highest intra-African immigration rates are, respectively, Gabon (17.3 per cent), Djibouti (10.9 per cent), Ivory Coast (9.4 per cent), The Gambia (8.7 per cent) and the Republic of Congo (6.6 per cent). Conversely, Algeria, Madagascar, Lesotho and Morocco show the lowest rates, below 1 per cent. These variations in immigration rates hide diverse microeconomic and macroeconomic motivations for migration within Africa, including

---

1 'Intra-African' migration refers to movements both within and between African states, including the movements of migrants who repeatedly leave from and return to their home countries.

female migrants.

Although the absence of microeconomic data limits understanding of the motivations for migration between African countries, the existence of aggregate data allows us to identify some important stylised facts linked to economic theory. The gravity models often used in empirical work on international trade offer an adequate framework for understanding the determinants of immigration.

Table 6.2: Immigration rate of African countries in 2020

Country	Immigration rate (%)					African immigration rate (%)				
	Rank	Total	Female	Male	Female ratio	Rank	Total	Female	Male	Female ratio
AGO	44	0.45	0.19	0.26	42.3	42	0.43	0.18	0.25	42.0
BDI	18	2.63	1.34	1.29	50.8	17	2.62	1.33	1.29	50.8
BFA	13	3.23	1.70	1.53	52.6	9	3.23	1.70	1.53	52.6
BWA	8	4.14	1.72	2.42	41.5	8	3.36	1.43	1.93	42.5
CAF	28	1.32	0.64	0.68	48.5	29	1.08	0.53	0.55	48.8
CIV	4	9.44	4.21	5.23	44.6	3	9.44	4.21	5.23	44.6
CMR	21	2.12	1.07	1.05	50.6	19	2.09	1.06	1.03	50.6
COD	32	1.03	0.52	0.50	51.1	31	1.03	0.52	0.50	51.1
COG	7	6.87	3.12	3.75	45.5	5	6.55	2.98	3.58	45.4
COM	30	1.18	0.62	0.56	52.4	28	1.13	0.60	0.53	52.9
CPV	19	2.53	1.25	1.29	49.1	21	1.86	0.90	0.96	48.4
DJI	3	11.42	5.45	5.97	47.7	2	10.89	5.17	5.71	47.5
DZA	50	0.11	0.05	0.06	47.0	51	0.03	0.02	0.02	45.7
EGY	46	0.37	0.18	0.19	48.4	46	0.14	0.07	0.08	48.0
ETH	35	0.92	0.47	0.46	50.4	33	0.92	0.46	0.46	50.4
GAB	1	18.23	6.53	11.70	35.8	1	17.29	6.21	11.08	35.9
GHA	29	1.31	0.59	0.72	45.1	26	1.28	0.58	0.71	45.1
GIN	38	0.84	0.35	0.49	41.4	38	0.73	0.30	0.43	41.6
GMB	5	8.66	4.11	4.55	47.5	4	8.66	4.11	4.55	47.5
GNB	37	0.85	0.43	0.42	50.5	36	0.80	0.41	0.40	50.5
GNQ	40	0.75	0.35	0.40	46.5	44	0.25	0.10	0.15	38.3
KEN	24	1.82	0.91	0.92	49.6	22	1.82	0.91	0.92	49.6
LBR	25	1.61	0.70	0.91	43.5	24	1.55	0.68	0.87	43.8
LBY	6	7.57	2.17	5.40	28.7	16	2.72	0.76	1.96	27.8
LSO	49	0.11	0.05	0.06	44.6	49	0.06	0.03	0.03	44.9
MAR	47	0.23	0.11	0.12	48.5	48	0.07	0.04	0.04	48.5
MDG	51	0.09	0.04	0.05	43.1	50	0.04	0.02	0.02	43.1
MLI	20	2.27	1.11	1.16	49.0	18	2.10	1.03	1.07	49.1
MOZ	33	0.97	0.49	0.47	51.2	32	0.94	0.48	0.45	51.7
MRT	15	3.13	1.33	1.80	42.6	13	3.09	1.32	1.77	42.6
MUS	23	1.87	0.78	1.09	41.9	45	0.19	0.09	0.10	46.1
MWI	39	0.80	0.41	0.39	51.4	37	0.79	0.41	0.38	51.5
NAM	10	3.86	1.76	2.10	45.5	15	2.85	1.25	1.60	43.8

Country	Immigration rate (%)					African immigration rate (%)				
	Rank	Total	Female	Male	Female ratio	Rank	Total	Female	Male	Female ratio
NER	26	1.38	0.73	0.65	53.1	25	1.38	0.73	0.65	53.1
NGA	43	0.57	0.26	0.31	45.5	41	0.57	0.26	0.31	45.5
RWA	9	3.90	1.93	1.97	49.6	6	3.90	1.93	1.97	49.6
SDN	17	3.08	1.55	1.53	50.3	14	3.07	1.55	1.52	50.3
SEN	27	1.38	0.63	0.75	45.9	27	1.26	0.57	0.69	45.5
SLE	41	0.66	0.29	0.37	43.5	39	0.63	0.27	0.36	43.4
SOM	48	0.22	0.10	0.12	46.8	47	0.14	0.06	0.07	46.9
STP	34	0.95	0.47	0.48	49.7	34	0.90	0.45	0.45	49.8
SWZ	31	1.10	0.47	0.64	42.4	30	1.07	0.45	0.62	42.0
SYC	2	12.53	3.69	8.84	29.4	20	2.05	0.70	1.36	34.0
TCD	14	3.23	1.77	1.46	54.8	10	3.23	1.77	1.46	54.8
TGO	16	3.12	1.52	1.59	48.9	12	3.10	1.52	1.58	49.0
TUN	45	0.41	0.19	0.21	47.7	43	0.27	0.13	0.14	47.8
TZA	42	0.65	0.33	0.33	50.0	40	0.63	0.32	0.31	50.2
UGA	11	3.76	1.95	1.81	51.9	7	3.74	1.94	1.80	51.9
ZAF	12	3.72	1.58	2.14	42.3	11	3.12	1.31	1.81	41.9
ZMB	36	0.89	0.43	0.46	48.5	35	0.83	0.40	0.42	48.8
ZWE	22	1.88	0.81	1.07	43.1	23	1.80	0.77	1.02	43.1
Africa		1.57	0.74	0.83	47.2		1.47	0.70	0.77	47.6

Source: Authors' adaptation of Abel and Cohen (2022: 173) migration data computations

Note: see Appendix for a key to the country abbreviations used.

FEMALE IMMIGRATION, SECTORAL PRODUCTIVITY AND INFORMAL EMPLOYMENT

The empirical framework adopted draws on several empirical studies in recent years, including the work of Ortega and Péri (2014: 231–251), Gnimassoun (2023: 785–817) and Coulibaly et al. (2020). However, this work does not distinguish the determinants of migration by gender, which could suggest that the motivations for migration of men and women are the same. The countries that attract migrants are the countries in which the living conditions of the populations are better and/or which offer a better institutional framework. In addition to economic and institutional motivations, geographical locations, networks or diaspora effects play a role in the dynamics of migration. Furthermore, conflicts and wars as well as increasingly significant climate change are potential causes of migration between countries.

In the context of this chapter, we propose to estimate a gravity model to better understand the determinants of immigration in Africa and South Africa for both female and male immigration. To this end, we explore the literature for insights into the various determinants:

- geographical (the distance between countries, the sharing of a common border);
- economic (the level of income per capita in the country of departure and the sharing of a common currency); and
- linguistic (the sharing of a common ethnic language).

To these traditional determinants, we added the trade openness rate as well as variables measuring political instability (the propensity for conflicts and wars) and climatic instability (the frequency of climate-related disasters). Indeed, conflicts and wars, as well as climatic disasters, are potential sources of migration from one African country to another, especially female migration.

The results of the empirical exercise undertaken in this chapter, which relate to 52 African countries over the period 1990 to 2020 with immigrant data available every five years, are summarised in Table 6.3. They confirm well-established empirical results in the literature while providing new lessons on the causes of immigration by gender, particularly in South Africa. For Africa as a whole, there is no fundamental difference in the determinants of immigration by gender. Factors that lead to an increase in female and male immigration rates include diaspora networks; the size of a country of origin; conflicts; wars in countries of origin; sharing of a common currency; a common border; and a common ethnic language with the country of origin. However, the intra-African immigration rate declines with distance and a relatively high level of per capita income in the country of origin. In other words, the immigration rate is higher when the standard of living in the country of origin is low, which is an expected result. This is also in line with neoclassical economics, which suggests migration of labour in search of better relative wages. Nevertheless, it seems that the diaspora effect is less for women than for men, while women seem to benefit more from geographical proximity. This observation is suggestive of the feminisation of the migration framework, that is, the drivers for men may not be exactly the same as drivers for women.

Women migrants may be migrating for reasons beyond accompanying their families or other male household representatives.

Table 6.3: Determinants of immigration – a gravity model

Variables	Immigration in Africa			Immigration in South Africa		
	Total	Female	Male	Total	Female	Male
Immigration rate in 1990	5.496***	5.266***	5.689***	2.184**	1.360	2.657***
	(0.399)	(0.416)	(0.393)	(1.005)	(1.064)	(0.997)
Ln distance	-0.905***	-0.931***	-0.882***	-1.034***	-0.941***	-1.114***
	(0.041)	(0.042)	(0.041)	(0.152)	(0.155)	(0.163)
Trade openness rate	0.004	0.006	0.002	0.515***	0.703***	0.379**
	(0.008)	(0.007)	(0.008)	(0.186)	(0.188)	(0.191)
Common currency	0.673***	0.613***	0.726***	0.037	0.174	-0.071
	(0.107)	(0.105)	(0.111)	(0.209)	(0.229)	(0.210)
Common border	2.039***	2.155***	1.946***	2.239***	2.355***	2.152***
	(0.102)	(0.104)	(0.103)	(0.399)	(0.413)	(0.405)
Common ethnic language	1.079***	1.074***	1.081***	0.924***	0.834***	0.982***
	(0.113)	(0.113)	(0.114)	(0.179)	(0.185)	(0.194)
Ln population, origin	0.164***	0.163***	0.165***	0.568***	0.597***	0.555***
	(0.048)	(0.050)	(0.048)	(0.102)	(0.118)	(0.096)
Ln GDP per capita, origin	-0.253***	-0.273***	-0.235***	-0.325***	-0.321***	-0.330***
	(0.048)	(0.049)	(0.048)	(0.089)	(0.092)	(0.092)
Conflicts/wars, origin	0.192***	0.199***	0.186***	0.108***	0.108***	0.105***
	(0.024)	(0.025)	(0.024)	(0.027)	(0.032)	(0.025)
Climate-related disasters freq., origin	-0.022	-0.024	-0.021	0.016	0.013	0.017
	(0.016)	(0.016)	(0.017)	(0.025)	(0.027)	(0.024)
Constant	0.521	0.030	-0.354	-4.229**	-6.404***	-3.856*
	(0.793)	(0.819)	(0.782)	(2.135)	(2.245)	(2.216)
Observations	16,890	16,890	16,890	333	333	333
R-squared	0.423	0.435	0.404	0.791	0.756	0.809

Source: Authors' own compilation

Note: Heteroskedasticity-robust standard errors are in parentheses. The symbols – *, ** and *** – denote significance at the 10 per cent, 5 per cent and 1 per cent confidence level, respectively. Regressions are performed using the PPML estimator to overcome the heteroskedasticity problem (see Silva and Tenreyro, 2006, 2010).

The results for South Africa show more marked differences in the determinants of immigration by sex. For example, the network effect, namely family relationships, acquaintances or friendships with former migrants (measured by the immigration rate in 1990), does not play a role at all for women, while it is decisive for men. This suggests an even stronger feminisation of migration is occurring when the focus is on South Africa alone. Furthermore, trade is an important determinant of immigration in South Africa although it is not decisive on a continental scale. In addition, bilateral trade favours female migration to South Africa more than male migration. Contrary to the results for Africa as a whole, the sharing of a common currency does not influence the immigration rate in South Africa, neither for female nor male immigration. Although climate poses an enormous challenge for Africa, the results of the empirical approach employed in this chapter show that climatic disasters in countries of origin have not been decisive in the dynamics of immigration rates in Africa in general and in South Africa in particular over the 1990 to 2020 period. But these results do not predict what could happen in the future with the runaway climatic phenomena.

Immigration status is decisive for the living and working conditions of migrant women. Yet, most intra-African labour migration, particularly low-skilled migration, occurs outside formal legal channels, which leads to undocumented status and the concentration of women in the informal economy (see UNCTAD, 2018). This irregular migration status is often made more by restrictions on the mobility of people such as temporary migration programmes, which increase the vulnerability of migrants. This is particularly true for female migrant workers, who are overrepresented in the informal sector and among undocumented workers (ILO, 2020). Furthermore, while formal recruitment offers greater job security, labour demand for female migrants is often the result of gender stereotypes and tends to exploit their marginalised social and economic situation in order to recruit a flexible workforce.

According to Ncube et al. (2020: 1165–1185), labour policies force many migrant women to take any available job even if these don't match their qualifications and skills. This situation accentuates the economic and social precariousness of female migrants and affects their productivity. This is the case in South Africa for migrant women from Zimbabwe. Although a majority of them have completed secondary and higher education, they are likely to take up low-skilled and low-paid jobs to facilitate their adaptation to the local labour market. This situation is mainly explained by the non-recognition of their foreign qualifications and prejudice against foreign education.

Across the continent, immigration is driven by economic sectors such as agriculture, mining and construction. Developments in services such as domestic work, cleaning, catering, hospitality and retail are also important drivers of immigration across Africa. Particularly in South Africa – the primary destination for African migrants – domestic work is one of the sectors driving female migration (see ILO, 2022).

The precariousness that characterises the situation of migrant women in host countries is likely to undermine their productivity regardless of their enormous potential. Despite the lack of disaggregated data on migration between African countries, empirical studies on macroeconomic data highlight relationships between immigration and labour productivity in Africa. Gnimassoun (2023), for example, shows that intra-African immigration has a significant and positive impact on labour productivity in Africa, particularly in the services sector. However, this study does not examine whether this relationship differs according to the sex of the migrants. Figure 6.3 represents the scatter diagrams relating labour productivity by sector, measured by the value added per worker in a particular sector, and the rate of immigration (total and female) in African countries in 2015. If the relationship between the rate of female immigration and labour productivity in agriculture is weak, there is a positive relationship between the rate of immigration and labour productivity in the service and industrial sectors. This relationship holds for both total immigration and female immigration. Although this type of relationship requires a solid empirical study to establish a causal relationship, it surely shows that the positive and significant impact established by Gnimassoun (2023) is undoubtedly carried by both male and female migrants.

Figure 6.3: Immigration rate and labour productivity by sector

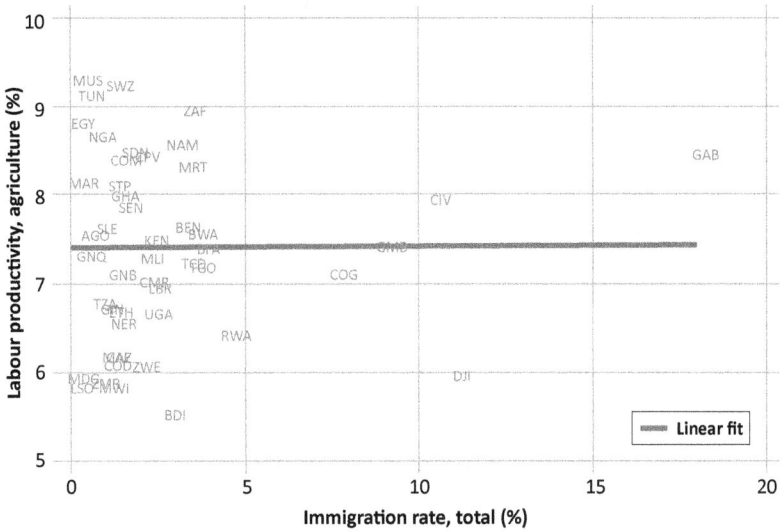

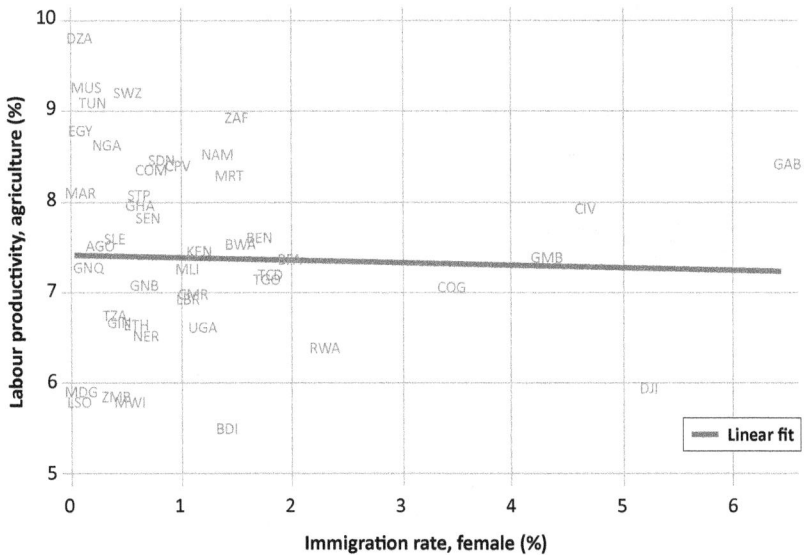

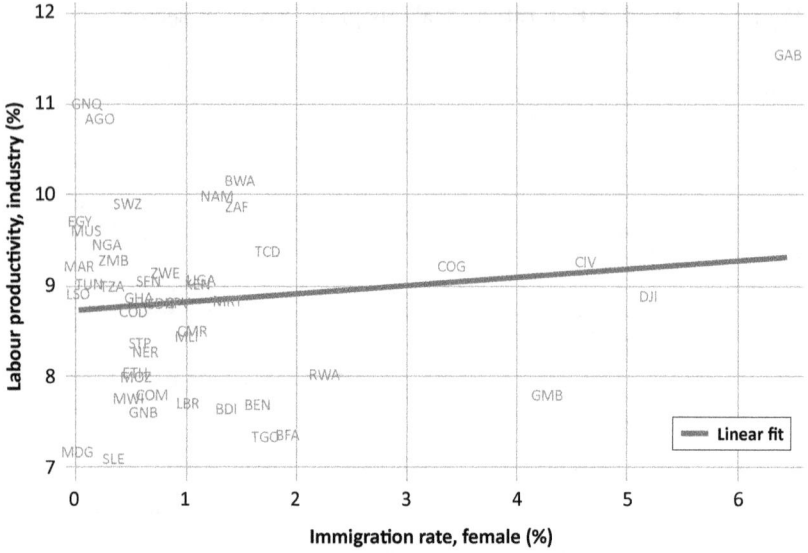

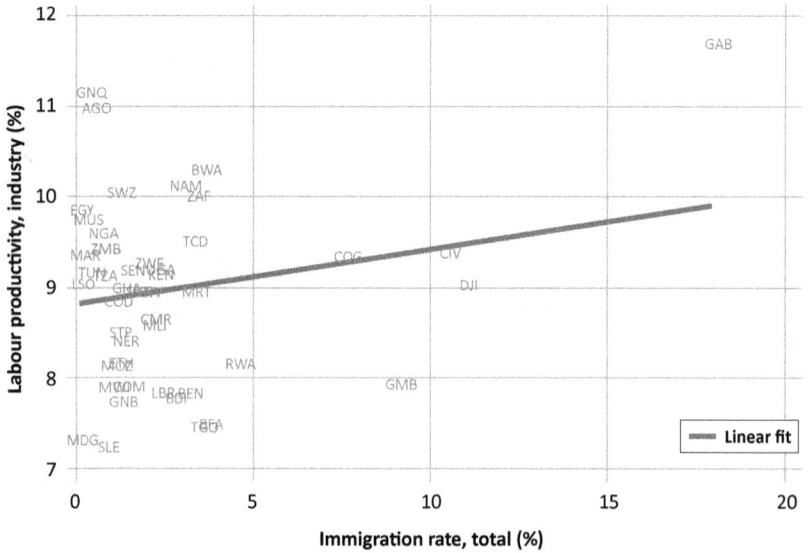

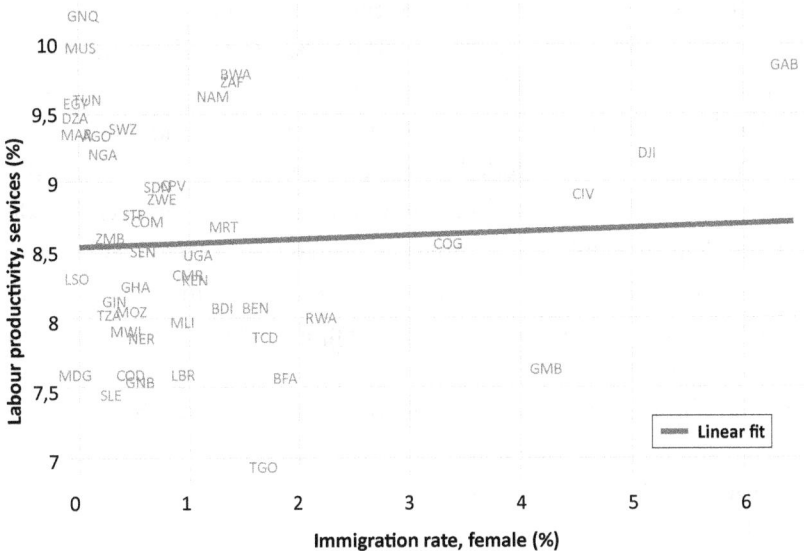

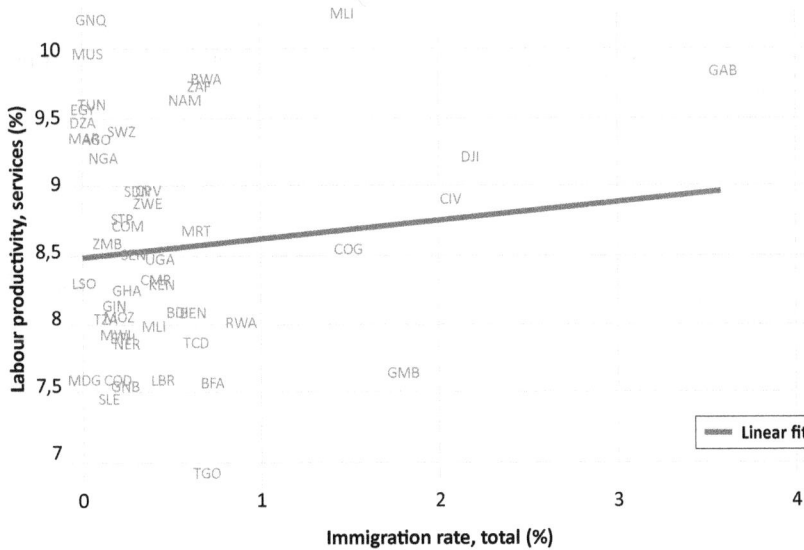

Source: Authors' compilation

Note: Labour productivity data (value added per worker in logarithm) is from the World Bank's WDI database.

In this section, we further examine the relationship between the ratio of informal employment by sector and the rate of female immigration. Employment in the informal sector is often associated with marginalised workers, particularly low-wage workers and immigrants. As women are often excluded from economic opportunities and the labour market, the expectation could be that the link between female immigration and informal employment would be stronger. Figure 6.4 represents the scatter plots showing the female immigration rate in Africa and the share of informal employment by sector. From this figure, no relationship emerges between the female immigration rate and the informal employment ratio, regardless of the sector of activity. In other words, female migrants in Africa are no more present in informal employment than in formal employment. However, the overall picture, across both male and female sectors, still reveals a wage-induced migratory channel.

Figure 6.4: Female immigration rate and share of informal employment by sector of activity

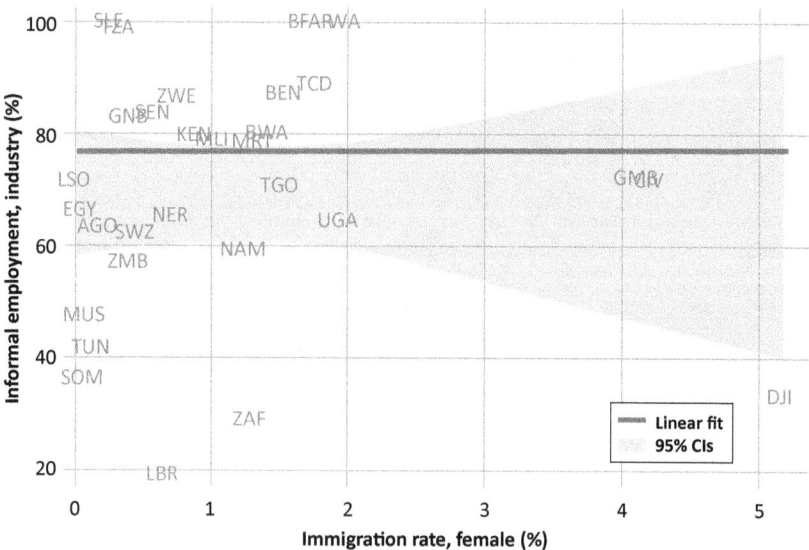

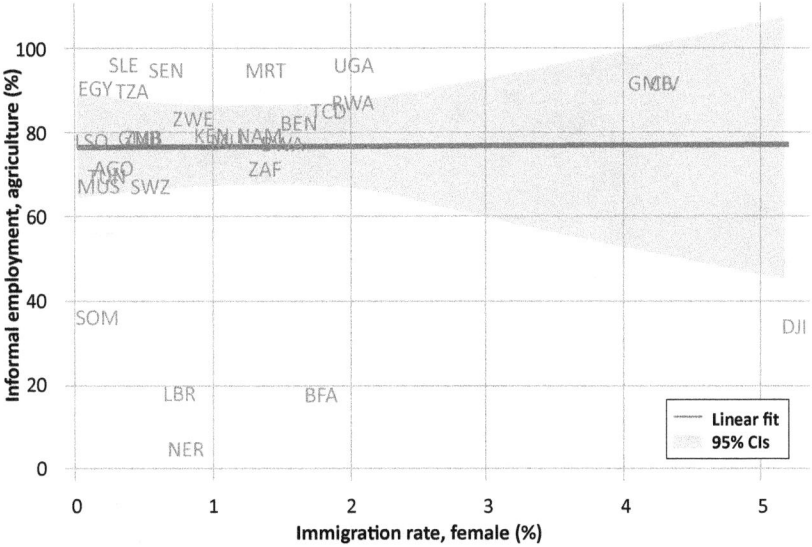

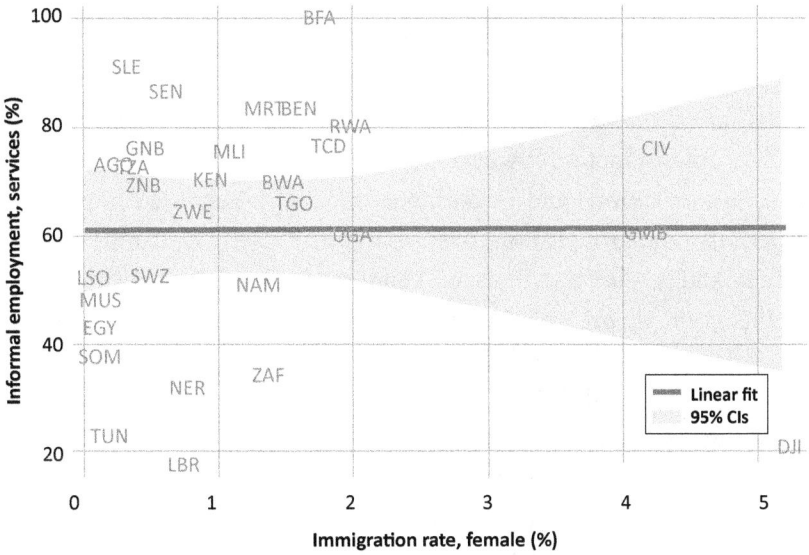

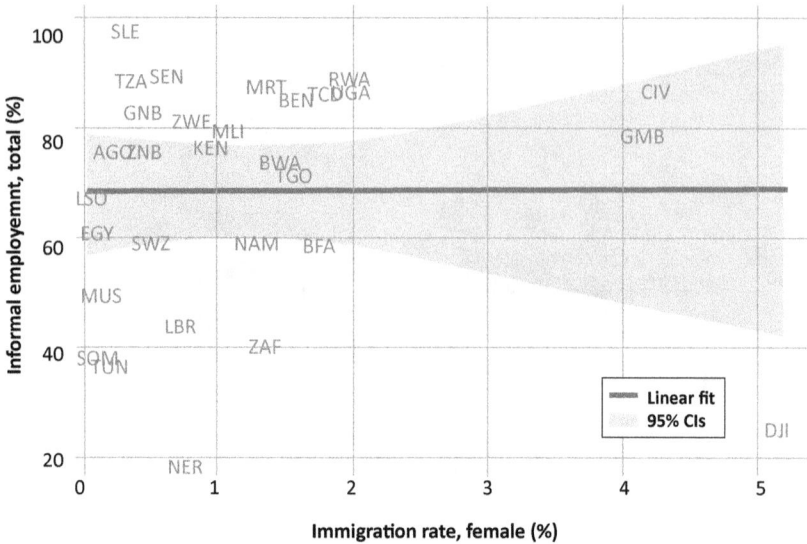

Source: *ILO (2022)*

Note: Data on the informal employment rate comes from the ILO database. It represents the percentage of informal employment in total employment.

INSTITUTIONS AND GOVERNANCE AS DRIVERS OF GENDERED MIGRATION

Thus far the chapter has examined economic drivers of migration, such as employment. However, it is also important to take cognisance of how institutions and governance impact on gendered migration, especially female migration. It is also important to consider the nature, extent and spillover effects of gendered migration. South Africa, in this context, presents a unique migration destination, while still falling under South–South migration. For example, while there might not be pronounced differences in terms of the quality of institutions across many SSA countries, South Africa's well-developed rule of law and the democratic principles enshrined in its constitution, are key factors that differentiate the country from others in the region. Thus, it is possible that female migration flows from other African countries to South Africa may be driven by similar dynamics as traditional South–North female migration flows.

There is a wide variation in the nature and quality of institutions, in their many ramifications, in Africa, including formal, informal, social, economic and political ones. Institutions have been shown to influence both South–North and South–South female migration decisions (Olesen, 2002; Ferrant and Tuccio, 2015). One well-adopted definition considers institutions as rules that shape and govern human interactions (North, 1990: 355–367). Another commonly used definition, and closer in context to gendered migration, is that given by Jütting et al. (2008: 65–86), in which institutions are defined as the formal and informal laws, social norm and practices that play an important role in shaping or restricting the decisions, choices and behaviours of groups, communities and individuals. Within this context, the provision of law – for protection from expropriation, or observance of contracts, or access to justice for both men and women – is an institutional phenomenon. And when either in law (de jure) or in practice/application (de facto), women are found to be less protected than their male counterparts, we want to understand, within the context of migration, how this may be a key driver.

It is possible that discrimination may be both a push factor for migration, entailing a search for better protection, governance and institutions, and also a preventative factor, whereby, because of the law, the ability to flee a place may be significantly curtailed (Ferrant and Tuccio, 2015: 240–254). For example, while the institutions in a country such as Eritrea are arguably known to be repressive, the same institutions prevent citizens from freely migrating. If this is the case, it may mask the gendered migration effects of the quality of governance, especially relative to other countries with poor institutions but without limitations on migration. Four measures are used to assess the quality of institutions as they pertain to female migrant flows from other African countries: access to justice for women, civil liberties, social group equality, civil and social rights, and equity (see Figure 6.6).

Table 6.4 presents the average number of migrants per year into South Africa. It draws on migration data computed by researchers Abel and Cohen (2022), who address the issue of a lack of gender information in migration data. There is a pronounced limitation on data on sex-specific international migration flows, which in turn limits quantitative inquiry into the drivers of gendered migration. This is important to note, as settlement experiences, networks available and the general foundations upon which life in the country of origin will be built are impacted by the sex of migrants (Abel and Cohen, 2022: 173). For this reason, complex computations are made with this data to extract the gender distribution of international migration flows. Specifically, use is made of the categorisation of migration numbers created by Azose and Raftery (2019: 116–122), which classifies migrant movements into emigration, return migration and transit migration. For the purpose of this chapter, we assume that emigration and transit migration are what matters, and the analysis is based on this. The data is computed on a five-year basis from 1990 to 2015. The average migration per country per year, and the total sum of migrants, based on gender, ratios are presented. International migration flows into South Africa from the global South, and specifically from African countries, yield interesting observations. The average number of migrants into South Africa from other African countries is 12,445 per country, and of this 5,375 are women.

Table 6.4: Five-year averages and the sum of transit migration flows from African countries to South Africa

Year	Female	Male	Female	Male	Total Sum	Female Ratio
	5-Yr Average		Sum			
1990	6433	4120	308792	197781	506574	61%
1995	3821	4602	183400	220903	404303	45%
2000	4983	8990	239190	431496	670687	36%
2005	6258	10293	300364	494082	794446	38%
2010	7788	11013	381629	539622	921251	41%
2015	2966	3400	145345	166586	311932	47%
Total	5375	7070	1558721	2050471	3609192	45%

Source: Authors' adaptation of Abel and Cohen (2022: 173) migration data computations

This is highly aggregated per country over the 25-year period for which the data was computed. The female ratio is below the male ratio at 45 per cent over this period. The total number of migrants into South Africa, computed through the method introduced by Azose and Raftery (2019: 116–122), stands at about 3.6 million, and female migrant flows account for about 1.56 million of these. However, this masks a lot of nuance, especially when considering the data relating to individual countries of origin.

Table 6.5 offers further inquiry into gender-disaggregated migration flows into South Africa for the period from 1990 to 2015. Notably, there are clear gender disparities in these migration patterns. Countries like Mozambique (MOZ) and Zimbabwe (ZWE) predominantly feature male migrants, as evidenced by their female ratios of 32 per cent and 40 per cent, respectively.

Table 6.5: Computed transit migration numbers by gender and origin country

Country	Female	Male	Female	Male	Total	Female Ratio
	Average		Sum		Total Sum	
AGO	1247	1315	7484	7890	15374	49%
BDI	1005	1004	6028	6022	12050	50%
BEN	14	19	85	116	201	42%
BFA	44	41	264	246	509	52%
BWA	2689	5134	16135	30803	46938	34%
CAF	159	116	953	699	1652	58%
CIV	472	559	2832	3353	6185	46%
CMR	299	389	1797	2337	4134	43%
COD	4250	4703	25498	28219	53717	47%
COG	2742	3445	16451	20672	37123	44%
COM	6	23	34	141	175	20%
CPV	1	0	4	2	6	67%
DZA	25	47	151	285	436	35%
EGY	340	233	2039	1398	3438	59%
ERI	83	69	500	415	915	55%
GAB	27	30	160	178	338	47%
GHA	649	636	3896	3814	7710	51%
GIN	60	44	363	264	627	58%
GMB	1	3	8	20	27	28%
GNB	6	2	34	12	47	74%
GNQ	0	0	0	0	0	53%
KEN	4804	4177	28823	25064	53888	53%
LBR	156	41	936	245	1181	79%
LBY	557	368	3340	2210	5550	60%

Country	Female	Male	Female	Male	Total	Female Ratio
	Average		Sum		Total Sum	
LSO	39728	36239	238369	217436	455805	52%
MAR	72	90	435	540	975	45%
MDG	23	22	137	135	272	50%
MLI	118	66	707	398	1105	64%
MOZ	34934	75806	209604	454835	664440	32%
MRT	11	28	64	170	234	27%
MUS	694	612	4165	3672	7837	53%
MWI	32110	34126	192658	204754	397412	48%
NAM	7364	4807	44183	28839	73023	61%
NER	42	7	252	42	294	86%
NGA	2847	5832	17081	34992	52072	33%
RWA	1352	1134	8109	6802	14911	54%
SEN	98	624	585	3746	4331	14%
SLE	76	32	455	194	650	70%
SOM	6296	6604	37776	39625	77402	49%
SSD	104	30	209	60	269	78%
SWZ	16208	13372	97248	80233	177480	55%
TCD	3	1	19	9	28	68%
TGO	10	1	61	7	68	89%
TUN	8	8	48	51	99	49%
TZA	6590	9108	39538	54645	94183	42%
UGA	2989	3235	17933	19411	37345	48%
ZMB	4543	2769	27257	16616	43873	62%
ZWE	84002	124809	504010	748855	1252865	40 %

Source: Authors' adaptation of Abel and Cohen (2022: 173) migration data computations

The data reveals patterns with strong historical elements, reflecting that, for much of apartheid-era South Africa, cheap migrant male labour was sourced from these countries (Tati, 2008: 423–440). Conversely, Liberia (LBR) and Niger (NER) display a predominance of female migrants, with strikingly high female ratios of 79 per cent and 86 per cent. Such variations in gender ratios across countries of origin point towards complex dynamics that may influence migration flows in a gender-sensitive manner. For example, while the southern African migratory patterns may follow neoclassical economic theory expectations, the observed numbers from Liberia and Niger could be gravity-driven or conflict-driven, following more closely the framework of gendered geographies of power. Figure 6.5 plots the scatter of the ratios of female migration into South Africa from all origin countries. When looking at the data in this way across all countries, the variation that exists in terms of the female composition of migrant flows becomes even clearer.

Figure 6.5: Distribution of countries by female migrant ratio

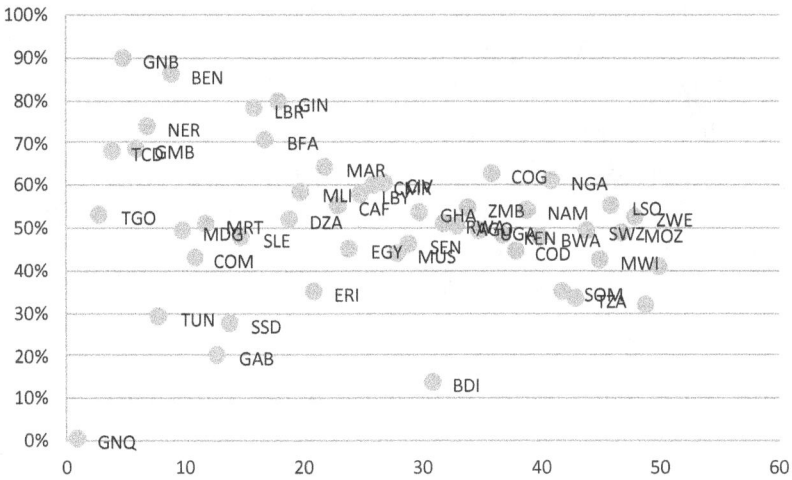

Source: Authors' adaptation of Abel and Cohen (2022: 173) migration data computations

A crucial aspect of this discussion involves acknowledging the geographical proximity of some countries to South Africa. Lesotho, Mozambique, Zimbabwe, eSwatini and Malawi share borders with South Africa, potentially accounting for the substantial migration flows from these countries. This geographical closeness may serve as a confounding factor that could obscure the true gendered nature of migration. The sheer volume of migrants from these neighbouring countries might overshadow more nuanced gender-specific migration patterns, making it imperative to consider geographical proximity when interpreting this data.

Adding another layer of complexity are the zero values observed for specific migration flows in the dataset, most notably Equatorial Guinea (GNQ). These zeros could signify multiple interpretations:

either an absence of recorded migration from these countries or potential data limitations. They could also represent specific policy or social conditions that discourage migration, thereby creating gaps in the gendered understanding of migration flows into South Africa. Regardless, these zero values cannot be overlooked as they may hold key insights into the broader landscape of gender and migration.

The column detailing female ratios further refines our understanding. While some countries, like Kenya (KEN) and Mauritius (MUS), display balanced female ratios of around 53 per cent, others such as Senegal (SEN) and Mauritania (MRT) show low female ratios of 14 per cent and 27 per cent respectively. When interpreting these percentages, one must also consider the absolute numbers of migrants from each country. A high or low female ratio in a country contributing a smaller number of total migrants may not have as significant an impact on the broader gender composition as would larger migration flows from countries like Mozambique or Zimbabwe.

Figure 6.6: Institutional dimensions of migration

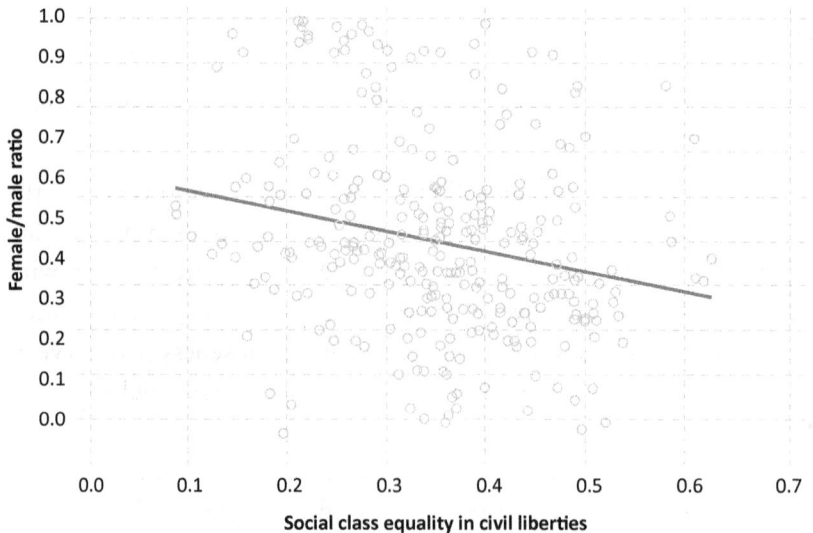

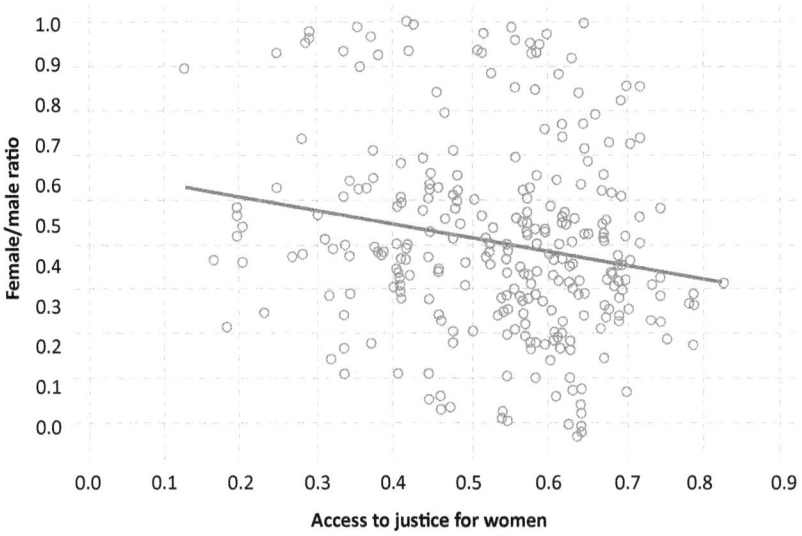

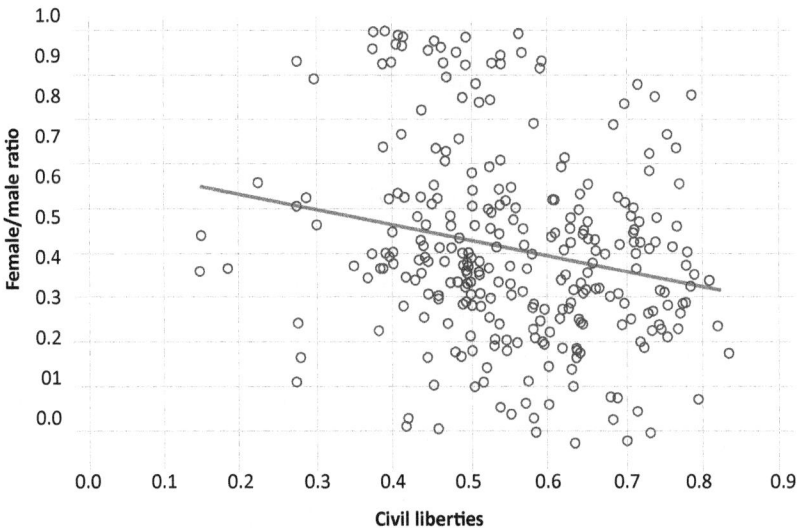

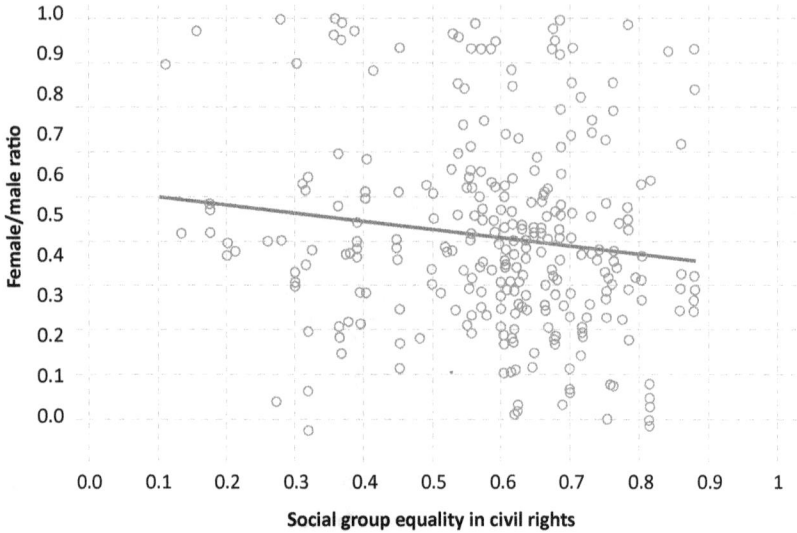

Source: Authors' adaptation of Abel and Cohen (2022: 173) migration data computations and V-DEM Democracy Indices

What this indicates is the multifaceted nature of gendered migration flows into South Africa, influenced by geographical proximity, absolute numbers and unrecorded flows represented by zero values. Such nuances necessitate an analytical approach that takes cognisance of these factors, in order to understand the nature of migration, and possibly better envisage the destination struggles as well. To do this, we borrow a commonly used tool in the trade and migration literature, known as the gravity model. The gravity model tool originated in physics and was later adopted, and adapted, for economic analysis (Tinbergen, 1962; Bergstrand, 1985; Mátyás, 1997). It was subsequently incorporated into the analysis of migration flows between countries (Vanderkamp, 1977; Karemera et al., 2000; Beine et al., 2016: 496–512). Its key value is as a tool to incorporate all possible economic, geographical, geopolitical and historical linkages when assessing cross-country flows and how they impact on outcomes.

In this regard, it is important to take into account that countries in Africa have significant differences in their institutional makeups, the colonial influence on them, and the evolutions of these institutions. For example, if we just plot the scatter of female migrant ratios across countries, Figure 6.6 shows a lot of variation which is informative. However, it is important to understand the drivers of this variation, especially in the context of institutions and governance. To explore this further, eight measures of institutions were examined for their relationship with the intensity of female migration into South Africa, namely: access to justice for women, civil liberties, social class equality in respect of civil liberties, social group equality, social rights and equality, freedom of discussion for women, freedom of movement for women, and gender equality.

Figure 6.6 presents four of these measures, which all relate to the quality of institutions in origin countries. It becomes immediately apparent that as institutions and governance in origin countries improve, the gendered intensity of migration from those countries is reduced. In addition, the intensity of gender migration declines when there is access to justice, legal remedies and civil liberties. As gender equality, or lack thereof, is taken as one of the most appropriate measures of social discrimination in societies, we also plot the relationship between this and female migration.

IMPLICATIONS FOR LIVELIHOODS OF WOMEN MIGRANTS

Women migrants from countries with weak governance reflect the fact that there is minimal protection of access to justice in their home nations. Their migration to South Africa may indicate that institutional environments are more favourable here than in their countries of origin. However, given the local context of South Africa, where the experience of the elite in comparison to the masses has often been likened to that of a dualistic economy (Lebert and Rohde, 2007; Thamaga-Chitja et al., 2010; Fergusson, 2013), it is possible that, due to the vulnerable nature of female migrants, they may not get access to the better-quality institutions they would have migrated for. Table 6.6, for example, shows that in all of the eight measures of governance considered pertaining to women, South Africa ranks more highly than comparative African countries. In fact, on average, across all the metrics of institutions considered, South Africa is about 4 per cent better, and, if we exclude 1990, it is 24 per cent better.

Table 6.6: Difference between South Africa and origin countries' quality of institutions

Governance Measure	1990	1995	2000	2005	2010	2015
Access to justice for women	-16%	30%	30%	29%	27%	22%
Civil liberties	-14%	30%	30%	24%	24%	20%
Freedom of discussion for women	-45%	24%	23%	20%	20%	21%
Freedom of domestic movement for women		46%	54%	6%	56%	17%
Gender equality	-39%	32%	33%	28%	26%	21%
Social group equality	-262%	12%	13%	12%	12%	12%
Social group equality in respect for civil liberties	-202%	15%	18%	17%	16%	17%
Social rights and equality	-203%	26%	26%	22%	22%	20%

Source: Authors' adaptation of Abel and Cohen (2022: 173) migration data computations

Migration patterns into South Africa, especially of women, are intricately tied to the quality of governance in origin countries with social group equality being a pivotal element, as evidenced in Table 6.7. This can be better understood within the feminisation-of-migration framework, which highlights the surge in female migrants that is uniquely different from overall global migration trends, as discussed by Donato and Gabaccia (2016). Their research accentuates the importance of recognising distinct migration motivations unique to women, such as evading gender-based violence or seeking improved prospects in care professions. Thus, it becomes imperative to delve deeper into understanding the quality of governance, specifically the institutions addressing social discrimination against women in both origin and destination countries. It is essential to reinforce better conditions in destination nations as mirroring discriminatory situations can exacerbate hardships for female migrants, especially where their socio-professional networks are already limited (see Table 6.7).

Table 6.7: Correlation between female migration and institutions as well as gravity variables

Variables	Female Migrant Ratio	Total Migration
Access to justice for women	-0.0873	0.0149
Civil liberties	-0.1081	0.0105
Social group equality	-0.1806*	-0.1709*
Social group equality in respect for civil liberties	-0.1186	-0.1370
Social rights and equality	-0.1323	-0.0869
Freedom of discussion for women	-0.1597	-0.0305
Freedom of domestic movement for women	0.0292	0.1241
Gender equality	-0.0738	0.0918
Distance	-0.1381	-0.6951*
Contiguity	0.1135	0.5972*
Common language	0.0266	0.5562*
Common ethnic	0.0651	0.4226*
Comon religion	0.1706*	0.6179*
Population	-0.0910	0.1263
Per capita GDP	0.0444	0.1357
GDP	-0.0540	0.1750*
Cost of entry	-0.0248	-0.1414
Trade flows (UNCOMTRADE)	0.1518	0.7097*
Trade flows (IMF)	0.1109	0.6499*
Trade flows (IMF)	0.1109	0.6499*

Source: Authors' adaptation of Abel and Cohen (2022: 173) migration data computations & CEPII

RECOMMENDATIONS

Immigration has taken various contextual forms across space and time while remaining a constant element of human activity and a fundamental factor in human history and evolution. The past decade has seen a surge in anti-immigrant rhetoric and its proponents. This is evident in both the global North and South. South Africa is no exception. In the midst of such sentiments, and some of the political elements and drivers of it, the key drivers of immigration may have become sidelined.

Migration within the global South, especially in the African context, is a phenomenon with significantly gendered facets. This results in a pressing need for policies that address the specific dynamics and challenges of intra-African female migration. Such strategies could involve creating more accessible legal pathways, simplifying visa processes or considering visa-free regimes within regional blocs. Gender-sensitive measures should ensure fair wages, safe conditions and access to social protection, all while addressing root causes such as economic disparities and conflicts. Mechanisms to integrate migrants into local labour markets are paramount given the potentially positive impacts of migrants on labour productivity. Policies that bridge trade and migration could yield mutual benefits for both of these sectors, particularly as bilateral trade seems to favour female migration to South Africa.

This study further highlights the need to diversify the study of South–South gendered migration and to move beyond the predominant focus on South–North dynamics. A deep understanding of institutional influences across African countries is critical, given their evident disparities and impacts on migration. There is a need to recognise and understand regional variations in gender migration, which suggest diverse determinants that demand customised policies. Collaboration among nations, research entities and policymaking institutions is vital, given the intricacies of gendered migration. Shared resources and knowledge can spearhead the creation of effective policies and research trajectories.

This becomes pertinent when looking at the immigration of women into South Africa. South Africa boasts one of the most inclusive constitutions on the continent, and this, as we have shown, may be a key driver of gendered, governance-driven immigration into South Africa. Given the country's role as a major destination within the South–South migration corridor, there is a need to develop tailored policies that specifically address its unique migration dynamics. Given the influence of geographical proximity, countries that share borders naturally have increased migration flows, which could overshadow specifically gendered patterns. Therefore, policies should not only be geared towards broader continental dynamics but should also cater to nuanced regional patterns. It is of paramount importance to address the potential of discrimination as both a driver of and a deterrent to migration in the South African context, with an emphasis on ensuring equitable protection for the vulnerable. Given the ties between bilateral trade and female migration to South Africa, trade policies should be crafted in tandem with migration policies, which would ensure mutual benefits for both sectors. Furthermore, South Africa should invest in improving data-collection mechanisms, focusing on gender-disaggregated data. This would be instrumental in understanding the motivations behind migration flows, as well as the long-term, lived outcomes of migration. It would also go a long way towards helping to refine targeted policies. Collaborative approaches, especially with neighbouring countries, can facilitate knowledge sharing and the joint tackling of challenges like irregular migration and its effects.

CONCLUSION

In this chapter, the gendered nature of migration is explored with a focus on women migrants. Relying on some existing theories and frameworks on general migration, and on the migration of women specifically, this chapter explores relative variation in the numbers and origins of women migrants into South Africa, their contributions and lived outcomes. It also explores the potential drivers of such migration into South Africa. Despite the paucity of micro-level data on migration, some useful insights are offered. Migration, as a transformative force, greatly impacts the global socioeconomic tapestry, with the South–South dynamic of notable significance. Our exploration reveals the multifaceted nature of migration, with a distinct emphasis on its potential to act as a catalyst for both individual and collective economic growth.

At continental level, there are gender variations in the determinants of immigration: network effects, such as family ties or prior migrant relationships, significantly influence male migration but not female.

This seems to be a role for trade as a pivotal driver, with a bias towards female migration. While economic sectors such as agriculture and domestic work drive migration across Africa, South Africa remains a primary destination. This is especially true for female migrants, but the nature of integration into the local labour market does not fully utilise the skill sets that female migrants come with, as many migrant women resort to low-skilled roles due to biases towards and lack of recognition of foreign credentials. This is despite the evidence of a positive correlation between immigration and labour productivity in Africa. While the literature suggests so, the evidence in this chapter finds no strong link between the female migration rate and informal employment across sectors.

In the context of institutions and governance, Africa's myriad institutional configurations play a decisive role in influencing migration trends. Institutions, both formal and informal, have the potency to shape and drive migration decisions. The pivotal role of these governance structures becomes even more pronounced when considering the migration choices of women. Specifically, institutions that provide access to justice and protection can serve as significant pull or push factors. South Africa, with its advanced rule of law and democratic fabric, stands out in the South–South migratory narrative. The country's appeal, especially to women, underscores a larger, pan-African aspiration for robust institutional frameworks.

It is essential to better understand the explicit triggers of female migration. The urgency for improved governance, protective measures and institutions is pertinent. This chapter emphasises the need to bolster and refine institutional structures across the African continent. By establishing institutions that advocate for justice, equality and economic opportunities, the challenges posed by migration can be addressed, inherently amplifying its potential benefits.

Lastly, migration's evolving role in shaping global dynamics necessitates a comprehensive exploration, especially within the lesser-examined realm of South–South migration. While this chapter has attempted to do so within the context of governance and institutional determinants, as well as the lived outcomes of female migration, the lack of granular data severely limits the analysis that can be carried out.

158

A much-needed policy intervention is the collection of trackable data on migration that can help with a more in-depth assessment of some of the questions posed in this chapter. This will enrich the discourse on migration, thereby guiding future policy frameworks and strategies. Particularly, the dynamics of female migration warrant attention, against the backdrop of global challenges like climate change and sociopolitical upheavals. The vast majority of African migration is intra-continental, with South Africa serving as a principal hub. Addressing these dynamics is crucial to ensuring the welfare and prosperity of both migrant communities and local economies in an ever-evolving global landscape.

REFERENCES

Abel, G. J. and Cohen, J. E. 2022. 'Bilateral international migration flow estimates updated and refined by sex'. *Scientific Data*, 9(1), 173.

Adepoju, A. 2006. 'Internal and international migration within Africa', in Kok, P. D., Gelderblom, J., Oucho, J. and Van Zyl, J. (eds), *Migration in South and Southern Africa: Dynamics and Determinants.* Cape Town: Human Sciences Research Council.

Azose, J. J. and Raftery, A. E. 2019. 'Estimation of emigration, return migration, and transit migration between all pairs of countries'. *Proceedings of the National Academy of Sciences*, 116(1), 116–122.

Beauchemin, C. and Bocquier, P. 2004. 'Migration and urbanisation in Francophone West Africa: An overview of the recent empirical evidence'. *Urban Studies*, 41(11), 2245–2272.

Beguy, D., Bocquier, P. and Zulu, E. M. 2010. 'Circular migration patterns and determinants in Nairobi slum settlements'. *Demographic Research*, 23, 549–586.

Beine, M., Bertoli, S. and Fernández-Huertas M. J. 2016. 'A practitioners' guide to gravity models of international migration'. *The World Economy*, 39(4), 496–512.

Bergstrand, J. H. 1985. 'The gravity equation in international trade: Some microeconomic foundations and empirical evidence'. *The Review of Economics and Statistics*, 67(3), 474–481.

Camlin, C. S., Snow, R. C. and Hosegood, V. 2014. 'Gendered patterns of migration in rural South Africa'. *Population, Space and Place*, 20(6), 528–551.

Chammartin, G. 2002. 'The feminisation of international migration'. International Migration Programme, International Labour Organization, 37–40.

Chun, J. J., Lipsitz, G. and Shin, Y. 2013. 'Intersectionality as a social movement strategy: Asian immigrant women advocates'. *Signs: Journal of Women in Culture and Society*, 38(4), 917–940.

Collinson, M. 2009. 'Age-sex profiles of migration: Who is a migrant?', in Collinson, M. A., Adazu, K., White, M. and Findley, S. (eds), *The Dynamics of Migration, Health and Livelihoods: INDEPTH network perspectives*. Surrey: Ashgate.

Collinson, M., Tollman, S., Kahn, K., Clark, S. and Garenne, M. 2006. 'Highly prevalent circular migration: Households, mobility and economic status in rural South Africa', in Tienda, M., Findley, S., Tollman, S. and Preston-Whyte, E. (eds), *Africa on the Move: African Migration and Urbanisation in Comparative Perspective*. Johannesburg: Wits University Press, 194–216.

Coulibaly, D., Gnimassoun, B. and Mignon, V. 2020. 'The tale of two international phenomena: International migration and global imbalances'. *Journal of Macroeconomics*, 66, 103241.

De Haas, H. 2010. 'The internal dynamics of migration processes: A theoretical inquiry'. *Journal of Ethnic and Migration Studies*, 36(10), 1587–1617.

Diop, B. and D'Aloisio, J. 2007. 'Migration and gender in the African context'. International Committee for the Red Cross Advisory Meeting Special Report.

Donato, K. M. and Gabaccia, D. 2016. 'The global feminisation of migration: Past, present, and future'. Migration Policy Institute, https://www.migrationpolicy.org/article/global-feminisationfeminisation-migration-past-present-and-future, accessed 12 November 2023.

Fergusson, L. 2013. 'The political economy of rural property rights and the persistence of the dual economy'. *Journal of Development Economics,* 103, 167–181.

Ferrant, G. and Tuccio, M. 2015. 'South–South migration and discrimination against women in social institutions: A two-way relationship'. *World Development*, 72(C), 240–254.

Flahaux, M. L. and De Haas, H. 2016. 'African migration: Trends, patterns, drivers'. *Comparative Migration Studies*, 4, 1–25.

Gnimassoun, B. 2023. 'The effect of intra-African immigration on productivity in Africa'. AERC Research Paper No 535, African Economic Research Consortium, Nairobi.

Gnimassoun, B. and Anyanwu, J. C. 2019. 'The diaspora and economic development in Africa'. *Review of World Economics,* 155(4), 785–817.

International Labour Organization (ILO). 2020. 'Protecting migrant workers during the COVID-19 pandemic: Recommendations for policy-makers and constituents'. *ILO Brief,* https://www.ilo.org/wcmsp5/groups/public/---ed_protect/---protrav/---migrant/documents/publication/wcms_743268.pdf, accessed 15 December 2023.

International Labour Organization (ILO). 2022. 'Migrant domestic workers in the SADC region –Intersecting decent work with safe, orderly and regular migration', https://resource.sammproject.org/wp-content/uploads/download-manager-files/Migrant-Domestic-Workers-Final-Report-1.pdf, accessed 7 September 2023.

International Organization for Migration. 2020. 'World Migration Report 2020', https://worldmigrationreport.iom.int/wmr-2020-interactive/#:~:text=Overall%2C%20the%20estimated%20number%20of,the%20estimated%20number%20in%201970.

Jütting, J. P., Morrisson, C., Dayton-Johnson, J. and Drechsler, D. 2008. 'Measuring gender (in) equality: The OECD gender, institutions and development data base'. *Journal of Human Development,* 9(1), 65–86.

Karemera, D., Oguledo, V. I. and Davis, B. 2000. 'A gravity model analysis of international migration to North America'. *Applied Economics*, 32(13), 1745–1755.

Kurekova, L. 2011. 'Theories of migration: Conceptual review and empirical testing in the context of the EU East–West flows in interdisciplinary conference on migration'. *Economic Change, Social Challenge*, 4, 6–9.

Lebert, T. and Rohde, R. 2007. 'Land reform and the new elite: Exclusion of the poor from communal land in Namaqualand, South Africa'. *Journal of Arid Environments*, 70(4), 818–833.

Masanja, G. 2012. 'The female face of migration in sub-Saharan Africa. Huria'. *Journal of the Open University of Tanzania*, 11, 80–97.

Mátyás, L. 1997. 'Proper econometric specification of the gravity model'. *The World Economy*, 20(3), 363–368.

McAuliffe, M. and A. Triandafyllidou (eds), 2021. 'World Migration Report 2022'. International Organization for Migration (IOM), https://publications.iom.int/books/world-migration-report-2022, accessed 5 October 2023.

Ncube, A., Bahta, Y. T. and Jordaan, A. J. 2020. 'Job market perceptions of African migrant women in South Africa as an initial and long-term coping and adaptation mechanism'. *Journal of International Migration and Integration*, 21(4), 1165–1185.

North, D. C. 1990. 'A transaction cost theory of politics'. *Journal of Theoretical Politics*, 2(4), 355–367.

Olesen, H. 2002. 'Migration, return, and development: An institutional perspective'. *International Migration,* 40(5), 125–150.

Ortega, F. and Peri, G. 2014. 'Openness and income: The roles of trade and migration'. *Journal of International Economics*, 92(2), 231–251.

Pew Research Center. 2 April 2015. 'The future of world religions: Population growth projections 2010–2050', https://assets.pewresearch.org/wp-content/uploads/sites/11/2015/03/PF_15.04.02_ProjectionsFullReport.pdf, accessed 15 September 2023.

Popoola, A. A., Akogun, O., Adegbenjo, O. T., Rampaul, K., Adeleye, B. M., Medayese, S., Chipungu, L. and Magidimisha-Chipungu, H. H. 2021.

'South African destination among African women immigrants', in Nyemba, F. and Chitiyo, R. (eds.), *Immigrant Women's Voices and Integrating Feminism Into Migration Theory.* Hershey: IGI Global, 214–235.

Reed, H. E., Andrzejewski, C. S. and White, M. J. 2010. 'Men's and women's migration in coastal Ghana: An event history analysis'. *Demographic Research*, 22, 771–812.

Sharp, M. 2021. 'The labour market impacts of female internal migration: Evidence from the end of apartheid'. *Regional Science and Urban Economics*, 91, 103624.

Silva, J. S. and Tenreyro, S. 2006. 'The log of gravity'. *The Review of Economics and Statistics*, 88(4), 641–658.

Silva, J. S. and Tenreyro, S. 2010. 'On the existence of the maximum likelihood estimates in Poisson regression'. *Economics Letters*, 107(2), 310–312.

Souza, E. 2020. 'Labour market incorporation of immigrant women in South Africa: Impacts of human capital and family structure'. *Population Studies*, 75(1), 111–131.

Tati, G. 2008. 'The immigration issues in the post-apartheid South Africa: Discourses, policies and social repercussions. Espace populations sociétés'. *Space Populations Societies*, 3, 423–440.

Thamaga-Chitja, J.M., Kolanisi, U. and Murugani, V. G. 2010. 'Is the South African land reform programme gender sensitive to women's food security and livelihood efforts?'. *Agenda*, 24(86), 121–134.

Tinbergen, J. 1962. *Shaping the World Economy: Suggestions for an international economic policy.* New York: Twentieth Century Fund.

United Nations Conference on Trade and Development (UNCTAD). 2018. 'Economic development in Africa report 2018: Migration for structural transformation', https://unctad.org/system/files/official-document/aldcafrica2018_en.pdf, accessed 8 September 2023.

United Nations (UN). 2023. Global Migration Database. 'UN data on migration stocks', https://www.un.org/development/desa/pd/content/international-migrant-stock, accessed 8 October 2023.

United Nations Department of Economic and Social Affairs, Population Division (UN DESA). 2020. 'International Migration 2020: Highlights', undesa_pd_2020_international_migration_highlights.pdf, accessed 4 October 2023.

Vanderkamp, J. 1977. 'The gravity model and migration behaviour: An economic interpretation'. *Journal of Economic Studies*, 4(2), 89–102.

Viruell-Fuentes, E. A., Miranda, P. Y. and Abdulrahim, S. 2012. 'More than culture: structural racism, intersectionality theory, and immigrant health'. *Social Science & Medicine*, 75(12), 2099–2106.

Virupaksha, H. G., Kumar, A. and Nirmala B. P. 2014. 'Migration and mental health: An interface'. *J Nat Sci Biol Med*, 5(2), 233–239.

APPENDIX: COUNTRY ABBREVIATIONS USED

Country	Abbreviation
Algeria	DZA
Angola	AGO
Benin	BEN
Botswana	BWA
Burkina Faso	BFA
Burundi	BDI
Cabo Verde	CPV
Cameroon	CMR
Central African Republic	CAF
Chad	TCD
Comoros	COM
Congo, Dem. Rep.	COD
Congo, Rep.	COG
Côte d'Ivoire	CIV
Djibouti	DJI
Egypt, Arab Rep.	EGY
Equatorial Guinea	GNQ
Eritrea	ERI
eSwatini	SWZ
Ethiopia	ETH
Gabon	GAB
Gambia, The	GMB
Ghana	GHA
Guinea	GIN
Guinea-Bissau	GNB
Kenya	KEN
Lesotho	LSO
Liberia	LBR
Libya	LBY
Madagascar	MDG
Malawi	MWI
Mali	MLI

Country	Abbreviation
Mauritania	MRT
Morocco	MAR
Mozambique	MOZ
Namibia	NAM
Niger	NER
Nigeria	NGA
Rwanda	RWA
São Tomé and Príncipe	STP
Senegal	SEN
Seychelles	SYC
Sierra Leone	SLE
Somalia	SOM
South Africa	ZAF
South Sudan	SSD
Sudan	SDN
Tanzania	TZA
Togo	TGO
Tunisia	TUN
Uganda	UGA
Zambia	ZMB
Zimbabwe	ZWE

SEVEN

Migrants' lived experience of the nutrition transition in Johannesburg: Understanding dietary change through participatory research

BRITTANY KESSELMAN

This article examines the lived experience of the nutrition transition among internal and cross-border migrants to Johannesburg, South Africa. Like many rapidly growing cities in the global South, Johannesburg faces high levels of food and nutrition insecurity alongside rising levels of non-communicable diseases. The research undertaken for this chapter entailed a mix of participatory arts-based methods and interviews to data on the childhood and contemporary food practices of participants to better understand what kinds of dietary changes migrants experienced and how they perceived those changes. Four types of dietary change are considered: foods consumed, food procurement, food preparation and consumption practices. Changes include an increase in consumption of processed foods, a shift from subsistence production to food purchasing, consumption of ready-made meals or fast foods and a decline in food sharing. The research examines individual and structural factors influencing the migrants' perceptions of those changes and reveals that while many of the migrants' dietary changes are the result of necessity – due to unavailability of foods, unaffordability or time constraints – others are choices based on status, identity or a desire for connection. A more nuanced understanding of how the nutrition transition is experienced could improve nutrition and health policy interventions for migrant populations in cities.

INTRODUCTION

South Africa is one of the countries in southern Africa experiencing a nutrition transition, a shift from traditional diets high in fibre and nutrients to increased consumption of energy-dense processed foods high in sugar, salt and fat (Popkin, 2002b; Stern et al., 2010). The nutrition transition is accompanied by rising rates of obesity and diet-related non-communicable diseases (NCDs) such as diabetes, cardiovascular diseases, hypertension and some cancers (Popkin et al., 2012; Wentzel-Viljoen et al., 2018). In many countries of the global South, including South Africa, the nutrition transition is happening at a rapid pace, and is occurring alongside persistent under-nutrition (hunger and food insecurity) (Ford et al., 2017; Popkin et al., 2002b, 2012). This co-existence of under- and over-nutrition, known as the 'double burden of malnutrition', places a significant burden on health systems and also detracts from people's quality of life and livelihoods (Steyn and Mchiza, 2014; Vorster et al., 2011; WHO, 2017). To address this double burden of malnutrition and its attendant health impacts, it is critical to find better ways to prevent or reverse the most damaging dietary changes of urban migrants.

While the nutrition transition is occurring everywhere, it is more pronounced in urban areas (Hawkes et al., 2017). It is occurring especially rapidly for migrants moving from rural areas, where they may still practise subsistence agriculture to urban areas where they adopt more sedentary lifestyles and 'Westernised' diets featuring processed foods, convenience foods, as well as fast food eaten outside the home (Delavari et al., 2013; Cohen et al., 2017; Peters et al., 2019). Thus, in terms of understanding the drivers and consequences of dietary change, migrants in cities of the global South are an important population to consider.

Very often, nutrition and health interventions focus on individual behaviour change through education about nutrition, or on national-level regulations to influence the food environment – a sort of agency or structure binary that fails to capture the multiple and inter-connected determinants of dietary practices (Igumbor et al., 2012; Iversen et al., 2012). These interventions are generally failing to slow the tide; indeed no country has successfully reversed the trend of rising obesity (Ford et al., 2017; Boatemaa et al., 2018).

For 30 years, research on the nutrition transition has focused on national, regional and global scales using population-level data from dietary surveys or production/sales statistics (Walls et al., 2018; Baker et al., 2020). This is useful for understanding large-scale trends, including political-economic drivers of the nutrition transition such as trade liberalisation, the spread of supermarkets and processed food advertising (Hawkes, 2006; Popkin and Ng, 2022). However, this macro-level research does not contribute to our understanding of the interplay of cultural, socioeconomic and identity-related factors that feed into people's food choices at individual and household levels (Satia, 2010; Nichols, 2017).

This research seeks to fill that gap in the literature, drawing on ethnographic data collected in participatory group sessions with internal and cross-border migrants to Johannesburg. This chapter argues that by examining individuals' perceptions and embodied experiences of dietary changes, it is possible to better understand individual agency within the constraints imposed by broader structural factors. In particular, the research finds that issues of identity, status and the desire for communal eating are under-appreciated factors influencing migrants' food practices. In this way, the study brings a new approach to the nutrition transition literature in South Africa and begins to highlight different kinds of nutrition and health interventions based on the actual needs and experiences of migrants.

THEORETICAL FRAMEWORK: UNDERSTANDING
THE NUANCES OF THE NUTRITION TRANSITION

The literature on the nutrition transition points to a number of political-economic drivers of the shift from traditional, nutrient-dense diets to diets higher in processed foods and fats, sugar and salt. These drivers include shifts in the global food system (for example, concentration and expansion of processed food manufacturers, the spread of food advertising and trade liberalisation) as well as trends such as urbanisation, time pressures and de-skilling in relation to cooking (Baker et al., 2020; Popkin and Ng, 2022). In a South African context, the THUSA study (Transition and Health during Urbanisation of South Africans) examined this process in the late 1990s and found higher fat intake, higher levels of obesity and associated risks of NCDs among urban populations (Vorster et al., 2005). Some of the factors associated with the transition to unhealthy diets in urban areas include poverty, time constraints, limited access to food retail outlets, lack of refrigeration facilities and high costs of cooking fuel (Crush et al., 2011). Other nutrition transition research in South Africa has yielded similar findings (Macintyre et al., 2002; Vorster et al., 2005; Stern et al., 2010; Stupar et al., 2012; Wentzel-Viljoen et al., 2018). Studies of rural-to-urban migrants in other African countries also indicate similar issues (Cockx et al., 2018; Peters et al., 2019).

Nutrition transition literature provides an overview of large-scale shifts, but it fails to capture the complexities of dietary change and the various cultural, historical, political and environmental factors that influence diets in specific places. More recently, some nutrition transition research has begun to focus on more localised areas and to use more qualitative approaches to try to capture some of this nuance (Finnis, 2007; Di Rocco and Cuvi, 2014; Leatherman et al., 2016; Nichols, 2017; Denham and Gladstone, 2020). These new studies add much-needed richness to the nutrition transition literature, helping us understand the complexities of locally specific but globally embedded nutrition transitions.

The main focus of this research article is migrants' lived experience of the nutrition transition; however, it also draws on the concept of dietary acculturation. This is 'the process that occurs when members of a migrating group adopt the eating patterns/food choices of their new environment' (Satia-Abouta, 2003). Unlike nutrition transition literature, many dietary acculturation studies focus on individuals or groups in specific localities, seeking to understand how and why dietary changes occur (Patil et al., 2009; Osei-Kwasi et al., 2017). However, most of the literature on acculturation examines the situation of cross-border migrants, rather than internal migrants, usually focusing on migrants moving from the global South to the global North (Abbots, 2016; Osei-Kwasi et al., 2023). It also seems to assume that the dietary cultures of sending and receiving countries are completely different. However, due to the effects of colonisation, as well as the global reach of multinational food manufacturing and retail companies, diets around the world are increasingly homogeneous (Tuomainen, 2009; Martínez, 2014).

A third body of relevant research is the anthropological literature on food and migration, which focuses on questions of identity and belonging that are largely absent from the nutrition transition literature. This literature examines how food can be used to (re)construct a migrant's identity and root them in their new home (Raman, 2011; Johnston and Longhurst, 2012; Abbots, 2016). For migrants, food can contribute to a sense of connection with those left behind and can also help to forge connections in their new residence (Sutton, 2001; Johnston and Longhurst, 2012; Bailey, 2017; Kudejira, 2021). The literature on food, identity and belonging tends to be silent with regard to political and economic questions and the material influence of poverty or food insecurity on migrants' diets (for an exception, see Kudejira, 2021).

In South Africa, there has been limited research conducted on the dietary changes of migrants, and what little there is has tended to focus on identity and cultural beliefs (Naidu and Nzuza, 2013; Hunter-Adams and Rother, 2016; Nyamnjoh, 2018; Lakika and Drimie, 2019). There is a need to bring together the political-economic with the anthropological approach, or broader structural issues from the nutrition transition literature with the particular cultural and identity issues highlighted in the dietary acculturation, migration and belonging literature. This will allow for a more comprehensive picture of how and why internal and cross-border migrants in South African cities adapt and change their diets. This study addresses a gap in the literature on food and migration by bringing these two concepts together. Further, understanding how changes are perceived, embraced or rejected should contribute to better policy interventions in Johannesburg and other cities that are experiencing rapid growth through in-migration.

CONTEXT AND METHODS

Research setting

Despite being the economic hub of South Africa, Johannesburg suffers high levels of food insecurity, with estimates of food insecurity ranging from 52 per cent in some low-income areas (Rudolph et al., 2012) to up to 90 per cent in the poorest wards (De Wet et al., 2008). Since virtually all food consumed is purchased in Johannesburg, high levels of unemployment – just over 34.6 per cent in the second quarter of 2022 (Statistics South Africa, 2022) – translate into limited food access (Rudolph et al., 2012). At the same time, the nutrition transition is bringing increasing levels of obesity and associated NCDs (Drimie et al., 2013). Low-income South Africans subsist on unhealthy diets, high in sugar and processed starch (bread and maize meal) but low in essential nutrients, which contribute to rising levels of obesity and NCDs (Department of Health, n.d.; Mchiza et al., 2015).

An estimated 11 per cent of Johannesburg residents were born in other countries and about 33 per cent were born in other South African provinces (Dallimore et al., 2021). Since its founding as a gold mining town in 1886, Johannesburg has attracted migrants from the rest of South Africa and neighbouring countries. The mines, and later other industries, actively recruited migrant labour from across southern Africa, and many more came in search of economic opportunities (Segatti, 2011). Others fled conflict, repression or food insecurity (Crush, 2012; Sadiddin et al., 2019). As traced in this book, these struggles have continued into the present day. Migrants often struggle to find decent housing and employment, and those from other countries often face prejudice, poor access to public services and violence (Peberdy et al., 2004; Hiropoulos, 2020). Owing to these and other challenges, migrants face food insecurity in South Africa (Tawodzera and Crush, 2016).

Research methods

The migrants who participated in this study were part of a crafts programme at a non-governmental organisation (NGO) located in the inner-city of Johannesburg, Hillbrow. The area of Hillbrow is densely populated and is home to many migrants, both South African and international. As part of a programme of research which offers reciprocity, I conducted weekly sessions of about two hours each at the NGO. These sessions featured different activities related to food knowledge and practices over the course of several months in 2018 and then again, with new participants, for several months in 2019 (see Kesselman, 2022 for a full description of activities). Attendance by the participants was entirely voluntary. I utilised a mixture of arts-based, creative methods (see below) to engage participants in the sessions, as well as to overcome differences of language, culture, education and, in some cases, mental disability. In addition, I provided a healthy, low-cost meal to share with the group at each session, and distributed recipe cards in case members wished to prepare it at home. This was both a method of inquiry, as well as a gesture of reciprocity (Johnston and Longhurst, 2012; Walker, 2023). Discussions around the meals provided rich data on people's food knowledge and practices.

This research paper primarily draws on data collected during three specific activities conducted in 2018 and 2019. The first was a food mapping exercise in which participants drew a map showing their current food procurement practices. The second was the mapping of their childhood food environment. After each of these, there were group discussions about what participants had drawn. The third activity was an in-person food history interview, conducted near the end of our sessions together. These interviews covered participants' historical relationship with food, including growing food, shopping, cooking, and typical and special-occasion foods. The interviews explored changes over time, as well as changes participants would like to make. Some of these were conducted in English, while others were conducted, via an interpreter, in other South African languages. All research interviews were transcribed.

Participants

The participants were very diverse (see Table 7.1). The majority of the participants were internal migrants from rural parts of South Africa, while others were cross-border migrants from other African countries. The migrants' length of stay in Johannesburg ranged from only a few months to over a decade. Some were staying in over-crowded inner-city flats in or near Hillbrow and others were staying in townships further away, such as Soweto or Alexandra. Almost all of the older participants had grown up in rural areas. Members of the group spoke different languages (such as isiZulu, isiXhosa, Tshivenda, Shona, Swahili, French, etc.), had different levels of education and literacy, and in some cases were living with physical or mental health challenges. Each participant signed an informed consent form. The project was granted ethical clearance by the University of the Witwatersrand Human Research Ethics Committee (non-medical). To protect the identities of the participants, the chapter uses pseudonyms. While the participants do not constitute a statistically representative sample, the diversity of participants is in many ways characteristic of the diversity of Johannesburg, and thus useful to illustrate the food practices of migrants in Johannesburg.

Table 7.1: Comparison of participants between year 1 and year 2

Description	Year 1 (2018)	Year 2 (2019)
Consistency of participation	Rotating group	Slightly more stable though some dropped out
Numbers	Varied (largest 20–25 people, smallest 6, usually 12–15)	Consistently small (largest 11 on the first day, smallest 2, usually 5)
Age	20s–60s	20s–40s
Gender	Mostly women	Mostly women
Country of origin	South Africa, Zimbabwe, Burundi, Democratic Republic of the Congo, Sudan	South Africa, Zimbabwe, Democratic Republic of the Congo
Province of origin (for SA)	Eastern Cape, Limpopo, Free State, KwaZulu-Natal	KwaZulu-Natal, Gauteng
Residence type	Flat, homeless shelter	Flat
Household size	2–6	1–7

Description	Year 1 (2018)	Year 2 (2019)
Education level	Some secondary through completion of matric	[not known for all] 1 had some technical training after matric
Employment status	Unemployed, some piece work and Community Work Programme participation	Unemployed, some piece work, 1 employed at Outreach
Special needs	Some with physical or mental disabilities	n/a
Literacy	Varying levels	All at least basic literacy

Limitations

While an interpreter was used for some of the sessions and interviews, language barriers represented a limitation of this research. Working in groups and using creative methods helped to overcome some language challenges, but the research would have benefited from full-time interpretation in multiple languages. A second limitation of the research was the fluctuation of participants. While having a mix of new participants each week limited our ability to build on previous discussions over the course of the sessions, it also enhanced the richness of our conversations as participants with new views and experiences joined.

FINDINGS: THE DIETARY CHANGES

The findings in this section are grouped into four types of dietary change: 1) which foods are eaten; 2) how and where foods are procured; 3) food preparation practices; and 4) eating practices. Within each of these, I examine the different factors affecting continuity or change in migrants' dietary practices and discuss their experience of those changes.

Changes in foods commonly eaten by migrants

The basic meal structure of a starch, meat and vegetable remained the same from rural childhoods to contemporary Johannesburg but there were additions and substitutions. For example, migrants added new forms of processed starch such as rice, pasta and bread, not only maize meal. Processed meats, spice mixes and cooking oil were added to urban diets. At the same time, many foods eaten in rural areas could not be found in the city. Vegetables and fruits that were foraged wild in rural areas were simply not available for sale in Johannesburg. One woman who grew up in Zimbabwe said she missed 'amarula [fruit]. I haven't seen it [here]' (Faith, 14 June 2019). Fruits tend to be expensive in Johannesburg for people on limited food budgets (Temple and Steyn, 2011). Attempts to substitute ingredients, and a shift away from traditional foods due to their inaccessibility, are in line with the models of dietary acculturation (Satia-Abouta et al., 2002; Patil et al., 2009).

Most participants indicated that they missed foods from their homes and wanted to continue eating their traditional diets. Even if financial constraints were removed, Lindiwe said she would want to eat 'what I have grown [up] eating. Like my traditional foods, I love them' (Lindiwe, 19 June 2019). Another participant referred to childhood foods fondly: 'My mother used to – even now she still does – grow okra. I know it from my young age, so I love it' (Buhle, 14 June 2019). Lesedi did not have access to wild greens in Johannesburg, but still harvested them when she went home to Limpopo 'because I love them. I grew up eating them' (Lesedi, 26 July 2018). Familiar foods are comforting, and people wish to keep eating them if they are available to maintain their identity and feel connected to their places of origin (Abbots, 2016; Bailey, 2017; Janowski, 2012; Nyamnjoh, 2018). However, many of these foods were not easily accessible to migrants in Johannesburg.

Foods that had been considered rare or special in childhood became normalised among migrants, due to their greater availability in the city. According to one participant, Buhle, she rarely saw rice where she grew up in Zimbabwe. 'We don't have rice around there where I grew up, so rice is something which comes with the people who come from towns, so it was special to us' (Buhle, 14 June 2019). Similarly, a woman from the rural Eastern Cape also enjoyed special treats when migrant relatives returned from cities: 'For Christmas, it was special to have bread, meat, … Illovo syrup. Ah, that was when we will eat the sweets' (Ruth, 31 July 2018).

While previously special occasion foods become commonplace,

some also disappear. In Johannesburg, the absence of livestock means, as one interviewee put it, that, 'Around here [we eat] normal food, but when we are back at home, we slaughter a goat' (Sarah, 27 July 2018). As the nutrition transition literature suggests, most of the home foods that become inaccessible to migrants are healthy, fresh produce, while most of the new foods available in urban areas are more processed and less healthy (Baker et al., 2020).

Changes in food procurement practices

The most dramatic shift was from household food production to purchasing. Participants who grew up in rural areas indicated that their households grew most of their own food, with all family members involved in food production.

> Since my father was not employed, so we used to grow food for ourselves ... everyone in the family, because that was the only source of food... The surplus was being sold so that my father can pay the school fees (Buhle, 14 June 2019).

Childhood food maps showed food gardens producing staples (such as maize and even wheat), legumes, vegetables and fruits. Participants had livestock, such as chickens, goats, pigs, sheep and cattle. In one or two cases, there was a river or dam where people could fish. Most, but not all, of the older, rural participants referred to gathering wild fruits and greens for food when they were younger. These largely self-sufficient rural South African households had access to a general dealer, where they purchased a few basic items such as sugar, tea and flour. Bigger shops were in towns, which might be hours away by public transport. See Figure 7.1 for a sample childhood food map from rural KwaZulu-Natal.

In Johannesburg, participants purchased most of their food, sourcing it from different shops based on considerations of price, quality, freshness, convenience and familiarity. For example, many participants purchased major staples at the large supermarkets, to take advantage of low prices and occasional specials, even if this trip required paying for public transport.

Figure 7.1: Childhood food map, rural KwaZulu-Natal, South Africa

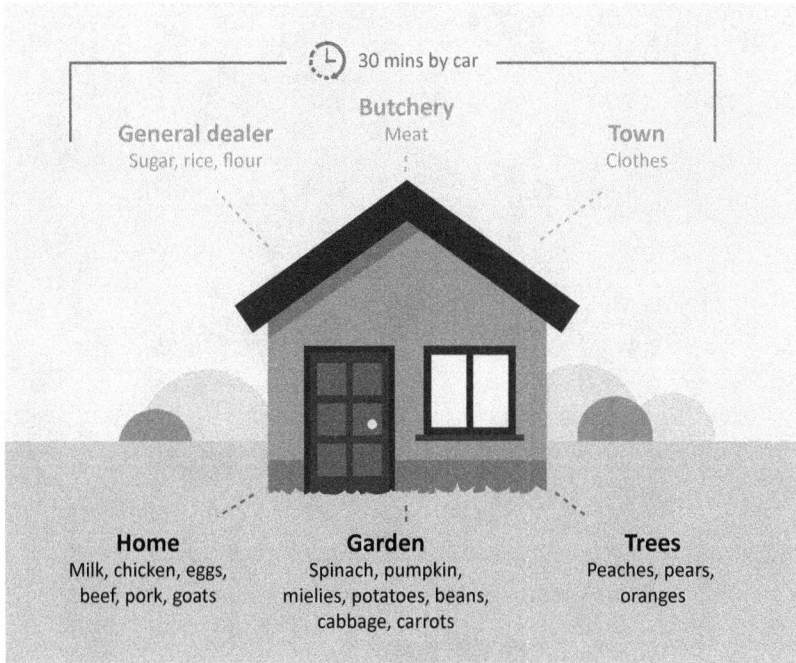

I buy [at] the local supermarket. Normally I find ... their veggies and that stuff are fresh. And I normally buy big things, like mealie meal, rice, flours and milk, those packs, 6-pack at a bigger supermarket (Ayanda, 31 July 2018).

Many participants used local spaza shops and street vendors, often located a short walk from where they stayed, to purchase vegetables, bread or other daily necessities. In a few cases, people went to specialised shops such as a butcher or a greengrocer to find better-quality foods, usually citing freshness or lack of contamination. 'I have to go far [to get] what I want because the shops around me, sometimes the food stays long there' (Thandeka, 31 July 2018). These mixed strategies for food purchasing are in line with other research on how low-income households source food in South African cities (Peyton et al., 2015; Petersen and Charman, 2018). Migrants from other countries made special efforts to buy foods from home not commonly eaten by South Africans, sourcing fufu, cassava and dried fish from Yeoville markets

Figure 7.2: Current food map of a cross-border migrant

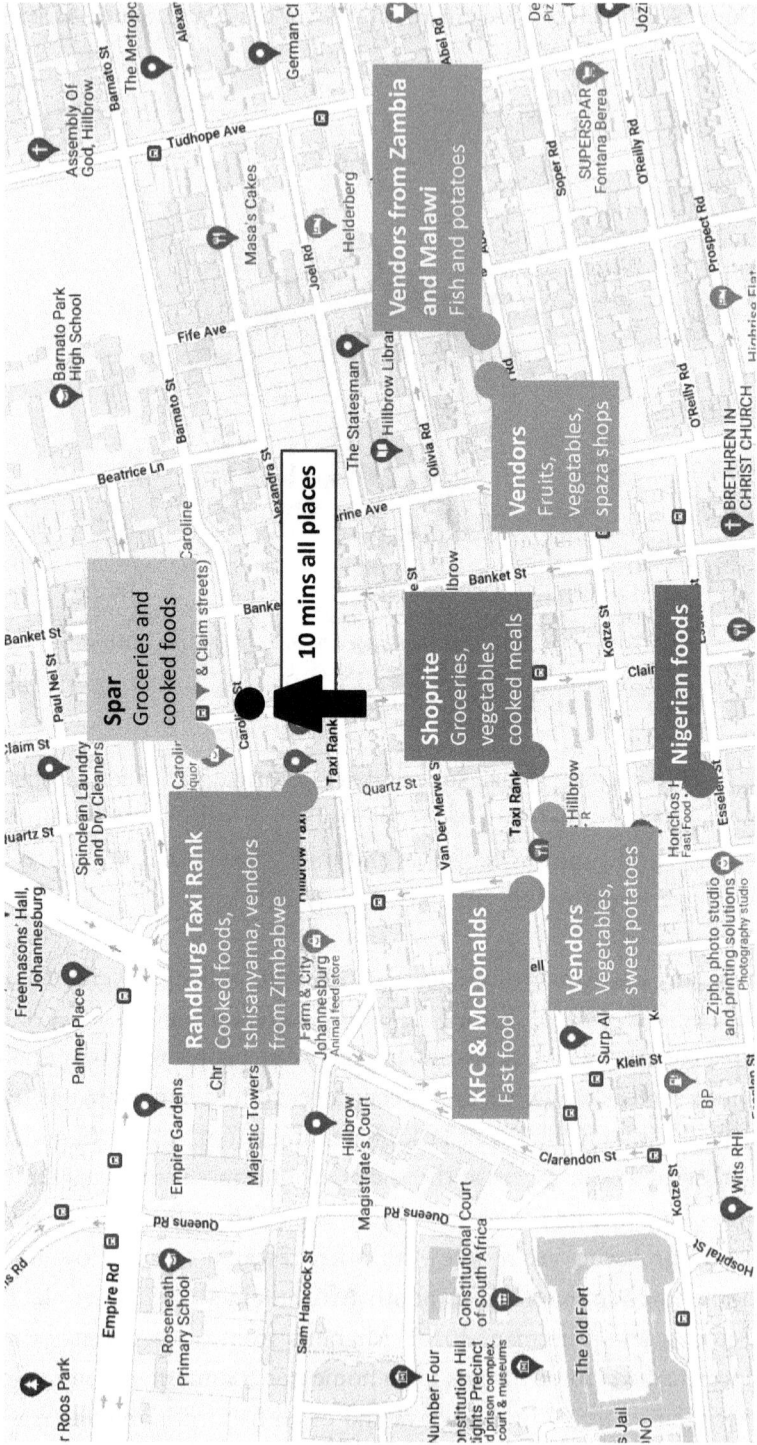

or specialised street vendors. See Figure 7.2 for a sample food map that shows the procurement of Nigerian foods, and fish from vendors from Zambia and Malawi. This practice of seeking out places to buy familiar foods may be seen as a means of maintaining identity and connections to home (Raman, 2011; Johnston and Longhurst, 2012).

Participants used these shopping strategies in the context of food budgets that were well below the cost of a healthy diet (BFAP, 2020). Not everyone shared their food budgets, but among those who did, people mentioned a range of R300–500 per person per month. As one woman explained:

> There are things that we wish we could have but we cannot afford ... like the vegetables that we normally have, we don't have enough [money], so we buy the cheapest, so we don't have variety ... and meat, we want to buy quality meat but since we don't have money, we just buy around and it's not quality meat (Buhle, 14 June 2019).

The exception to the rule of all food being purchased in Johannesburg was food received from family members in rural areas. This flow of food from rural to urban areas happened in different ways. In one case, a woman from Zimbabwe received food from her mother. The woman's brother drove a bus, so her mother was able to send many foods from home – peanuts, honey, sorghum, sweet potatoes and others (Sithabile, 26 July 2018). The direction of this flow, from the migrant-sending household in Zimbabwe to the migrant in Johannesburg, contradicts much of the literature on remittances (Pendleton et al., 2006; Makina, 2013; Tawodzera and Crush, 2016), though there is some evidence of bidirectional food flows between internal migrants in cities and their families in rural areas (Frayne, 2005; Abbots, 2016; Crush and Caesar, 2016; Bailey, 2017). Among South African internal migrants to Johannesburg, it was more common to bring food from the rural area back to the city after visits. As one woman from KwaZulu-Natal indicated, 'In December we can go and take some [mealies, spinach, butternut]' (Ayanda, 31 July 2018).

Participants lamented the fact that they must purchase all their food in Johannesburg. An older woman from the rural Eastern Cape explained, 'At home we had livestock, we could drink milk… Now we have to buy if we want milk. Nothing is for free' (Sarah, 27 July 2018). Several participants expressed a wish to grow their food in Johannesburg but indicated they did not have sufficient space.

> I love to plough and grow things there, and then at the end of the day I don't buy, I don't spend any money, I just pick it from my garden and use them. Otherwise here in Joburg, I'm suffering because when I want a vegetable I must go to the shop and buy it (Lesedi, 26 July 2018).

Participants recognised that the freshly produced and foraged foods of their childhoods were healthier than the food they buy in Johannesburg. A woman from the rural Eastern Cape explained:

> That time, when I was growing up, healthy eating was natural, because we ate … wild spinach, we didn't have even this one that we plant. There was wild spinach … we ate the pumpkin buds, for the veggies. … It was healthy (Ruth, 31 July 2018).

Participants also indicated that foraging was on the decline in the rural areas. This was due to the arrival of formal food retail, and the reduction of 'wild' spaces due to other land uses, as well as a matter of status. In KwaZulu-Natal, one participant said people still gather wild plants 'because some people, they're still struggling' (Ayanda, 31 July 2018).

Changes in food preparation practices

A major change in food preparation was a shift from making foods from scratch to consuming more convenience foods, again in line with the literature on the nutrition transition. The childhood food maps showed that most participants grew maize at home, and then either ground it into mealie meal at home or took it to a local mill to grind. Similarly, some mentioned making jam at home, using fruit from their own fruit trees. Others mentioned making steamed maize bread. Vegetables and beans from the garden were cooked from scratch, and even livestock was butchered at home on special occasions. In contrast, contemporary food preparation involves buying prepared and processed items like processed starch, tinned beans, jam, bread and processed meats.

A second shift had to do with the use of cooking oil and spice mixes. As Thandeka explained:

> We used to boil, not fry, not putting spices, not putting all those things. When we are there in the rural area, we just put the water and salt and boil and then we eat. Now you're putting oil, you're putting Rajah [a brand of spice mix], you're putting spices, you put all those things. You end up not tasting the food anymore. You're tasting the spices (Thandeka, 31 July 2018).

Like many participants, Thandeka felt this change was unhealthy. 'I eat too much oily food, seriously honestly. I want to change, maybe to eat steamed vegetables, no oil ... because I want to lose weight also. And oil makes you sick' (Thandeka, 31 July 2018). Some participants indicated that they could feel it in their bodies when they ate unhealthy foods, that they didn't feel 'right' after eating them. In comparison, they told me they did feel 'right' in their bodies after eating healthy meals together during our sessions.

The infrastructure for cooking is also different. In the childhood food mapping some people indicated going to the river or the well to fetch water, and to the bush to fetch firewood, in order to cook. In Johannesburg, people used electricity to cook, or in a few cases paraffin. Some participants stayed in overcrowded flats without access to full kitchens, with just a small stove or hot plate in their rooms. The costs associated with cooking fuel led to dietary changes; for example, one female participant who cooked on a paraffin stove indicated that fuel was too expensive to make foods such as samp and beans, which need to cook for a long time. Several participants missed some of their traditional dishes but said these simply took too much time and fuel to cook. The shift from traditional foods to convenience foods is a well-documented aspect of the nutrition transition (Popkin, 2002a; Crush et al., 2011; Steyn et al., 2011).

Changes in consumption practices

A major change from participants' rural homes to their lives in Johannesburg was the shift to eating outside the home. This included prepared food from street vendors as well as the occasional visit to a fast-food restaurant.

> At home there, we didn't have things like pizza because in rural areas you know, there are no such things, so when I came here, yeah, I ate a lot of things. ... Pizza is one of them ... it's shameful for someone to be seen buying cooked food, at home, unless if you are a traveller... So, if you buy you are considered as a lazy person (Buhle, 14 June 2019).

While there was stigma attached to eating outside the home when Buhle was growing up, the opposite is true in Johannesburg. Eating at a fast-food restaurant is seen as aspirational (Steyn et al., 2011; Kroll, 2017). Most participants indicated that they did so when they were able and considered it a treat.

> Sometimes I go to Nando's, I go to McDonald's for burgers, sometimes, once in a blue moon a burger, ne? It's not always ... once a month (Lesedi, 26 July 2018).

Another change in eating practices was related to sharing food with people outside of the household. In the rural areas, such sharing was more common. Ayanda talked about the neighbours insisting on giving her food in the rural areas. 'And the food, [they] say no no no, you can't go without eating, eat. It's Christmas. Eish those days, I miss them' (Ayanda, 31 July 2018). Lesedi explained that such practices were common in the past, but have declined even in rural areas today:

> My mother told us that she used to cook with a big pot, and then maybe three families are going to come and eat there at home. And then sometimes the other family again will cook, and then those families must go there and eat. It was just like that. ... Now, that thing doesn't happen anymore. Or just because the elders

are now gone, they are dead, so it's us who have gone away. Somebody's in Cape Town, somebody's in Durban, somebody's there. We don't meet anymore (Lesedi, 26 July 2018).

Even in rural areas, the practice of sharing among households faded as the elders died and the younger people migrated to cities. The concept of 'eating from one pot' also faded as economic conditions in rural areas worsened (Mosoetsa, 2011). Migrants could not take the practice with them to Johannesburg where food is too expensive to share with others. Participants indicated that they regretted this loss of communal eating, though some sought to connect with family members by eating out at a (fast-food) restaurant occasionally when finances allowed. Commensality, or eating together, helps to solidify social bonds and relations of reciprocity, so the inability to share meals may contribute to a sense of social isolation (Johnston and Longhurst, 2012; Bailey, 2017; Kudejira, 2021).

DISCUSSION: ISSUES OF STATUS, HEALTH, IDENTITY AND COMMENSALITY AMONG MIGRANTS

In line with the literature on the nutrition transition and dietary acculturation, participants in this study experienced a shift from more wholesome traditional diets to more processed foods (Baker et al., 2020). Many of the factors influencing these shifts are also what one might expect from the literature, such as lack of availability of traditional foods, prohibitive costs, time constraints, limited kitchen infrastructure and fuel costs (Crush et al., 2011; Patil et al., 2009).

A more interesting aspect of the research study emerged from participants' experiences of dietary changes in relation to questions of status and identity. The aspirational nature of certain foods, or ways of eating, is a factor in their rejection or adoption. Research suggests that in South Africa, fast foods are considered high status and modern (Kroll, 2017). At the same time, traditional foods may be seen as old-fashioned or associated with poverty (Modi et al., 2006; Stern et al., 2010). In a conversation with the participants about traditional healthy diets, one said, 'We thought it was because we were poor, that's why we were eating like that.' In addition, several participants mentioned that even in the rural areas, only those who could not afford to buy vegetables would go and harvest wild ones. This suggests that perceived status is an important aspect of acculturation, and of the nutrition transition. A long colonial history of disparaging indigenous foods in favour of 'modern', 'Western' foods needs to be actively counteracted.

The fact that many participants still long for those 'poverty foods' as familiar and healthy indicates that there is still interest in them. Indeed, participants frequently commented on the healthfulness of traditional foods, and how they felt 'right' when eating them, compared to when they ate processed or fast foods. Time, fuel and cost constraints were barriers to eating healthier traditional foods, where these items were available.

While most participants referred to some food items they missed from their homes, only international migrants mentioned going to special vendors to seek out foods from home. Research on acculturation, and on migration and belonging, points to the maintenance of identity as a reason to continue eating traditional foods (Morasso and Zittoun, 2014; Abbots, 2016; Bailey, 2017; Nyamnjoh, 2018). However, another factor may be that international migrants were less able to visit home to eat and bring back traditional foods than internal migrants.

The loss of the sense of connection that came from more communal ways of eating in rural areas was another important aspect of participants' experiences. The shift from food production to purchasing, and from rural homesteads to urban flats, meant that hosting large gatherings and sharing food was not possible in Johannesburg. Getting out of cramped accommodation to sit and eat fast food with family members at month-end was one way of finding some connection. While the fast foods eaten are neither traditional nor healthy, they provide a space for commensality that may help overcome the alienation of migration (Johnston and Longhurst, 2012; Bailey, 2017).

CONCLUSION AND RECOMMENDATIONS

By examining individuals' perceptions and experiences of dietary changes shaped by global and national forces, we are better able to

182

see the local uniqueness and complexity of the nutrition transition. Food/nutrition and health interventions by government or civil society organisations need to address the full spectrum of internal and cross-border migrants' changing food practices. Such interventions must recognise that people's responses to their environments, despite constraints, involve questions of status, health, identity and a desire for community.

In group discussions, the participants considered possible solutions to some of the food challenges they faced. A proposed intervention was to have community kitchens or subsidised canteens that serve healthy, traditional foods. This would address the longing for traditional foods, issues of access and affordability, as well as the desire for more connection around food. It might also address some of the migrants' challenges related to kitchen infrastructure and fuel costs.

Another proposal was to have more space for community gardens, which would enable migrants to produce some of their own food rather than purchasing it, and to grow foods they missed from home. Many researchers have rightly criticised the over-reliance of government on urban agriculture programmes to the detriment of other food security interventions (Battersby et al., 2015). However, past research indicates that some cross-border migrants in Johannesburg brought seeds to an urban garden nearby so that they could access foods from their home countries (Kesselman, 2017). While studies in other countries have highlighted the value of urban agriculture in providing culturally appropriate foods to migrants (Peña, 2006), there is limited research on this in a Johannesburg context (Lewis, 2013).

Policy responses to the nutrition transition tend to focus on individual behaviour change, often through education, or on shifting food environments through national-level regulations and taxes (Roberto et al., 2015; Hawkes et al., 2017;). Yet the experiences of these migrants suggest that local-level, collective solutions such as community kitchens and community gardens, with a focus on traditional foods, might be a more effective approach.

In terms of further research, three issues emerged. First, it would be enlightening to explore the dietary shifts happening in the rural areas that the migrants left behind. Second, it would also be useful to compare changes in rural South Africa with changes in the rural-sending areas of cross-border migrants (such as Zimbabwe, DRC and Burundi). Finally, additional research exploring the two-way flow of foods and food practices between urban and rural areas would help to get a better sense of how these spaces are mutually shaping each other's diets.

REFERENCES

Abbots, E. J. 2016. 'Approaches to food and migration: Rootedness, being and belonging', in Klein, J. and Watson, J. (eds), *The Handbook of Food and Anthropology*. London: Bloomsbury, 115–132.

Bailey, A. 2017. 'The migrant suitcase: Food, belonging and commensality among Indian migrants in the Netherlands'. *Appetite*, 110, 51–60.

Baker, P., Machado, P., Santos, T., Sievert, K., Backholer, K., Hadjikakou, M., Russell, C., Huse, O., Bell, C., Scrinis, G., Worsley, A., Friel, S. and Lawrence, M. 2020. 'Ultra-processed foods and the nutrition transition: Global, regional and national trends, food systems transformations and political economy drivers'. *Obesity Reviews*, 21(12), 1–22.

Boatemaa, S., Drimie, S. and Pereira, L. 2018. 'Addressing food and nutrition security in South Africa: A review of policy responses since 2002'. *African Journal of Agricultural and Resource Economics*, 13(3), 264–279.

Battersby, J., Haysom, G., Kroll, F., Tawodzera, G. and Marshak, M. 2015. 'Looking beyond urban agriculture: Extending urban food policy responses'. Policy Brief – South African Cities Network (SACN).

Bureau for Food and Agricultural Policy (BFAP). 23 March 2020. 'How South Africans spend their food budgets', https://www.grainsa.co.za/upload/files/2020.03.23%20BFAP%20COVID%2019%20Brief%202%20-%20How%20South%20Africans%20spend%20their%20food%20budgets.pdf, accessed 5 October 2023.

Cockx, L., Colen, L. and De Weerdt, J. 2018. 'From corn to popcorn? Urbanization and dietary change: Evidence from rural–urban migrants in Tanzania'. *World Development*, 110, 140–159.

Cohen, E., Amougou, N., Ponty, A., Loinger-beck, J., Nkuintchua, T., Monteillet, N., Bernard, J. Y., Saïd-Mohamed, R., Holdsworth, M. and Pasquet, P. 2017. 'Nutrition transition and biocultural determinants of obesity among Cameroonian migrants in urban Cameroon and France'. *International Journal of Environmental Research and Public Health*, 14, 696.

Crush, J. 2012. 'Migration, development and urban food security'. Urban Food Security Series No. 8, https://scholars.wlu.ca/cgi/viewcontent.

cgi?article=1008&context=afsun, accessed 5 October 2023.

Crush, J. and Caesar, M. 2016. 'Food remittances: Migration and food security in Africa'. Southern African Migration Programme Migration Policy Series No. 72, https://scholars.wlu.ca/samp/26/, accessed 5 October 2023.

Crush, J., Frayne, B. and McLachlan, M. 2011. 'Rapid urbanization and the nutrition transition in Southern Africa'. Urban Food Security Series No. 7, https://afsun.org/wp-content/uploads/2013/09/AFSUN_7.pdf, accessed 5 October 2023.

Dallimore, A., De Kadt, J., Hamann, C. and Mkhize, S. 2021. 'Quality of Life Survey 6 (2020/ 21): Municipal report: City of Tshwane'. Gauteng City Region Observatory, Johannesburg.

De Wet, T., Patel, L., Korth, M. and Forrester, C. 2008. 'Johannesburg poverty and livelihoods study'. Centre for Social Development in Africa University of Johannesburg, https://www.ncr.org.za/documents/pages/research-reports/mar08/Livelihoods%20study.pdf, accessed 18 November 2023.

Delavari, M., Sønderlund, A. L., Swinburn, B., Mellor, D. and Renzaho, A. 2013. 'Acculturation and obesity among migrant populations in high income countries – a systematic review'. *BMC Public Health*, 13, 458.

Denham, D. and Gladstone, F. 2020. 'Making sense of food system transformation in Mexico'. *Geoforum*, 115, 67–80.

Department of Health. (n.d.). *National Strategic Plan for the Prevention and Control of Non-Communicable Diseases 2020–2025*. Pretoria: Department of Health.

Di Rocco, A. M. and Cuvi, N. 2014. 'An ethnographic approach to the nutrition transition in Ecuador'. *The Journal of Global Health*, 4(1), 6–9.

Drimie, S., Faber, M., Vearey, J. and Nunez, L. 2013. 'Dietary diversity of formal and informal residents in Johannesburg, South Africa'. *BMC Public Health*, 13, 911.

Finnis, E. 2007. 'The political ecology of dietary transitions: Changing production and consumption patterns in the Kolli Hills, India'. *Agriculture and Human Values*, 24, 343–353.

Ford, N. D., Patel, S. A. and Narayan, K. M. V. 2017. 'Obesity in low- and middle-income countries: Burden, drivers, and emerging challenges'. *Annual Review of Public Health*, 38, 145–164.

Frayne, B. 2005. 'Survival of the poorest: Migration and food security in Namibia', in Mougeot, L. (ed.), *Agropolis: The social, political, and environmental dimensions of urban agriculture*. London: Routledge, 31–50.

Hawkes, C. 2006. 'Uneven dietary development: Linking the policies and processes of globalization with the nutrition transition, obesity and diet-related chronic diseases'. *Globalization and Health*, 2, 1–18.

Hawkes, C., Harris, J. and Gillespie, S. 2017. 'Urbanization and the nutrition transition'. *Global Food Policy Report*, 4, 34–41.

Hiropoulos, A. 2020. 'South Africa, migration and xenophobia: Deconstructing the perceived migration crisis and its influence on the xenophobic reception of migrants'. *Contemporary Justice Review: Issues in Criminal, Social, and Restorative Justice*, 23(1), 104–121.

Hunter-Adams, J. and Rother, H. A. 2016. 'Pregnant in a foreign city: A qualitative analysis of diet and nutrition for cross-border migrant women in Cape Town, South Africa'. *Appetite*, 103, 403–410.

Igumbor, E., Sanders, D., Puoane, T., Tsolekile, L., Schwarz, C., Purdy, C., Swart, R., Durão, S. and Hawkes, C. 2012. '"Big Food" the consumer food environment, health and the policy response in South Africa'. *PLoS Medicine*, 9(7), 1–7.

Iversen, P., Marais, D., Du Plessis, L. and Herselman, M. 2012. 'Assessing nutrition intervention programmes that addressed malnutrition among young children in South Africa between 1994–2010'. *African Journal of Food, Agriculture, Nutrition and Development*, 12(50), 5928–5945.

Janowski, M. 2012. 'Introduction: Consuming memories of home in constructing the present and imagining the future'. *Food and Foodways*, 20(3/4), 175–186.

Johnston, L. and Longhurst, R. 2012. 'Embodied geographies of food, belonging and hope in multicultural Hamilton, Aotearoa New Zealand'. *Geoforum*, 43(2), 325–331.

Kesselman, B. 2017. 'Sowing the seeds of food sovereignty or cultivating consent? The potential and limitations of Johannesburg's community gardens'. PhD Thesis, University of KwaZulu-Natal.

Kesselman, B. 2022. 'Participatory action research for food justice in Johannesburg: Seeking a more immediate impact for engaged research', in Bezuidenhout, A., Mnwana, S. and Von Holdt, K. (eds), *Critical Engagement with Public Sociology: A Perspective from the Global South*. Bristol: Bristol University Press, 171–191.

Kroll, F. 2017. 'Foodways of the poor in South Africa: How poor people get food, what they eat, and how this shapes our food system'. Institute for Poverty, Land and Agrarian Studies (PLAAS), https://repository.uwc. ac.za/xmlui/bitstream/handle/10566/4302/pb_48_foodways_of_the_ poor_in_south_africa_2017.pdf?sequence=1&isAllowed=y, accessed 4 December 2023.

Kudejira, D. 2021. 'The role of "food" in network formation and the social integration of undocumented Zimbabwean migrant farmworkers in the Blouberg-Molemole area of Limpopo, South Africa'. *Anthropology Southern Africa*, 44(1), 16–32.

Lakika, D. and Drimie, S. 2019. 'The food we eat here weakens us': Food practices and health beliefs among Congolese forced migrants in South Africa – a case study of Yeoville in Johannesburg'. *African Journal of Food, Agriculture, Nutrition and Development*, 19(2), 14372–14392.

Leatherman, T., Hoke, M. and Goodman, A. 2016. 'Local nutrition in global contexts: Critical biocultural perspectives on the nutrition transition in Mexico', in Zuckerman, M. and Martin, D. L. (eds), *New Directions in Biocultural Anthropology*. New Jersey: John Wiley & Sons, 49–65.

Lewis, M. 2013. 'Urban agriculture, livelihood strategies and commodity networks in inner-city Johannesburg: A case study of a vegetable co-operative in Bertrams', in Greenberg, S. (ed.), *Smallholders and Agro-Food Value Chains in South Africa: Emerging practices, emerging challenges*. Institute for Poverty, Land and Agrarian Studies (PLAAS), University of the Western Cape, 74–79.

Macintyre, U., Kruger, H. S., Venter, C. and Vorster, H. 2002. 'Dietary intakes of an African population in different stages of transition in the North West Province, South Africa: The THUSA study'. *Nutrition Research*, 22, 239–256.

Makina, D. 2013. 'Migration and characteristics of remittance senders in South Africa'. *International Migration*, 51(SUPPL.1), e148–e158.

Martínez, A. 2014. 'Reconsidering acculturation in dietary change research among Latino immigrants: Challenging the preconditions of US migration'. *Ethnic Health*, 18(2), 115–135.

Mchiza, Z., Steyn, N., Hill, J., Kruger, A., Schönfeldt, H., Nel, J. and Wentzel-Viljoen, E. 2015. 'A review of dietary surveys in the adult South African population from 2000 to 2015'. *Nutrition*, 7, 8227–8250.

Modi, M., Modi, A. and Hendriks, S. 2006. 'Potential role for wild vegetables in household food security: A preliminary case study in KwaZulu-Natal, South Africa'. *African Journal of Food, Agriculture, Nutrition and Development*, 6(1), 1–13.

Morasso, S. G. and Zittoun, T. 2014. 'The trajectory of food as a symbolic resource for international migrants'. *Outlines*, 15(1), 28–48.

Naidu, M. and Nzuza, N. 2013. 'Food and maintaining identity for migrants: Sierra Leone migrants in Durban'. *Journal of Sociology and Social Anthropology*, 4(3), 193–200.

Nichols, C. 2017. 'Millets, milk and Maggi: Contested processes of the nutrition transition in rural India'. *Agriculture and Human Values*, 34(4), 871–885.

Nyamnjoh, H. M. 2018. 'Food, memory and transnational gastronomic culture among Cameroonian migrants in Cape Town, South Africa'. *Anthropology Southern Africa*, 41(5), 25–40.

Osei-Kwasi, H., Boateng, D., Asamane, E. A., Akparibo, R. and Holdsworth, M. 2023. 'Transitioning food environments and diets of African migrants: Implications for non-communicable diseases'. *Proceedings of the Nutrition Society*, 82, 69–79.

Osei-Kwasi, H., Powell, K., Nicolau, M. and Holdsworth, M. 2017. 'The influence of migration on dietary practices of Ghanaians living in the United Kingdom: A qualitative study'. *Annals of Human Biology*, 44(5), 454–463.

Patil, C., Hadley, C. and Djona, P. 2009. 'Unpacking dietary acculturation among new Americans: Results from formative research with African refugees'. *Journal of Immigrant and Minority Health*, 11, 342–358.

Peberdy, S., Crush, J. and Msibi, N. 2004. 'Migrants in the city of Johannesburg'. Southern African Migration Project.

Peña, D. G. 2006. 'Farmers feeding families: Agroecology in south central Los Angeles'. *Keynote Address Presented to the National Association for Chicana and Chicano Studies*, 1–15.

Pendleton, W., Crush, J., Campbell, E., Green, T., Simelane, H., Tevera, D. and de Vletter, F. 2006. 'Migration, remittances, and development in Southern Africa'. Southern African Migration Project.

Peters, R., Amugsi, D. A., Mberu, B., Ensor, T., Hill, A. J., Newell, J. N. and Elsey, H. 2019. 'Nutrition transition, overweight and obesity among rural-to-urban migrant women in Kenya'. *Public Health Nutrition*, 22(17), 3200–3210.

Petersen, L. M. and Charman, A. J. E. 2018. 'The scope and scale of the informal food economy of South African urban residential townships: Results of a small-area micro-enterprise census'. *Development Southern Africa*, 35(1), 1–23.

Peyton, S., Moseley, W. and Battersby, J. 2015. 'Implications of supermarket expansion on urban food security in Cape Town, South Africa'. *African Geographical Review*, 34(1), 36–54.

Popkin, B. M. 2002a. 'An overview on the nutrition transition and its health implications: The Bellagio meeting'. *Public Health Nutrition*, 5(1a), 93–103.

Popkin, B. M. 2002b. 'The dynamics of the dietary transition in the developing world', in Caballero, B. and Popkin, B. (eds), *The Nutrition Transition: Diet and disease in the developing world*. Cambridge: Academic Press, 111–128.

Popkin, B. M., Adair, L. S. and Ng, S. W. 2012. 'Global nutrition transition and the pandemic of obesity in developing countries'. *Nutrition Reviews*, 70(1), 3–21.

Popkin, B. M. and Ng, S. W. 2022. 'The nutrition transition to a stage of high obesity and noncommunicable disease prevalence dominated by ultra-processed foods is not inevitable'. *Obesity Reviews*, 23(1), 1–18.

Raman, P. 2011. 'Me in place, and the place in me'. *Food, Culture and Society*, 14(2), 165–180.

Roberto, C. A., Swinburn, B., Hawkes, C., Huang, T. T. K., Costa, S. A., Ashe, M., Zwicker, L., Cawley, J. H. and Brownell, K. D. 2015. 'Patchy progress on obesity prevention: Emerging examples, entrenched barriers, and new thinking'. *The Lancet*, 385(9985), 2400–2409.

Rudolph, M., Kroll, F., Ruysenaar, S. and Dlamini, T. 2012. 'The state of food insecurity in Johannesburg'. Urban Food Security Series No. 12, https://scholars.wlu.ca/cgi/viewcontent.cgi?article=1011&context=afsun, accessed 15 December 2023.

Sadiddin, A., Cattaneo, A., Cirillo, M. and Miller, M. 2019. 'Food insecurity as a determinant of international migration: Evidence from Sub-Saharan Africa'. *Food Security*, 11(3), 515–530.

Satia, J. A. 2010. 'Dietary acculturation and the nutrition transition: An overview'. *Applied Physiology, Nutrition and Metabolism*, 35(2), 219–223.

Satia-Abouta, J. 2003. 'Dietary acculturation: Definition, process, assessment and implications'. *International Journal of Human Ecology*, 4(1), 71–86.

Satia-Abouta, J., Patterson, R. E., Neuhouser, M. L. and Elder, J. 2002. 'Dietary acculturation: Applications to nutrition research and dietetics'. *Journal of the American Dietetic Association*, 102(8), 1105–1118).

Segatti, A. 2011. 'Migration to South Africa: Regional challenges versus national instruments and interests', in Segatti, A. and Landau, L. (eds), *Contemporary Migration to South Africa: A regional development issue*. New York: World Bank and Agence Française de Development, 9–30.

Statistics South Africa. 2022. *Quarterly Labour Force Survey* (2nd quarter). Statistics South Africa.

Stern, R., Puoane, T. and Tsolekile, L. 2010. 'An exploration into the determinants of noncommunicable diseases among rural-to-urban migrants in periurban South Africa'. *Preventing Chronic Disease*, 7(6).

Steyn, N., Labadarios, D. and Nel, J. 2011. 'Factors which influence the consumption of street foods and fast foods in South Africa: A national survey'. *Nutrition Journal*, 10, 104.

Steyn, N. P. and Mchiza, Z. J. 2014. 'Obesity and the nutrition transition in Sub-Saharan Africa'. *Annals of the New York Academy of Sciences*, 1311, 88–101.

Stupar, D., Eide, W. B., Bourne, L., Hendricks, M., Iversen, P. O. and Wandel, M. 2012. 'The nutrition transition and the human right to adequate food for adolescents in the Cape Town metropolitan area: Implications for nutrition policy'. *Food Policy*, 37(3), 199–206.

Sutton, D. 2001. *Remembrance of Repasts: An anthropology of food and memory*. Oxford: Berg.

Tawodzera, G. and Crush, J. 2016. 'Migration and food security: Zimbabwean migrants in urban South Africa'. Urban Food Security Series No. 23, https://scholars.wlu.ca/cgi/viewcontent.cgi?article=1031&context=hcp, accessed 15 December 2023.

Temple, N. and Steyn, N. 2011. 'The cost of a healthy diet: A South African perspective'. *Nutrition*, 27, 505–508.

Tuomainen, H. 2009. 'Ethnic identity, (post)colonialism and foodways'. *Food, Culture and Society*, 12(4), 525–554.

Vorster, H., Venter, C., Wissing, M. and Margetts, B. 2005. 'The nutrition and health transition in the North West Province of South Africa: A review of the THUSA (Transition and Health during Urbanisation of South Africans) study'. *Public Health Nutrition*, 8(5), 480–490.

Vorster, H. H., Kruger, A. and Margetts, B. M. 2011. 'The nutrition transition in Africa: Can it be steered into a more positive direction?'. *Nutrients*, 3, 429–441.

Walker, A. C. 2023. 'Let us govern around the kitchen table: Embodying the guild's anti-colonial commitments: Presidential Address 2023 Annual Meeting. *Religious Education*, 1–9.

Walls, H. L., Johnston, D., Mazalale, J. and Chirwa, E. W. 2018. 'Why we are still failing to measure the nutrition transition?'. *BMJ Global Health*, 3(1), 1–3.

Wentzel-Viljoen, E., Lee, S., Laubscher, R. and Vorster, H. H. 2018. 'Accelerated nutrition transition in the North West Province of South Africa: Results from the prospective urban and rural epidemiology (PURE-NWP-SA) cohort study, 2005 to 2010'. *Public Health Nutrition*, 21(14), 2630–2641.

World Health Organization (WHO). 2017. 'The double burden of malnutrition'. Policy brief, World Health Organization, Geneva.

EIGHT

Exploring the structural nexus between migration, retail conglomerates and township spaza shops

AMUZWENI NGOMA AND
WANDILE M. NGCAWENI

INTRODUCTION

The year 2023 marked the 60th anniversary of the African Union (AU). At its 50th anniversary in 2013, eminent scholar Amina Mama contended that for Africans, political independence was intricately 'rooted in very clear material and political interests' and that African economies remained structurally and 'deeply unequal' (Mama, 2014: 60). She called on African leaders and states to recover a Pan-African vision embedded in 'the freedom to organise' African economies to suit Africa, including the freedom to choose 'how to organise labour, production and consumption' processes (Mama, 2014: 61).

The spread of supermarkets, which includes their sales of food products, has been referred to as the 'supermarket revolution' or 'supermarketisation' (Das Nair, 2019: 4). Supermarkets have become the key source of food consumption in rural and urban areas and across all income groups (Das Nair, 2019: 4; Ashman, 2023). Supermarketisation has also taken place alongside internationalisation (Das Nair, 2019). Under the liberal and free trade economic regime of the southern African region, foreign direct investment (FDI) has been one of the key conduits of supermarketisation. Through traders in the Southern African Development Community (SADC) region, 'the expansion of supermarkets is driving important changes in the trade of food and household products' (Das Nair, 2019: 25).

This chapter is an exploration of the broad evolution of the southern African political economy. It explores how the structure of the southern African economy affects the township economy, with a particular focus on informal and formal traders (including spaza shops, supermarkets, etc.). This has significant implications and outcomes for the livelihoods of both foreign and South African nationals. Conceptually, the chapter draws on the intersecting concepts of regional integration, internationalisation, supermarketisation, and the informal and township economy. It explores the ways in which internationalisation and supermarketisation affect foreign and South African national traders operating in South African townships. The chapter also discusses the dual structure of the South African economy in order to give a sense of the contexts in which the economy operates.

This chapter calls for a macro strategy linking the development of SADC's informal economy and local township economies as the region's trading class. It argues for concerted efforts to reorganise migrant relations in the regional trading class. This would promote bottom-up integration that would build productive capabilities, including among precarious population groups across countries. The chapter concludes that for local enterprises to thrive, it is important to review national industrial, agricultural and competition policies as well as regional integration objectives. The chapter argues that the increasing financialisation of the South African economy, deindustrialisation and missed opportunities for regional support of agro industries affect local economies and enterprises, in negative and positive ways, that economic and migration policies have not caught up with.

The remainder of the chapter is structured as follows: the chapter provides a brief overview of trade in specific sectors and follows with a section that details the informal and formal economic structures of South Africa, the performance of informal enterprises in the country's townships and the challenges they face. The chapter ends by synthesising recommendations aimed at support for regional enterprises.

THE EVOLUTION OF THE SOUTHERN AFRICAN POLITICAL ECONOMY

Snapshot of international migration

South Africa has a dynamic history of domestic and trans-border migration. From before the discovery of diamonds in Kimberley in 1867 and gold in Johannesburg in 1886, the country has been a global site of economic and labour migration. In the post-apartheid period, the country's domestic and trans-border migration flows have been highly dynamic and subject to change. South Africa is recognised as the '"the southern hub" for international migration in Africa and a principal migrant-receiving country in the African Union' (AU, 2022: 13), and is among the top 20 destinations for international migrants globally (World Bank, 2019). In 2015 it became the largest host for international migrants on the continent, having been the second largest host in 2000 (DEL, 2022: 16).

Citing migration estimates by the United Nations Department of Economic and Social Affairs (UNDESA), South Africa's Department of Employment and Labour (DEL) (2022: 16) reports that in 2019 there were about '7,481,000 migrants in the SADC region'. This estimate excluded irregular migrants. South Africa received much of this SADC migrant flow, with 4,036,696 migrants or 54 per cent going to the country. The International Organization for Migration (IOM, 2020) estimated that the total number of migrants living in South Africa in 2019 was 4.22 million or 7.2 per cent of the population. The migrant flow was mixed, comprising asylum seekers, economic migrants and trafficked and smuggled persons, with over 90 per cent of asylum and refugee seekers in South Africa being economic migrants (DEL, 2022: 16). Importantly, the World Bank provides the caveat that international migration 'statistics do not account for irregular or undocumented migrants' (World Bank, 2019: xvi). It cautions that 'anecdotal evidence and unofficial estimates suggest that almost all major migrant-receiving countries face the 'challenge of irregular migration' (2019: xvi).

Post-apartheid South Africa attracts skilled migrants, refugees and asylum seekers (AU, 2022). Migrant flows to South Africa are shaped by intersecting push-and-pull factors. Pull factors include the promise of employment, business, education and training opportunities while push factors include migrants seeking refuge from crises or challenging circumstances in their home countries (AU, 2022). Other main drivers of migration include climate change, social inequality and demographic imbalances. In addition, the World Bank notes that 'policy changes in both origin and destination countries can influence migration decisions and demand for migrant workers' (World Bank, 2019: xvi).

While SADC migration dominates, South Africa has received new migration flows from the rest of the continent and several parts of Asia. This includes economic migrants from 'India, Pakistan, Bangladesh and China, as well as a continuation of immigration from Europe' (DEL, 2022: 16). While South Africa's migrant flow is mixed, most migrants are in search of economic opportunities and are attracted by real and perceived opportunities. Many of them are low-skilled; inflows from the SADC are dominated by unskilled and semi-skilled women. Many are unable to secure formal-sector jobs and instead are employed or self-employed in the urban informal sector. This has resulted in the diversification of the urban informal sector in significant ways, which has, until recently, been inaccessible and received little to no attention from policymakers.

SOUTH AFRICA'S MIGRATION POLICY

The South African government has consistently sought to formulate and implement policy and legislation appropriate to changing global and regional political economies. The government has also sought out more effective developmental responses to amplify the positive benefits

Table 8.1: Total and work-related arrivals in 2015 and 2020 by country of origin

	Total arrivals in South Africa from other African countries, 2015–2020		Work-related arrivals in South Africa from other countries, 2015–2020	
SADC	**2015**	**2020**	**2015**	**2020**
Angola	53,213	16,913	2,017	293
Botswana	1,139,370	277,167	6,081	9,486
Comoros	231	179	14	3
DRC	33,683	10,363	2,122	377
eSwatini	1,649,731	70,933	5,511	27,205
Lesotho	3,369,272	1,029,654	9,491	33,698
Madagascar	3,262	1,026	295	233
Malawi	153,978	63,412	2,747	1,151
Mauritius	20,480	5,556	563	213
Mozambique	1,988,328	628,170	3,198	9,424
Namibia	274,073	90,529	1,058,	3,067
Tanzania	42,198	12,898	767	238
Seychelles	6,615	1,406	67	17
Zambia	183,284	71,430	4,398	3,464
Zimbabwe	3,313,649	1,062,522	91,722	63,966
SADC sub-total	**12,231,337**	**3,742,218**	**130,566**	**152,835**
East and Central Africa	80,160	21,178	5,692	1,261
West Africa	105,912	22,940	6,852	293
North Africa	18,629	5,977	1,626	416
Sub-total	**204,701**	**50,095**	**14,170**	**2,970**
Total	12,436,038	3,792,313	144,706	155,805

Source: AU (2022: 30)

of migration into South Africa while minimising or mitigating the risks and challenges to the country, migrants and nationals (MISTRA, 2022). Migration is also an 'important factor in long-term development planning, income generation, education, and health facilities, among other things' (MISTRA, 2022: 110). Consequently, the post-apartheid migrant policy has been reviewed and amended several times since 1998. For example, the Refugees Act of 1998 has undergone six amendments in 2002, 2008, 2011, 2015, 2017 and 2020 (AU, 2022). In the post-

Covid-19 period, the DEL initiated a review process of South Africa's labour migration policy and published a draft for public engagement in 2022. The DEL acknowledges that South Africa's migration policies have addressed the dynamic change in migration flows into South Africa 'haphazardly and with limited attention paid to the guidance provided by international and regional standards and frameworks' (DEL, 2022: 7). In tandem with the many changes in migration flows into the country, South African social attitudes to migrants have been affected and have attracted critiques from many quarters, including academia and mainstream media.

Table 8.1 indicates the total number of arrivals in South Africa and work-related arrivals for 2015 and 2020 by country of origin. This was a period of significant reduction in the granting of asylum and refugee permits. For the SADC region, the highest numbers of arrivals were from Lesotho in 2015 and from Zimbabwe in 2020. The highest work-related arrivals in 2015 and 2020 were also from Zimbabwe, with Lesotho coming in second and eSwatini third.

Southern African region: Power and economic performance

The economic structure of SADC is closely bound up with that of South Africa. Schoeman (2003: 363) asserts 'South Africa is now often labelled an emerging power, apparently referring to its position as a regional leader and its position in the broader or global political system as a possible middle power' (Schoeman, 2003: 349). The National Development Plan (NDP) contends that South Africa is an emerging economy, which aims to be a developmental state (NPC, 2011). The Macro-Social Report (MISTRA, 2022) also measures South Africa as a developing country compared with its counterparts. In the post-apartheid era, South Africa has grown into a regional big power. An International Futures model reveals that by 2040 South Africa and Angola will be the region's heavyweights, with South Africa leading. Tanzania is expected to be the third biggest regional power (Lipper and Benton, 2020: 19).

In the post-apartheid era, South Africa rapidly expanded into the African market economy (Daniel et al., 2003: 372–373). The international gradual liberalisation of trade policies was beneficial for South Africa's rapid 'economic penetration of the African market' (Daniel et al., 2003: 373). It facilitated South Africa's penetration of regional economic structures, which were characterised by a 'deregulated market economy with minimal state/government intervention' (Daniel et al., 2003: 374). Africa's agricultural value chain analysis shows that South Africa 'is a "hub" country and is by far the most important single player in the sector, and the most important exporter' (Tralac, 2022).

Although the SADC economy is tightly integrated, this does not benefit countries and populations equally. The African Development Bank (AfDB) reports that in the current period, the region's economic performance is subdued, and heavily affected by South Africa's low economic growth and energy crisis. South Africa is the SADC's largest economy and trading partner (AfDB, 2023). Growth in SADC 'decelerated the most, to about 2.5 per cent in 2022 from 4.3 per cent in 2021. This slowdown reflects subdued growth in South Africa, as higher interest rates, weak domestic demand, and persistent power outages weighed on the economy' (AfDB, 2023: 2). The AfDB asserts that with 'the right policy interventions, growth could recover to 2.7 per cent in 2024' (2023: 2).

While an open SADC economy has benefited South African firms, the SADC region continues to struggle with serious structural issues. The SADC Industrialisation Strategy and Roadmap (SISR) 2015–2063 targets a regional GDP rate of 7 per cent. The region's sectoral structure is dominated by the service sector. The manufacturing sector's share of GDP is about 12 per cent, with a target of 30 per cent by 2030. According to the SISR report, in 2015, intra-SADC trade was still around 20 per cent (23 per cent by 2022): far less than other regions such as Asia (30 per cent) and the EU (60 per cent). Low intra-regional trade is associated with a low share of manufactured exports to total exports of around 3 per cent, a far cry from the target of 50 per cent of total exports by 2030.

The constraints on the SADC region's infrastructure impede economic development and regional trade. Efforts to improve transboundary infrastructure through the Regional Infrastructure Development Master Plan (RIDMP) 2012–2027 have not had the desired effect on trade. The AfDB estimates that Africa has an annual

Figure 8.1: Real GDP growth: Annual per cent change

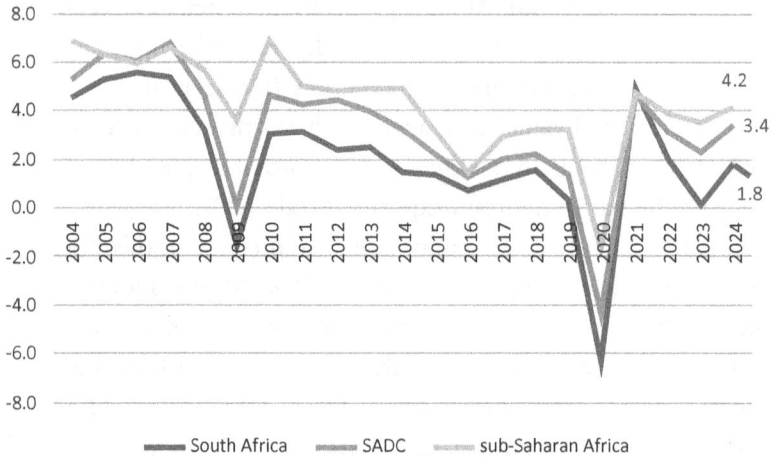

Source: IMF (2017)

infrastructure shortfall of US$130–170 billion (AfDB, 2018). This gap directly affects SADC member states' abilities to meet the aspirations of the African Union's Agenda 2063 and to achieve Sustainable Development Goal (SDG) targets.

The structure of the South African economy has changed over time. In the post-apartheid era, it is characterised by deindustrialisation and de-agrarianisation. This has been accompanied by a rise in the service sector, dominated by finance, with the digital sector also rising. New retail and telecom conglomerates have emerged to dominate the southern African economy.

South Africa's corporate power dominates the southern African region, as illustrated in Table 8.2. A survey cited by Ford (2023)[1] shows South African companies contributing 67 per cent of the top 250 companies in the southern African region. The top 20 companies in the region are in the sectors of finance, consumer non-cyclicals, consumer services, telecommunications and non-energy materials.

---

1 This is the total value by market capitalisation on Africa's stock exchanges at 31 March 2023. These are companies that have African heritage and earn more than 50 per cent of their revenues from Africa.

Table 8.2: Top 20 companies in southern Africa by market value, 2022–2023

Regional ranking	Name	Sector	Market Value 31/03/22 (US$m)	Market Value 31/03/23 (US$m)	Revenue, (latest) (US$m)	Net Income (latest) (US$m)
1	Naspers	Consumer Non-Cyclicals	49,619	80,865	7,940	12,223
2	FirstRand	Finance	29,739	19,09	6,178	1,868
3	Standard Bank Group	Finance	20,915	16,347	7,183	1,866
4	Vodacom Group	Telecomm	20,102	14,292	6,334	1,058
5	Anglo American Platinum	Non-Energy Materials	36,429	14,265	9,056	2,713
6	MTN Group	Telecomm	24,5	13,537	11,381	1,063
7	Gold Fields	Non-Energy Materials	13,909	11,936	4,287	711
8	Capitec Bank Holdings	Finance	18,604	11,044	1,861	587
9	AngloGold Ashanti	Non-Energy Materials	10,032	10,196	4,501	297
10	Absa Group	Finance	11,048	8,686	5,438	1,13
11	Sasol	Non-Energy Materials	15,354	8,638	17,92	1,753
12	Kumba Iron Ore	Non-Energy Materials	14,446	8,163	4,058	988
13	Impala Platinum Holdings	Non-Energy Materials	13,062	7,874	6,842	1,853
14	Bid Corp	Consumer Services	7,3	7,533	8,686	289
15	Shoprite Holdings	Consumer Non-Cyclicals	9,577	7,408	10,658	331
16	Sanlam	Finance	11,003	7,075	5,257	584
17	Nedbank Group	Finance	8,153	6,252	3,496	785

Regional ranking	Name	Sector	Market Value 31/03/22 (US$m)	Market Value 31/03/23 (US$m)	Revenue, (latest) (US$m)	Net Income (latest) (US$m)
18	Sibanye Stillwater	Non-Energy Materials	11,581	5,844	7,534	1,019
19	Investec	Finance	6,716	5,503	n/a	n/a
20	Discovery	Finance	8,393	5,333	3,39	316

Source: Ford (2023)

Note: Listed companies with less than 50 per cent of their revenues in Africa and companies that are not listed or dual-listed on an African exchange are excluded.

There have been significant foreign direct investment flows from South African firms to SADC and the rest of the African continent (Arndt and Roberts, 2018: 298). These have largely been in the retail, banking, insurance, transport and business support services (Arndt and Roberts, 2018: 298). This growth in FDI has been accompanied by a rapid growth in trade in goods and services, in sectors such as retail, banking, insurance, transport and business support services.

HOW THE STRUCTURE OF THE SOUTHERN AFRICAN ECONOMY AFFECTS THE TOWNSHIP ECONOMY

Supermarkets at the regional level

The growth in South African exports of diversified manufactured goods to SADC countries has been led by food products and machinery and equipment (Arndt and Robets, 2018) but the food product exports are generally under-reported (Arndt and Roberts, 2018: 298). On the African continent, there has been a spread of supermarkets led by foreign direct investment from larger African economies (Das Nair, 2019).

Drawing from value chain analysis, Arndt and Roberts (2018) highlight the importance of the spread of supermarket chains in the region. They argue that SADC needs 'to address transport and logistics, and value chains whose competitive advantages are inherently regional, as in the cases of poultry and mining' (Arnd and Roberts, 2018). Their

Figure 8.2: Revenue (latest) by sector (in US$ millions)

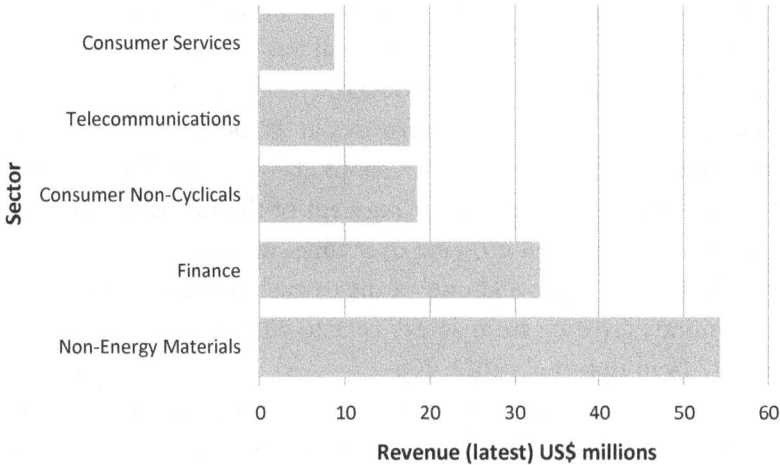

Source: Ford (2023)

research focuses on regional supermarkets, poultry, trucking and mining equipment and related services value chains as these 'offer high potential for growth and mutually beneficial trade and are critical to the nature and dimensions of regional integration' (Arndt and Roberts, 2018: 298).

Township and informal economy competition and performance

There are various estimates of the South African township economy, with over 500 townships in the country. South Africa's Department of Small Business Development (DSBD) estimated that the number of micro and informal businesses is around 3.3 million (DSBD, 2021), and also found there could be as many as 4.8 million when using the broad definition of survivalist entrepreneurs (DSBD, 2021). One estimate valued the township economy at R900 billion with approximately 60 per cent of this market considered formal and 40 per cent informal (News24, 2023). National Treasury finds that 'South African SMMEs contribute more than 40 per cent of the total GDP and accounts for more than 87 per cent of all employment; more than 60 per cent of people who start an informal business do so because they are unemployed and have no alternative source of income' (National Treasury, 2023: 10; Finmark Trust, 2020: 7). Economic activity in the township comprises retail trade, transportation and government services (Pernegger and Godehart, 2007: 11). There are enterprises in health services such as traditional healers and doctors, personal services (edu-care such as creches, beauty such as hair and nail salons) and street vendors. Liquor retailers dominate township enterprises at 19 per cent, followed by hair salons at 15 per cent and spaza shops at 7 per cent (Van Eyk et al., 2022: 21). Spaza shops are a large segment of the township economy, a segment that has been growing over time. In the pre-Covid-19 era, spaza shops were the 'backbone' of the township-retail component of the economy, growing from 45 per cent to 53 per cent between 2016 and 2017 (Van Eyk et al., 2022: 20).

Citing the 2016 Nielson South African report on consumer behaviour, Madubela (2021) reports that the South African informal or independent retail trade sector was worth R46 billion in annual sales. The spaza shop market in South Africa contributed 5.2 per cent to GDP and employed 2.6 million people (Madubela, 2021).

The DSBD has seen the relevance of small, medium and micro enterprises (SMMEs) and the need for supporting, growing and creating a conducive market environment for small business development. The Department of Small Business Development Strategic Plan 2020–2025 sets out the following objectives (DSBD, 2020: 2–3):

- Grow the contribution of SMMEs to GDP from 35 per cent to 50 per cent by 2024. The plan is to upscale support for SMMEs and cooperatives through the provision of blended finance instruments.
- To facilitate the increase of small businesses in sectors historically dominated by a few large companies, or concentration (township economies and rural development). This is to be achieved through collaboration with different government departments, such as the Department of Trade, Industry and Competition (DTIC), in order to open up entry to SMMEs in concentrated economic sectors.
- To prioritise and increase the number of businesses owned by women to a target of 40 per cent; by persons with disabilities to 7 per cent; and by youth to 30 per cent.

The retail trade sector comprises traditional trade stores in 'brick and mortar' outlets in fixed locations, while informal traders are at unofficial locations and are independently owned. Malls have been built in the townships, with large retailers taking up market space in townships. Importantly, Pernegger and Godehart (2007: 12) argued early on that there was a need to balance the activities of large retailers and malls with the small, survivalist formal and informal enterprises operating in townships. Informal retailers suffered negative impacts from shopping malls operating in proximity to their businesses (Pernegger and Godehart, 2007). Small and survivalist formal and informal enterprises have lost out. Madubela (2021) asserts that even though South African formal retailers have the power and access to resources enjoyed by large-scale vendors when they enter the township market, they structure themselves using characteristics similar to informal traders operating in the townships. For example, Mr Price and Shoprite have shipping-container style stores in some townships, while Pick n Pay (worth R900 billion in 2021, 60 per cent formal and 40 per cent informal market) has been investing in spaza shops. This means that large retailers are going into head-to-head competition with informal traders for the township economy, with many small players finding themselves outcompeted and forced to shut down (Das Nair, 2019). In South Africa's grocery retail market, Pick n Pay, Shoprite, Spar and Woolworths take up a 50 per cent market share.

The presence of these supermarkets in townships is seen to reinforce the concentration in markets suited to informal trading, thus impacting on the livelihoods available to migrants. For instance, Buthelezi et al. (2018: 1) note that competitive markets benefit small businesses, entrepreneurs, consumers, workers and the economy more generally but several indicators suggest the persistence of market concentration in many of South Africa's economic sectors. There has also been the complicated issue of mergers and acquisitions between big, listed conglomerates buying localised, small players. This has continued the trend of supermarketisation of the players in the margins, such as the Pick n Pay acquisition of Boxer Superstores. Note that the persistence of high levels of market concentration may also be a product of merger and acquisition activity (Buthelezi et al., 2018).

Table 8.3: Structural market challenges faced by local formal and informal SMMEs

Limited access to finance	• Accessing finance with favourable terms and the conditions necessary for building a sustainable informal or formal business is generally difficult.
	• Funding institutions have not adequately responded to the economic and cultural conditions of informal enterprises. This is exemplified by the requirements for securing loan finance from formal financing institutions which tend to exclude informal enterprises.
	• South Africa's venture capital industry is underdeveloped, making the pool of funding limited.
Lack of access to markets	• Informal and formal small businesses struggle to access markets beyond their localities.
	• Reaching wider markets is important for accessing growth capital and other resources; lack of capacity to do so thus constrains the viability and sustainability of businesses.
Poor infrastructure	• Lack of infrastructure is a key impediment to business growth and adds to the costs of doing business.
	• Infrastructure is seen as a key enabler for SMME development; this includes land/retail space at affordable prices, reasonable utilities and transport and communication infrastructure which can be instrumental in the success of a small business.
Onerous labour laws	• South Africa's labour laws have been found to be significant regulatory obstacles to business growth, particularly when it comes to laying off staff.
	• The country's labour regime is criticised by business owners for its inflexibility and negative impact on employment; it is seen as having a direct impact on growth in formal businesses, and as being a deterrent to formalisation in informal ones.

Inadequately educated workforce	• The NDP notes that small businesses, particularly in the services sector, are affected by a shortage of skills.
	• This affects the biggest SMME businesses in the trade and accommodation sector.
	• Skills shortages in the workforce are ranked as one of the main impediments to the growth of small businesses.
	• The prevailing critique is that there is inadequate education in entrepreneurship. The shortage of skills acts as a constraint to employment.
Red tape	• Government policies are instrumental in enhancing favourable entrepreneurial activity and provide the platform needed to start and sustain businesses.
	• The procedures and costs associated with registering a business and acquiring necessary permits have been identified by both formal and informal SMMEs as obstacles that cost valuable time and money.

Source: BER (2016)

Post-apartheid South Africa has seen large inflows of migrants, who have also been establishing themselves in the informal and formal sectors (Rogerson, 1997).

Deconcentrating the region's informal and local economies
Scheba and Turok (2020) argue that township businesses are necessity-based and unable to grow beyond a storefront or small-scale operation. These businesses often operate informally with low financial returns and rates of employment (Scheba and Turok, 2020). ANDE (2021) has found that 'only 15 per cent of township enterprises are formally registered, compared with 30 per cent of similar enterprises in the urban areas'. In addition, their services are often localised and do not reach a market outside of their immediate locations or create jobs that will benefit their community in any substantive way (Scheba and Turok, 2020).

Table 8.4: Why foreign-owned spaza shops are more 'successful' than locally owned ones

Ownership dynamics and vertical integration between spaza shops and wholesalers	Foreign traders, unlike local traders, tend to operate their spaza shops in partnerships rather than under sole ownership. They tend to have links to a wholesaler, also foreign owned, operating in the CBD. They adopt a network-based approach to operating their spaza shops in contrast to the micro-scale, survivalist business approach of most locally owned spaza shops. Foreign nationals employ ownership strategies which include: • Shareholding or operational ties to other township retail outlets (horizontal models) • Spaza shops as an outlet for a formally registered wholesaler (vertical linkages) • Cooperative strategies for working with separate but allied retail outlets to share opportunities for bulk purchasing and deliveries • Maintaining multiple retail outlets under central control in a separate location
Price competition	Price is at the centre of the claims that foreign-owned shops have outcompeted the local shop owners. Foreign-owned shops say they are cheaper than most national supermarket chains because of their procurement strategies, which include buying from diverse wholesalers at lower prices. There are generally more foreign-owned shops in townships than locally owned ones.
Procurement of goods	It has been found that foreign-owned spaza shops share transport among themselves and also rotate the sourcing of goods. In some cases, they have national partnerships of up to 20 stores, which allow them to buy stock in bulk and take advantage of volume discounts that can in turn be passed on to customers. Foreign traders generally have clear strategies for being as competitive as possible, especially on prices and varieties of products.
Trading hours and location	As spaza shops are, by nature, convenience stores, their location and proximity are crucial for the consumer. Foreign-owned shops are often strategically located in intersections with high pedestrian traffic. They are also open throughout the year, including holidays. The managers of the foreign-owned shops tend to be men with no family in South Africa, while local shops are often run by women who are more likely to have young children. Foreign-owned shops also capitalise on their longer trading hours.

Counterfeit goods	The sale of counterfeit goods has also influenced competitiveness. This has been raised as an issue of concern by local shop owners. Cigarettes have been found to be the prevalent counterfeit good. Foreign traders have access to these products and sell them at low prices to the detriment of local traders who cannot access them. The prevalence of counterfeit goods in spaza shops suggests strong supply chain links between wholesalers and the black and grey markets.
Stock diversity, product choice and packaging	Foreign-owned shops supply a wider variety and larger volume of groceries than those supplied in locally owned spaza shops. Locally owned shops are seen to offer items that customers find expensive and readily available more cheaply at supermarket chains, while foreign-owned spaza shops supply products that are more frequently demanded by consumers, with a shorter shelf life.

Source: CCSA (2019: 168)

The SMME sector is a necessary catalyst for development and growth in the region. The structural realities of trade and markets in the SADC region, as demonstrated above, reveal a dominance of big corporations with a concentration that has devastating effects on the small business sector's growth, profitability and sustainability. South Africa reflects the realities of the region, including in its domestic economic structures and the impacts of these on formal and informal SMMEs.

The domination of South Africa's large corporations in the regional economy influences migration flows into South Africa and the wider region. South Africans and foreign nationals experience conflict with each other, often expressed as violent xenophobia as locals and migrants scramble for access to resources, as explored in chapter 3. Charman and Piper (2012: 82) note 'the micro-context from which violence against shopkeepers, for instance, can be understood against the entrepreneurship linked to economic competition in the informal economy'. In contrast, other scholars bring out the macro contexts, as does this chapter. In particular, the gap is highlighted between national policy positions (which emphasise the rights of both locals and migrants) (Crush 2008; Landau, 2008) and the grassroots expectations of inclusion and participation in the economy. These expectations are

Figure 8.3: Manufacturers, processors and suppliers in the retail sector

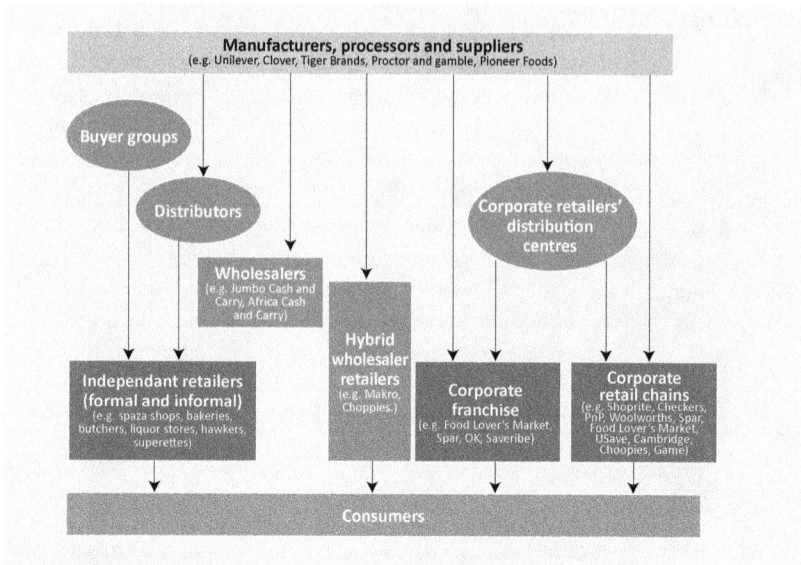

Source: CCSA (2019: 47)

despite the economic environment across the region, in which parasitic capitalist conglomerates dominate operations. Our contention is that regardless of the formal or informal nature of SMMEs in the country, they have to contend with the reality of a concentrated economy. This duality of the structure of the South African economy is necessary to explain. In this next section, we therefore explore the duality of the South African economy.

DUALITY AND STRUCTURE OF THE SOUTH AFRICAN ECONOMY

Former South African president Thabo Mbeki purported that the country had a dual economy, made up of formal and informal economies (Mbeki, 2003). The dual economy consists of the informal economy which operates as a sector on the periphery separate from the formal economy but working to support the economic security and interests of the marginalised, peripherised and poor (Mbeki, 2003). The informal sector is considered secondary in the dual economy nexus of

Figure 8.4: Size of the informal sector in selected SADC countries

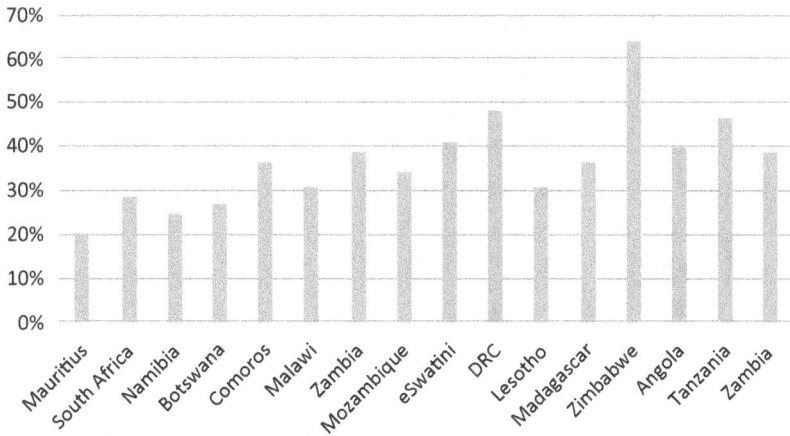

Source: Finmark Trust (2020)

South Africa. Some have tried to highlight the linkages between the two economies. Scholars have argued, for instance, that the informal economy is not on the periphery as believed but is rather a 'diverse subset of the economy that fosters entrepreneurship with great potential to revive growth and generate employment, and livelihood opportunities' (Sparks and Barnett, 2010). The World Bank makes an observation on the impact and consequence of the dual economy in South Africa's agricultural sector (World Bank, 2022: 4):

> Land inequality resulted in dual agricultural systems, which combine large-scale, commercial farms and resource-poor, subsistence-oriented smallholdings. The bulk of agricultural land belongs to large-scale farmers, while most people who depend on land for their livelihoods struggle on less than one hectare per family in the face of worsening terms of trade. By and large, they do not use modern agricultural practices and cannot afford to invest in machinery and inputs. This means that their agricultural productivity remains low, which perpetuates their low incomes and further entrenches inequality.

The inequalities described above mean that formal and informal SMMEs in farming have to compete with heavily resourced and concentrated farms whose owners have designed the value chain for their own benefit, with little chance for small, informal players to break the power of this monopoly.

The informal economy consists of unpaid workers in family enterprises, casual wage employment, home-based workers or service providers and street vendors. It is an economic site of survival for poor people (Etim and Daramola, 2020: 2). South Africa has one of the highest unemployment rates on the African continent at 32.9 per cent (Stats SA, 2023). However, despite South Africa's informal economy accounting for 3 million or 20 per cent of the country's total employment, many of the unemployed remain underrepresented there. (Pooe and Ngcaweni, 2022: 425). Tables 8.1 and 8.2 reflect the various structural barriers that affect participation in the informal sector.

Supermarket vs SMMEs

The Competition Commission (2019) recognises the limited participation of SMMEs in the South African grocery market: '... the entry, expansion, and diversification by the national supermarket chains into townships, peri-urban and rural areas, and the more recent direct entry by these players in the informal spaza shop segment, has ... contributed to the observed decline in the number of the small and independent grocery retailers' (Competition Commission, 2019: 22). All small and independent grocery retailers have struggled to adapt and compete, including those run by migrants.

Locals have had to contend with competitive players in various forms which have proved to be extremely difficult to out-compete. As the chapter argues, migrants in the SMME sector have been out-competing locals because of the methods they employ to keep prices lower than those of local competitors. The emergence of shopping complexes and malls has posed competition to township retailers, especially the more recent development of the big retailers opening small outlets in the township in order to compete with SMME retailers, both locally and foreign owned (Competition Commission, 2019: 22):

The change in the competitive environment and its negative impact on the sustainability and participation of locally owned small and independent grocery retailers is exacerbated by the competitive pressure emanating from, among others, the participation of foreign nationals in the informal segment, mainly the spaza shop segment. As a result, the inquiry found that there is a need for the development and deployment of a competitiveness support strategy to assist these businesses to become more competitive and thriving businesses, particularly in a context where the lack of employment opportunities and economic inequality are on the rise.

The SMME retail sector sources most of its products from formal retail supermarkets because of the nature of the economy in South Africa and the region. The non-productive nature of the SMME sector in particular has made it vulnerable to concentrated retail supermarkets who have managed to build monopolistic value chains for their own benefits. The demand for many products sold in formal supermarkets is driven by the informal economy. Products and companies that have benefited include cigarette companies. Coca-Cola has also increased its domination and benefited from its products being pushed by SMMEs, formal or informal (Competition Commission, 2019: 26):

> The retail level of the value chain is segmented between the formal and informal channels. The formal retail segment is characterised by the presence of the incumbent national supermarket chains, speciality stores and emerging challenger retailers, while the informal segment mostly has an active presence of small and independent retailers including general dealers and spaza shops. The sale of grocery products takes place through both the formal and informal retail channels. The formal channel is the larger and more important distribution segment. Within the formal channel, a large proportion of grocery product sales (over 50 per cent) takes place in shopping centres which are primarily occupied by national supermarket chains as the anchor tenants.

Improvements in SMME productivity would help small shop owners to regain some of the market share lost to supermarket retail stores. A productive SMME sector in South Africa has the potential for spillover effects in the region, encouraging vibrant competition, trade and industriousness to build the regional economy.

The Competition Commission has argued that we need to get the 'South African grocery retail sector on the path towards the realisation of inclusive economic participation, an innovative sector and wider choice for consumers at competitive prices' (Competition Commission, 2019: 23). At the core is the productive/manufacturing capacity required for SMMEs to be able to maintain their competitive advantage.

LINKING THE DEVELOPMENT OF THE SADC INFORMAL ECONOMY AND TOWNSHIP ECONOMIES

It is important to apply macro-strategic thinking to the development of SADC's informal economy and township economies as the region's trading class in the context of migration.

Recommendations
- A holistic framework of regional integration should be developed, through the refinement of skills capacities in the informal and township sectors. Large-scale surveys should be conducted to establish the skills needed in the informal sector, and development programmes should be tailored accordingly. Active steps should be taken to harness the potential and opportunities presented by the SADC region's informal and township economies.
- Careful attention should be paid to supporting social organisations that build the competencies in micro-manufacturing and production, and also promote informal market regional integration.
- Macroeconomic interventions, such as the encouragement of foreign direct investment, should be undertaken to benefit SMMEs in informal and township economies.
- Support for informal and township economies across the region should be one of the strategies for catalysing structural

transformation and removing barriers, such as concentrated markets and oligopolistic structures.

- Regional infrastructure projects of all sizes should be linked with value addition, enterprise development and employment creation for the benefit of formal and informal SMMEs.
- Both the Southern African Customs Union (SACU) and the wider SADC should formulate synergistic macro strategies for the development of informal and township economies and the SMMEs therein. Regional linkages of township economies would revitalise the regional economy but are currently not prioritised in SADC funding and development projects.
- The region has an opportunity to create sustainable livelihood, employment and business opportunities for its most vulnerable and excluded cohorts. To achieve this, a nexus of policy approaches are necessary. Southern Africa's large source of labour requires a structured and highly coordinated regional strategy. This strategy would necessarily be anchored in capacity building and training, to ensure value addition.

The region should develop policies and institutions that foster regional integration, collaboration and cooperation. Hirsch (2023) makes the point that while South Africa's Department of Trade, Industry and Competition (DTIC) recognises the importance of regional integration to South Africa's structural transformation efforts, it has not yet allocated the resources necessary to develop the required regulatory, policy, programmatic and institutional supports.

CONCLUSION

This chapter recognises that the political economies of South Africa and the broader southern African region intersect in complex ways, producing a nexus of paradoxical livelihood outcomes for both foreign and South African nationals.

It sought to explore the mega trends in the southern African region and how these interact with changes in South Africa's post-apartheid economic structure, migration, migration attitudes and local economies.

For local enterprises to thrive, it is important to review national industrial, agricultural and competition policies as well as regional integration objectives. We argue in this chapter that the increasing financialisation of the South African economy, deindustrialisation and missed opportunities for the regional support of agro industries are affecting local economies and enterprises in both negative and positive ways. It is argued that economic and migration policy has not caught up with the implication of this just yet.

Migrant and informal traders should be supported to challenge the retail, digital and finance sector penetration of local economies by investing in online, digital platforms. Local networks of producers must be supported for a more equitable distribution of the benefits emerging from the regional economy, ensure inclusive participation and drive structural transformation. The economic aspirations of Africans are closely tied. This makes the aspirations of South Africans inseparable from their neighbours.

REFERENCES

African Development Bank (AfDB). 2018. 'African economic outlook report', https://www.afdb.org/fileadmin/uploads/afdb/Documents/Publications/African_Economic_Outlook_2018_-_EN.pdf, accessed 9 August 2023.

African Development Bank Group (AfDB). 2023. 'Africa's macroeconomic performance and outlook', https://www.afdb.org/en/documents/publications/africas-macro-economic-performance-and-outlook-report, accessed 12 March 2023.

African Union (AU). 2022. 'Expanding the use of administrative data sources and new data types for labour migration statistics: A pilot study of South Africa', https://au.int/sites/default/files/documents/42165-doc-Labour_migration_Statistics_Pilot_study_-_Expanding_The_Use_Of_Administrative_data_SourcesRepublic_of_South_Africa.pdf, accessed 5 August 2023.

Arndt, C. and Roberts, S. 2018. 'Key issues in regional growth and integration in Southern Africa'. *Development Southern Africa,* 35(2), 297–314.

Ashman, S. 2023. 'Beyond the MEC? Limits and prospects in the development of South African capitalism', in Mohamed, S., Ngoma, A. and Baloyi, B. (eds), *The Evolving Structure of South Africa's*

Economy: Faultlines and futures. Johannesburg: Mapungubwe Institute for Strategic Reflection.

Aspen Network of Development Entrepreneurs (ANDE). 2021. 'Entrepreneurial ecosystem snapshot: Township economies in South Africa', https://ecosystems.andeglobal.org/south_africa_townships. pdf, accessed 15 January 2024.

Bureau for Economic Research (BER). 2016. 'The small, medium and micro enterprise sector in South Africa'. Commissioned by the Small Enterprise Development Agency (SEDA), Stellenbosch University.

Buthelezi, T., Mtani, T. and Mncube, L. 2018. 'The extent of market concentration in South Africa's product markets'. Competition Commission Working paper CC2018/05, https://www.compcom. co.za/wp-content/uploads/2020/03/Working-paper_The-extent-of-South-Africas-concentration-problem-13082018.pdf, accessed 25 August 2023.

Charman, A. and Piper, L. 2012. 'Xenophobia, criminality and violent entrepreneurship: Violence against Somali shopkeepers in Delft South, Cape Town, South Africa'. *South African Review of Sociology*, 43(3), 81–105.

Competition Commission South Africa (CCSA). 2019. 'The grocery retail market inquiry: Final report', https://www.compcom.co.za/ wp-content/uploads/2019/12/GRMI-Non-Confidential-Report.pdf, accessed 1 December 2023.

Crush, J. (ed.). 2008. 'The perfect storm: The realities of xenophobia in South Africa'. Southern African Migration Project, http://www. genocidewatch.org/images/South_Africa_09_03_30_the_perfec storm. pdf, accessed 5 May 2023.

Daniel, J., Naidoo, V. and Naidu, S. 2003. 'The South Africans have arrived: Post-apartheid corporate expansion into Africa', in Daniel, J., Habib, A. and Southall, R. (eds), *State of the Nation: South Africa 2003–2004.* Pretoria: HSRC Press, 368–390.

Das Nair, R. 2019. 'The internationalisation of supermarkets and implications on suppliers in Southern Africa', https://unctad.org/ system/files/non-official-document/unda1617ld05_supermarkets_ SA_en.pdf, accessed 12 March 2023.

Department of Employment and Labour (DEL). 2022. 'Draft national labour migration policy for South Africa', https://www.labour.gov.za/ DocumentCenter/Publications/Public%20Employment%20Services/ National%20Labour%20Migration%20Policy%202021%202.pdf, accessed 12 March 2023.

Department of Small Business Development (DSDB). 2020. 'Strategic Plan 2020–2025', http://www.dsbd.gov.za/sites/default/files/documents/ strategic-plan2020-25.pdf, accessed 2 May 2023.

Department of Small Business and Labour (DSBD). 2021. 'Impact of Covid-19 on micro and informal businesses: South Africa 2021', https://www.dsbd.gov.za/sites/default/files/reports/Impact-of-covid19-on-businesses.pdf, accessed 15 January 2024.

Etim, E. and Daramola, O. 2020. 'The informal sector and economic growth of South Africa and Nigeria: A comparative systematic review'. *Journal of Open Innovation*, 6(4), 134.

Finmark Trust. 2020. 'Finscope MSME survey: South Africa 2020', https://www.finmark.org.za/Publications/FS%20MSME%202020.pdf, accessed 1 April 2023.

Ford, N. 11 May 2023. 'Southern Africa's top companies in 2023'. *African Business,* https://african.business/2023/05/finance-services/southern-africas-top-companies-in-2023, accessed 6 June 2023.

Hirsch, A. 2023. 'South Africa: Regional integration and structural transformation', in Mohamed, S., Ngoma, A. and Baloyi, B. (eds), *The Evolving Structure of South Africa's Economy: Faultlines and futures.* Johannesburg: Mapungubwe Institute for Strategic Reflection.

International Monetary Fund (IMF). 2017. 'The informal economy in sub-Saharan Africa: Size and determinants'. IMF Working Paper No. 2017/156, https://www.imf.org/-/media/Files/Publications/WP/2017/wp17156.ashx, accessed 12 March 2023.

International Organization for Migration (IOM). 2020. 'World Migration Report 2020', https://publications.iom.int/system/files/pdf/wmr_2020.pdf, accessed 20 August 2023.

Landau, L. 2008. 'Attacks on foreigners in South Africa: More than just xenophobia?'. Institute for Strategic Studies, University of Pretoria. Unpublished.

Lipper, L. and Benton T. G. 2020. 'Mega-trends in the Southern African region'. SADC futures: developing foresight capacity for climate resilient agricultural development knowledge series, CCAFS Report, https://cgspace.cgiar.org/server/api/core/bitstreams/2dbd4249-02ca-4f0d-9601-87c715741863/content, accessed 20 August 2023.

Madubela, A. 16 October 2021. 'A bigger slice of the pie: Retailers find ways to cash in on township economy'. *Mail & Guardian,* https://mg.co.za/business/2021-10-16-a-bigger-slice-of-the-pie-retailers-find-ways-to-cash-in-on-township-economy/, accessed 6 May 2023.

Mama, A. 2014. 'Pan-Africanism: Beyond survival to renaissance'. *New Agenda*, 53, 60–63.

Mapungubwe Institute for Strategic Reflection (MISTRA). 2022. *Macro-Social Report.* Johannesburg: MISTRA.

Mbeki, T. 11 November 2003. 'Address to the National Council of Provinces', http://www.dirco.gov.za/docs/speeches/mbeki.htm, accessed 5 February 2023

National Planning Commission (NPC). 2011. 'National Development Plan (NDP): Vision for 2030', https://www.gov.za/sites/default/files/gcis_document/201409/devplan2.pdf, accessed 2 August 2023.

National Treasury. 2023. 'An inclusive financial sector for all', https://www.treasury.gov.za/comm_media/press/2023/2023112701%20An%20Inclusive%20Financial%20Sector%20for%20all%202023.pdf, accessed 14 January 2023.

News24. 23 June 2023. 'The rise and rise of the township economy'. *News 24*, https://www.news24.com/news24/partnercontent/the-rise-and-rise-of-the-township-economy-20230621, accessed 25 August 2023.

Pernegger, L. and Godehart, S. 2007. 'Township in the South African geographic landscape: Physical and social legacies and challenges', https://www.treasury.gov.za/divisions/bo/ndp/ttri/ttri%20oct%202007/day%201%20-%2029%20oct%202007/1a%20keynote%20address%20li%20pernegger%20paper.pdf, accessed 2 August.

Pooe, T. K. and Ngcaweni, W. 2022. 'When theory and policy miss the transformational opportunity: South Africa's untapped informal sector potential for addressing youth unemployment'. *Journal of Public Administration*, 57(3), 421–439.

Rogerson, C. M. 1997. 'African immigrant entrepreneurs and Johannesburg's changing inner city'. *Africa Insight*, 27(4), 265–273.

Scheba, A. and Turok, I. 2020. 'Informal rental housing in the south: Dynamic but neglected'. *Environment and Urbanisation*, 32(1), 109–132.

Schoeman, M. 2003. 'South Africa as an emerging middle power: 1994–2003', in Daniel, J., Habib, A. and Southall, R. (eds), *State of the Nation: South Africa 2003–2004*. Pretoria: HSRC Press, 349–367.

Sparks, D. L. and Barnett, S. T. 2010. 'The informal sector in sub-Saharan Africa: Out of the shadows to foster sustainable employment and equity?'. *International Business & Economics Research Journal (IBER)*, 9(5), 1–11.

Statistics South Africa (Stats SA). 2023. 'Key findings – Quarterly Labour Force Survey (QLFS): Quarter 1', https://www.statssa.gov.za/?page_id=1856&PPN=P0211&SCH=73571, accessed 15 August 2023.

Trade Law Centre (Tralac). 30 December 2022. 'The agribusiness value chain in Africa', https://www.tralac.org/resources/infographics/15897-the-agribusiness-value-chain-in-africa.html, accessed 12 March 2023.

Van Eyk, M., Amoah, F. and Yase, T. 2022. 'Sustaining the township economy: An investigation into the factors influencing the shopping experience of spaza shop customers in South Africa'. *Journal of Economics and Behavioural Studies*, 14(3), 20–32.

World Bank. 2019. 'Leveraging economic migration for development. A briefing for the World Bank Board', https://www.knomad.org/sites/

default/files/2019-08/World%20Bank%20Board%20Briefing%20
Paper-leveraging%20economic%20migration%20for%20
development_0.pdf, accessed 6 May 2023.

World Bank. 2022. 'Inequality in Southern Africa: An assessment of the
Southern African customs union', http://hdl.handle.net/10986/37283,
accessed 6 May 2023.

NINE

Rethinking migrant human settlement as an advantage to township dwellers: The case of Soweto

MALAIKA LESEGO SAMORA MAHLATSI

Migration has been an intrinsic component of the developmental process of southern Africa and since the Mineral Revolution has played an instrumental role in the building of the South African nation. But throughout the colonial and apartheid eras, foreign migrant workers were permitted in specified industries, essentially mining and agriculture. This, along with the restrictive measures on the recruitment of foreign workers, would later result in a considerable reduction of the flows of migrants from peripheral labour reserves in neighbouring countries. This changed at the dawn of the democratic dispensation when South Africa, regarded as an emerging economy within the new global structures of production, became a preferred destination for various categories of migrants. Over time, this increase in the immigrant population, occurring alongside poverty and rising levels of structural inequality and unemployment, set parameters for native hostilities anchored on the narrative of migrants as threatening and parasitic. Employing critical theory and using Soweto as a case study, this chapter explores how the dynamic relationship between migrants and locals in townships challenges this narrative. By focusing on the migrant tenant-local landlord relationship that is a growing feature of township geographies, it demonstrates how the migrant tenant community is instrumental in facilitating township economic development and social cohesion. It illustrates how the township economy is strengthened by the participation of migrant communities who respond to the demand for goods and services and create employment opportunities. The chapter concludes that migrant entrepreneurialism and tenant/migrant relations are crucial forces in facilitating local economic and human development in South African townships.

INTRODUCTION

From dusk until dawn, taxis speed through Main Road, transporting the working class from various parts of Soweto West and Roodepoort to the Johannesburg central business district. Just before Durban Deep, a gold mine long abandoned and around which an informal settlement has been established, the taxis take a left turn on a double-laned tarred road towards Dobsonville. A few kilometres down, to the left, lies the vast Marie-Louise landfill site that is located just north of a section of Meadowlands known as Soteba. To the left lies Braamfischerville, a Reconstruction and Development Programme (RDP) settlement that was established by the democratic government to address the urban housing crisis that confronts the post-apartheid dispensation. The RDP was a socioeconomic framework that was implemented by the first democratic government, whose primary aim was to address the colossal socioeconomic problems that South Africa had inherited from centuries of colonialism and apartheid. One of these problems was housing. Mahlatsi (2022) acknowledges the scholarship on the effects of land dispossession and policies – such as the Group Areas Act of 1950 – which meant that millions of black South Africans had no access to land and housing. Low-cost houses were built to address this housing crisis, and they came to be known as RDP houses or RDPs.

Braamfischerville is divided into four phases and a section just across the road from Soteba known as the Braamfischerville Extension. This part of the township consists of bond houses that are constructed in the layout typical of Extension sections of townships across Soweto – a kitchen, lounge, bathroom and three bedrooms. The RDP houses in Braamfischerville do not look too different from the matchbox houses just across the road in Meadowlands and Dobsonville that were built for black people by the apartheid government – except that the RDP houses are much smaller. According to Moolla (2011), they are generally a 30m² house on a 250m² plot, comprising an open lounge, a single bedroom and a kitchen area, with no dividing wall, and a small toilet. While some of the houses in Braamfischerville have been extended by the owners, many are still in the condition in which the government provided them. But in a significant number of yards, shacks have been erected – sometimes as many as five. In some yards, the shacks are occupied by members of the family that owns the RDP house, but who could not be accommodated in the small dwelling that can barely house a family of three. But in many yards, the shacks are occupied by tenants – both locals and immigrants. This feature of Braamfischerville can be seen across Soweto, including in Extensions – parts of the township that were developed in the 1980s to accommodate the middle class of the time: teachers, nurses, government administrators and police officers, etc. Houses in the Extensions are much larger in size than RDPs and the matchbox houses that were built by the apartheid government. These houses were once regarded as being affluent and were rarely ever sites of informal backyard dwellings and shacks. This is no longer the case.

From Dobsonville in the far west to Diepkloof in the far east, yards in townships within Soweto are increasingly filling with informal dwellings and shacks that are being rented out for residential as well as commercial purposes. This is the reality across the Gauteng province. According to Webster (2018) and a Gauteng City Region Observatory study by Hamann et al. (2018), backyard shacks in the province have increased by 204.7 per cent. In Soweto, more than a quarter of the population lives in backyard shacks (Crankshaw et al., 2000). These shacks operate as both living quarters and places of business. Spaza shops – informal convenience shops common in townships – operate from shacks and repurposed shipping containers. This reconstruction of township space has produced a socio-spatial dialectic that is rarely studied. The socio-spatial dialectic is a conceptualisation of the complex inter-relationship between spatial and social structures. In his seminal work titled, 'The socio-spatial dialectic', Soja (1980) contends that the spatialities that are produced by social processes have causal influence over those processes. Simply put, space shapes and is shaped by societal constructs. The socio-spatial differentiation in Soweto, at whose centre scholars such as Bonner and Segal (1998) place the growing number of informal dwellings, has impacted its geomorphologies, geographies and economies.

This chapter will analyse the migrant tenant–local landlord relationship that is a growing feature of township geographies, with the Soweto townships of Braamfischerville, Meadowlands and Dobsonville as focus areas. With a population of just over 1.3 million located within a land area of 200.03km^2 (Statistics South Africa, 2011), Soweto is the biggest and one of the most ethnically diverse townships in South Africa. It also has a rich political history that is rooted in activist communities. These features of Soweto make it an important case study as an evolving and growing urban settlement. In addition to this, the migrant tenant–local landlord relationship in Soweto provides a basis for a critique of the democratic government's policy of turning South Africa into a nation of homeowners as a response to the disenfranchisement wrought by apartheid policies that placed significant impediments on home ownership for black people in particular. Crankshaw et al. (2000) posit that the unintended consequence of this policy is that it forced households in need of rental accommodation to turn to informal markets. This is corroborated by Beall et al. (2003) who contend that the demand for this rental accommodation led to the complete transformation of formal housing in Soweto, with backyard shacks emerging on the properties of houseowners. This critique is important in making sense of how and why backyard shacks have become a conveyor belt of the migrant tenant–landlord relationship in the township. It also provides a foundation for understanding the attitudes and relationships of South African locals towards tenant immigrants.

RESEARCH METHODOLOGY

A qualitative approach was used to understand the experiences, ideas, meanings, interpretations, values and beliefs (Babbie, 2001) of migrant tenants, local landlords and broader community members in Soweto, who are negotiating relationships that are constantly evolving in post-apartheid South Africa. The study embraces the idea of multiple realities and uses this lens to view and interpret the local–migrant relations in townships. The primary research design uses case studies with a focus on the township of Soweto. Case studies contribute uniquely to our knowledge and understanding of social and political phenomena and enable the investigation of holistic and meaningful characteristics of real-life events. Secondary data was collected through official and scholarly literature, all of which was reviewed with the employment of critical theory. Primary data was gathered over a period of five weeks in Dobsonville, Meadowlands and Braamfischerville, through the use of semi-structured interviews.

A total of forty (40) individuals were interviewed and were selected using non-probability purposive sampling. This sampling method was used to create a subjective study population from whom source data was required. Participants were identified with the assistance of community forum leadership, with the selection/inclusion criteria for tenants being that they are migrants above the age of 18. The selection/inclusion criteria for landlords were that they were South African citizens (by birth or naturalisation); owned the properties they were leasing out; and were aged 18 or older. In Meadowlands, eight landlords and a corresponding number of migrant tenants were interviewed. In Braamfischerville, seven landlords and a corresponding number of migrant tenants were interviewed. And in Dobsonville, five landlords and a corresponding number of migrant tenants were interviewed. In 60 per cent of the cases, migrant tenants were leasing space from local landlords for commercial purposes, while in 40 per cent of the cases, migrant tenants were renting rooms and shacks from local landlords for residential purposes. Of the 20 landlords interviewed, 15 were women aged between 35 and 76, while 5 were men aged between 45 and 70. Of the 20 immigrants interviewed, 17 were men aged between 22 and 43, while 3 were women aged between 25 and 38.

In Meadowlands and Dobsonville, the average monthly rental fee is R2,000 for a backroom, while in Braamfischerville, it is R1,800. The distinction in prices is informed by two factors: size of the room/shack and access to an outdoor toilet. According to the landlords in Meadowlands and Dobsonville, the availability of a toilet outside the main house means the tenants have better access to sanitation, which necessitates the higher rentals. A landlord in Zone 8 Meadowlands also argued that she factors in the relatively lower rates of crime in the township when pricing her rooms – one which is occupied by a Mozambican immigrant and two by locals. Six of the eight tenant immigrants interviewed stated that they are in the country illegally, with only one being in possession of the Zimbabwe exemption permit (ZEP) and another having asylum status. Three tenants are Zimbabwean nationals, two are from Lesotho, two are from Mozambique and one is Malawian. All stated that they opted to live in Soweto due to its cheap rentals and close proximity to industries in Johannesburg, Roodepoort and Lenasia to the south. The remaining 60 per cent of the participants, comprising 12 landlords and 12 tenants, have commercial rental agreements. The landlords are renting space to the tenants for businesses that include spaza shops and a hair salon. Eight of the tenants are from Ethiopia, one from Mozambique and three from Somalia. The Mozambican hair salon owner rents a shack in Braamfischerville, while the rest of the migrant tenants are operating from used shipping containers that are erected on the front yards of the households from where they are renting space. The average monthly rental fee for the spaza shop owners is R2,500 across Dobsonville, Meadowlands and Braamfischerville. Almost all migrant spaza shop owners indicated that they had purchased the shipping containers themselves rather than found them already erected. This is corroborated by the landlords, who indicate that they are only renting out working space in the yard but do not own any implements and equipment. According to the tenants, Soweto was the logical destination due to its large working-class market.

INFORMAL HOUSING IN SOWETO: A RESPONSE TO GOVERNMENT FAILURE TO PROVIDE HOUSING FOR MIGRANTS?

Under the apartheid system, the legal regime governing spatial planning was orientated towards separate and uneven development. Consequently, in the democratic dispensation, the legal regime governing spatial planning is tasked with addressing the ills of apartheid and simultaneously striving towards the goal of sustainable development (Kimberley, 2015). While at the heart of this spatial planning is also the legal commitment and responsibility to guarantee migrants, specifically displaced persons and refugees, with access to adequate housing, the issue of housing for immigrants is grossly under-studied. In his study on immigration and homelessness in democratic South Africa, McDonald (1998) contends that the existing housing backlog for locals and myriad structural challenges such as poverty has pushed the immigrant housing issue to the background of political discourse. This, he argues, begs for critical reflection as the denial of housing to immigrants is a violation of their human rights. Under international law, obligations imposed on South Africa include but are not limited to the extension of the fundamental rights and freedoms contained in the 1951 Convention Relating to the Status of Refugees (the Refugee Convention) to refugees and asylum seekers. These include the right to have access to adequate housing. Article 21 of the Refugee Convention, to which South Africa is a signatory, states:

> As regards housing, the Contracting States, in so far as the matter is regulated by laws or regulations or is subject to the control of public authorities, shall accord to refugees lawfully staying in their territory treatment as favourable as possible and, in any event, not less favourable than that accorded to aliens generally in the same circumstances.

In a 2019 study titled 'Housing and Integrating Refugees: South Africa's Exclusionary Approach', Kavuro contends that the South African government employs an exclusionary approach towards housing refugees and asylum seekers, and to integrating them into the economy. The study illustrates that policy issues are acting as barriers to refugees and asylum seekers accessing housing programmes. It is these challenges that are leading to migrants becoming backyard dwellers and living in informal housing in Soweto. The fact that some of the participants in this study are asylum seekers provides evidence of Kavuro's contention.

THE MAKING OF SOWETO AND THE MIGRANT LABOUR SYSTEM

Like many townships across South Africa, Soweto is the product of the apartheid regime and the spatial planning policies that it had developed from the colonial dispensation. One of the defining features of the colonial dispensation was the discovery of gold on the Witwatersrand in 1886 – a development that followed the discovery of diamonds in Kimberley nearly two decades prior. This period, known as the Mineral Revolution, set parameters for the rapid industrialisation that would see South Africa transition from an agricultural society to becoming the world's largest producer of gold and one of the largest producers of diamonds (Nieftagodien and Gaule, 2012). But the changes brought by the Mineral Revolution extended beyond the nature of the economy. The period resulted in significant changes to the spatiality and demography of South Africa and, specifically, the Gauteng province.

The emergence of industrial-scale mining on the Witwatersrand necessitated the provision of labour. This labour was provided by African men within and beyond the borders of South Africa – migrants who initially travelled to the mines seasonally. The unsustainability of this practice resulted in the decision by mining corporations and the colonial regime to create a permanent labour force on the Witwatersrand. Various instruments were used to achieve this, including the introduction of the hut tax that facilitated the proletarianisation of rural men in particular, through de-agrarianisation (Ntsebeza and Kepe, 2012). Another important instrument used was the direct recruitment of young men from African countries, including Lesotho, Mozambique, Angola, Zambia, Swaziland (now eSwatini) and as far afield as Tanzania. In their study titled 'A century of migrant labour in the gold mines of South Africa', Harington et al. (2004) examine the changing numbers of the total black workers on the gold mines over the century from 1896 to 1996 and posit that migrant labour from outside South Africa accounted for over 60 per cent of the total labour force in the Witwatersrand gold mines. This is significant in understanding the complex history of the relationship between migrants and 'locals' that would ultimately shape the relations between locals and immigrants in townships like Soweto. The complexity in this history is explored by Neocosmos (2006: 23) who contends that those who deemed themselves 'locals' on the basis of being from the Bantustans (which were also termed 'homelands') that historically formed part of the Union of South Africa were themselves regarded as foreigners by apartheid legislation that de-nationalised them. According to the Bantu Homelands Citizenship Act of 1970, homelands were regarded as independent, self-governing authorities, and those residing in them were denied South African citizenship. Lawrence (1994) and Neocosmos (2006) contend that this relationship between the apartheid state and its subjects in the homelands, structured around 'ethnic' nationalities, was reproduced by mining companies.

The birth of Soweto can be traced back to 1891 when the colonial government established Kliptown, the oldest township in Soweto. By 1903, Kliptown was full of informal settlements that housed people who were working in the gold mines of the Witwatersrand, a majority of whom were black, Indian and coloured. When the bubonic plague broke out in the informal settlements of Langlaagte and Kliptown in 1904, the colonial government decided to clear the areas and implement segregated housing policies (Bonner and Segal, 1998). These would see black people resettled in Klipsruit, a township in the heart of modern-day Soweto. Within three decades, the population of Klipspruit, Alexandra and other townships had increased exponentially owing to the rapid industrialisation of Johannesburg and surrounding areas as a result of mining and related sectors. These developments necessitated the increase of housing for the army of black labour that was required to sustain the growing economy of Johannesburg. This resulted in the decision by the City Council to expand Soweto and, by 1931, the first council houses were completed and rented out to black people. These matchbox houses would become the blueprint for housing in Soweto and black townships across the Union of South Africa. Soweto as we now know it was thus created in the 1930s when the colonial government established black townships across the country as a means of differentiating the black working class from the white. The parameters for this differentiation had been set legislatively through the Urban Areas Act of 1923, which had its origins in the pass laws of the Cape Colony.

The migrant labour system played an instrumental role in the construction of Soweto. According to Delius (2017), the spatial inequalities wrought by the migrant labour system include but are not limited to the development of townships on the peripheries of industrial cities such as Johannesburg. Underdeveloped and overpopulated, these townships continue to serve as reserves for labour as was the case during colonialism and apartheid. This concentration of Africans in townships provides a blueprint for dealing with urbanisation. As with the townships under apartheid, in democratic South Africa, the poor are being concentrated in informal settlements and tenements. Townships and other compounds such as hostels that were built under colonial and apartheid regimes, protected white communities against the perceived threat posed by the thousands of African men working in the mines and staying in relative proximity to them (Demissie, 1998). This is a model that the post-apartheid city has assumed. Delius (2017) argues that the uniqueness of the said system lies in the extent to which it modelled not only rural transformation and industrialisation but urbanisation as well. According to Delius, the forms of urban systems and governance which emerged out of the migrant labour system are responsible for the forms of segregation existing in the post-apartheid urban space, in great part because migrancy and racism are intertwined (Neocosmos, 2006; Terreblanche, 2002; Kaziboni, 2022).

With the abolishment of the apartheid regime, black Africans who had been stripped of their citizenship were reintegrated back into South Africa. Consequently, with the complete abolition of laws governing movement for Africans in 1994, millions of people began to migrate to cities and towns where there were better economic opportunities after decades of separate development policies which centralised resources to urban South Africa. According to Tewolde (2021), these migrants were not only black South Africans but also Africans from other parts of the continent. This resulted in the advent of capital flight – the migration of industries and companies out of the city centre of Johannesburg to the northern suburbs. According to Tewolde (2021), this resulted in a majority of inner-city neighbourhoods across the Gauteng province being black-dominated and in the overpopulation of townships such as Soweto. It consequently gave rise to black South Africans and African immigrants living as segregated racialised groups and equally experiencing the brutal legacies of historical racial segregation. In Soweto, these experiences have forged both solidarity and native hostilities.

MIGRATION IN SOWETO

Native hostilities that are increasingly characterising the relations between black South African locals and immigrants in urban areas are anchored on the argument that the country is experiencing a 'migrant influx' that is impacting on the economy, and, specifically, on job prospects for locals. This narrative is examined in a policy brief titled 'Migration and employment in South Africa' by Budlender and Fauvelle-Aymar (2016). One of the key findings of the report is that migrants were more likely than locals to be employed, and unemployment rates for the migrants are noticeably lower than for those born in South Africa. However, this is mitigated by the fact that immigrants were much more likely than locally born residents to work in the informal sector, in precarious employment, and accessed far fewer benefits (Budlender and Fauvelle-Aymar, 2016). This aspect of the study is particularly significant because it explains, in part, why more migrants are opting to reside in the outskirts of cities, in peri-urban areas and informal settlements, and in townships like Soweto. They are part of the super-exploited working class that is also found in these areas with their status often taken advantage of through low wages and inferior working conditions.

Further to this, the 'migrant influx' narrative creates a false perception that migration is occurring only in South Africa. But according to Wickramage et al. (2018), there are increasing levels of international and internal migration specifically in low- and middle-income countries located in the global South. Internal migration or urbanisation in particular refers to the movement of people within a country's borders. The movement of people from rural to urban areas in particular results in a substantial increase in the proportion of people in cities and has been increasing more rapidly on the African continent than in any other region in the world. According to the UN, the urban population on the African continent is expected to increase from 43 to 59 per cent by the year 2050. This increase has colossal implications for the urban landscape, which has already been undergoing significant observable changes. While there has been a proliferation of studies on how migration is changing the urban landscape in Africa, many of these studies have been on the impacts of urbanisation and development on conservation. And very little of this research is focused on the ways in which migrants are positively disrupting township economies in ways that enfranchise locals.

The South African Cities Network (SACN) (2014) has revealed that these observed patterns of migration have implications for urban governance in South Africa. In its report on migration, mobility and urban vulnerabilities in South African cities, the network found that urban areas in places like Johannesburg are to a great degree spaces of improved access to better opportunities for livelihood generation, as well as the attainment of basic services, owing to their relatively better resources. Nevertheless, they are also zones of intra-urban inequalities where the poor, including migrants, battle to negotiate their existence. The report states that: 'There is evidence that in many of the country's cities, migration and mobility have resulted in different forms of socioeconomic and political instability and urban vulnerabilities, such as ethnic tensions, violent political rivalries, violent service delivery protests, xenophobic violence, livelihood insecurity, poor health outcomes, and a lack of access to services and opportunities. These have led to an urban penalty for the urban poor' (SACN, 2014: 5–6). These tensions and instabilities can be seen in Soweto, where anti-immigrant sentiments have resulted in outbursts of violence (Simelane and Nicolson, 2015) and the growth of xenophobic movements like Operation Dudula, which aims to rid townships of undocumented immigrants, often using violence and intimidation.

However, the narrative of native hostilities is only one aspect of the relations between locals and migrants. In the same Soweto, there is also a different relationship playing itself out – one of solidarity and mutual benefit between locals and migrants. This is particularly evident in the migrant tenant-local landlord relationship that is a growing feature of township geographies. There is observable evidence that the migrant tenant community is instrumental in facilitating township economic development, contributing to the alleviation of challenges, including but not limited to food security and poverty.

THE MIGRANT TENANT-LOCAL LANDLORD RELATIONSHIP IN SOWETO

Soweto ranks among the poorest areas in the City of Johannesburg metropolitan municipality – a result of colonial and apartheid policies that placed strict restrictions on enterprises in the township. According to Beavon (1997) these restrictions, which were in place from the early 1920s through to 1976, limited enterprise in Soweto to the operation of general shops and consequently the sale of hawked goods and informal trading in the township developed outside the legally recognised activities. This meant that until the late 1970s, households had no legal means of creating wealth. Compounded by the township's underdevelopment and the low income of households, this facilitated the reproduction of generational poverty in Soweto. This has resulted in Soweto having one of the highest levels of poverty in South Africa. The township also has high levels of unemployment, particularly among its youth. According to a study by the University of KwaZulu-Natal, in 2004, approximately 62 per cent of residents in the townships of Pimville and Orlando were either unemployed or pensioners. While data on the current rate of unemployment in Soweto is scant, it is logical to deduce that it is in alignment with the soaring rate of unemployment in the country, which presently stands at 32.7 per cent and 42.6 per cent based on the expanded definition of unemployment (Statistics South Africa, 2023), which includes those who have given up on searching for work. This profile makes Soweto fertile ground for low-skilled and semi-skilled migrants searching for economic activities in the diverse economy of the Gauteng province. Additionally, the location of Soweto on the outskirts of the City of Johannesburg, coupled with the availability of a somewhat integrated public transport network, means there is a relatively easy (albeit expensive) commute in and out of the city and other hubs of economic and industrial activity.

THE TOWNSHIP ECONOMY IN SOUTH AFRICA

The term 'township economy' refers to all the economic activities that occur in formally promulgated urban areas known as townships. Mahlatsi (2022) describes townships as underdeveloped residential spaces that were designed by the colonial regime and later the apartheid government to function as segregated dormitories supplying labour to economic centres in the city. Under apartheid, townships were reserved for black, coloured and Indian people and, in the democratic dispensation, this racialised spatial construct persists. The township economy, which encompasses the production, distribution, exchange and consumption of goods and services, is thus a spatial concept. Scheba and Turok (2019) contend that the township economy is different to the informal economy, which refers to unregulated economic activities irrespective of their location. The Sustainable Livelihoods Foundation (SLF) conducted the most comprehensive study on township economies in 2016, encompassing over 10,000 township enterprises across all nine provinces in the country. According to the study, grocery, food and liquor services comprise 54 per cent of all township businesses, followed by local services at 34 per cent (SLF, 2016). The latter includes car washes, hair salons/barber shops, traditional healers, mechanical/electrical repairs, recycling, churches and early childhood education centres. The study noted that manufacturing and production make up only 2 per cent of township enterprises (SLF, 2016) indicating that the township economy is not anchored on locally produced goods. This is corroborated by a 2018 study by the Cities Support

Programme, which states that products sold in the informal retail trade in townships, which is the dominant economic activity that includes spaza shops, shebeens and street vendors, are almost exclusively produced by firms based elsewhere.

RESULTS OF STUDY

Migrant tenants and income supplementation
All 20 landlords interviewed indicated that they were leasing rooms/ shacks and space in their yards as a means of supplementing the little income that their household has. Eleven of the landlords are pensioners and while some of them receive a state pension and/or money from their employed relatives, they stated that this was not enough to cover their expenses. Six of the landlords are unemployed, with most of their source of income being child support grants for their younger children and grandchildren. They all expressed that at R480 per child, the grant was not sufficient to purchase even the most basic of necessities. Three landlords indicated that while they are employed, their salaries are very low and cannot cover their monthly needs. Renting out rooms supplements their income, enabling them to have disposable cash for savings and investments. One uses the rental money to pay stokvel and funeral policies while another stated that she uses it to supplement school fees for her child who is attending a multi-racial school in the suburb of Westridge, Roodepoort.

Migrant tenants and food security
The benefits of migrant tenants in Soweto extend beyond providing supplementary incomes for their landlords. Community members benefit from the migrant enterprises, particularly on the issue of food security. The United Nations Food and Agriculture Organization defines food security as: 'A situation that exists when all people, at all times, have physical, social and economic access to sufficient, safe and nutritious food that meets their dietary needs and food preferences for an active and healthy life' (FAO, 2002: 4). While interventions such as social grants and other social protections by the state provide the financial means by which to attain nutritious foods, the physical and

233

social access to this food is provided by migrant spaza owners who ensure its availability in townships. According to the migrant spaza shop owners, members of the community take food on credit during the month and repay the debt when they have resources, usually from social grants. In Braamfischerville, where a significant proportion of households rely solely on child support grants and pensions, migrant spaza shop owners provide a critical intervention by extending credit for food and other goods, for which no interest is paid at the end of the month. This practice has shielded many households from hunger, especially as the income they receive is usually below the food poverty line. While the practice has resulted in many households being dependent on this food credit facility, sustaining a cycle of borrowing, it does provide temporary relief from hunger. One of the migrant tenant spaza shop owners indicated that school-going children benefit most from this practice as their parents often take food to make school lunchboxes on credit. Infant food is also a common food taken on credit.

Migrants, job creation and skills transfer

Migrant tenant spaza shop owners in Soweto contribute to employment as they employ some locals. In a migrant-owned hair salon in Braamfischerville, the Mozambican migrant employs three South African women who do braids and dreadlocks. In this process, there is also skills transfer as the migrant tenant indicated that he taught the three young women how to braid and do other hairstyles. Additionally, one of the women also does acrylic nails in the salon, which essentially means she has acquired and is practising a new skill that will aid in her income generation and employability. In spaza shops, locals are employed to cook and make *kotas*. The migrant tenant spaza shop owners also stated that they employ locals as security guards not only to create employment, but because locals are more conversant with the happenings in the township.

Migrant tenants and security for the elderly and women

A number of landlords interviewed indicated that the migrant tenants provide some form of security for them. Four landlords who are pensioners and whose own children are at work during the day stated that the presence of migrant tenants was a deterrent for criminals who sometimes committed residential burglaries in the neighbourhood. A landlord who is renting a shack to a migrant in Braamfischerville stated that his presence in the yard makes her feel safer as she is a single mother who is vulnerable to criminals who often target households where they know that there are no male figures.

Migrant tenants and community diversity

Some of the landlords interviewed indicated that the presence of migrants in their homes has led to them understanding migrants in general better, and thus, changing their previously held prejudicial ideas about immigrants. A landlord in Meadowlands stated that she has learned Shona, one of the national languages of Zimbabwe, as a result of having a tenant from Masvingo renting in her yard. Communities, broadly, are benefiting from learning about the different cultures and traditions of migrants, which is a necessary step towards integration and tolerance in a South Africa that is battling with xenophobia and related intolerance.

RECOMMENDATIONS

Transitional housing provision for refugees and asylum seekers

South Africa does not have an encampment policy for dealing with asylum seekers and refugees. This means that under section 27 of the Constitution, refugees and asylum seekers have the right to freedom of movement within South Africa and are not limited or confined to certain spaces but may go to any area (Scalabrini Centre, 2023). While this is progressive in the sense that it enables better integration of these categories of immigrants into local communities, it also places them in a precarious position where they do not have means and adequate opportunities to access housing and other services (Kavuro, 2019). The National Housing Code and the National Housing Policy and Subsidy Programme state that beneficiaries of individual, consolidation, institutional, or rural subsidies and residential development programmes must have either citizenship or permanent residence. No provision is made for refugees and asylum seekers in these programmes. To resolve this, the South African government, with multilateral partners such as the United Nations High Commissioner for Refugees (UNHCR) and development partners, must source financial resources and utilise available financial infrastructure to build low-cost transitional housing for refugees and asylum seekers. Programmes to transition them and integrate them into the economy, which agencies such as the UNHCR already provide on a limited scale, must then be instituted to ensure their full integration.

Strengthen the township economy

The township economy in South Africa has the potential to bring significant transformation in townships such as Soweto. However, there is a range of municipal by-laws, regulations and procedures that inhibit township enterprises from operating legitimately and obtaining the associated benefits (Scheba and Turok, 2019). While there is recognition that inappropriate standards and complex approval procedures and bureaucracy inhibit the formalisation and expansion of many township enterprises, there is still a conservative approach to the implementation of the Business Act of 1991, which makes allowance for informal trade, by municipalities. This needs to be addressed at Council level to ensure that councillors and municipal authorities apply the law as intended. Another important factor to note is the low manufacturing capacity of township enterprises, which has led to township enterprises performing a complementary role in enabling formal retailers and major wholesalers access into the low-income consumer segment in townships, rather than creating locally manufactured products. It is recommended that a framework for building manufacturing capacity in townships be developed through the establishment of manufacturing hubs. Resources must be availed by the Department of Trade, Industry and Competition as well as provincial and municipal governments for this undertaking.

CONCLUSION

This study illustrates that the spatial ordering of the post-apartheid dispensation perpetuates the marginalisation of certain sectors of the urban population, particularly in townships. Linked to this is the dire economic state of townships such as Soweto, where unemployment and poverty are significantly high. This has set parameters for locals finding alternative ways of income and livelihood generation outside the formal economy. The leasing of backyard dwellings and yard space is an attempt by landlords to survive in an economy that is hurling them at the margins, as well as a way for immigrants, asylum seekers and refugees who are not included in housing policies to negotiate their own survival and existence. There are some notable positive aspects of the migrant tenant-local landlord relationship, such as the supplementing of income, transfer of skills, job creation and the provision of access to food and nutrition. But there is also an empowerment component to this relationship. However, the relationship also enables the dereliction of duty on the part of government, both towards locals and migrants. The slow pace of economic transformation is deepening racialised inequalities, which affect working-class people in townships like Soweto the most. Furthermore, the policy issues posing an impediment to migrant refugees and asylum seekers accessing housing programmes is creating an untenable situation where migrants are being left to their own devices, sometimes in hostile and violent environments, without any meaningful legal and social protection. This demands a paradigm shift in how the government engages the issue of housing, which is part of a chromatin network of which an untransformed and stagnant economy is the nucleus.

REFERENCES

Babbie, E. 2001. *The Practice of Social Research*. Belmont: Wadsworth Thompson Learning.

Beall, J., Crankshaw, O. and Parnell, S. 2003. 'Social differentiation and urban governance in Soweto: A case study of post-apartheid Meadowlands', in Tomlinson, R., Bureauregard, R. A., Bremner, L. and Magcu, X. (eds), *Emerging Johannesburg: Perspectives on the post-apartheid city*. New York and London: Routledge.

Beavon, K. 1997. 'Johannesburg: A city and metropolitan area in transformation', in Rakodi, C. (ed.), *The Urban Challenge in Africa: Growth and management of its large cities*. Tokyo: United Nations University Press.

Bonner, P. and Segal, L. 1998. *Soweto: A history*. Cape Town: Maskew

Miller Longman.

Budlender, D. and Fauvelle-Aymar, C. 2016. 'Migration and employment in South Africa'. *MiWORC Policy Brief 2*, https://www.ilo.org/wcmsp5/groups/public/---ed_protect/---protrav/---migrant/documents/publication/wcms_379445.pdf, accessed 5 December 2022.

Crankshaw, O., Gilbert, A. and Morris, A. 2000. 'Backyard Soweto'. *International Journal of Urban and Regional Research*, 24(4), 841–857.

Delius, P. 2017. *Migrant Labour in South Africa (1800–2014): Oxford research encyclopaedia of African history*. Cape Town: Oxford University Press.

Demissie, F. 1998. 'In the shadow of the gold mines: Migrancy and mine housing in South Africa'. *Housing Studies*, 13(4), 445–469.

Food and Agriculture Organization (FAO). 2002. 'The State of Food Insecurity in the World 2021'. Rome, 4–7.

Hamann, C., Mkhize, T. and Götz, G. 2018. 'Backyard and informal dwellings (2001–2016)'. Gauteng City Region Observatory, https://www.gcro.ac.za/outputs/map-of-the-month/detail/backyard-and-informal-dwellings-2001-2016/, accessed 17 May 2023.

Harington, J. S., McGlashan, N. D. and Chelkowska, E. Z. 2004. 'A century of migrant labour in the gold mines of South Africa'. *The Journal of the South African Institute of Mining and Metallurgy*, 104(2), 65–71.

Kavuro, C. 2019. 'Housing and integrating refugees: South Africa's exclusionary approach'. *Obiter*, 40 (1).

Kaziboni, A. 2022. 'Apartheid racism and post-apartheid xenophobia: Bridging the gap', in Rugunanan, P. and Xulu-Gama, N. (eds), *Migration in Southern Africa*. IMISCOE Research Series. Johannesburg: Springer.

Kimberley, J. 2015. 'The nature, scope and purpose of spatial planning in South Africa: Towards a more coherent legal framework under SPLUMA'. Master's thesis, University of Cape Town.

Lawrence, P. G. 1994. 'Class, colour consciousness and the search for identity: Blacks at the Kimberley diamond diggings 1867–1893'. Master's thesis, University of Cape Town.

Mahlatsi, M. L. S. 2022. 'Gentrification and the displacement of vulnerable communities in the post-apartheid city: A case study of the Maboneng Precinct and Braamfontein'. Master's thesis, University of Johannesburg.

McDonald, D. A. 1998. 'Hear no housing, see no housing: Immigration and homelessness in the new South Africa'. *Cities*, 15(6), 449–462.

Moolla, R., Kotze, N. and Block, L. 2011. 'Housing satisfaction and quality of life in RDP houses in Braamfischerville, Soweto: A South African case study'. *Urbani Izziv*, 22(1), 138–143.

Neocosmos, M. 2006. *From 'Foreign natives' to 'Native foreigners': Explaining Xenophobia in Post-apartheid South Africa- Citizenship and Nationalism, Identity and Politics. Monograph* series. Dakar: CODESRIA.

Nieftagodien, N. and Gaule, S. 2012. *Orlando West, Soweto: An Illustrated*

History. Johannesburg: Wits University Press.

Ntsebeza, L. and Kepe, T. (eds). 2012. *Rural Resistance in South Africa: The Mpondo revolts after fifty years*. Cape Town: University of Cape Town Press.

Scalabrini Centre. 2023. 'World refugees day: Assessing South Africa's refugee protection system', https://sihma.org.za/Blog-on-the-move/world-refugees-day#:~:text=Furthermore%2C%20South%20Africa%20does%20not,(Scalabrini%20Centre%2C%202023), accessed 1 December 2023.

Scheba, A. and Turok, I. N. 2019. 'Strengthening township economies in South Africa: The case for better regulation and policy innovation'. *Urban Forum*, 31, 77–94.

Simelane, B. C. and Nicolson, G. 2015. 'Hour-by-hour, Soweto xenophobia spirals into disgrace'. *Daily Maverick*, https://www.dailymaverick.co.za/article/2015-01-23-hour-by-hour-soweto-xenophobia-spirals-into-disgrace/, accessed 17 May 2023.

Soja, E. W. 1980. 'The socio-spatial dialectic'. *Annals of the Association of American Geographers*, 70(2), 207–225

South African Cities Network (SACN). 2014. *Migration, mobility and Urban Vulnerabilities: Implications for urban governance in South Africa*. Braamfontein: SACN.

Statistics South Africa. 2011. 'Census 2011', https://www.statssa.gov.za/?page_id=3839, accessed 20 February 2023.

Sustainable Livelihoods Foundation (SLF). 2016. 'South Africa's informal economy: Research findings from nine townships'. Cape Town: Sustainable Livelihoods Foundation.

Terreblanche, S. 2002. *A History of Inequality in South Africa 1652–2002*. Durban: UKZN Press.

Tewolde, A. I. 2021. 'Migrating into segregated majority-black inner cities: Racialised settlement patterns of African migrants in Pretoria, South Africa'. *Cities*, 113.

Webster, D. 2018. 'Gauteng separates into shacks and gated estates'. *New Frame*, https://www.newframe.com/gauteng-separates-shacks-and-gated-estates/, accessed 15 May 2023.

Wickramage, K., Vearey, J., Zwi, A. B., Robinson, C. and Knipper, M. 2018. 'Migration and health: A global public health research priority'. *BMC Public Health*, 18(1), 987.

TEN

Internal migration, spatial divisions and the redistribution dilemma in South Africa

Eddie M. Rakabe

INTRODUCTION

International migration has and continues to receive significant scholarly and political attention, yet by far the largest movements of people are between places in the same country, not always from the villages to cities, but also from economically lagging to leading rural areas (World Bank, 2009). Internal migration forces are responsible for the transformation of economic geography throughout countries around the world. Classic economic literature suggests that factors of production (capital and labour) move to places where they are concentrated and likely to earn the highest returns. Producers and workers in developed economies have sought and often found their fortunes in towns and cities (Vanables, 2003). The movement of industry and people to concentrated towns and cities recognises that 'the world is not flat' i.e., the rate of development across the geographic scale is not smooth nor linear. Some places develop earlier and faster than others (World Bank, 2009). These places are called 'leading areas'. Economic development in leading areas fosters greater market integration, which in turn attracts waves of people and capital inflows that promote inclusive and sustainable spatial transformation.

People's and firms' concentration in leading areas fuels agglomeration economies, which in turn reinforces migration exoduses to leading areas. Development models, however, suggest that the process of agglomeration plateaus at some point and starts to be offset by diseconomies of agglomeration[1] and, importantly, disquiet over uneven spatial development (World Bank, 2009). The presence of agglomeration diseconomies does not necessarily halt or reverse the process of migration. Movement from lagging to leading areas continues as long as the centripetal force outweighs the centrifugal force. In the process, spatial disparities present redistribution dilemmas to countries juggling circular migration, large rural populations and ambitious agglomeration ideals. Spatial disparities manifest broadly through levels of economic activity and income as well as variations in factor endowments and infrastructure, which affect the accessibility and quality of basic and social services such as education and healthcare (Shilpi et al., 2018).

Uneven spatial development matters for several reasons. First, it is part of overall, undesirable national inequality. Second, it reinforces this inequality when migrant-sending and -receiving regions are divided along political, ethnic and religious lines. Third, it matters on account of enormous public policy interest in addressing spatial divisions through progressive taxes, transfers, provision of basic services, infrastructure and incentives at source and destination areas. Lastly, spatial disparities shape settlement and development patterns (Kambur and Vanables, 2005). These, in turn, influence or reinforce the concentration of economic activity in a given area and the investment decisions of respective governments to either expand the capacity of leading areas to attract and accommodate increased migrants (and

---

1 Including but not limited to pollution, congestion, sprawl and slum development, the high cost of living and crime.

industry) or to reduce the social and economic push factors in lagging areas (Vanables, 2003).

When people migrate from one area to another – either voluntarily or through coercion – attempts are made to create spatial policies that will reduce the factors causing spatial divisions, such as poor planning or use of land, and market failures. Such policies are usually aimed at improving state provision of developmental services, such as schools, healthcare, housing, water, roads and public employment programmes (PEPs). Other spatial policies incentivise firms to locate or remain in lagging areas in the hope of creating conducive economic conditions (generally employment) similar to those in destination towns and cities. Development studies, in particular, have especially placed significant emphasis on employment and wages (labour migration) as the key forces driving internal migration and shaping economic geography.

The first generation of studies departing from the rural, agrarian growth model to an urban, manufacturing sector model postulated that people move because of differences in wages between source and destination areas. In this conjecture, high wages at the destination are presumed to reflect a shortage of labour relative to capital, and the arrival of job-searching migrants is expected to slow down wage growth while capital accumulation at the source areas is projected to increase wage growth for the remaining workers. Eventually, the incomes of the two areas converge, leading to either a slowdown or ceasing of migration processes (Krugman, 1991). The second generation and popular classic framework dubbed the Harris and Todaro Model theorised that prospective migrants' decision to move is based on the expected future differential income they could earn in destination cities compared with that in rural-sending areas, after considering relocation and job-search costs.

In this formulation, migration from rural to urban areas continues as long as urban expected wages exceed rural wages. This model created a phenomenon called the Todaro Paradox – namely, that policies to improve urban wage and development could paradoxically cause or worsen urban surplus labour (unemployment) or increase urban informal sector activity by attracting more job-seeking migrants from the rural areas. Accordingly, urban migration must be managed to avoid negative social impacts and urban employment disequilibrium (Todaro, 1996). Based on this model, many developing countries adopted place-based redistribution policies such as integrated rural development programmes, which, among other things, encouraged rural wage increases to reduce migration outflows. Admittedly, the focus of conventional theories on economic disparities as a key determining factor of spatial mobility has been criticised by De Haas (2010a) as inadequate, static and narrow in its treatment of migration as a single action rather than a process of transformation.

Acknowledging these limitations, this chapter departs from the premise that economic disparities generally trigger redistribution policies to reduce spatial divisions as part of broader regional development, which may in turn influence migration in either direction, i.e. from lagging to leading areas, and contrariwise. Spatial disparities are especially acute in South Africa, originating from apartheid racialised spatial transformation policies, which encouraged industrial concentration and deliberately curtailed the free movement of people and labour. Specifically, these policies suppressed urban and rural wages for African workers. With the advent of democracy and the subsequent easing of movement restrictions South Africa finds itself undergoing yet another unique spatial transformation in which internal migration coexists with spatial mismatch (physical separation of where people live and work).

This geographic transformation is accompanied by rising levels of unemployment and poverty in both the source (mainly rural) and destination (cities) areas: urban decline and deindustrialisation in destination areas, and deeply entrenched if not worsening underdevelopment in source areas (COGTA, 2016). As the transformation of economic geography unfolds, tensions arise over whether to invest in lagging areas or to promote further agglomeration, thus creating a redistribution dilemma. This chapter therefore assesses the intersection between internal migration, spatial disparities and redistribution policies with particular emphasis on how redistribution policy responds to or shapes subsequent migration and spatial patterns in South Africa.

MIGRATION AS A PROCESS OF
SPATIAL TRANSFORMATION

Migration is an integral part of societal change, and it has always been an important contributor to and a result of spatial transformation – which refers to changes in the sectoral and spatial distribution of economic activity and people over a period of time. A typical manifestation of this process, popularised by advocates of the core-periphery development model, entails a gradual shift from agricultural economic activities (in the rural areas) to a modernised economy based initially on manufacturing and then on services (in the urban area) occurring alongside agglomeration economies[2] (Mercandalli et al., 2019). While there have been sustained shifts from industrialising towards the services sectors, there remain significant variations in the nature and extent of this transformation across geography within countries (Takeda, 2022).

Spatial transformation and agglomeration economies occur and continue at different paces in accordance with prevailing regional characteristics or comparative advantages. Badiane et al. (2022) is of the view that spatial transformation is successful when accompanied by the migration of labour out of the rural agriculture sector into the urban industrial sector – bringing into sharp focus the causal and dynamic relationship between the two. Historically, the phenomenon of migration has not always been associated with spatial transformation. Movement of people, as Mercandalli et al. (2019) note, was initially associated with the search for safe and suitable land for settlement, pasture and farming in response to climate variations, changing social formations and political circumstances, such as warfare and slavery.

As people moved, they discovered natural factor endowments and other locational characteristics, which became the basis for industrial activity, thereby setting in motion a mutually reinforcing process of concentration between firms and people or agglomeration in general. The World Bank (2009) sees this transformation as comprising three

---

2   Co-location and concentration of firms and workers.

dimensions: density,[3] distance[4] and division[5], which continuously intersect to affect or drive migration. Table 10.1 illustrates the transformation process by order of importance along three geographic scales, namely, local, national and international. Accordingly, density or concentration is the most important dimension at local scale while distance to density (between areas of high economic activity) matters the most at the national geographic scale in the process of spatial transformation. The key enabling and driving factors of national spatial transformation are labour mobility and lower transportation costs, which are made possible by infrastructure investments.

Table 10.1: Dimensions of spatial transformation

	Geographic scale		
	Local	National	International
	Area	Country	Region
First importance	Density	Distance	Division
	Rural and urban areas	Between lagging and leading areas	Between countries
Second importance	Distance	Density	Distance
	Due to congestion	Of population and poverty in lagging areas	To major world markets
Third importance	Division	Distance	Distance
	Between formal and informal settlements	Between areas within a country	No large economy in the neighbourhood

Source: World Bank (2009)

As evidenced, migration is not a single action, but an integral part of the spatial and structural transformation process accompanied and inspired by technological change and sectoral restructuring. The changes

---

3 Compactness of people and geographic activity within a defined geographic area.

4 Relates to distance between areas of economic concentration and lagging areas to facilitate easy access to markets.

5 Concerns international divisions on free movement of people and capital across borders and differences in currencies and regulations.

emanate from scattered agricultural activities to concentrated urban industry, and from labour migrations from rural areas to cities made possible by advances in transport and communication linkages. Migration flows continue, almost incessantly driven by push factors at places of origin, i.e., population pressures, land use inefficiency, low productivity and mechanisation (of agriculture) shortage of amenities and pull factors at destination areas, including high wage and job expectations, the lure of 'city lights', better and further education opportunities, and higher living standards (Kaya, 2015). In this way, push and pull factors intersect to create cumulative causation between migration and spatial transformation.

The process of human and economic concentration continues for as long as regions and countries develop. The pace of development, however, varies according to geographic scale. For instance, the growth of economic and population density is faster at local levels and at lower incomes – below US$4,255 per capita per annum (World Bank, 2022b) – a level that has been surpassed by leading/urban areas in most developing countries, including in Africa. Economic density increases faster in some places as new waves of people move to live near new towns and cities, following what De Haas (2010b) calls pioneer migrants.

According to the World Bank (2022b), the proportion of urban populations globally continues to rise steeply from 10 per cent to over 50 per cent as different countries transition from a low- to middle-income status of about US$4,255 (2022) per capita. The process of concentration slows down when the income level reaches US$13,205 per capita – mainly associated with middle-income countries – and starts stalling at higher income levels above US$13,205 per capita (see also Friedmann, 1966). As income rises together with migration, in the process of spatial transformation, living standards are expected to converge between leading and lagging areas. However, convergence is neither linear nor guaranteed. Spatial disparities are inevitable, especially in developing countries, which may still have inadequate infrastructure and institutions at different regional levels.

Redistribution policies for spatial disparities
While there has been sustained concentration of people and industry in leading areas, there is significant variation in the extent of this

spatial transformation across the geographic scale within any given country (Takeda, 2022). Once a significant number of migrants settle in leading areas, other forces come into play (De Haas, 2021), manifesting as economic and social problems. These forces, as theorised by Krugman (1991), result in cumulative circular, divergent and asymmetric development in which certain regions or areas gain a 'core' status while others become peripheries. Factors contributing to this process are centripetal forces, including market sizes, high wages or incomes, free labour movement and positive external environments, as well as centrifugal forces, which are generally immobile, i.e., natural resources, competition and positive external factors. Dominance in any one of the forces leads to extreme spatial disparities (Andrzej and Magdalena, 2019). According to Krugman (2011), centripetal forces (concentration) are generally stronger than centrifugal forces (spatial dispersion) and this inevitably leads to stark variations in levels of socioeconomic development across spaces.

The ensuing disparities manifest in three ways: through wages and income; household consumption patterns; and access to basic (public) services. Differences between areas in household consumption and access to basic services are generally more persistent, although convergence tends to happen faster at a local level, as with economic concentration. Wage and income disparities between source and destination areas grow wider as countries transform from low- to lower-middle-income status. These disparities manifest and vary on a geographic scale. For instance, there are fewer disparities within low-income countries than between different regions and countries.

Similarly, highly urbanised areas display asocial deficiencies, such as the prevalence of slum areas, even when income levels are high (World Bank, 2009). This challenge is generally attributable to faster population growth resulting from migration. An inability to manage the disparities not only creates and compounds the redistribution dilemma but also reproduces poverty, inequality, agglomeration diseconomies and underdevelopment (Peter, 2015).

Farole and Sharp (2017) assert that spatial inequality is normal. Similarly, the World Bank (2015) notes that economic growth (and development) is inherently unbalanced and therefore spreading such development over large geographical areas discourages it. By this logic, the process of human and economic concentration must be supported even if it produces spatial inequalities. While the Organisation for Economic Co-operation and Development (OECD) (2019) and Fintel (2018) argue that spatial disparities arise because of rapid industrialisation, Farole and Sharp (2017) attribute the imbalance to disproportionately mobile capital, specifically in relation to the movement of people or labour. For Kohler (2015) the growing concentration of wealth and income stands in stark contrast to the ideals of balanced, shared and sustainable growth in an ever-more interdependent, segmented and dispersed production process. The disparities therefore imply a lack of aggregate economic efficiency and an inability to produce within the region's potential. When this combines with self-reinforcing institutional failures, the result is an unending cycle of underdevelopment in lagging areas and threats to social and political cohesion where regions are divided along ethnic and political lines. The conception of inequality as a natural and temporary phenomenon likely to converge over time with economic growth, as predicted in certain theories, has proved unattainable for most economies in transition. This gap then leads to contestation over policies to address spatial inequalities.

Spatial policy for lagging areas

Deepening spatial disparities tend to provoke irresoluble policy debates concerning the appropriateness of spatial policies (broadly, redistribution policies) to promote inclusive and equitable spatial transformation. One school of thought (Castells-Quintana and Royuela, 2018) argues that government must avoid spatially targeted policies and instead adopt space-neutral policies, which enable vulnerable people to access opportunities when they arise. According to this conjecture, leading areas develop almost naturally, driven by market forces, and subsequently narrow spatial gaps through trade and migration linkages to lagging areas. Large cities function as engines of growth because of agglomeration economies. This approach advocates for the removal of regulations and spatial interventions as they distort market signals, limit capital and labour mobility, undermine economic efficiency, suppress growth and limit welfare benefits (Mel'nikova, 2015; Todes and Turok, 2016).

Conversely, another strand of literature (Krugman, 2011), based on new economic geography and endogenous growth theory, argues for explicit, spatially targeted policies to maximise the growth potential of regions and areas beyond the cities. As markets are prone to failure, government intervention is often required to improve the fortunes of lagging areas and create an enabling environment for the concentration of economic activity and people. Government should actively drive decisions about business locations and migration flows to avoid the formation of inefficient spatial development patterns. In this regard, spatial policies must exploit untapped local social, institutional and economic attributes, and remedy constraints on local and regional development (Neumark and Simpson, 2014). This strategy requires an integrated approach (including planning for stakeholder involvement and financing) based on the holistic development of regional capabilities, rather than on a narrow sectoral approach.

Place-based policies are synonymous with another approach called spatial rebalancing, an approach differentiated by rationales, areas of focus and instruments. While place-based policies are concerned with improving conditions across a wider cluster of regions through an endogenous process, spatial rebalancing seeks to narrow the wealth gap between regions with a focus on poor areas. Spatial rebalancing generally involves diverting economic activity from leading to lagging areas and attracting external investments through policies such as subsidies for firms and infrastructure. It has attracted major criticism for being overly centralised, reinforcing dependency and failing to engender self-sustaining growth in the wake of initial interventions (Todes and Turok, 2016). The adoption of any one of the approaches to spatial policies within an environment of high spatial divisions may aggravate inefficient spatial transformation, e.g., neglect of infrastructure in declining rural areas or holding back agglomeration economies.

SPATIAL DEVELOPMENT AND MIGRATION PATTERNS IN SOUTH AFRICA

Social and economic injustices (and divisions) represent a significant part of South Africa's historical spatial development patterns and are partly attributable to the country's unique spatial transformation trajectory (Giraut and Vacchiani-Marcuzzo, 2009; Fintel, 2018). These patterns are strongly correlated with race and remain largely the same to this day, as exemplified by the remnants of apartheid city social tapestries and low racial integration across space (see Figures 10.1 and 10.2). Southern Africa's pre-colonial industrial and migration patterns were closely related to the industrialisation process, which entailed exploiting natural resources (land and minerals) and labour (migrants), epitomised by the remains of the famous Mapungubwe kingdom/ settlement, among others. The discovery of diamonds in 1867 and gold in 1886 in South Africa stimulated the Mineral Revolution and unprecedented spatial transformation. This was first characterised by vast labour movement to the mining areas and later a process of industrial modernisation and concentration, dubbed the Mineral Energy Complex, to support and profit from the minerals value chain (Turok, 2012).

Figure 10.1: Social tapestry (Nelson Mandela Bay Metro)

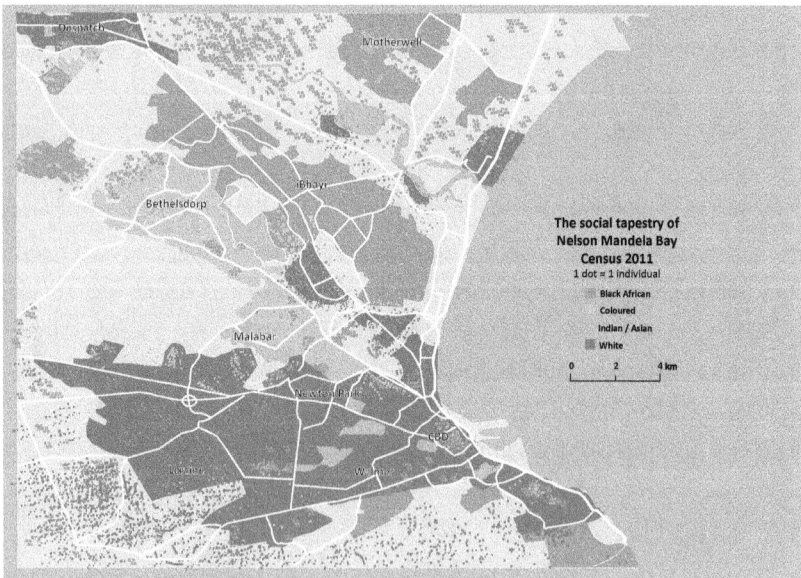

Source: StatsSA (2016a)

Figure 10.2: Segregation index of six cities

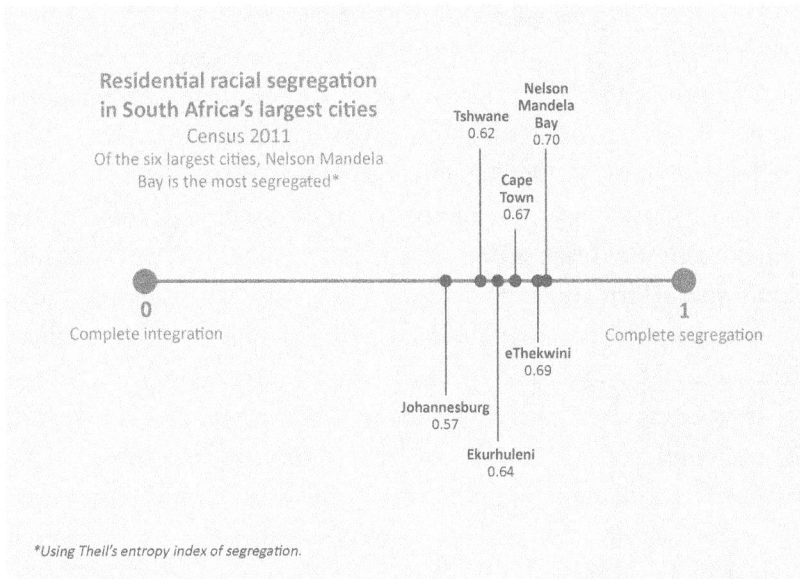

Residential racial segregation
in South Africa's largest cities
Census 2011
Of the six largest cities, Nelson Mandela
Bay is the most segregated*

Nelson
Mandela
Bay
0.70

Tshwane
0.62

Cape
Town
0.67

0
Complete integration

1
Complete segregation

eThekwini
0.69

Johannesburg
0.57

Ekurhuleni
0.64

*Using Theil's entropy index of segregation.

Source: StatsSA (2016a)

The need for a cheap and regular flow of African labour to the mines and industry, on the one hand, and the desire to maintain white minority political and economic control as well as separate development, on the other hand, led to the introduction of various forms of draconian social and spatial engineering laws (apartheid spatial planning) to control the spatial distribution of population and industry (Giraut and Vacchiani-Marcuzzo, 2009). A transient labour system (underpinned by pass laws) was created for African workers to migrate to (mining) cities for work purposes only. The Land Act of 1913 and Group Areas Act of 1950 maintained racially segregated areas, with the African majority forced to live in lagging areas without economic activity and social services. The system had a profound influence on rural dispersion and how cities are organised, therefore causing spatial mismatch, i.e., industrial concentration with restricted labour mobility (dislocated urbanisation) and misalignment between density and housing, amenities and skilled labour (Shilpi et al., 2018).

At the dawn of democracy in 1994, South Africa had a total population of 40 million, of which 53 per cent already lived in the urban areas and 43 per cent lived in the Bantustans[6] or lagging areas (see Figure 10.1). Mining expansion and the resulting urban industrial growth created a strong impetus for the de-facto permanent urban residency of African workers and a resulting need for housing to accommodate black families in the townships, rendering influx control policies ineffective (Turok, 2012; Shilpi et al., 2018). The abolition of mobility restrictions in the wake of the democratic transition accelerated the migration flow of black people, in particular, out of the Bantustans into urban South Africa under racially inclusive political and administrative boundaries towards core urban centres (towns, cities and metropolitan areas) during the 1990s and 2000s (Bakker et al., 2016).

In tracking post-apartheid migration patterns between 1996 and 2001, Shilpi et al. (2018) observe that a substantial number of the Bantustan population did not move to large urban cities but to towns closer to their areas of origin. Figure 10.3 illustrates the population shift from the periphery towards core areas in the city of Tshwane[7] between 2000 and 2011. This is partly explained by the gravity principle, which implies that a town or leading area located closer to a homeland will attract more migrants than a town further away because of considerations about the costs of distance (Bakker et al., 2016). By 2001, the total South African urban population increased to 56.3 per cent with only 47 per cent of black people urbanised while the corresponding figure for white, coloured and Indian people was 90, 87 and 97 per cent respectively (Kok et al., 2006). Since then, migration to leading areas (urbanisation) has been increasing steadily at an annual average rate of 1 per cent, reaching 68 per cent in 2021 (see Figure 10.6).

Notwithstanding the gravity argument above, the general trend in migration portrays a shift from the Bantustans (which constituted a large part of post-apartheid provincial boundaries) and mostly rural and underdeveloped provinces, including the Eastern Cape (EC), Limpopo (LP), KwaZulu-Natal (KZN), Northwest (NW) and parts of Mpumalanga (MP), to highly urbanised and industrialised provinces,

---

6 Territories (constituting 7 per cent of the land) reserved for black people under apartheid.
7 The population density increased from 340 to 463 people per km² between 2001 and 2011 (StatsSA, 2016a).

Figure 10.3: Population density shifts between 2001 and 2011 (City of Tshwane)

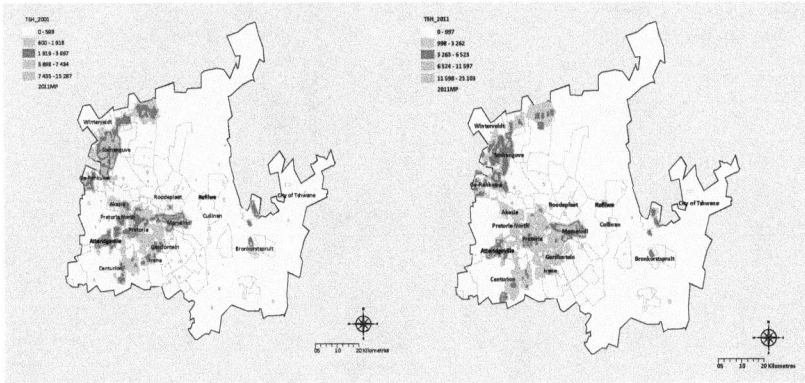

Source: StatsSA (2016a)

including Gauteng (GP) and the Western Cape (WC) (shown in Figure 10.4). This pattern resembles a greater part of colonial/apartheid capital accumulation and economic protectorates and generally reinforces a deep-seated spatial mismatch (see next section).

The analysis reveals other noteworthy observations about South Africa's spatial transformation discussed earlier. First, urbanisation stalled during the apartheid era despite rising incomes, thus constraining the urban dividend. Second, urbanisation started increasing steadily in the aftermath of 1994 in line with rising income as expected and as a consequence of the complete abolition of 'influx control' laws and practices. However, this increase was characterised by rising subnational disparities in income and production (see next section). The World Bank (2009) attributes this phenomenon to underdeveloped infrastructure and institutions. Third, urbanisation has been accompanied by deindustrialisation, illustrated by the declining share of manufacturing to total output[8] (Rodrik, 2020), high urban informal economy[9] (Rogan,

---

8   Manufacturing as a share of total output peaked to 25 per cent in 1980 and started a declining trend to 12 per cent in 2020 (Reserve Bank, 2020).
9   Informal employment as a proportion of total employment across eight major cities is 24 per cent and highest in eThekwini (Durban) and Johannesburg at 26 and 25 per cent respectively.

Figure 10.4: Bantustan territories, new provinces and cities

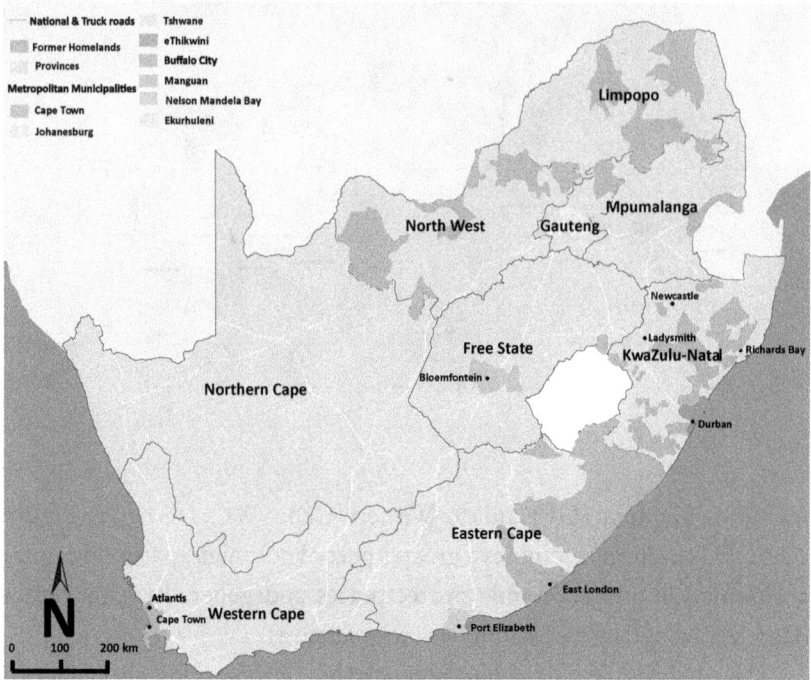

Source: Ali (2016)

Figure 10.5: Migration destination (2016–2021)

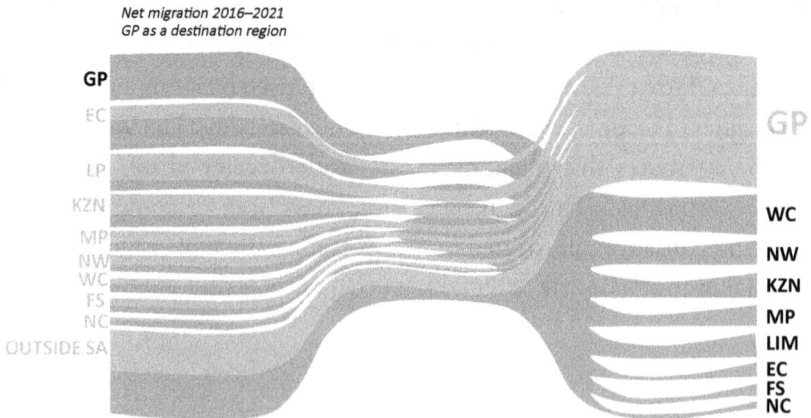

Source: StatsSA (2021a)

Figure 10.6: Rate of urbanisation and levels of income trend

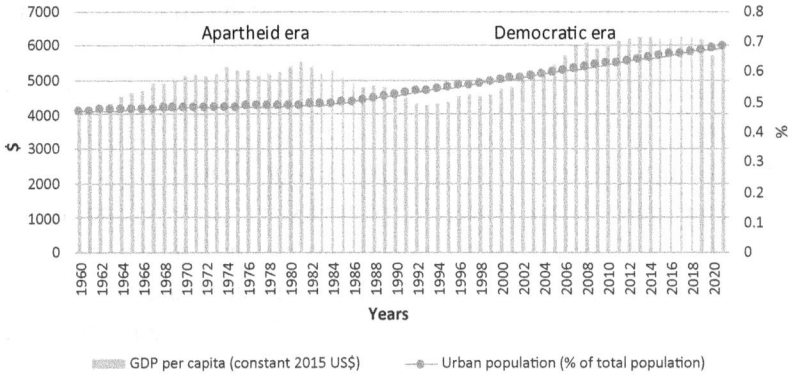

Source: World Bank (2022b)

Note: US$ applied for ease of reference to country income level in relation to the previous discussion.

2019), acute poverty[10] and agglomeration diseconomies. Urban areas are experiencing premature agglomeration diseconomies because of a cumulative lag in investments and a lack of structural change, especially a corresponding concentration of a skilled workforce and technology-intensive industry (Kebede, 2018; Reserve Bank, 2020).

Tables 10.2 and 10.3 give a detailed breakdown of internal migration patterns by provinces of origin and destinations over two waves of migration – 2006–2011 and 2011 and 2022 – driven by various spatial development fundamentals and myriad other forces explained in previous sections. The data illustrates that migration patterns are not one-directional despite the general movement towards the two most urbanised provinces of Gauteng and the Western Cape. Several other important patterns emerge: Gauteng province has remained the leading destination for migrants across the two waves, with the highest numbers of migrants originating from Limpopo, KwaZulu-Natal and Eastern Cape provinces. The number of migrants from rural provinces has decreased slightly over the period resulting in a lower negative net migration. For instance, Eastern Cape net migration amounted to a negative 352,000 between

---

10 17 per cent of households in metropolitan areas experience food hunger (StatsSA, 2021b).

2006 and 2011 and a further 63,000 between 2011 and 2022 (see Figure 10.7 and Table 10.2). This may be partly attributable to the gravity and agglomeration diseconomies arguments made above.

Gauteng, the Eastern Cape and Limpopo have a relatively high proportion of mobile populations. Cross-boundary (provincial) migration tends to follow historical patterns of labour demand and the gravity principle. For instance, the Eastern Cape is the second-highest contributor of in-migration to North West province despite the long-distance factor, partly because of what Nomvete (2021) describes as 'ina-ethe[11] migration' – high status historically placed on migration and mining labour by Xhosa men to meet their traditional customs as providers and heads of households. Similarly, the largest share of out-migrants from the Northern Cape settle in North West because of cultural and family ties, as well as geographical proximity. The same pattern is also observable between neighbouring Limpopo and Mpumalanga, KwaZulu-Natal and Mpumalanga as well as Free State and the Eastern Cape provinces as can be seen by the number of people who moved between the neighbouring provinces in Table 10.2 (the figures in rows show the total number of people who moved from once province to another between 2011 and 2022).

Figure 10.7: Net migration differentials per province (2006–2011 and 2011 and 2022)

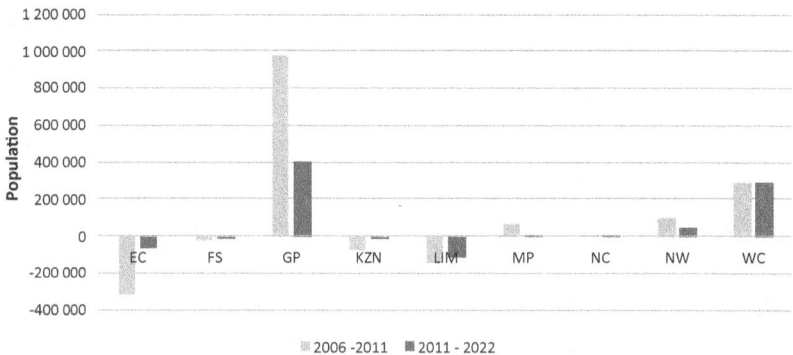

Source: StatsSA (2016a, 2022)

---

11 'Give and take' (in South Africa's Xhosa language), describing the reciprocal relationship between male migrant workers and their housewives.

Table 10.2: Provincial migration patterns, Census 2011 and 2022

	WC	EC	NC	FS	KZN	NW	GP	MP	LP	In-migrants	Out-migrants	Net migration
WC	6,706,820	60,082	8,916	3,564	7,615	2,400	25,780	1,825	2,338	406,549	112,520	294,029
EC	124,225	6,792,242	2,823	8,051	38,941	10,226	54,323	5,153	3,100	184,213	246,842	-62,629
NC	11,098	2,751	1,272,160	3,738	1,046	5,198	6,576	897	978	44,376	32,282	12,094
FS	12,823	7,457	5,339	2,778,654	5,200	9,879	36,289	3,940	2,594	73,643	83,521	-9,878
KZN	25,730	21,091	1,358	6,337	1,1793,136	3,835	100,052	17,505	3,342	169,183	179,250	-10,067
NW	8,344	4,935	9,249	6,478	2,578	3,522,544	56,780	3,184	7,439	146,262	98,987	47,275
GP	97,972	46,820	8,184	24,183	53,810	58,128	13,734,733	42,394	64,486	795,330	395,977	399,353
MP	8,176	3,922	1,325	3,956	9,154	5,796	70,811	4,852,153	16,669	132,459	119,809	12,650
LP	7,540	3,457	1,510	2,629	3,495	14,424	161,877	20,342	6,197,192	100,946	215,274	-114,328
Outside SA	110,641	33,698	5,672	14,707	47,344	36,376	282,842	37,219	50,411			

Source: StatsSA (2022)

SOUTH AFRICAN SPATIAL
DIVISIONS IN PLAIN SIGHT

Spatial divisions manifest at different geographical scales (regional to local) and various functional units (administrative or economic borders) through different physical, social and economic attributes. This formulation can result in different permutations of spatial disparities where divisions occur within a region, across sub-regions and local areas, and between local areas or towns in functional economic or administrative borders. This section focuses on high-level spatial inequalities at a national geographical scale. The aim is not so much to discuss the underlying causes as to illustrate the existence of the spatial gaps using mainly economic indicators.

South Africa is one of the most unequal and visibly polarised territories in the world (The Presidency, 2012; David et al., 2018). This uneven concentration of economic activity is the most glaring and disconcerting indicator of spatial division. Three provinces, including Gauteng, KwaZulu-Natal and the Western Cape, account for two-thirds of the total economic output as seen in Figure 10.8. Regional growth concentration patterns correspond with the trends in per-capita gross regional domestic product (GRDP) as seen by high incomes in Gauteng and Western Cape provinces which are the top-most economically dominant provinces.

Variation in per-capita GRDP at the local scale is more dynamic as the better-resourced municipalities are mostly rural agricultural towns (formerly white only) such as Matlosana (formerly Klerksdorp) in North West, Modimolle (Nylstroom) in Limpopo, Steve Tshwete (Middelburg) in Mpumalanga and Knysna in the Western Cape (David et al., 2018). Notwithstanding the skewed concentration of economic activity, unemployment in both the leading and lagging provinces is high. For example, Gauteng has the third-highest unemployment rate at 37 per cent after the Eastern Cape (44 per cent) and Mpumalanga (38 per cent) while the Western Cape boasts the second-lowest unemployment rate (25.2 per cent) after the Northern Cape (24.9 per cent) (StatsSA, 2022). The rest of the other former Bantustan territories or migrant-sending areas such as Limpopo,[12] KwaZulu-Natal and the North West display unemployment rates below the national average. Overall, migration patterns or broader factor mobility continue to display path dependency, but the post-democratic era waves have not resulted in income convergence, presumably owing to the lasting effect of colonial/apartheid era divergent development patterns.

Figure 10.8: GRDP share per province, 1996 and 2021

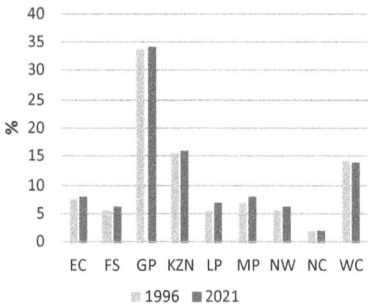

Figure 10.9: Per capita GRDP, 2021

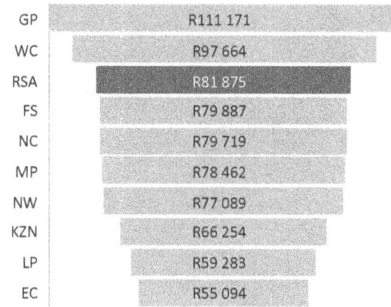

GP	R111 171
WC	R97 664
RSA	R81 875
FS	R79 887
NC	R79 719
MP	R78 462
NW	R77 089
KZN	R66 254
LP	R59 283
EC	R55 094

Source: StatsSA (2021a)

Source: StatsSA (2021a)

Uneven spatial distributions of growth and development are further characterised by high poverty, coinciding with high inequality across provincial and local geographic scales. Figure 10.10 shows that poverty and inequality are acute in regions that correspond with former homeland areas. While income poverty depicts stark geographical concentration, income inequality, measured by the Gini coefficient, shows wider prevalence and variation across the national scale. The high spatial income divisions straddle both the lagging and the leading areas.

Spatial divisions are also manifested in access to basic services and the enabling delivery/network infrastructure across the regions, as illustrated in Figures 10.11 and 10.12. While South Africa has made significant progress in improving household access to basic water (88 per cent), electricity (89 per cent), sanitation (84 per cent) and refuse (60 per cent), there remains extensive spatial variation in the quality and

---

12 Slightly above national average with fourth-highest unemployment rate.

Figure 10.10: Spatial distribution of poverty and income (local scale)

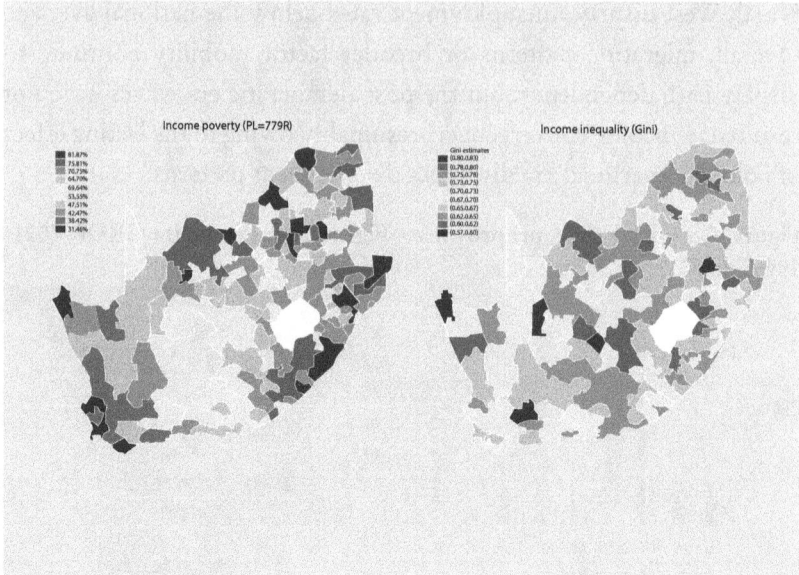

Source: StatsSA (2016b)

reliability of the services (StatsSA, 2021b). Rural provinces generally experience high service delivery interruptions (StatsSA, 2016a). Using a Multiple Deprivation Index,[13] Noble and Wright (2013) also show that the most deprived regions in South Africa correspond with the former Bantustan areas, which remain relatively deprived to this day.

Experience of spatial policies and resulting redistribution paradox
South Africa has introduced numerous spatial policies since 1995 that seem to straddle spatial rebalancing, targeting and neutrality at the same time, perhaps signifying the stubborn legacy of apartheid spatial planning and the difficulties in defining a new vision of economic geography. Migration and industrial concentration patterns discussed earlier create new challenges for spatial policies as people continue to migrate to leading areas where the number of jobs available per jobseeker is declining and economic activity is rapidly shifting towards the services sector. At the same time, a significant majority remains

---

13 Comprises material deprivation, employment deprivation, education deprivation and living environment deprivation.

Figure 10.11: Percentage of households with access to piped water

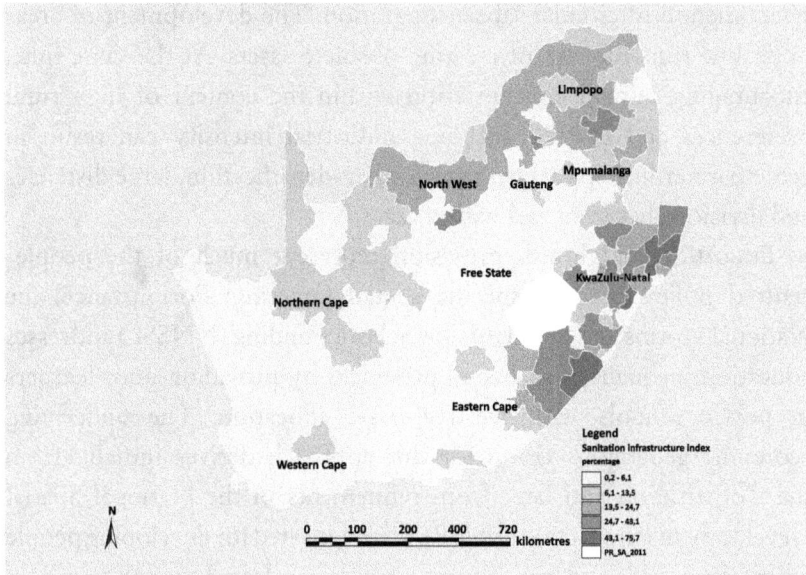

Source: StatsSA (2016b)

Figure 10.12: Sanitation infrastructure quality index

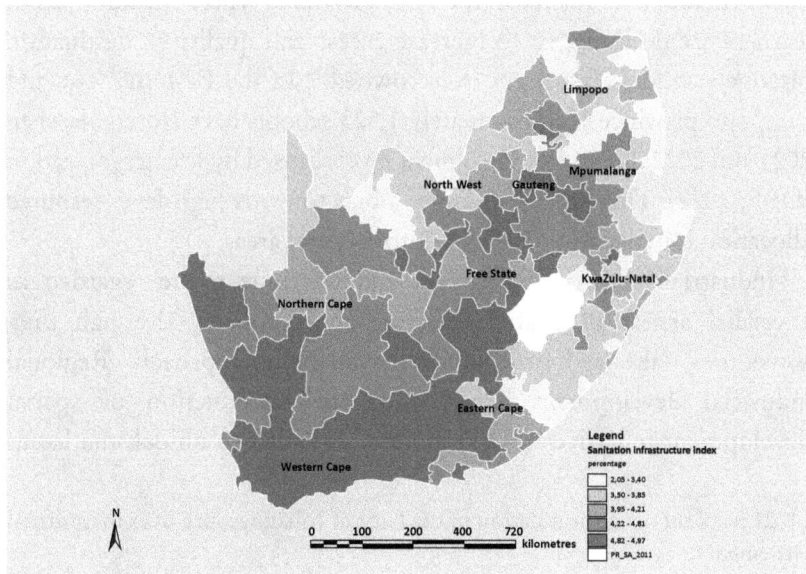

Source: StatsSA (2016b)

rural bound because of historical and cultural ties and the strong phenomenon of circular labour migration. The development of areas in decline runs the risk of creating obsolete assets. At the same time, encouraging human concentration within the context of high rural preferences and low or declining industrial intensity can result in growth-retarding spatial patterns, i.e., de-densification, large distances and divisions between and within areas.[14]

Education and health provision represent much of the people-centred policy without specific spatial targeting. For instance, the National Norms and Standards for School Funding (NNSSF) addresses education inequalities across all provinces by providing poor learners in public schools with fee-free basic education. The underlying economic geography vision for this approach derives initially from the Constitution and later from refinements in the National Spatial Development Perspective (NSDP): this advocated for developing people where they reside and targeting investment in selected growth corridors to which skilled migrant labour can move (The Presidency, 2006). With the changing patterns of migration from single men to families and the (perceptions of) poor education conditions in rural provinces, space-neutral policies produce tensions over whether to improve education infrastructure and quality in the rural provinces where the numbers of learners are declining or to increase access and quality in destination provinces where classes are overcrowded.[15] In the Eastern Cape and Limpopo provinces, approximately 1,523 schools have closed between 2021 and 2022 due to low enrolment levels caused by learner migration (DBE, 2022). This happens despite a bias towards high-level resource allocation for education infrastructure in rural areas.

Industrialisation policies were and continue to be regarded as a crucial aspect of spatial transformation policies although they sometimes take a hybrid and unsystematic approach. Regional industrial development began with the introduction of spatial development initiatives (SDIs) in 1996 intended to unlock the latent

---

14 21 per cent of the population in the City of Johannesburg lives in informal settlements.

15 Gauteng receives over 100,000 new learners from outside the province per annum.

growth potential of 11 corridors across the country. This was to be achieved through a combination of targeted local infrastructure investment, incentives to attract private firms (rebalancing) and a broad range of institutional interventions to improve the business climates and skills (place-based). SDIs were conceptualised as 12–18-month initiatives that would later be transferred to the relevant provinces and municipalities. The SDI morphed into a spatial rebalancing programme of industrial development zones (IDZs) around the year 2000, aimed at building industrial precincts to increase the exportation of value-added commodities via key ports. Dissatisfaction with the IDZ over its failure to attract investors and other, wider institutional weaknesses led to the introduction of the special economic zones (SEZs) in 2014. These promised a wider regional focus and the promotion of distinctive local industrial clusters. Eleven SEZs were subsequently created across all nine provinces (Todes and Turok, 2016).

The implications of an industrialisation-focused spatial transformation for economic and redistribution policies are threefold. The first is the inefficiencies associated with spreading industrial activity in areas experiencing population decline. The second relates to the diverting of resources and investments from cities as key drivers of national growth and competitiveness. The third relates to the investment of public funds in areas with low prospects for generating self-sustaining commercial activity and development (Farole and Sharp, 2017). Reviews of the IDZs by Chinguno (2009) found that similar incentive packages were available outside of the designated industrial zones while Nel and Rogerson (2014) maintain that SEZ incentives do not respond holistically to the bidding constraints affecting rural provinces, such as thin markets, poor infrastructure and low skills bases.

The spatial division-induced redistribution dilemma and the unwavering political pressure for expedient spatial transformation are nowhere more evident than in the introduction of myriad spatially targeted initiatives, consistent with place-based ideals, since 1994. The Special Integrated Presidential Projects were launched in 1994 as part of the Reconstruction and Development Programme (RDP) to fast-track public service delivery in areas ravaged by political violence. In

2001, President Mbeki launched the Urban Renewal Programme and the Integrated Sustainable Rural Development Programme as the first nodal development scheme of the new government to reduce poverty and deprivation in eight township nodes and 15 rural nodes (largely overlaying former Bantustan boundaries). In the intervening years, attempts to formalise, legislate and set a broader vision for spatial integration led to the enactment of the Spatial Planning and Land Use Management Act (SPLUMA) of 2013. Among other things, this laid out requirements for national, provincial and local spatial development frameworks and principles for spatial justice. Section 7 (a) (ii) of the Act states:

> Spatial development frameworks and policies at all spheres of government must address the inclusion of persons and areas that were previously excluded, with an emphasis on informal settlement, former Bantustan areas and areas characterized by widespread poverty and deprivation.

As the legacy of apartheid spatial divisions endures, the number of new place-based initiatives has proliferated. These include a gamut of conditional fiscal transfers, reincarnation of old policies and programmes and a cumulative layer of new policies.

In general, fiscal transfers to provinces and municipalities generally embrace equalisation principles to the benefit of lagging areas. Conditional grants such as the Neighbourhood Development Partnership Grant (NDPG), the Urban Settlements Development Grant (USDG) and the School Infrastructure Backlog Grant (SIBG)[16] have been designed specifically to unlock the potential of marginalised urban (mainly township) and rural nodes through a combination of infrastructure and institutional support. Financial support for spatial targeting also includes the Urban Renewal Tax Incentive within designated urban development zones to attract investments (mainly property) to the inner city. Some of these interventions have been

---

16 Grant intended to replace inadequate school facilities (mud schools) in the Eastern Cape province.

retrospectively appended to the newly revised spatial transformation policies such as the Cities Support Programme and the Integrated Urban Development Framework – seen as the overarching basis for guiding future growth and management of urban areas (COGTA, 2016).

The National Development Plan (NDP), first published in 2011, further outlines a national scheme for spatial targeting consisting of five corridors of national importance and three special intervention areas classified as job intervention zones, growth management zones and green economy zones – each requiring a unique form of state intervention. For instance, the jobs intervention zones are areas that have experienced more than a 20 per cent reduction in employment over a 10-year period in which the state may seek to stimulate the growth of new sectors, invest in new skills or promote depopulation (The Presidency, 2012). These areas generally coincide with rural restructuring corridors or densely populated peripheries, which according to the NDP require 'management, institutional development, land and tenure reform, infrastructure provision and economic stimulu'. Yet, the 2009 Comprehensive Rural Development Programme (CRDP) sought to drive a participatory and non-interventionist approach to rural development by decongesting and rehabilitating overcrowded former homelands while promoting the emergence of rural industrial and financial sectors at the same time.

With a seemingly total disregard for the NSDP, the NDP advocated for the development of a national spatial framework to coordinate and integrate programmes that create and shape the functioning of places. Subsequently, the new National Spatial Development Framework was enacted into law in 2023, as per section 13(5) of SPLUMA, setting out a new vision for national spatial development that is premised on a combination of nodal development, spatial rebalancing and targeted approaches (DRDLR, 2023). Figure 10.13 gives a schematic illustration of the new spatial vision. In 2019, the government adopted the District Development Model, yet another intervention, embodying spatial targeting features in which 44 district municipalities and eight metropolitan areas become the focal point for joint planning and delivery of public services and private investments.

Figure 10.13: New national spatial transformation logic

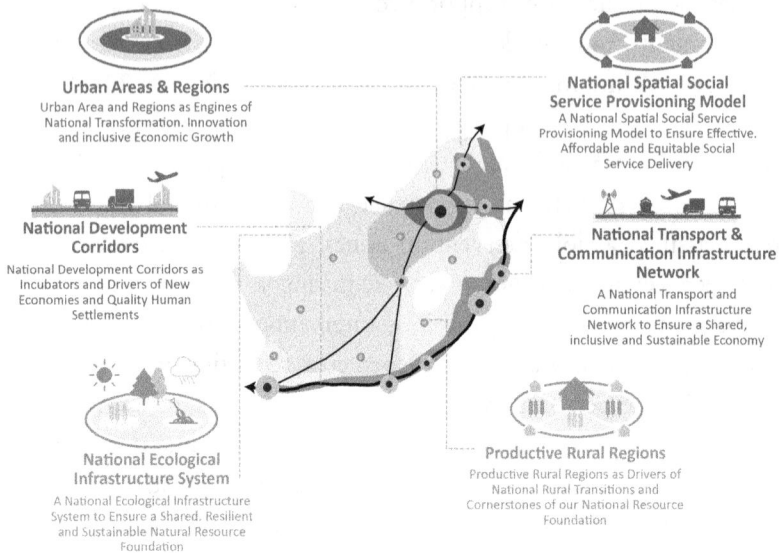

Urban Areas & Regions
Urban Area and Regions as Engines of
National Transformation. Innovation
and Inclusive Economic Growth

**National Spatial Social
Service Provisioning Model**
A National Spatial Social Service
Provisioning Model to Ensure Effective.
Affordable and Equitable Social
Service Delivery

**National Development
Corridors**
National Development Corridors as
Incubators and Drivers of New
Economies and Quality Human
Settlements

**National Transport &
Communication Infrastructure
Network**
A National Transport and
Communication Infrastructure
Network to Ensure a Shared,
inclusive and Sustainable Economy

**National Ecological
Infrastructure System**
A National Ecological Infrastructure
System to Ensure a Shared. Resilient
and Sustainable Natural Resource
Foundation

Productive Rural Regions
Productive Rural Regions as Drivers of
National Rural Transitions and
Cornerstones of our National Resource
Foundation

*Source: Department of Agriculture, Land Reform and Rural Development
(2023)*

The policy framework does not seem to explicitly promote agglomeration economies (even at the sub-regional scale) as the overarching vision for driving growth and spatial transformation. At most, the entire package seems to drive an agenda of spreading growth and development throughout the country – presumably because of the decentralised system of government – which requires equitable treatment of all provincial and local territories. Not only does this create redistribution disorder but it also results in the neutral impact of spatial policies and reinforces undesirable patterns of spatial transformation.

CONCLUSION

This chapter sought to highlight the distributional tensions arising from an unsystematic spatial transformation agenda. Historical development and migration patterns affect the subsequent formation of economic geography in which certain regions or areas stagnate while others thrive. Spatial policies correct the ensuing spatial division by either encouraging the concentration of industry and people in big towns and cities to maximise agglomeration economies, or by supporting development in lagging peripheral areas to promote inclusion. The slow pace of spatial transformation, however, often leads to and reinforces suboptimal organisation of economic geography or spatial mismatch where industry concentrates without creating sufficient jobs or attracting the right skills. A combination of the resultant incorrect migration signals and remedial spatial policies directs people to areas experiencing urban decline while confining others within latent areas.

An institutionalised system of dispossession, racial segregation, mobility restrictions and deliberate deprivation of Bantustans in South Africa has created a lasting legacy of country-wide spatial divisions, which continue to aggravate undesirable spatial development patterns. Former Bantustans remain largely underdeveloped and characterised by low economic activity and poor socioeconomic status. Migration patterns generally portray path dependency – seemingly following social networks rather than economic opportunities. The province that is the top choice as a destination for migrants has the third-highest rate of unemployment, juxtaposed with extensive deprivation in the sending provinces and wide income inequalities across the national scale.

The government has found it difficult to develop appropriate policy responses to vastly complex socio-spatial inequalities, sometimes conflicted by the equality and equity ideals espoused in the Constitution. The approaches adopted by the South African government overlap between all these spatial policies. Consequently, resources are spread thinly, with efforts to both develop rural areas beyond the provision of basic services and, at the same time, support urban areas in becoming thriving centres of growth. South Africa needs to develop a common vision for economic geography to achieve successful and growth-enhancing spatial transformation.

REFERENCES

Ali, S. M. S. 2016. 'GIS time series mapping of a former South African homeland'. Master of Technology in Cartography thesis, Cape Peninsula University of Technology, https://etd.cput.ac.za/bitstre am/20.500.11838/2506/1/214319954-Ali-Salih%20Mohamed%20

Sidahmed-M.Tech-Cartography-Eng-2017.pdf, accessed 15 May 2023.

Badiane, O., Collins, J., Glatzel. K. and Tefera, W. 2022. 'The rise of Africa's processing sector and commercialization of smallholder agriculture', in Jenane, C., Ulimwengu, J. M. and Tadesse, G (eds), *Annual Trends and Outlook Report: Agrifood Processing Strategies for Successful Food Systems Transformation in Africa.* Kigali: International Food Policy Research Institute, 6–22.

Bakker, J. D., Parson, C. and Rauch, F. 2016. 'Migration and urbanisation in post-apartheid South Africa'. IZA Discussion Paper No. 10113, https:// docs.iza.org/dp10113.pdf, accessed 15 May 2023.

Castells-Quintana, D. and Royuela, V. 2018. 'Spatially blind policies? Analysing agglomeration economies and European investment bank funding in European neighbouring countries'. *The Annals of Regional Science*, 60(3), 569–589.

Cooperative Governance and Traditional Affairs (COGTA). 2016. 'Integrated urban development framework: A new deal for South African cities and towns'. Republic of South Africa, Pretoria.

David, A., Guilbert, N., Hamaguchi, N., Higashi, Y., Hino, H., Leibbrandt, M. and Shifa, M. 2018. 'Spatial poverty and inequality in South Africa: A municipality level analysis'. SALDRU Working Paper Number 221, SALDRU, University of Cape Town.

De Haas, H. 2010a. 'The internal dynamics of migration processes: A theoretical inquiry'. *Journal of Ethnic and Migration Studies*, 36(10), 1587–1617.

De Haas, H. 2010b. 'Migration transitions: A theoretical and empirical inquiry into the developmental drivers of international migration'. *IMI/DEMIG Working Paper No 24*, Oxford University: International Migration Institute.

De Hass, H. 2021. 'A theory of migration: The aspirations-capabilities framework'. *Comparative Migration Studies*, 9(8), 1–35.

Department of Rural Development and Land Reform (DRDLR). 2023. 'National Spatial Development Framework'. Republic of South Africa, Pretoria.

Farole, T. and Sharp, M. 2017. 'Spatial industrial policy, Special Economic Zones (SEZ), and cities in South Africa', https://www. ukesa.info/download/N0pLMrXBAWfF84hu9iszKj6Vkv2J7PGS/ Paper-5-SEZs-and-Cities.pdf, accessed 15 May 2023.

Fintel, D. V. 2018. 'Long-run spatial inequality in South Africa: Early settlement patterns and separate development'. Stellenbosch Economic Working Papers WP16/2018, University of Stellenbosch.

Friedman, J. R. 1966. *Regional Development Policy: A case study of Venezuela.* Cambridge: MIT Press.

Gaspar, J. M. 2021. 'New economic geography: History and debate'. *The European Journal of the History of Economic Thought*, 28(1), 46–82.

Giraut, F. and Vacchiani-Marcuzzo, C. 2009. *Territories and Urbanisation in South Africa: Atlas and geo-historical information system (DYSTURB)*. Marseille: IRD Editions.

Kambur, R and Vanables, A. J. 2005. 'Spatial inequality and development: An overview of UNU-Wider project'. *GSDRC Applied Knowledge Services*, https://gsdrc.org/document-library/spatial-inequality-and-development-an-overview-of-unu-wider-project/, accessed 15 May 2023.

Kaya, G. 2015. 'Internal migration and its effects in one of the underdeveloped regions of Turkey'. *International Journal of Humanities and Social Science*, 5(3), 71–80.

Kebede, G. 2018. 'Understanding and promoting cities as drivers of economic development'. Stellenbosch Institute for Advanced Study, https://stias.ac.za/2018/04/understanding-and-promoting-cities-as-drivers-of-economic-development-fellows-seminar-by-gulelat-kebede/, accessed 15 May 2023.

Kohler, P. 2015. 'Redistributive policies for sustainable development: Looking at the role of Assets and Equity'. UN DESA Working Paper No. 139, https://www.un.org/ar/desa/redistributive-policies-sustainable-development-looking-role-assets-and-equity, accessed 15 July 2024.

Kok, P., Collinson, M., Van Tonder, L. and Roux, N. 2006. 'Migration and urbanization in South Africa'. Report 03-04-02, Statistics South Africa, Pretoria.

Krugman, P. 1991. 'Increasing returns and economic geography'. *Journal of Political Economy*, 99(3), 483–499.

Krugman, P. 2011. 'The new economic geography, now middle-aged'. *Regional Studies*, 45(1), 1–7.

Mel'nikova, L. V. 2015. 'Space-neutral and place-based regional policies: The problem of choice'. *Regional Research of Russia*, 5, 1–9.

Mercandalli, S., Losch, B., Belebema M. N., Bélières J. F., Bourgeois R., Dinbabo M. F., Fréguin-Gresh S., Mensah, C. and Nshimbi, C. C. (eds), 2019. *Rural Migration in Sub–Saharan Africa: Patterns, drivers, and relation to structural transformation*. Rome: FAO and CIRAD.

Nel, E. L. and Rogerson, C. M. 2014. 'Re-spatializing development: Reflections from South Africa's recent re-engagement with planning for Special Economic Zones'. *Urbani Izziv*, 25(supplement, S24 – S35).

Neumark, D. and Simpson, H. 2014. 'Place-based policies'. Working Paper No. 20049, National Bureau of Economic Research, Cambridge.

Noble, M. and Wright, G. 2013. 'Using indicators of multiple deprivation to demonstrate the spatial legacy of apartheid in South Africa'. *Social Indicators Research*, 112(1), 187–201.

Nomvete, S. 2021. 'The emergence of Ina-ethe migration: Mpondo men and continued migrant labour post-apartheid'. PhD Thesis: University of Pretoria.

Peter, E. 2015. 'Dilemmas of urban governance and infrastructure deficit in Africa', in Condie, J. and Cooper, A. N. (eds), *Dialogues of Sustainable Urbanisation: Social science research and transitions to urban context.* Sydney: University of Western Sydney.

Reserve Bank, 2020. 'South African Reserve Bank Occasional Bulletin of Economic Notes, OBEN/20/02'. Reserve Bank: South Africa.

Rodrik, D. 2020. 'Industrialization, de-industrialization and growth strategy for South Africa'. The Presidency, https://www.thepresidency.gov.za/sites/default/files/01.%20Industrializatio%20 Deindustrialization%20and%20Growth%20Strategy%20for%20 SA%20March%202020.pdf, accessed 15 May 2023.

Shilpi, F., Xu, L., Behal, R. and Blankespoor, B. 2018. 'People on the move: Spatial mismatch and migration in post-apartheid South Africa'. World Bank Group, file:///C:/Users/Machete/Downloads/ Paper-1-People-on-the-Move.pdf , accessed 15 May 2023.

Statistics South Africa (StatsSA). 2016a. 'GHS series volume VII, housing from a human settlement perspective, In-depth analysis of the General Household Survey Data 2002–2014'. Pretoria.

Statistics South Africa (StatsSA). 2016b. 'The state of basic service delivery in South Africa: In-depth analysis of the community survey 2016 data'. Pretoria: South Africa.

Statistics South Africa (StatsSA). 2021a. 'General Household Survey'. Pretoria: South Africa.

Statistics South Africa (StatsSA). 2021b. 'Mid-year population estimates'. Pretoria: South Africa.

Statistics South Africa (StatsSA). 2022. 'Quarterly labour force survey'. Pretoria: South Africa.

Takeda, K. 2022. 'The geography of structural transformation: Effects on inequality and mobility'. Discussion Paper, Centre for Economic Performance, The London School of Economics and Political Science.

The Presidency. 2006. 'National Spatial Development Perspective'. Republic of South Africa, Pretoria.

The Presidency, 2012. 'National Development Plan (NDP), Vision 2030'. Republic of South Africa, Pretoria.

Todaro, M. P. 1996. 'Income expectations, rural–urban migration and employment in Africa'. *International Labour Review* 135(3/4), 421–444.

Todes, A. and Turok, I. 2016. 'Spatial inequalities and policies in South

Africa: Place-based or people-centred?'. *Progress in Planning*, 123, 1–31.

Turok, I. 2012. 'Urbanisation and development in South Africa: Economic imperatives, spatial distortions and strategic response'. Urbanization and Emerging Population Issues Working Paper 8, International Institute for Environment and Development United Nations Population Fund.

Vanables, T. 2003. 'Spatial inequality and development'. *Widerangle,* https://www.wider.unu.edu/publication/spatial-inequality-and-development-0, accessed 15 May 2023.

World Bank. 2009. 'World Bank development report 2009: Reshaping economic geography'. Washington D.C.: The World Bank Group

World Bank. 2015. 'Global economic prospects: Having fiscal space and using it', https://www.worldbank.org/content/dam/Worldbank/GEP/GEP2015a/pdfs/GEP15a_web_full.pdf, accessed 15 January 2024.

World Bank, 2022a. 'World Bank database'. Washington D.C.: World Bank.

World Bank, 2022b. New World Bank country classifications by income level: 2022-2023. Washington D.C.: World Bank.

Section Three

The State and Migration Governance

ELEVEN

Migration governance in South Africa

EDDIE M. RAKABE, WANDILE M. NGCAWENI AND GABRIEL LUBALE

INTRODUCTION

Background on migration governance in South Africa
Migration governance in South Africa has been and remains a complex and challenging issue for politicians and government officials. The complexity and primacy of migration governance in the country has escalated in the post-democratic era due to the multiple economic, geopolitical and environmental issues affecting the African continent and the sub-Saharan African region in particular (Ehiane, 2023). As the country grapples with the inflow of migrants from the region and the need to embrace free peoples movement principles, the South African government is often found wanting, receiving criticism from citizens over the inability to manage porous borders, while at the same time taking blame for violating international migration treaties

and securitising the borders. The result is an ambiguous migration governance framework, which, as Maunganidze (2023) argues, is balanced on paper, but tilts towards deterrence, enforcement and exclusivity in practice.

The ambiguity has historical precedence in the apartheid-era Aliens Act of 1937, which excluded Indians, Jews, Catholics and black Africans, from obtaining long-term residence outside of designated locations and homelands. It is also evident in the post-democratic era in the treatment of irregular migrants from different countries, with those from Zimbabwe and Lesotho enjoying exemption permits[1] while others are excluded (Hirsch, 2024). Governance challenges are further compounded by the inefficiency and maladministration of the institutions responsible for overseeing and implementing migration policies.

This chapter provides an overview of migration governance in South Africa and assesses the policy measures undertaken to manage migration in the post-democratic era, and the impact of these on attaining a holistic migration governance regime. It further aims to highlight key challenges and opportunities associated with implementing state policies on migration in the context of public outcries over the weakness of migration governance and the strong advocacy to regularise undocumented migrants (Government of South Africa, 2002; DHA, 2017). It also provides the South African government's perspective on migration governance as conceived in the White Paper on International Migration. The chapter concludes that migration governance in South Africa will require a long-term commitment from the government and other stakeholders to work together in addressing perceptions about the causes, consequences and threats of migration.

THEORETICAL BACKGROUND

Migration governance is a combination of two concepts: migration and governance. Migration is generally accepted terminology. However, the term governance when it relates to migration has no common

---

1   These exemptions are a subject of ongoing legal action between civil rights movements and the government of South Africa over the termination date and the granting of permanent residence to permit holders.

understanding. This is unsurprising because governance develops meaning from the intended ideas, processes and practices rather than any prior conceived meaning it possesses (Geddes, 2022). Fukuyama (2016: 2) describes governance as comprising three dimensions, namely, governance as a synonym for public administration (good governance); governance as international cooperation through non-sovereign bodies outside the state system (international governance); and governance as the regulation of social behaviour through networks and other non-hierarchical mechanisms (governing without government). Drawing from these dimensions, migration governance can therefore be regarded as a complex set of laws, regulations and partnerships adopted by national, subnational and international institutions to manage and shape migration across countries (European Commission, 2021).

Migration governance interacts with several non-institutional actors in both countries of origin and destination but is also applicable to different categories of migration, including regular and irregular migration, labour migration, child migration, forced migration, refugees migration and family migration (European Commission, 2021). These categories are regulated differently by different actors and institutions. By creating these categories and allocating people accordingly, governance not only shapes migration but also has a decisive effect on who is eligible to migrate. For this reason, Geddes (2022) argues that migration governance is about inclusion but also strongly about exclusion. The process of inclusion or exclusion can occur at the stage of departure, entry, transit and stay. This underscores the point that migration governance does not apply only at the point of destination, as some of the migration studies suggests.

Migration studies have had the tendency to depict the migration policy strategies of non-European actors as neat, fixed or two-dimensional, without explaining how actors oscillate between positions and domestic political demands, resulting in tensions and unlikely alliances (De Haas et al., 2019); or analysing how bureaucratic dynamics such as civil servants' interpersonal networks and staff turnover within ministries shape policy outcomes 'on the ground' (Lebon-McGregor, 2020).

The International Organization for Migration (IOM) defines

migration governance as 'the traditions and institutions by which authority on migration, mobility and nationality in a country is exercised, including the capacity of the government to effectively formulate and implement sound policies in these areas' (IOM, 2015: 1). The state is regarded as the primary actor in migration affairs and therefore commands sovereign right to determine conditions of entry and stay in its territory, albeit within the confines of international laws. Recognising the participatory nature of migration, the IOM (2015) further acknowledges that other actors such as citizens, migrants, civil movements, international organisations and academia can contribute to migration governance through interaction with the state and each other.

Accordingly, the overarching thrust of governance must seek to ensure that migration is humane, safe, and orderly, and benefits migrants and the society by adhering to international standards and fulfilling migrants' rights. It should also seek to address the socioeconomic wellbeing of migrants and mobility dimensions of crises. Migration governance thus has both a national and global dimension. Global governance refers to the norms, rules, principles, decision-making procedures and organisational structures that regulate the behaviour of states and other transnational actors (Betts and Kainz, 2017: 5). In the domain of international migration, governance assumes a variety of forms. These include the migration or immigration policies, labour migration policies and programmes of individual countries, as well as inter-state discussions and agreements, multilateral (forums) and consultative processes, the activities of international organisations, as well as relevant laws and norms (IOM, 2019: 150–151).

Some migration studies have characterised migration governance in South Africa as vague, inconsistent, populist and highly securitised, without explaining how different actors vacillate between domestic political and international demands, resulting in tensions and unlikely alliances, or analysing the effects of bureaucratic changes on migration policy outcomes. Migration governance intersects with long and complicated histories of mobility, state formation and colonial domination, as chapter 1 in this volume has indicated.

It also interacts with local actors who have agency and strategies of their own, to accommodate, obstruct or resist attempts to externalise migration policy or project international aspirations of migration governance. The scholarship on migration tends to avoid these complexities to the detriment of understanding that migration politics is an area where local and transnational interests collide and overlap, thus producing unexpected and sometimes irrational architecture of governance. In sum, migration governance is not just ex-post reaction to migration flows and patterns, but importantly a field where power, legitimacy and sovereignty are actively created and negotiated (Geddes, 2022).

MIGRATION GOVERNANCE FRAMEWORK

The IOM's conceptual framework for managing migration contains three elements: policy, legislation and administrative organisation. First, the policy determines the approach of the state at the highest level, based on national objectives that are linked to other national policies such as labour migration and foreign and investment policies. The second element, legislation, gives concrete expression to policy and provides both authority and the required measures, including regulations. The third, administrative organisation, assigns and allows for the coordination of functions in a framework for managing migration that upholds responsibility, accountability, compliance with laws and adherence to the code of ethics. These three elements make it possible for governments to manage migration by applying principles, directions and commitments (Lubale, 2024) across four migration management areas, including migration for development; facilitating migration; regulating migration; and forced migration as well as across several cross-cutting activities illustrated in Figure 11.1.

Figure 11.1: Conceptual framework of the IOM's approach to migration management

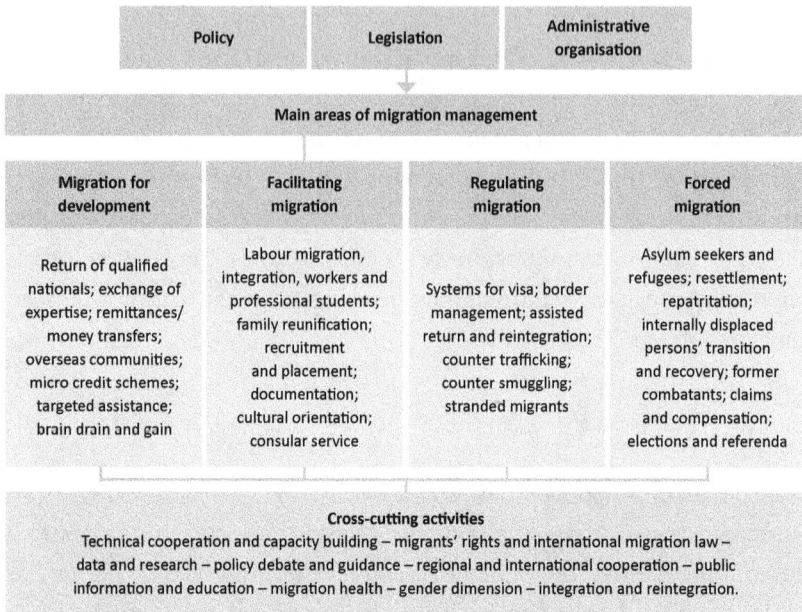

Policy	Legislation	Administrative organisation

Main areas of migration management

Migration for development	Facilitating migration	Regulating migration	Forced migration
Return of qualified nationals; exchange of expertise; remittances/ money transfers; overseas communities; micro credit schemes; targeted assistance; brain drain and gain	Labour migration, integration, workers and professional students; family reunification; recruitment and placement; documentation; cultural orientation; consular service	Systems for visa; border management; assisted return and reintegration; counter trafficking; counter smuggling; stranded migrants	Asylum seekers and refugees; resettlement; repatritation; internally displaced persons' transition and recovery; former combatants; claims and compensation; elections and referenda

Cross-cutting activities
Technical cooperation and capacity building – migrants' rights and international migration law – data and research – policy debate and guidance – regional and international cooperation – public information and education – migration health – gender dimension – integration and reintegration.

Source: Dimanche (2021)

GLOBAL MIGRATION GOVERNANCE FRAMEWORKS

Migration is a cross-cutting policy issue, extending beyond the regulation of human movement across international borders (World Bank, OECD and UNDP, 2020: 15). The growing complexity of international migration across the world is testing current migration management systems (Popova and Panzica, 2017: 4). These migration flows have often generated contradictory reactions and interests in different parts of the world. Concerns are raised regarding security, cultural differences and integration (Popova and Panzica, 2017: 10).

Global migration governance is largely driven by the United Nations 1951 Refugee Convention and its 1967 Protocol Relating to the Status of Refugees (UN, 2018b) and the International Convention on the Protection of the Rights of All Migrant Workers and Members of their Families (ICRMW). The Organisation of African Unity adopted its own convention in 1969 to address peculiar circumstances of migrants and refugees in Africa. These regulations outline the rights of refugees such as the right to identity documents, public education and wage-earning employment as well as the legal obligations of states to protect them. The conventions further obliges countries to uphold the principle of non-refoulement which prohibits expulsion and extradition of asylum seekers and refugees to a place where they face prosecution or danger, but also provides for exclusions on certain grounds, i.e., asylum seeker involvement in war crimes.

These documents set out a binding global diplomatic deal to guarantee dignity and equality. Additionally, these treaties take into account the principles embodied in the basic instruments of the United Nations concerning human rights, in particular, the Universal Declaration of Human Rights (UDHR), the International Covenant on Economic, Social and Cultural Cultural Rights, the International Covenant on Civil and Political Rights, the International Convention on the Elimination of All Forms of Racial Discrimination, the Convention on the Elimination of All Forms of Discrimination against Women, and the Convention on the Rights of the Child.

The UN Refugee Convention (1951) and Protocol (1967) have been ratified by 149 state parties wholly or in part, either by incorporating them into their constitutions or through legislation. Some countries interpret these instruments as a guiding framework within which member states of the United Nations (UN) can structure and domesticate their own policies and therefore have acceded to the treaties with reservations or limitations, as per article 42. Below are examples of reservations filed by Malawian, Mozambican and Ugandan governments, respectively, according to the White Paper on Citizenship, Immigration and Refugee Protection and the 1951 UN Refugee Convention (DHA, 2023; UN, 1951).

Malawi

The government of Malawi considers the provisions in articles 7 (exemption from reciprocity), 13 (movable and immovable property), 15 (right of association), 19 (liberal professions), 22 (public education) and 24 (labour legislation and social security) as recommendations only and not legally binding obligations. Furthermore, the government of

Malawi does not consider itself bound to grant a refugee, who fulfils any of the conditions, automatic exemption from the obligation to obtain a work permit or to extend more favourable rights to wage-based employment than those granted to aliens generally in respect of article 17 (wage-earning employment). The government of Malawi and many others also reserve the right to designate the place or places of residence of the refugees and to restrict their movements whenever considerations of national security or public order so require in terms of article 26 (freedom of movement).

Mozambique

The government of Mozambique only takes provisions of the 1951 Convention as simple recommendations not binding it to accord to refugees the same treatment as is accorded to Mozambicans with respect to elementary education and property. The government of Mozambique interprets the provisions as not requiring it to grant an exemption from the obligation to obtain a work permit.

Uganda

The government of Uganda understands provisions of article 7 (exemption from reciprocity) as not conferring any legal, political or other enforceable right upon refugees who, at any given time, may be in Uganda. Because of this understanding, the Ugandan government shall accord refugees such facilities and treatment as the government shall in its absolute discretion deem fit in terms of its own security, economic and social needs. The government reserves the right to abridge article 13 (movable and immovable property) without recourse to courts of law or arbitral tribunals, national or international, and obligation to provide legal assistance, if the government deems such abridgement to be in the public interest. In respect of article 15 (right of association), the government of Uganda has the full freedom to withhold any or all rights conferred by the Convention from any refugees as a class of residents within its territory. The government also insulates itself from incurring expenses on behalf of refugees in connection with the granting of assistance except in so far as such assistance is requested.

There are also non-binding agreements that inform migration

practices in the management of migration cycles in countries of origin, transit and destination at various stages of the migration process, including pre-departure, departure, arrival, residence, return/reintegration. Examples include the Global Compact for Migration (UN, 2018a) and the International Labour Organization Multilateral Framework on Labour Migration (ILO, 2006).

MIGRATION GOVERNANCE IN SOUTH AFRICA: THE GOVERNMENT PERSPECTIVE

The Department of Home Affairs published the White Paper on Citizenship, Immigration and Refugee protection in November 2023 with a view to undertaking a comprehensive review of migration governance in South Africa, as outlined in the Citizenship Act of 1995, the Refugees Act of 1988 and the Immigration Act of 2002. The White Paper provides an important background to the gravity of migration governance challenges facing South Africa. It notes that asylum seekers and refugees have been acquiring permanent residence prematurely and inappropriately; that criminal syndicates are exploiting the refugee and permit system and therefore placing South Africa at loggerheads with other countries and the UN's International Residual Mechanism for Criminal Tribunals. The White Paper further claims that the asylum regime is often conflated with economic migrants, thus overburdening the asylum system. It also attributes several migration governance challenges, such as the delay in processing of visa applications and enforcement of migration laws, to corrupt activities, inadequate structures within government and cumbersome legislation (DHA, 2023).

The next section contextualises migration governance challenges and reforms based on an interview with the then Minister of Home Affairs, Dr Aaron Motsoaledi, conducted on 29 May 2004.

South Africa's migration governance regime has largely been shaped by the colonial and apartheid policies which in the main sought to deprive the black majority of their citizenship and restrict African migrant worker flows into South Africa. This is eloquently captured by Justice Khampepe in *Chisuse and Others v Director General, Department of Home Affairs* (Constitutional Court of South Africa, 2020):

> The systematic act of stripping millions of South Africans of their citizenship was one of the most pernicious policies of the apartheid regime, which left many as foreigners in the land of their birth. The advent of constitutional dispensation established South African citizenship as precept based on equality.

The country undertook significant migration governance reforms in the wake of democracy to restore the citizenship of some of the former Transkei, Bophuthatswana, Venda and Ciskei (TBVC) state residents, the exiles as well as migrant mine workers (Simelane and Modisha, 2008). At the forefront of these reforms was the constitutional Bill of Rights, which guarantees and protects the human rights of asylum seekers and refugees who hitherto were not recognised in South Africa while immigration policy generally favoured white migrants, mostly from Zimbabwe, Mozambique and Portugal (DHA, 2023).

With this background of exclusion in mind, South Africa approached migration governance from a humanitarian, Pan-Africanist and neighbourly perspective, not only codifying migrants' human rights in the Constitution but also assented to the UN and OAU conventions without filing any reservations. Motsoaledi reiterates (interview, 2024):

> We used to have heavy security and electric fences along our borders especially with Mozambique. When Madiba came in, we said we cannot live like this with our neighbours. Which was fine, but the problem is that the fences were replaced with nothing... No country in the world can claim that their borders are not managed. Because borders are there to manage human trafficking, counterfeit goods, drugs, etc. Borders are not just to manage refugees. In 2009 there is a structure called NICC (National Intelligence Co-ordinating Committee), which coordinate military intelligence, crime intelligence of police, national security, financial intelligence, etc., which picked up

that our borders were not safe. They identified mechanisms that all failed and came up with the idea of a Border Management Authority (BMA), but it took 12 years for Parliament to pass an Act because of political differences.

Motsoaledi also makes the point that South Africa assented to the UN and OAU conventions without reservations and therefore the White Paper seeks to correct some of the past mistakes and importantly streamline the Citizenship Act, the Refugees Act and the Immigration Act. He argues that the country is not reneging on its obligations to protect human rights. Migration governance challenges are amplified by numerous court cases in which regulations have been found to be incoherent and unconstitutional. This is evident in the matter between Alex Ruta, a Rwandan national, and the Department of Home Affairs, and Muriel Watchenuka, a Zimbabwean national, and the Minister of Home Affairs (Motsoaledi, interview, 2024).

Ruta came into the country and did not announce himself, he did not try to register himself anywhere as required by the Immigration Act. Ruta was arrested 15 months after entering the country and subjected to deportation, at which point he applied for asylum under the Refugee[s] Act citing threat to life in the home country. Home Affairs rejected the application on the grounds that he failed to do so within the prescribed period and therefore subject to criminal conviction. Ruta tried the matter through the courts and found relief in section 2 of the Refugees Act (1998) which provides as follows:

Notwithstanding any provision of this Act or any other law to the contrary, no person may be refused entry into the Republic, expelled, extradited or returned to any other country or be subject to any similar measure, if as a result of such refusal, expulsion, extradition, return or other measure, such person is compelled to return to or remain in a country where—

(a) he or she may be subjected to persecution on account of his or her race, religion, nationality, political opinion, or membership of a particular social group; or

(b) his or her life, physical safety or freedom would be threatened on account of external aggression, occupation, foreign domination, or other events seriously disturbing or disrupting public order in either part or the whole of that country.

The Judge in the order acknowledges that this (section 2 of the Refugees Act) is extra ordinary, as it even goes beyond international conventions on non-refoulement. The judge was commending the human rights culture in South Africa, how it even supersedes the United Nations conventions. I do not agree because there is no country that can pride itself going beyond what the whole world can do because we would be lying. In the ruling, the judge said this man (Ruta) must be allowed to apply for asylum, regardless of him violating the immigration act. That is the part we want to change.

On the other hand, Watchenuka, a Zimbabwean female national who came to South Africa in 2002 seeking asylum, went to court to demand the right to work and for her son to study (partly because there were no refugee camps for her to stay in) as per article 17 of the UN Convention and the Bill of Rights. The court granted relief to Watchenuka pending application for her asylum and further instructed the government to set conditions relating to work and study under an asylum seeker permit. Motsoaledi remarked (interview, 2024):

The problem is that you cannot wake up and make these definitions or make changes to the current laws as required because you do not have reservations with United Nations (statutes). By the way all SADC countries have reservations on jobs.

The Watchunuka case partly explains the proposal in the White Paper to withdraw from UN conventions and re-enter with reservations, which is allowed in terms of article 42. According to Motsoaledi (interview, 2024):

> The biggest reservation we wish to make is on article 17 (right to employment). In 2021 the president was attacked on issues of migration and jobs. Political parties blamed the ruling party for grossly mishandling the issue and fuelling the tensions between the locals and migrants. The president appointed an inter-ministerial committee chaired by me (Minister of Home Affairs) and Thulas Nxesi (Minister of Labour) to deal with this issue. We have drawn the Act, but it is at Nedlac. You are aware of the continuous truckers protests over foreign drivers, etc.

Citing Uganda as an example of one of the African countries with a high population of migrants and the difference in obligations to refugees between countries with and without UN conventions reservations, Motsoaledi makes the following observation (interview, 2024):

> Uganda has refugee camps but equally they are regarded as a poor country and therefore receive assistance from the UN and other international organisations. These organisations build schools and clinics at the refugee camps and the Ugandan citizens can use them. So having a refugee camp next to your village becomes a benefit because you have access to infrastructure they would otherwise not have. Adding to their reservations, their constitution can control the refugees ... they have a right to determine anything over a refugee and they cannot be taken to court.
>
> All we are saying is that South Africa is an international liar. Believing that we can provide all these things is not practical and it is not true. We are promising to provide things we are not able to provide. When you do not provide, you are taken to court or called xenophobic. When you provide, we are already borrowing money to run the country and causing war between the citizens and migrants.

Another important reason behind the White Paper is to address refugee administration weaknesses alongside fraudulent activities within government in the administration of the three Acts. An internal investigation authorised by the Minister of Home Affairs in 2021 found that 36,647 applications for visas, permits and refugee status were issued fraudulently over a 16-year period under investigation (Hirsch, 2024). Motsoaledi (interview, 2024) said:

> The design of refugee administrative processes is weak. When you arrive at refugee centres you are received by the Refugee Status Determination Officer. These are junior clerks making judgements on very complex international laws where they must integrate three conventions, the South African Constitution, PAJA [Promotion of Administrative Justice Act of 2000] and Refugee[s] and Immigration Act[s]. Thus, everyone whose application is rejected, appeals. This is the reason for the high backlogs … it is not because people are not being seen, it is that there is a backlog of appeals. The appeal process has a blue-sky approach, which means it's unending … it goes on and on and when you are tired you can go back to a lower court … people never leave the country regardless of an RSDO's [refugee status determination officer] decisions. That is the reason it took long years to deport refugees who were camping at the Cape Town Methodist Church situation. It is not fair to the country to have an unending process. Part of the change in the White Paper [relates to] who must hear you when you arrive in South Africa … that is why we are making proposals of an immigration board that may include even retired judges who are experienced enough to adjudicate. And where they adjudicate, it must be at the boarder not in a faraway province.

The White Paper of 2023, like the minister, also notes that 'refugee and immigration structures, including appeal bodies are not occupied by suitable qualified persons to carry out efficiently their statutory duties' (DHA, 2023: 10).

Motsoaledi (interview, 2024) revealed that governments in other African countries are quarrelling with South Africa about its weak migration management. Among other issues that these African governments cite is that South Africa sometimes harbours wanted criminals, people with treasonous or regime change motives and so on.

> There is a worry in other African countries that South Africa is becoming very liberal because there are guys that cause problems in their home countries and then run to South Africa to make noise about their home governments. Anyone that wants to get involved in the political affairs of their home country must ask for permission from the Minister of Home Affairs. These are some of the things we want to change, and it is not true that we want to take human rights away.
>
> The introduction of BMA has improved our borders already. Their presence has made a huge difference because for instance, we do not have to fight criminals fleeing their country inside of SA, we get them at the borders and deal with them from there.

The White Paper has faced opposition from some quarters, including civil society organisations, academia and political parties, which have raised concerns about the potential impact of the policy on the rights of migrants and refugees (Lebon-McGregor, 2020: 72; Moyo, 2020: 1). Landau and Walker (2023) argue that the policy is based on false claims and poor logic while Hirsch (2024) has characterised the reform as a mess. The minister confirmed that there are significant challenges that exist with regard to various policy documents that guide migration governance in the country, which is a similar admission found in the 2023 White Paper. These challenges include contradictions that exist between acts and the interpretation of stipulations in the acts, even up to the Constitution of the country. Other challenges relate to corruption and incompetence within the department to an extent that the courts are imposing personal cost orders against the minister.

> We have got Acts which are very complex, which have been amended several times such that even the people who apply them no longer know what they mean, and lately more often than not they are clashing.

I was charged personal cost by the Constititional Court. The issue was section 34 of the Immigration Act. In 2016 the Lawyers for Human Rights went to the High Court to declare it unconstitutional; I agree with them, it says without a need of a warrant an immigration officer is allowed to make arrests etc... The Constitutional Court confirmed in 2017, and gave government 24 months to amend and remove unconstitutionality in the Act. Parliament decided it won't be an executive bill but a parliamentary bill and the date to correct eventually lapsed in June. In 2021, immigration officers arrested 2,000 people in Diepsloot who were here illegally, but they were then released by the court because there is no law. Our own lawyer submitted an affidavit with wrong information, which resulted in me being charged costs. The court gave the department a further 12 months to fix the amendment (Motsoaledi, interview, 2024).

Critics such as Hirch (2024) are of the view that government must focus its attention on implementing existing laws and fixing operational weakness within the Department of Home Affairs rather than securitising migration further and trampling on asylum seeker and refugee rights. For Hirsch (2024), rooting out and prosecuting the corrupt officials, improving IT systems, integrating systems and appointing the right staff is a sensible approach to improve migration governance.

To address these challenges, the government has taken steps to strengthen the capacity of government agencies responsible for migration management, including the Department of Home Affairs (DHA), the Department of Employment and Labour (DEL), the South African Police Service (SAPS) and the Department of International Relations and Cooperation (DIRCO) (Lebon-McGregor, 2020: 76). The government has also engaged with civil society organisations and other stakeholders to ensure that the policy reflects the needs and concerns of all stakeholders. The task is admittedly a huge one as evidence suggests there is a need to revisit our commitments to international policies and ensure that our domestic policies are also streamlined and complementary to each other. As the minister noted, there is a need for us to eventually have one master policy on migration because the current experience with different acts is not effective. The 2023 White Paper also notes that 'it has become an international trend to develop a single policy and legislative measures dealing with citizenship, immigration and refugee protection' (DHA, 2023: 8).

Dr Aaron Motsoaledi acknowledged that there are challenges of capacity at the Department of Home Affairs, especially when dealing with refugees, but he also argued that the law sometimes hinders the department's ability to be efficient in its processes. Motsoaledi further stated that the changes in the White Paper on Migration introduces an interdepartmental approach to migration governance where all departments dealing with migration are consolidated under the auspices of the BMA.

As a signatory to numerous international and continental accords on migration, South Africa has been criticised on countless occasions for failing to manage irregular migration, prevent and condemn human rights violations and attacks on migrants, carrying out illegal detention and deportation of irregular migrants and failing to recognise the rights of asylum seekers (Human Rights Watch, 2009: 6; Vearey et al., 2017: 1; Hunter-Adams and Rother, 2017: 1; Zihindula et al., 2017: 1; Vanyoro, 2019: 9). Legal disputes against the Department of Home Affairs' system of migration governance are a common occurrence. At the time of writing, the department was involved in a protracted legal battle to terminate the Zimbabwe exemption permit programme (Broughton, 2024). Similar legal battles were also unfolding in the UK following the government's passing of the Rwanda Act of 2024 to transfer asylum seekers to Rwanda in exchange for development aid (Phrabat, 2023).

The foregoing discussion illustrates that migration governance is a terrain where power, legitimacy and sovereignty are actively created and negotiated, as Geddes (2022) notes. Governments are actively shaping migration patterns by limiting the rights of migrants based on the countries' perceived capacity to meet relevant international migration treaties or obligations. At the same time, both migrants and civil society organisations are using available legal avenues to assert their legitimacy amidst a fragile environment in which migration governance is caught between the global open immigration discourse, humanitarianism and rising nationalism. It is here where local and transnational interests collide and overlap, thus calling for partnerships between national, subnational and international institutions to manage and shape migration governance across countries.

MIGRATION GOVERNANCE INDICATORS TOOL

The IOM worked with The Economist Intelligence Unit and developed the Migration Governance Indicators (MGI) to operationalise the Migration Governance Framework (MiGOF). It includes a standard set of approximately 90 indicators to assist countries in assessing their migration policies and to advance the conversation on what constitutes well-governed migration (ILO, 2019a: 8).

The Migration Governance Indicators (MGI) tool is a process that entails the evaluation of these six domains of the MGI:

- migrants' rights;
- whole-of-government approach;
- partnerships;
- socioeconomic wellbeing of migrants;
- mobility dimensions of crises; and
- safe and orderly migration.

How does the MGI contribute to better migration governance? First, it generates a government-wide dialogue on migration governance, and second, it uses the findings to inform policy change. Finally, it establishes baselines to track and report progress on national and international commitments, such as the GCM and SDGs (IOM Global Migration Data Analysis Centre [GMDAC], 2022). The MGI Country Report helps governments, upon request, to take stock of their migration policies and strategies to identify good practices and areas with the potential for further development (GMDAC, 2022). The country profile is first endorsed by the government in question and then published on the Migration Data Portal. There is no report yet available online for South Africa and countries with reports on the portal from SADC are Angola, eSwatini, Lesotho, Zimbabwe, Zambia, Malawi, Botswana and Namibia.

CONCLUSION

Migration governance in South Africa remains a complex and challenging issue, requiring a comprehensive, coordinated and integrated approach from government and other stakeholders, described as a whole-of-society and government approach and partnerships (Opon and Nzau, 2021: 98). The implementation of the White Paper on International Migration for South Africa (DHA, 2017) has the potential to address many of the challenges associated with migration governance in the country and the SADC region but will require the allocation of adequate resources and the participation of critical stakeholders to balance domestic and transnational interests. Ultimately, effective migration governance in South Africa will require a long-term commitment from the government and other stakeholders to address the causes, consequences and dynamics of different dimensions of migration. South Africa could take a step towards this by giving consideration to participating in the Migration Governance Indicators (MGI) assessment process.

REFERENCES

Betts, A. and Kainz, L. 2017. 'The history of global migration governance'. Refugee Studies Centre, Working Chapter Series No 122, https://www.rsc.ox.ac.uk/publications/the-history-of-global-migration-governance/@@download/file, accessed 15 August 2023.

Bjerre, L., Helbling, M., Römer, F. and Zobel, M. 2015. 'Conceptualizing and measuring immigration policies: A comparative perspective'. *The International Migration Review*, 49(3), 555–600.

Broughton. 2024. 'Home Affairs minister takes Zimbabwean permit battle to the Constitutional Court'. *GroundUp*, https://groundup.org.za/article/motsoaledi-appeals-to-constitutional-court-in-his-bid-to-scrap-zimbabwe-permits/, accessed 24 May 2024.

Constitutional Court of South Africa. 2020. 'Chisuse and Others v Director-General, Department of Home Affairs and Another'. ZACC 20, Case CCT 155/19, https://collections.concourt.org.za/bitstream/handle/20.500.12144/36628/Judgment%20CCT%20155-19%20Chisuse%20and%20Others%20v%20Director-General%2c%20Department%20....pdf?sequence=47&isAllowed=y, accessed 25 May 2024.

De Haas, H., Czaika, M., Flahaux, M. L., Mahendra, E., Natter, K., Vezzoli, S.

and Villares-Varela, M. 2019. 'International migration: Trends, determinants, and policy effects'. *Population and Development Review*, 45(4), 885–922.

Department of Home Affairs. 2017. 'White Paper on International Migration for South Africa', http://www.dha.gov.za/WhiteChapteronInternationalMigration-20170602.pdf, accessed 1 September 2023.

Department of Home Affairs. 10 November 2023. 'Publication of the White Paper on citizanship, Migration and Refugee Protection: Towards a Complete Overhaul of the Migration System in South Africa', https://www.gov.za/sites/default/files/gcis_document/202311/49690gon4061.pdf, accessed 24 May 2024.

Dimanche, S. 10 December 2021. 'Essentials of migration management' [Lecture].

Ehiane, S. 8 May 2023. 'Fostering fair labour migration governance in South Africa: Policy implications'. Democracy Development Programme, https://ddp.org.za/blog/2023/05/08/fostering-fair-labour-migration-governance-in-south-africa-policy-implications/, accessed 24 May 2024.

European Commission. 2021. 'International migration governance', https://knowledge4policy.ec.europa.eu/migration-demography/topic/international-migration-governance_en, accessed 24 May 2024.

Fukuyama, F. 2016. 'Governance: What do we know, and how do we know It?'. *Annual Review of Political Science*, 19(1), 89–105.

Geddes, A. 2022. 'Migration governance', in Scholten, P. (ed.), *Introduction to Migration Studies*. IMISCOE Research Series. Springer, Cham, https://doi.org/10.1007/978-3-030-92377-8_20.

Global Migration Data Analysis Centre (GMDAC). 2022. 'Migration governance indicators and country profiles', https://www.migrationdataportal.org/overviews/mgi, accessed 1 May 2023.

Government of South Africa. 1998. Refugees Act, No. 130 of 1998 402. https://www.gov.za/sites/default/files/gcis_document/201409/a130-980.pdf, accessed 24 May 2024.

Government of South Africa. 2002. Immigration Act, No. 13 of 2002 43. https://www.gov.za/sites/default/files/gcis_document/201409/a13-020.pdf, accessed 14 August 2023.

Hirsch, A. 2024. 'South Africa country study: Migration trends, policy implementation and outcomes'. New South Institute Government and Public Action, https://nsi.org.za/wp-content/uploads/2024/01/South-Africa-Country-Study-%E2%80%93-Migration-trends-02-12-2023-V5.pdf, accessed 24 May 2024.

Human Rights Watch. 2009. 'No healing here: Violence, discrimination and barriers to health for migrants in South Africa', https://reliefweb.int/report/south-africa/no-healing-here-violence-discrimination-and-barriers-health-migrants-south, accessed 24 May 2024.

Hunter-Adams, J., and Rother, H. A. 2017. 'A qualitative study of language barriers between South African health care providers and cross-border migrants'. *BMC Health Services Research*, 17(1), 97.

ILO International Migration Programme. 2006. 'ILO Multilateral framework on labour migration; non-binding principles and guidelines for a rights-based approach to labour migration (First)'. *International Labour Office*, https://www.ilo.org/asia/publications/WCMS_146243/lang--en/index. htm, accessed 15 September 2023.

International Organization for Migration (IOM). 2015. 'Migration governance framework', https://www.iom.int/sites/g/files/tmzbdl486/files/about-iom/migof_brochure_a4_en.pdf, accessed 24 May 2024.

International Organization for Migration (IOM). 2019. 'International migration law: Glossary on migration', https://publications.iom.int/system/files/pdf/ iml_34_glossary.pdf, accessed 15 September 2023.

Landau, L. B. and Walker, R. 2023. 'South Africa's immigration proposals are based on false claims and poor logic-experts'. *The Conversation*, https:// theconversation.com/south-africas-immigration-proposals-are-based-on-false-claims-and-poor-logic-experts-217941, accessed 24 May 2024.

Lebon-McGregor, E. 2020. 'A history of global migration governance: Challenging linearity'. IMI Working Chapter Series No 167, International Migration Institute, Amsterdam.

Lubale, G. W. 2024. 'Migration governance in South Africa'. *International Journal of Innovative Research and Development,* 12(10), 70–79.

Maunganidze, O. A. 2023. 'The irregular distraction in the new pact'. Foundation for European Progressive Studies Policy Brief, https://library. fes.de/pdf-files/bueros/aethiopien/20756.pdf, accessed 24 May 2024.

Moyo, I. 2020. 'On decolonising borders and regional integration in the Southern African Development Community (SADC) region'. *Social Sciences*, 9(4), 32.

Opon, O. and Nzau, M. 2021. 'The impact of migration governance on national security in Africa: A case of Kenya', http://erepository.uonbi. ac.ke/handle/11295/160868, accessed 14 August 2023.

Phrabat, D 2023. 'Supreme Court rules Rwanda plan unlawful: a legal expert explains the judgment, and what happens next'. *The Conversation*, https:// theconversation.com/supreme-court-rules-rwanda-plan-unlawful-a-legal-expert-explains-the-judgment-and-what-happens-next-217730, accessed 24 May 2024.

Popova, N. and Panzica, F. 2017. 'General practical guidance on promoting coherence among employment, education, training and labour migration policies (First)'. International Labour Organization, http://www.ilo.org/ global/topics/labour-migration/publications/WCMS_614314/lang--en/ index.htm, accessed 14 August 2023.

Simelane, X and Modisha, G. 2008. 'From formal to informal migrant labour system: The impact of changing the nature of migrant labour system on mining communities in Lesotho and Mozambique'. Paper presented at the XIV SASA Congress, Stellenbosch University, https://repository.hsrc.ac.za/bitstream/handle/20.500.11910/5014/5682.pdf?sequence=1&isAllowed=y, accessed 24 May 2024.

United Nations. 2018a. 'Global compact for migration', https://refugeesmigrants.un.org/sites/default/files/180713_agreed_outcome_global_compact_for_migration.pdf, accessed 14 August 2023.

United Nations. 2018b. 'Global compact on refugees', www.unhcr.org/media/37797, accessed 14 August 2023.

Vanyoro, K. P. 2019. '"When they come, we don't send them back": Counter-narratives of "medical xenophobia" in South Africa's public health care system'. *Palgrave Communications*, 5(1), 1.

Vearey, J., Modisenyane, M. and Hunter-Adams, J. 2017. 'Towards a migration-aware health system in South Africa: A strategic opportunity to address health inequity'. *2014 SAHR – 20 Year Anniversary Edition*, https://www.hst.org.za/publications/South%20African%20Health%20Reviews/9_Towards%20a%20migration%20aware%20health%20system%20in%20South%20Africa_a%20strategic%20opportunity%20to%20address%20health%20inequity.pdf, accessed 1 January 2024.

World Bank, OECD and UNDP. 2020. 'Measuring policy coherence for migration and development: A new set of tested tools', https://www.knomad.org/sites/default/files/2020-08/Measuring%20Policy%20Coherence%20for%20Migration%20and%20Development%20-%20A%20new%20set%20of%20tester%20tools.pdf, accessed 2 March 2023.

Zihindula, G., Meyer-Weitz, A. and Akintola, O. 2017. 'Lived experiences of Democratic Republic of Congo refugees facing medical xenophobia in Durban, South Africa'. *Journal of Asian and African Studies*, 52(4), 458–470.

Interviews

Motsoaledi, A. 30 May 2024. Interview with the authors, Johannesburg.

TWELVE

Securitisation of borders and migration in the context of uneven regional development in southern Africa

INNOCENT MOYO

INTRODUCTION

This chapter discusses borders and migration in the context of uneven regional development in the southern African region. Nation states in the region are at different levels of economic development, which has led to South Africa, an economic hegemon, being a destination of choice for cross-border migrations, including undocumented ones and even human smuggling. This has ignited debates in South Africa about its porous borders with neighbouring Southern African Development Community (SADC) nation states like Mozambique and Zimbabwe, among others, and also about how these borders are governed. The assumption is that such porous and ineffectively governed borders pose a cross-border security issue and undermine the socioeconomic stability of South Africa (Neocosmos, 2006; Nyamnjoh, 2006; Crush and Ramachandran, 2014; DHA, 2017; Dodson, 2000; Moyo, 2020a). Such concerns are valid and have led to the establishment of the Border Management Authority (BMA), which is predicated on the Border Management Authority Act of 2020. The Border Management Authority (BMA), which started operations in April 2023, is a public entity under the Department of Home Affairs and its primary function is to enforce integrated border law. It needs to be emphasised that South Africa, like other SADC nation states and indeed any country in the world, has the constitutional responsibility to uphold its sovereignty and territorial integrity and the BMA demonstrates this commitment. The BMA is therefore expected to enhance cross-border security and halt undocumented migration while at the same time enhance legitimate trade and related cross-border commerce (Moyo, 2020a).

However, in the case of South Africa, the BMA will effectively lead to border securitisation and militarisation because of, among other factors, the use of border guards who have the power to arrest and detain any person deemed to have transgressed the new law. Border guards have extensive powers like the authority to search any person, premises, goods or vehicles and to question any person about any matter related to the passage of people, goods or vehicles through a port of entry or across the borders (Moyo, 2020a). This brings to the fore governance of borders and migration and animates this contribution. Two propositions are advanced. The first is that in a region like the SADC, border militarisation and securitisation do not amount to effective management and governance of borders; if anything, they lead to and exacerbate cross-border security challenges by entrenching underground and sophisticated cross-border illegalities.

Second, border militarisation and securitisation only deal ineffectively with symptoms, leaving untouched and hidden the causes of the problem of people crossing borders illegally. SADC nation states should not construct cross-border illegalities as a cross-border security problem. In this regard, I invoke the argument by Wendt (1999: 395) that:

Anarchy is what states make of it. This is because there is

no 'logic' of anarchy apart from the practices that create and instantiate one structure of identities and interests rather than another; structure has no existence or causal powers apart from process. Self-help and power politics are institutions, not essential features of anarchy.

The meaning of this is that nation-states' assessments and determinations of threats and/or insecurities are socially constructed.

For instance, 'if society "forgets" what a university is, the powers and practices of professors and students cease to exist; if the United States and erstwhile Soviet Union decide that they are no longer enemies, "the Cold War is over". It is collective meanings that constitute the structures that organise our actions' (Wendt, 1999: 397). In the context of this chapter, Wendt's argument is used to advance the idea that nation-states in the southern African region must forget that people who cross borders are the problem, requiring border militarisation and securitisation. Instead, these states must remember that the problem is a lack of cooperation and partnership in managing borders and migration, and a lack of decisive actions, which lead to migration and the displacement of people. Seen thus, borders (even if they are porous) are not the *actual* problem, but the causes and drivers of migration. The construction of migration as a security issue leads to the securitisation of borders and the occlusion of the actual cross-border security issues and thus derails attempts at effective border governance, migration, regional development and integration. The governance of borders implicates the institutions charged with responsibility for this and it is therefore necessary to reflect on the issues raised through the lenses of institutional liberalism.

INSTITUTIONAL LIBERALISM

Institutional liberalism advances that 'institutions and rules can facilitate mutually beneficial cooperation – within and among states. The social purpose of institutional liberalism is to promote beneficial effects on human security, human welfare and human liberty as a result of a more peaceful, prosperous and free world' (Keohane, 2012: 125–126).

In this sense, institutional liberalism advocates for the establishment of robust institutions for resolving problems that degrade the living conditions of people. The fundamental tenet of institutional liberalism is that both domestic and foreign institutions must offer a platform for the advancement of human security and liberty. This implies that institutions, whether national or international, ought to advance and defend all people's rights, with the former enhancing or articulating into the latter (Keohane, 2012). This suggests that at the international level, such as the SADC region, the sovereignty of member states should not be curtailed; member states should rather cooperate for the advancement of humankind through the application of pertinent national and international laws that govern intra-state and inter-state actions. This is why Keohane (2012: 131) is correct in stating that 'democratic forms of governance are based on and justified by moral principles, and the relevance of these principles hardly diminishes when democratic states project power outside their borders'. Nonetheless, institutional liberalism has come under fierce criticism for several perceived shortcomings, including the fact that it is utopian, for equating individual morality with public morality or morality on a global scale. The point is that 'people do not accept the principle of individual equality on a global scale and therefore do not put the interests of the global community above those of their own nations' (Keohane, 2012: 131). Additionally, it might be argued that without a deeper grasp of the forces behind the legalism of these institutions, it is too simplistic to view institutions as capable of furthering social purpose. In other words, 'we need to peer through the veil of rhetoric and law, to discern the power and interest structures that lie below'. Hence, another way to look at this is that 'institutions rest on power and changes in power generate changes in institutions' (Keohane, 2012: 135–136). This implies that established institutions could be the result of power systems that are not always supportive of social justice, and vice versa. In this regard, it can be naive to assume that institutions will always fulfil their commitments to justice, human security and growth without being aware of the institutions' underlying principles.

Taking into consideration these contestations around institutional liberalism, it is helpful to ask whether or not there are institutions with a responsibility for managing borders at national and international levels in nation-states and SADC respectively, and the extent to which these organisations promote and safeguard human welfare and security – and thus comprehensively address the push and pull factors. The reality is that there are no regional institutions that control borders and migration at the SADC regional level. The only effort is SADC's 2005 draft Protocol on the Facilitation of Movement of Persons (SADC, 1992), which is the legal instrument that enforces the terms of the SADC treaty on the movement of persons in the region. The overarching objective of the Protocol is the development of policies that will progressively eliminate obstacles to human mobility into and within SADC members' territories (SADC, 2005). However, the Protocol is not in full force (it has not reached the required two-thirds majority threshold of member state ratifications) because only six SADC states – namely, Botswana, Lesotho, Mozambique, South Africa, eSwatini and Zambia – have ratified it (Nshimbi and Fioramonti, 2013, 2014). Consequently, individual nation-states implement the management of borders and migration. This is the context within which SADC nation-states promulgate disparate border management approaches that have a national rather than regional focus. In the case of South Africa, this is best exemplified by the Border Management Act [Act 2 of 2020] and the establishment of the Border Management Authority. Taking into consideration and accepting the argument by Keohane (2012) that institutions are a product of power and not innocent and simple edifices that enforce the enhancement of human security, it is possible to understand that the South African Border Management Authority is an outcome of the power of stakeholders like parliamentarians who have called for the securitisation of South Africa's borders. It would be naive to expect institutions like the Border Management Authority to always uphold the rights of cross-border actors. At the same time, however, it is important to consider whether such an institutionally driven effort to secure borders is not in and of itself a source of insecurity in the context of migration and uneven regional development.

The point being made here is that even if laws that regulate institutions are intended to promote human security, liberty and welfare, they can also act as a source of insecurity if they fail to do so. That then becomes an added layer of complexity in the governing of borders and migration in the context of uneven development. This is more the case when many people attempt to cross borders as undocumented migrants because of a failure to do so formally. This means that stringent borders, migration and immigration controls lead to people opting for illegal ways of crossing borders (Musoni, 2020). A good example of this is the cases recorded at the South Africa–Zimbabwe border at Beitbridge in which Zimbabweans attempt to cross the border into South Africa (Moyo, 2016a, 2020a, 2020b, 2020c, 2022; Tshabalala, 2019; Musoni, 2020). The reason such Zimbabweans cross the Beitbridge border into South Africa, in some cases as undocumented migrants, is firstly because of their failing to do so legally as a result of difficulties in securing long-term residence visas (Tshabalala, 2019; Musoni, 2020). Secondly, it is due to the difficult conditions in their country of origin which push them to engage in such cross-border actions (Moyo, 2016b, 2020a). The insights from institutional liberalism, when applied to the management of borders and migration in the context of unequal regional development as is the case in the SADC region, suggest that the focus of institutions must be on regional migration and immigration regimes or the lack of them. Emphasis should be on the regional challenges and problems, which uproot people and lead to cross-border problems, and not on the victims who have been uprooted. In any event, regional security complex theory, as advanced by Buzan (1991), suggests that the security of a nation-state is dependent on the security of other states at both micro and macro levels. This means that 'security is a relational phenomenon. Because security is relational, one cannot understand the national security of any given state without understanding the international pattern of security interdependence in which it is embedded' (Buzan, 1991: 187). Mozambique can be used to illustrate this point. Parts of Mozambique are currently unstable, and this necessarily links to the SADC regional complex and the opposite is true: if the current volatility in Mozambique persists, it will have an impact on the SADC region in terms of cross-border migration. To press the point further, if a SADC nation-state faces problems that lead to the displacement of people and thus migration, those problems need to be addressed by the SADC collective before it focuses on the people who cross borders.

In this sense, the focus must be on what uproots people because trying to stop them when they cross borders hardly works. Migrants always find ways to breach borders, no matter how securitised and militarised these are. What is happening at the EU/Spanish border at Ceuta and Melilla and in the Mediterranean Sea illustrates this fact. The securitisation of the EU/Spanish border has involved the implementation of the Integrated System of External Surveillance (SIVE), and the creation of the European Border and Coast Guard Agency (FRONTEX) (Ferrer-Gallardo, 2008; 2010). In addition, technologies such as sensors were installed that could identify the heartbeat of a migrant from a certain distance (Ferrer-Gallardo, 2008). This is the context within which Papadopoulos and Tsianos (2013) suggest that the securitisation of borders has led to the regulation of migration being seen through the lens of sovereignty and citizenship and to the placing of limits on the freedom of people who want to migrate. Such a fortification of the Moroccan borders with the EU has been characterised as the 'Schengenisation of Spain's borders' with Africa at Ceuta and Melilla. This fortification has also led to the creation of so-called 'limboscapes' (Ferrer-Gallardo and Albet-Mas, 2013: 528), which are 'territories of exception' characterised by the 'discriminatory granting of access to the EU', which is characteristic of 'human-blacklisting bureaucratic machinery of the Schengen regime' (Van Houtum, 2010 cited in Ferrer-Gallardo and Albet-Mas, 2013: 530). For those who managed to irregularly cross the border onto EU soil, there were detention centres, which are 'a space of oblivion between the heaven of regularisation and the hell(s) of repatriation/ deportation/expulsion' (Ferrer-Gallardo and Albet-Mas, 2013: 529). Migrants in these detention camps 'have not yet received the baptism or the conviction of the Schengen law' (Ferrer-Gallardo and Albet-Mas, 2013: 529).

Yet, these border securitisation paraphernalia have not stopped migration. People continue to breach these borders and some drown in the Mediterranean Sea. The point is that the focus has been placed on the people who cross borders and not on the conditions that cause them to migrate. The importance of this case is that it demonstrates that the management and governance of borders in the context of uneven development are problematic if the (under)development problems that drive people to migrate are not addressed. People who attempt to cross the EU-securitised border at Ceuta and Melilla generally come from Africa to Europe and the EU. Africa is generally at a lower level of economic development compared to Europe and the EU, which drives people to migrate from the continent. Seen thus, border securitisation addresses the symptoms and not the problems, which cause people to migrate, and this is why it does not work.

THE SADC BORDERS AND
MIGRATION CONUNDRUM

In the southern African region, the governance of borders and migration is focused on nation-states and not the region, based on the assumption that the interests of the former supersede the latter. As suggested in the preceding discussion, this lack of coordination and partnership creates a gap for undocumented migration, particularly from less economically developed countries to more economically developed ones in SADC. This undocumented migration is made possible for two main reasons. The first is that the lack of a regional approach that regulates regional mobility yields undocumented migrants as those who fail to migrate within the limits of immigration law do so illegally. There is no efficient way of monitoring and accounting for this because of migration governance approaches, which are focused on the nation-state. This lack of coordination of the governance of borders and migration has led to the growth of human smuggling networks (Tshabalala, 2019; Moyo, 2020b; Musoni, 2020). These human smuggling networks transport people from less economically developed SADC nation-states to those that are developed. Examples of this include human smuggling at the Beitbridge border between South Africa and Zimbabwe. In this border region, human smugglers transported undocumented migrants from different parts of Zimbabwe to the Beitbridge border town in Zimbabwe. From there these undocumented migrants then crossed the South

Africa–Zimbabwe border at undesignated points of entry and exit. Upon reaching South Africa, the human smugglers transported them to different destinations in the country (Araia, 2009; Moyo, 2020a, 2020b, 2020c). This suggests that the lack of coordination between South Africa and Zimbabwe at this border made this undocumented migration possible in addition to the fact that people always find means to circumvent the border. This amplifies the point made earlier that whenever a border (be it a fence or a wall or both) was erected, people devised ways of breaching it (Laine, 2020), and the 'higher the wall – be it of concrete or paper – the higher the stakes' (Moyo and Laine, 2021: 96). This is more the case in the southern African region where people migrating from economically underdeveloped countries find ways to cross borders rather than stay in their countries of origin. This is further complicated by the fact that cross-border migration in the region has a long and well-entrenched history. For instance, Mozambicans migrated to South Africa in the late 1800s to work on farms in the then Cape Colony (Wentzel, 2003; Crush et al., 2005; Wentzel and Tlabela, 2006). Migrant workers from present-day Mozambique, Malawi and Zambia worked in the mines in the then Southern Rhodesia, which is now Zimbabwe. The discovery of diamonds in Kimberley in the 1860s and gold on the Witwatersrand in the 1880s resulted in migration to South Africa from Mozambique, Botswana, Lesotho, Malawi, eSwatini and Zimbabwe in search of employment (Crush et al., 2005; Wentzel and Tlabela, 2006; Nshimbi and Fioramonti, 2013, 2014). Thus, an entrenched history of migration plus the fact that there is no regional approach and mechanism to manage migration leads to nation-states unsuccessfully trying to manage borders and migration in isolation, resulting in this conundrum.

The second reason is that migration from those countries, which are not economically developed, has led to the instrumentalisation of borders and the establishment of a private economy by cross-border officials. Cross-border officials cash in on the migrants, including those who are undocumented from less economically developed countries like Zimbabwe, who are desperate to cross the border to countries like South Africa, which are relatively better developed economically. The point being made here is that disparities in economic development in

SADC have entrenched neopatrimonial tendencies at cross-border points of entry and exit. Neopatrimonialism can be defined as 'a type of political domination which is characterised by *insecurity* about the behaviour and role of state institutions (and agents)' (Erdmann and Engel, 2007: 105). This insecurity is predicated on the view that state institutions and/or their agents operate along both formal and informal channels with the result that 'formal state institutions cannot fulfil their universalistic purpose of public welfare. Instead, politics and policies are determined by particularistic interests and orientations' (Erdmann and Engel, 2007: 105). The distinctive feature of neopatrimonialism is that 'officials hold positions in bureaucratic organisations with powers which are formally defined but exercise those powers … as a form … of private property' (Clapham, 1985: 48). State bureaucrats may use the law to operate informally for their own benefit (Chabal and Daloz, 1999; Van de Walle, 2001) suggesting that neopatrimonialism 'is a mix of two types of political domination. It involves a conjunction of patrimonial and legal-rational bureaucratic domination. The exercise of power in neopatrimonial regimes is erratic and unpredictable, as opposed to the calculable exercise of power embedded in universal rules' (Erdmann and Engel, 2007: 105, 114). As such, 'public norms under neopatrimonialism are formal and rational, but their social practice is often personal and informal' (Erdmann and Engel, 2007: 105, 114) through the diversion of the authority of a state to meet private interests and not those of the state (Van de Walle, 2001). This involved the use of bureaucratic powers as defined by the appointing authority, which is the government, 'as a form … of private property' (Clapham, 1985: 48).

Moyo (2022, 2023) has convincingly shown that in the context of cross-border regions, this involved cross-border officials soliciting and receiving bribes from different categories of desperate cross-border actors such as, among others, informal cross-border traders (ICBTs). The result of this is that there was a sale of 'state-administered benefits … to economic and social actors' (Trantidis and Tsagkroni, 2017: 265), based on the fact that cross-border actors had to pay cross-border officials to illegally cross the border and/or transport goods. This typifies neopatrimonialism given that it also entails state bureaucrats utilising state institutions for their own gain and thus failing to fulfil their intended goal of promoting the general good and welfare (Erdmann and Engel, 2007). To this extent, cross-border officials amassed benefits 'by extraction *through* the state [... because] state actors draw material benefits directly from the private economy by taking advantage of their decision-making positions within public administration. Extractive actors receive bribes ... in exchange for preferential treatment in various decisions' (Trantidis and Tsagkroni, 2017: 266). The entrenchment of neopatrimonial tendencies in cross-border points of entry and exit in the southern African region complicates the management of borders and migration in the context of uneven development. This is because, for as long as development disparities exist, people will migrate from poor to relatively economically developed countries, but the lack of a coordinated regional approach for managing migration means that nation-states manage migration disparately. This creates gaps for undocumented/ unregulated migration as well as neopatrimonial tendencies.

CONCLUSION

In conclusion, it is worth reiterating that the SADC region is characterised by uneven development, and this has necessarily meant that some countries like South Africa, which are economically developed, attract migrants from those countries that were less economically developed and afflicted by several socioeconomic and political challenges. The mere fact of uneven development stands in the way of regional integration on the score of a coordinated regional migration approach. This is because economic hegemons will tend to have nationalistic and inward-looking migration and immigration approaches in defence of territorial sovereignty and economic and political stability. This can be seen in the migration approaches of countries like Botswana, Namibia and South Africa, but perhaps a good example is that of South Africa, which now has the BMA with a securocratic outlook. This BMA does not have a SADC regional focus as is the case for border and migration governing institutions in several other SADC nation-states.

What comes to the fore therefore is that in such a situation it becomes difficult to manage borders and migration. In the absence of a regional migration approach and given the fact that people migrate from less economically developed to more economically developed countries like South Africa (or from socially unstable environments to more stable ones), managing borders and migration becomes difficult, if not impossible. As South Africa tries to securitise its borders, cross-border actors also try to find ways of breaching the borders. This tug-of-war between nation-states securitising borders and cross-border actors breaching the same borders shows how and why managing borders in the context of unequal development continues to be problematic. This is not to condemn South Africa's migration and immigration control and the governing and managing of its borders. On the contrary, this is intended to problematise and show the complexities inherent in border and migration control in a region characterised by uneven economic development. In any event, cross-border migration in the southern African region has a long and entrenched history and therefore there is a need for less emphasis on the securitisation of borders and migration. Complex histories of migration bind people in the southern African region. To this extent, the political process of memory and remembrance of the issues of borders and migration is necessary to underscore the fact that the complex history of migration in the southern African region is an essential part of the current and future realities.

More than that, the problem with border securitisation is that it addresses the symptom and not the problem. People seen crossing the border illegally or engaged in human smuggling are uprooted by more difficulties like circumstances in their countries of origin. Seen thus, arresting and detaining people at borders does not necessarily stop them from attempting to cross the border. Events in the Mediterranean Sea have repeatedly taught us that. Does that mean that nation-states like South Africa must not do anything about their borders? Not at all. Clearly, all nation-states have the constitutional obligation to protect their territorial sovereignties, but that, unfortunately, does not and cannot stop the problem of cross-border migration, and herein lies the problem of how difficult it is to control and manage borders in the wake of uneven economic development and other manifestations of human insecurity. Nation-states cannot sit back and do nothing, and yet doing something like securitising borders does not solve the problem; it complicates it further, leading to underground cross-border activities as well as neopatrimonial relations. The solution could be a coordinated, regional approach to the problem of cross-border movement as well as regional development challenges, yet SADC nation states are not willing to commit to this regional imperative. Nonetheless, before a regional approach to migration becomes a reality, countries like South Africa are forced to respond to the challenges that undocumented migrants have caused or are causing. This is why it is suggested that a diplomatic and political approach could reduce the problem of undocumented migration. As an economic hegemon and perhaps even a regional leader, South Africa could contribute to solving those problems that displace people, forcing them to migrate to South Africa undocumented.

REFERENCES

Araia, T. 2009. 'Report on human smuggling across the South Africa/ Beitbridge border'. MRMP occasional paper, Forced Migration Studies Programme, University of the Witwatersrand.

Buzan, B. 1991. *People, States, and Fear: An agenda for international security studies in the post-Cold War era.* Colchester: ECPR Press.

Chabal, P. and Daloz, J. P. 1999. *Africa Works. Disorder as political instrument.* Oxford: James Currey.

Clapham, C. 1985. *Third World Politics.* London: Helm.

Crush, J. and Ramachandran, S. 2014. 'Xenophobic violence in South Africa: Denialism, minimalism and realism'. Migration Policies Series No 66, Southern Africa Migration Project and International Migration Research Centre, Cape Town and Canada.

Crush, J., Williams, V. and Peberdy, S. 2005. 'Migration in Southern Africa'. Paper prepared for Policy Analysis and Research Programme of the Global Commission on International Migration.

Department of Home Affairs. 2017. 'Border post and borderline security: Presentation to the portfolio committee on police'. Parliamentary Monitoring Group, https://static.pmg.org.za/docs/2011/111108bBorderpost. pdf, accessed 8 January 2020.

Dodson, B. 2000. 'Porous borders: Gender and migration in southern Africa'.

South African Geographical Journal, 82(1), 40–46.

Erdmann, G. and Engel, U. 2007. 'Neopatrimonialism reconsidered: Critical review and elaboration of an elusive concept'. *Commonwealth and Comparative Politics,* 45(1), 95–119.

Ferrer-Gallardo, F. 2010. 'Territorial (dis)continuity dynamics between Ceuta and Morocco: Conflictual fortification vis-à-vis co-operative interaction at the EU border in Africa'. *Tijdschrift voor Economische en Sociale Geografie,* 102(1), 24–38.

Ferrer-Gallardo, X. 2008. 'The Spanish-Moroccan border complex: Processes of geopolitical, functional and symbolic rebordering'. *Political Geography,* 27, 301–321.

Ferrer-Gallardo, X. and Albet-Mas, A. 2013. 'EU-Limboscapes: Ceuta and the proliferation of migrant detention spaces across the European Union'. *European Urban and Regional Studies,* 23(3), 527–530.

Keohane, R. O. 2012. 'Twenty years of institutional liberalism'. *International Relations,* 26(2), 125–138.

Laine, J. 2020. 'Ambiguous bordering practices at the EU's edges', in Bissonnette, E. and Vallet, A. (eds), *Borders and Border Walls: In-security, symbolism, vulnerabilities.* London: Routledge, 69–97.

Moyo, I. 2016a. 'The Beitbridge–Mussina interface: Towards flexible citizenship, sovereignty and territoriality at the border'. *Journal of Borderlands Studies,* 31(4), 427–440.

Moyo, I. 2016b. 'Changing migration status and shifting vulnerabilities: A research note on Zimbabwean migrants in South Africa'. *Journal of Trafficking, Organised Crime and Security,* 2(2), 108–112.

Moyo, I. 2020a. 'On borders and the liminality of undocumented Zimbabwean migrants in South Africa'. *Journal of Immigrant and Refugee Studies,* 18(1), 60–74.

Moyo, I. 2020b. 'Southern Africa's porous borders pose a problem for containing the corona virus'. *The Conversation,* https://theconversation. com/southern-africas-porous-borders-pose-a-problem-for-containing-the-coronavirus-135386n, accessed 14 November 2020.

Moyo, I. 2020c. 'On decolonising borders and regional integration in the Southern African Development Community (SADC) region'. *Social Sciences,* 9(4), 1–14.

Moyo, I. 2022. 'COVID-19, Dissensus and de facto transformation at the South Africa–Zimbabwe border at Beitbridge'. *Journal of Borderlands Studies,* 37(4), 781–804.

Moyo, I. 2023. 'The vacuity of informal cross-border trade facilitation strategies in the SADC region'. *Political Geography,* 101, 1–8.

Moyo, I. and Laine, J. P. 2022. 'Human mobility in the Southern African Development Community region: Some best practices for migration management from the European Union', in Moyo, I., Laine, J. P. and

Nshimbi, C. C. (eds), *Intra-Africa Migrations: Reimaging borders and migration management*. London: Routledge, 89–105.

Musoni, F. 2020. *Border Jumping and Migration Control in Southern Africa*. Bloomington: Indiana University Press.

Neocosmos, M. 2006. *From 'Foreign Natives to Native Foreigners'. Explaining Xenophobia in Post-Apartheid South Africa: Citizenship and nationalism, identity and politics*. Dakar: CODESIRA.

Nshimbi, C. C. and Fioramonti, L. 2013. 'MiWORC Report N°1. A region without borders? Policy frameworks for regional labour migration towards South Africa'. Johannesburg: African Centre for Migration and Society, University of the Witwatersrand.

Nshimbi, C. C. and Fioramonti, L. 2014. 'The will to integrate: South Africa's responses to regional migration from the SADC region'. *African Development Review*, 26(1), 52–63.

Nyamnjoh, F. B. 2006. *Insiders and Outsiders: Citizenship and xenophobia in contemporary South Africa*. Dakar, London and New York: CODESIRA and Zed Books.

Papadopoulos, D. and Tsianos, V. S. 2013. 'After citizenship: Autonomy of migration, organisational ontology and mobile commons'. *Citizenship Studies*, 17(2), 178–196.

Southern African Development Community (SADC), 1992. 'Declaration and Treaty of SADC', https://www.sadc.int/document/declaration-treaty-sadc-1992#:~:text=The%20Declaration%20and%20Treaty%20 specify,resources%20and%20environment%3B%20social%20 welfare%2C, accessed 20 September 2022.

Southern African Development Community (SADC). 2005. 'Protocol on Facilitation of Movement of Persons', https://www.sadc.int/ document/protocol-facilitation-movement-persons-2005, accessed 20 September 2022.

Trantidis, A. and Tsagkroni, V. 2017. 'Clientelism and corruption: Institutional adaptation of state capture strategies in view of resource scarcity in Greece'. *The British Journal of Politics and International Relations,* 19(2), 263–281.

Tshabalala, X. 2019. 'Hyenas of the Limpopo: "Illicit labour recruiting", assisted border crossings, and the social politics of movement across South Africa's border with Zimbabwe'. *Journal of Borderlands Studies,* 34(3), 433–450.

Van de Walle, N. 2001. *African Economies and the Politics of Permanent Crisis, 1979–1999*. New York, N.Y.: Cambridge University Press.

Wendt, A. 1999. *Social Theory of International Politics*. Cambridge: Cambridge University Press.

Wentzel, M. 2003. 'Historical and contemporary dimensions of migration between South Africa and its neighbouring countries'. HSRC migration workshop, Pretoria.

Wentzel, M. and Tlabela, K. 2006. 'Historical background to South African migration', in Kok. P., Gelderblom, D., Oucho, J. O. and Van Zyl, J. (eds), *Migration in South and Southern Africa: Dynamics and determinants.* Cape Town: Human Sciences Research Council, 71–95.

THIRTEEN

The digital policy on asylum protection in South Africa

LINDOKUHLE MDABE

INTRODUCTION

It has been a huge psychological shift to realise that the use of digital tools in the asylum system, which were implemented to limit the impact of the Covid-19 pandemic, will stay with us for a long time to come (Beirens, 2022: 7). For instance, in April 2021, South Africa's Department of Home Affairs (DHA) relied on the existing legislative and policy framework regulating the use of digital tools in public administration to introduce an online email application system at its five Refugee Reception Offices (RROs) located in Durban, Tshwane, Musina, Cape Town and Gqeberha. Initially, this digital tool was used to issue and extend visas for asylum seekers and refugees who were already in the country. This practice was later extended, on 3 May 2022, to conduct (a) front-end online registration of asylum applications from newly arrived asylum seekers (newcomers); (b) the online issuing and extension of asylum seeker and refugee visas; and (c) verification of the status of asylum seekers and refugees (Chitengu, 2022: 2).

While the reliance on the existing legislative and policy framework was not misconceived, there is a need for a context-specific and coherent digital policy to regulate the digital practice in the asylum system, particularly the use of digital tools to manage asylum applications, visas and asylum status. This asylum digital policy must be sensitive to the cardinal principles of asylum protection, namely, the non-refoulement principle (the idea that asylum seekers and refugees should not be vulnerable to arbitrary state- and non-state-driven measures, which would result in them being returned to countries where they will face persecution);[1] the prevention of unlawful detention, arrest and deportation of asylum seekers and refugees;[2] and the ability of asylum seekers and refugees to exercise their basic human rights to access public and private goods and services.[3]

This chapter briefly outlines the legislation and policy implementation regarding digital tools in the asylum system and provides guidelines for creating an asylum digital policy that complies with the asylum protection principles in policymaking, implementation and protection. This model of interpretation is borrowed from the Constitutional Court's adjudicative model in several cases involving

---

1 The 1951 Convention Relating to the Status of Refugees; the 1967 Protocol Relating to the Status of Refugees; the 1969 Organisation of African Unity Convention Governing the Specific Aspects of Refugee Problems in Africa; and the Refugees Act of 1998.
2 The 1951 Convention Relating to the Status of Refugees; the 1967 Protocol Relating to the Status of Refugees; the 1969 Organisation of African Unity Convention Governing the Specific Aspects of Refugee Problems in Africa; and the Refugees Act of 1998.
3 The 1951 Convention Relating to the Status of Refugees; the 1967 Protocol Relating to the Status of Refugees; the 1969 Organisation of African Unity Convention Governing the Specific Aspects of Refugee Problems in Africa; and the Refugees Act of 1998. Therefore, asylum seekers can access socioeconomic rights through the combination of the 1966 International Covenant on Economic, Social and Cultural Rights (ICESCR); the International Convention on the Elimination of All Forms of Racial Discrimination; the Convention on the Rights of the Child; the African Charter on Human and People's Rights; the Constitution; and the Refugees Act of 1998. These include the right to work, housing, education, healthcare services, and access to banking, social assistance and the legal system.

asylum protection in South Africa.[4] Secondly, the chapter provides a discussion of current digital practices implemented at the RROs and reflects on whether these comply with the asylum protection principles. Finally, recommendations are offered for asylum digital policy.

CONTEMPLATING A CONTEXT-SPECIFIC AND COHERENT ASYLUM DIGITAL POLICY

South Africa has not carved out a context-specific and coherent asylum policy, despite having a progressive legislative and policy framework to support digitalised public administration more broadly. The existing legislative and policy framework requires careful legal interpretation to reconcile it with the cardinal principles of asylum protection, namely, the non-refoulement principle; the prevention of unlawful detention, arrest or deportation of asylum seekers and refugees; and the ability of asylum seekers and refugees to exercise their basic human rights to access public and private goods and services. This model of an interpretive process was adopted by the Constitutional Court in several cases involving asylum protection in South Africa.[5] The interpretative reconciliation takes place in three aspects of the legislative and policy framework regulating digitalisation in South Africa, namely, policymaking, implementation and protection.

The first aspect relates to policymaking. Given that policymaking requires a policy problem (that is, policy is not designed in a vacuum but

---

4　On the non-refoulement principle, unlawful detention and deportation, please see *Abore v Minister of Home Affairs and Another* (CCT 115/21) [2021] ZACC 50; 2022 (4) BCLR 387 (CC); 2022 (2) SA 321 (CC) (30 December 2021); and *Ruta v Minister of Home Affairs* (CCT02/18) [2018] ZACC 52; 2019 (3) BCLR 383 (CC); 2019 (2) SA 329 (CC) (20 December 2018); and on extension of asylum visas, see *Saidi and Others v Minister of Home Affairs and Others* (CCT107/17) [2018] ZACC 9; 2018 (7) BCLR 856 (CC); 2018 (4) SA 333 (CC) (24 April 2018). Sections 27 and 27A of the Refugees Act on the rights.

5　*Abore v Minister of Home Affairs and Another* (CCT 115/21) [2021] ZACC 50; 2022 (4) BCLR 387 (CC); 2022 (2) SA 321 (CC) (30 December 2021); *Ruta v Minister of Home Affairs* (CCT02/18) [2018] ZACC 52; 2019 (3) BCLR 383 (CC); 2019 (2) SA 329 (CC) (20 December 2018); and *Saidi and Others v Minister of Home Affairs and Others* (CCT107/17) [2018] ZACC 9; 2018 (7) BCLR 856 (CC); 2018 (4) SA 333 (CC) (24 April 2018).

aims to address a problem), a digital policy in the asylum system must strive to facilitate the cardinal principle of non-refoulement, prevent arbitrary detention, arrests and deportation, and must promote the basic human rights of asylum seekers and refugees. To begin with, the powers conferred on the Minister of Public Service and Administration to facilitate the use of information and communication technologies in the public service must be guided by the cardinal principles of asylum protection (Government of South Africa, 1997). In addition, South Africa's existing e-governance vision and strategy, as set out in the National e-Government Strategy and Roadmap to promote universal access to electronic communications and to encourage the use of e-government services, must be implemented in conformity with the asylum cardinal principles (Government of South Africa, 2002). Finally, the education and training provided by the Sector Education and Training Authorities (SETAs) to public administrators in the use of digital tools must draw from the cardinal principles of asylum protection (Government of South Africa, 1998).

The second aspect relates to the implementation of legislation and policy. For instance, data messaging (which includes electronic mail) is currently being used by the RROs as evidence of acknowledgement of receipt of asylum seekers and refugee front-end online registration. This is part of the process of issuing and extending asylum visas and conducting the verification of status (DHA, 2021). An administrator at an RRO must comply with the stringent rules of legal compliance to accord this administrative process a legally binding status. For instance, the process must be in writing and supported by an advanced electronic signature, its integrity must not be altered, and it must be original. However, RROs are currently using an online email application system without guidelines on when an administrator should provide a turnaround response, and without a complaint-and-alert mechanism where asylum seekers and refugees may lodge governance-related complaints, on instances of malfunction and non-response. As a result, asylum seekers and refugees could go for months without visas and any engagement from the RROs (Lemekwana, interview, 2023; Mtshatsha, interview, 2023; Manyusa, interview, 2023), thus placing them at the risk of refoulement measures, arbitrary detention, arrest and deportation, and ultimately frustrating the exercising of their rights. This digital tool is intended to improve compliance with the cardinal principles of asylum protection by establishing guidelines on the time an administrator should take to provide a turnaround response, and a complaint mechanism for asylum seekers and refugees to lodge governance-related complaints.

The third aspect relates to data protection. For instance, the Promotion of Access to Information Act of 2000 gives effect to citizens' constitutional right to access information held by the state and by non-state actors. In contrast, the Protection of Personal Information Act of 2013 seeks to protect personal information held by public and private bodies. The Refugees Act further underscores this by guaranteeing the right to confidentiality of the asylum procedure, and disclosure of records required by applicants to exercise their rights (Government of South Africa, 1998). Given that prevention of arbitrary refoulement, detention, arrest and deportation and ensuring access to rights are urgent matters,[6] a request for records conducted in terms of the Promotion of Access to Information Act may prejudice vulnerable asylum seekers and refugees as these requests take time to process. Therefore, there is a need to adopt shorter timeframes for disclosure of relevant records.

Based on the above, South Africa has a solid legislative and policy foundation at the level of policymaking, implementation and protection when using digital tools to provide public services (Kariuki et al., 2022: 146). However, there is a need for a context-specific and coherent policy on the digitalisation of asylum procedures. This policy must integrate the cardinal principles of asylum protection. The section that follows discusses how the current digitalisation practice of the RROs, adopted in terms of the above legislative and policy framework post-Covid, compromises these cardinal principles of asylum protection.

---

6 *Zimbabwe Exiles Forum and Others v Minister of Home Affairs and Others (27294/2008) [2011] ZAGPPHC 29* (17 February 2011) at para 9.

POST-COVID DIGITALISATION PRACTICE
OF REFUGEE RECEPTION CENTRES

Covid-19 accelerated the move in the use of digital tools in asylum processes in Europe (Jean-David and Testi, 2021), Canada (Reid, 2021) and South Africa (Kariuki et al., 2022). According to Beirens (2022), this move can be best understood under three themes: the suspension of operations; the ad hoc implementation of specific measures to reduce pressure on the system; and the psychological shift from 'adaptation to necessity' to 'adaptation for innovation' (Beirens, 2022: 6). In the South African context, the DHA announced an email online application (Garber, 2022). Initially, this digital tool was limited to issuing and extending visas and conducting online verifications of applicants' status through email without having to physically go to the RRO. This digital tool was only available to holders of visas that expired during the Covid-19 lockdown. It was not until 3 May 2022 that newcomers could apply for asylum. This digital tool produces three possible outcomes once the application is made, namely, a PDF permit (if the application is done correctly), an additional information response (if the application is incomplete), and a request to appear in person (where the application cannot be completed online). Several public interest organisations (Garber, 2022) in South Africa have documented cases where their client community of asylum seekers and refugees go for months and years without valid documents, despite having made online applications to register claims, extend visas or verify asylum status (Lemekwana, interview, 2023).

Front-end online registrations

The Covid-19 pandemic accelerated two ad hoc digital processes in the asylum procedure, namely, the pre-registration and self-registration stages (Jean-David and Testi, 2021: 9–11). The former usually entails an intention to apply for asylum, and not the application itself. The latter entails an application by a new asylum applicant in countries such as Greece, the Netherlands and Norway, through self-registration booths using accessible languages (Jean-David and Testi, 2021: 9–11). Pre-registration is the antithesis to the principle that applicants 'should have prompt effective access to the asylum procedure', and there is no legal basis for it (Jean-David and Testi, 2021: 9–11). In international law, the right to secure swift access to the asylum procedure, including through new digital tools, is derived from the state's duty to provide public administration that is impartial and operates within reasonable timeframes; the principle of non-refoulement; and the right to asylum (Jean-David and Testi, 2021: 9–11). In some countries, including the United Kingdom, Greece, Belgium, Italy, Spain and France, asylum applicants who made pre-registrations through telephone calls, skype and emails experienced delays in lodging their applications (Beirens, 2022: 12).

Similarly, in the South African context, a newly arrived person who is seeking asylum in South Africa must make an online pre-registration (by filling in their details and those of their family members on the online application form, attaching scanned copies of their transit visas, passports or affidavits, and emailing this form to the RRO within their jurisdiction). This digital tool generates an automatic response indicating that the application has been received and that the applicant will be informed of the next steps in due course. What usually follows is an invitation letter indicating the time, date and place for an appointment. Therefore, this tool serves to allocate appointments, and RROs leverage it to accommodate their lack of administrative capacity (Amit, 2015: 6). While this tool facilitated greater access to the RROs, it had several shortfalls that forced the RROs to revert to in-person services.

To begin with, this digital tool created an added administrative layer to the asylum procedure; this contravenes the rule in the Refugees Act that an application must be conducted in person (Government of South Africa, 1998). It was also impractical for newcomers because key processes, which were previously at the core of claims conducted in person, were now conducted online (including the collection of biometric information; a detailed BI-1590 application form capturing the basis of the refugee claim; the opening of digital files; and the status determination interview) (Government of South Africa, 1998b). This meant that the asylum process was, and still remains, divided into a front-end, online pre-registration stage and an in-person registration stage. Additionally, in the absence of quantitative data, public-interest organisations working with asylum seekers and refugees reported that many of their clients were not assisted through the digital tool in periods between 2022 and 2023 (PMG, 2022). This tool did not provide guidelines on deadlines for responses. This glaring omission coincided with a lack of a complaint mechanism. In conclusion, given that the output of the tool was a mere invitation to apply, newcomers remained vulnerable to arbitrary deportation, detention and arrests.

The online issuing and extension of visas

This issuing and extension of visas are also done through an online email application system. And in the same way as the front-end online registration, it omits critical safeguards. It does not provide key guidelines on how long it should take for visas to be issued or extended, and it also does not establish a complaint mechanism for governance-related complaints. Several public interest organisations have recorded individual complaints from asylum seekers and refugees of having gone for more than three months or a year without a valid permit (Lemekwana, 2023). During this time people were not formally recognised as asylum seekers and refugees, despite having made online applications. Therefore, this digital tool placed asylum seekers and refugees at risk of unlawful deportation, detention and arrest, and it also frustrated their ability to exercise their right to gain access to private and public services.

Verification of the status of asylum seekers and refugees

Private and public institutions are often invited to verify the validity of an asylum seeker's status and refugee's status (Government of South Africa, 2002). This verification can be conducted by the immigration authorities, the South African Police Service (SAPS), financial and banking institutions, education authorities, healthcare authorities, employers and other public/private institutions. The DHA introduced a 24-hour line, which is linked to the National Immigration Information System (NIIS) for verification on the spot. However, practice also shows that the digital tool for verification does not trigger an immediate response, and this unresponsiveness can continue for an extended period as there is no guideline on turnaround time and or a complaint mechanism. Therefore, despite the availability of digital tools to conduct verification, there is evidence to suggest that asylum seekers and refugees have been arbitrarily detained and arrested, while others have not been able to access public and private services because of being undocumented (Amit, 2015: 18–22; Gander, 2019: 23–33; Ncube, 2020: 30–34). The RRO may improve the protection of asylum seekers and refugees by generating automated responses with track and trace of status (detailing where a person is on the asylum stage), and by updating website information, on the following issues:

- Verification to prevent detention, arrests and deportation, which must be conducted by the South African immigration authorities and SAPS.[7] This automated advisory message must underscore the principle of non-refoulement (Government of South Africa, 1998), the obligation placed on immigration officers and SAPS officers to verify asylum status (Government of South Africa, 2002), and the right of asylum seekers and refugees not to be detained, arrested or deported in the process of pursuing asylum protection (Government of South Africa, 1998).
- Verification to facilitate access to banking. An automated advisory message may draw its authority from the existing negotiated settlement between an NGO representing migrants and refugees and Banking Association South Africa (BASA). This states that bank accounts will not be blocked merely due to expired documentation, pending attempts to regularise asylum status.
- Verification for schools. An automated advisory message may draw its authority from three sources, namely, constitutional rights, the South African Schools Act of 1996 read with its regulations and the South African Human Rights Commission, in its Position Paper on Access to Basic Education for Undocumented Learners in South Africa.[8]
- Verification for hospitals. An automated advisory message must

---

7   *Zimbabwe Exiles Forum and Others v Minister of Home Affairs and Others (27294/2008) [2011] ZAGPPHC 29* (17 February 2011) at paras 29 to 34.
8   *Minister of Home Affairs and Others v Watchenuka and Another 2004 (4) SA 325 (SCA).*

underscore the importance of the right to access healthcare in terms of section 27(1)(a) of the Constitution of the Republic of South Africa, which guarantees that everyone has the right to access healthcare services in South Africa. 'Everyone' has been explicitly interpreted to include non-citizens and even undocumented individuals.[9]

• Verification to facilitate employment may be promoted through data messaging to employers. Such an advisory message could draw its authority from the right to employment (SA Constitution, 1996).

Collectively, the proposed verification interventions aim to prevent arbitrary refoulement, detention, arrest, deportation and violation of the rights of asylum seekers and refugees. They serve to facilitate access to private and public services. Considering the above discussion, I make recommendations in the section that follows.

RECOMMENDATIONS

A context-specific and coherent digital policy

The existing legislative and policy framework as discussed and interpreted above must be used to create a context-specific and coherent digital policy for asylum processes. The use of digital tools must eradicate any practice or measures that might violate the non-refoulement principle. In addition, such tools must prevent the unlawful detention and deportation of asylum seekers and refugees, and facilitate the exercising of their basic human rights. This should occur at the level of policymaking, strategy, norms, standards and institutional frameworks, as well as in the training and education of public administrators in digital tools.

At the level of implementation, digital tools adopted must improve compliance with the cardinal principles of asylum protection by establishing guidelines on the time an administrator should take to provide a response, and by setting up complaint mechanisms for

---

9   *Minister of Home Affairs and Others v Watchenuka and Another 2004 (4) SA 325 (SCA).*

asylum seekers and refugees to lodge governance-related complaints. At the level of protection, there should be a shorter turnaround time for responses to requests for the disclosure of documents to avoid prejudicing the applications of asylum seekers and refugees.

Guidelines for turnaround responses, complaint mechanisms and assistance

The RROs must introduce guidelines on turnaround responses to the online email application system. These must also establish a complaint mechanism for governance-related complaints, as well as telephonic digital assistance in conducting online applications. These guidelines must be implemented at three stages of the asylum process, namely the application stage; the issuing and extension of visas stage; and the status verification stage.

Discontinue front-end online applications

The RROs must discontinue the front-end online application, which creates an added administrative layer to the asylum procedure; this contravenes the rule in the Refugees Act that this application must be done in person. The RROs may adopt the self-registration online application, which may accommodate the collection of biometric information, a detailed BI-1590 application form capturing the basis of the refugee's claim, the opening of digital files and digitally enhanced status determination interviews, which may be conducted virtually.

Verification of the status of asylum seekers and refugees

The RROs may improve the protection of asylum seekers and refugees by generating verification automated responses with track and trace of status (detailing where a person is on the asylum stage), and updating website information, on issues including: the prevention of detention, arrests and deportation of asylum seekers and refugees; access to banking, schooling and hospitals; and employment rights.

CONCLUSION

There is a need for a context-specific and coherent digital policy strategy to regulate digital practices in the asylum system in South Africa, particularly the use of digital tools to manage asylum applications, issue and extend visas, and verify asylum status. This digital policy must be sensitive to the qualitative indicators of the organising principles of asylum protection. At the level of policymaking, digital policies must eradicate any practice or measures that may violate the non-refoulement principle; they must also prevent the unlawful detention and deportation of asylum seekers and refugees, and facilitate the exercise of their basic human rights. At the level of implementation, digital tools adopted must improve compliance with the cardinal principles of asylum protection by establishing guidelines on the time an administrator should take to provide a response, and by providing complaint mechanisms, which enable asylum seekers and refugees to lodge governance-related complaints. Lastly, at the level of protection, the turnaround time for responses to requests for the disclosure of documents must be shorter to avoid prejudicing the applications of asylum seekers and refugees. Without this asylum-specific digital policy, the RROs will continue to use digital tools without timeframes on turnaround responses, complaint-and-alert mechanisms or additional support. In addition, the RROs will continue with the front-end online applications, despite this entailing contravention of the Refugees Act. The policy recommended would provide guidelines on a just and fair verification process to prevent unfair detention, arrest and deportation, and to promote the rights of access to education, healthcare, employment and banking services.

REFERENCES

Amit, R. 2015. *Queue Here for Corruption: Measuring Irregularities in South Africa's Asylum System.* Johannesburg: Lawyer for Human Rights and African Centre for Migration and Society.

Beirens, H. 2022. 'Rebooting the asylum system? The role of digital tools in international protection'. Migration Policy Institute, www.migrationpolicy.org/research/asylum-system-digital-tools, accessed 21 October 2023.

Chitengu, C. 17 August 2022. 'Strengthening online systems to make asylum and refugee permits accessible across the digital divide'. Alt Advisory Africa, https://altadvisory.africa/2022/08/17/online-systems-asylum-and-refugee-permits/, accessed 1 November 2023.

Department of Home Affairs (DHA). April 2021. 'Online extension of asylum seekers and refugees visas', www.dha.gov.za/index.php/notices/1441-online-extension-of-asylum-seekers-and-refugees-visas, accessed 21 October 2023.

Jean-David, O. and Testi, E. 2021. 'Digitalisation of asylum procedures: Risks and benefits'. Asylum Information Database, https://asylumineurope.org/wp-content/uploads/2022/01/Digitalisation-of-asylum-procedures.pdf, accessed 19 October 2023.

Gander, S. 2019. '"They treat me as if I was nothing": Research report on the gendered impact of the decision to close the Cape Town refugee reception office'. Sonke Gender Justice, Cape Town.

Garber, J. 15 November 2022. 'Asylum seekers face challenges with DHA's online system – Lawyers for Human Rights (LHR)'. *News 24*, https://www.news24.com/news24/politics/parliament/asylum-seekers-face-challenges-with-dhas-online-system-lawyers-for-human-rights-20221115, accessed 19 June 2023.

Kariuki, P., Goyayi, M. and Ofusori, L. O. 2022. 'COVID-19, migration and inclusive cities through e-governance: Strategies to manage asylum seekers in Durban, South Africa'. *Digital Policy, Regulation and Governance*, 24(2), 145–146.

Lemekwana, C. 2023. 'Report from the Desmond Tutu Refugee Reception Centre stakeholders' meeting', Tshwane.

Ncube, W. 2020. *Monitoring Policy, Litigious and Legislative Shifts in Immigration Detention in South Africa*. Johannesburg: Lawyers for Human Rights.

Parliament Monitoring Group (PMG). 2022. 'Migrant issues, opening of refugee offices, statelessness: Stakeholder engagement with ministry; Electoral Amendment Bill: summary of public input', https://pmg.org.za/committee-meeting/35586/, accessed 22 June 2023.

Reid, K. 2021. 'Digital inclusion of refugees resettling to Canada: Opportunities and barriers'. International Organization for Migration (IOM), https://publications.iom.int/books/digital-inclusion-refugees-resettling-canada-opportunities-and-barriers, 19 October 2023.

Government of South Africa Acts, all accessed 2 August 2023

Electronic Communication and Transaction Act 25 of 2002. 2 August 2002. Chapter 3, https://www.gov.za/sites/default/files/gcis_document/201409/a25-02.pdf.

Electronic Communication and Transaction Act 25 of 2002. 2 August 2022, https://www.gov.za/sites/default/files/gcis_document/201409/a25-02.pdf,

Immigration Act No. 13 of 2002. 31 May 2002. 'Section 34 and 41'. https://www.gov.za/sites/default/files/gcis_document/201409/a13-020.pdf.

Public Service Commission Act of 1997. 17 December 1997, https://www.326. gov.za/sites/default/files/gcis_document/201409/a93-97.pdf.

Refugees Act No. 130 of 1998. 2 December 1998b. Section 1, 21(1A), https:// www.gov.za/sites/default/files/gcis_document/201409/a130-980.pdf.

Refugees Act No. 130 of 1998. 2 December 1998. 'Section 21', https://www. gov.za/sites/default/files/gcis_document/201409/a130-980.pdf.

Refugees Act No. 130 of 1998. 2 December 1998. 'Section 21(4)', https://www. gov.za/sites/default/files/gcis_document/201409/a130-980.pdf.

Refugees Act No. 130 of 1998. 2 December 1998. 'Section 2', https://www. gov.za/sites/default/files/gcis_document/201409/a130-980.pdf, Section 2

Republic of South Africa. 1996. 'Constitution of the Republic of South Africa: Section 22', https://www.gov.za/documents/constitution/chapter-2-bill-rights#22.

Skills Development Act 97 of 1998. 20 October 1998, http://www. nationalskillsauthority.org.za/wp-content/uploads/2015/11/skills-development-act.pdf.

Court Cases

Abore v Minister of Home Affairs and Another (CCT 115/21) [2021] ZACC 50; 2022 (4) BCLR 387 (CC); 2022 (2) SA 321 (CC) (30 December 2021).

Minister of Home Affairs and others v Watchenuka and Another 2004 (4) SA 325 (SCA).

Ruta v Minister of Home Affairs (CCT02/18) [2018] ZACC 52; 2019 (3) BCLR 383 (CC); 2019 (2) SA 329 (CC) (20 December 2018).

Saidi and Others v Minister of Home Affairs and Others (CCT107/17) [2018] ZACC 9; 2018 (7) BCLR 856 (CC); 2018 (4) SA 333 (CC) (24 April 2018).

Zimbabwe Exiles Forum and Others v Minister of Home Affairs and Others (27294/2008) [2011] ZAGPPHC 29 (17 February 2011) at paras 29 to 34.

Interviews

Lemekwana, C. 16 September 2023. Interview with a lawyer at Lawyers for Human Rights, Johannesburg.

Manyusa, N. 16 September 2023. Interview with a lawyer at Lawyers for Human Rights, Durban.

Mtshatsha, H. 16 September 2023. Interview with a lawyer at Lawyers for Human Rights, Tshwane.

FOURTEEN

Conclusion: Whole-of-route approach to migration

EDDIE M. RAKABE

The compilation of chapters in this volume contends with contemporary patterns and policy debates on migration in South Africa, juxtaposing these with developments across the African continent and the global village. The authors have examined the complex intersection between migration, social cohesion and economic interests; the realities and perceptions of migrant livelihood strategies; and the tensions or unity and solidarity between locals and migrants that result. Lastly, this volume explores the intricate relationship between migration governance and border controls. The book presents various theoretical perspectives, including from dual labour market theory, network theory and institutional theory. Other ancillary theories straddle migration and belonging or social cohesion; in short, migration and economic development and the securitisation of migration.

Southern Africa and many regions across the continent are making stop-start progress towards the free movement of people (and goods) across the nation-states. These processes are aimed at facilitating Pan-African ideals and territorial, cultural and economic sovereignty.

However, they also generate protective barriers in the form of strict border controls and other kinds of discrimination also known as invisible borders. Under colonialism, African states were established through the arbitrary partitioning of borders. This resulted in the separation of families and ethnic communities, who constantly find themselves clashing over territorial trespassing in the post-colonial era (Gashaw, 2017). This book is published at a time when South Africa is juggling long-standing perceptions and sporadic incidents of xenophobia, a deteriorating economic and political climate accompanied by populist and nationalist rhetoric, and reckoning with its declining historical status as a regional employment hub, despite remaining a preferred destination for migrant workers.

These factors create a milieu of analytical challenges and false narratives, socioeconomic precarity and complexities for forging social cohesion beyond the confines of nation-state belonging and migration governance in a region characterised by uneven economic development. To make sense of these tensions and challenges, this book argues for and marshals evidence that migration in the context of Africa is a colonial construct that continues to be contentious not only for South Africa but also for regions promising better livelihoods and respect for human rights. The findings in this book suggest that certain social actors have been declared undesirable to engage in cross-border mobility due to the long history of social divisions and hierarchisation. These social actors generally belong to the 'Africa of the labour reserves' as coined by Amin (1972) – a belonging that does not recognise multi-layered identities.

WHEN THE POLITICS OF BELONGING CLASH WITH ECONOMIC INTERESTS

In tracing the genealogy and motivations of migration, this volume acknowledges that cross-border shifts have always been an intrinsic part of development rather than a temporary reaction to economic, social, political and environmental disequilibrium. Migrants do not change habitual residence across borders to assimilate into or append the nationalities of the hosting nations but rather do so to fulfil economic aspirations, re-establish social networks and, increasingly, to escape political and environmental vulnerabilities. The primacy of economic significance in migration is articulated in the African Union Protocol on Free Movement of Persons in this way (AU, 2018):

> ... the free movement of persons, capital goods and services will promote integration, Pan-Africanism, enhance science, technology, education, research and foster tourism, facilitate inter-African trade and investment, increase remittances within Africa, promote mobility of labour, create employment, improve the standards of living of the people of Africa and facilitate the mobilization and utilization of the human and material resources of Africa in order to achieve self-reliance and development...

Yet for Africa, and South Africa in particular, patterns and processes of migration have evolved somewhat counterintuitively to the idea envisaged above of maximising the full benefits of open borders. Colonial authorities created migrant-labour governance systems, which forcibly uprooted people from their habitual territories and traditional means of production into servitude and a wage economy for capitalist interests. Migrants were reduced to unproductive workers, sub-humans and temporary sojourners who must, by decree, return to their countries once declared 'expired workers' and 'rejects'[1] by an exploitative capitalist system (Moyo and Laine, 2021). Nshimbi in chapter 2 argues strongly that the fundamental structure, networks and mechanisms through which contemporary migration flows have become increasingly conflated with the politics of belonging and economic ownership and opportunities. South Africa continues to attract migrants from neighbouring countries, many engaged in path dependency as the network theory postulates, battling to find a place in the rainbow nation-building project.

In chapter 6, Fadiran and Amusa dispel the myth of unproductive migrant workers, which dehumanises migrant workers and confines

---

1 Dehumanising terminology used by the apartheid system to refer to the weak and sick workers who can no longer work in the mines.

them to low-paid jobs. Their findings are especially intriguing as productivity is analysed from a feminisation perspective. They argue that labour migration in Africa among low-skilled workers generally occurs outside of formal channels. This leads to undocumented status and a perceived overconcentration of women in the informal economy and the sectors associated with low productivity, as examined in chapter 3. In some instances, women are forced to deskill and self-demote, instead of using their qualifications, to the detriment of their productivity. However, chapter 6 not only finds no discernible variation in productivity between migrant men and their female counterparts but also concludes that migrant women are no more present in the informal sector than in the formal sector. This chapter challenges the orthodox and patronising view, consistent with the new economics of migration theory, that women migrate to join husbands and families. Both single and married women are now migrating independently in search of jobs in richer countries or regions, thus redefining traditional gender roles within families and societies. However, class dynamics often result in complex experiences of social cohesion for migrant women in the context of contested meaning and belonging in post-apartheid South Africa.

In chapter 5, Munakamwe sheds light on the intricate intersection between acceptance, class and economic power relations, drawing on lessons from migrant employees' experiences of accessing compensation for occupational injuries and diseases. She contrasts the experiences of skilled migrant workers who reside in affluent areas and are likely to be spared, but not entirely excluded from, anti-immigrant attitudes and violence and those in low-skilled occupations, such as domestic work, who encounter workplace discrimination, labour rights subjectivity and patronising power dynamics that reinforce passivity and exploitation. In the places where unskilled migrants reside, violence and fear of deportation are common occurrences, creating apathy towards advocacy and participation in movements aimed at asserting human and labour rights. Yet, in some instances the enduring legacy of systemic and cross-cutting capitalist economic exclusion directly and indirectly forges unity and solidarity between local and migrant workers, cultivating a sense of shared belonging and economic struggle. Munakamwe suggests that trade union leaders, who also struggle with recognition for organising in low-skilled occupations, are at the centre of forging Pan-African worker unity to minimise wage undercutting and curb exploitation.

The research in this volume reasserts the significance of capital in attracting migrants while at the same time highlighting its impact on reproducing regional paradigms of uneven development, inequality and local migrant tensions in impoverished communities. Ngoma and Ngcaweni in chapter 8 reflect on the market domination of South Africa's large retail corporations to underline the significance of a centralised capital structure, or parasitic capitalist conglomerates, in driving migration flows. Colonial and apartheid systems of capital accumulation have enabled and facilitated the growth of multinational conglomerates that rely on market and financial muscle to expand beyond South African borders and into local markets or dwellings (townships) generally served by local small businesses and occupied by migrants. Corporate expansion coincides with the growing phenomenon of foreign-owned spaza shops, operated mainly by migrants from Somalia, Bangladesh and Pakistan, and the concentration of informal street trading by African migrants in townships and villages. The penetration of large conglomerates, on the one hand, and the emergence of foreign-owned informal businesses, on the other, causes a 'scramble for opportunities' between locals and migrants that expresses itself as conflict and xenophobic attacks. Concerns about foreigners taking jobs and opportunities manifest in violent protest and an accentuation of the 'struggle to be a South African'.

Ndlovu in chapter 4 strongly argues that the struggle to be a South African is a historical project that has remained an elusive ideal to native ethnic groups. This is the context within which the intricate interface between politics of belonging and economic interest should be understood. Ndlovu eloquently describes how this understanding may be sought, namely by tracing the challenges of the idea of South Africa through a historically grounded approach. This approach appreciates that migrants come into a context in which there are long-standing challenges of harnessing complex identities into a normatively constructed post-apartheid identity of a rainbow nation. These complex identities emerged along fault lines well captured by scholars such as Neocosmos (2010) as involving a process of constructing 'foreign natives' out of black, indigenous people and 'native foreigners' out of white settlers. Migrants then come into this context as an added layer of complexity, where nation-building and social cohesion are long-standing, post-apartheid challenges, and the idea of being South African remains an illusion for the majority of black South Africans who are experiencing social and economic hardships.

Debates and discussions on migration in South Africa are overwhelmingly overshadowed by xenophobic assertions and fears. This construction, however necessary and germane, often overlooks daily grassroots-level social and economic interactions that help to reclaim, reassert and reinforce social cohesion or a multi-layered sense of belonging in communities and workplaces. As indicated earlier, Munakamwe's chapter observed how local and migrant worker solidarity against wage undercutting can foster a common sense of belonging. Malaika Mahlatse in chapter 9 also shows how the reconstruction of township space has produced a socio-spatial dialectic in which complex inter-relationships between spatial and social structures result in ethnic tensions; violent service delivery protests; livelihood insecurity; and a lack of access to housing, social and basic services. These have led to a penalty for the urban poor, she argues.

However, even as both the local and migrant poor navigate the urban spatial transformation deficit in an effort to access incomes and affordable housing, the communities they reside in benefit from learning about the different cultures and traditions of migrants through tenant-landlord relationships. These interactions are a necessary step towards integration and tolerance. Mahlatsi observes that a landlord in Soweto, Meadowlands section has learned Shona, the national language of Zimbabwe, due to hosting a tenant from Masvingo in Zimbabwe. Myriad social interactions of this nature do not attract scholarly and media attention to the extent that anti-immigration sentiments do. Kesselman in chapter 7 employs an anthropological approach to demonstrate how food can be used to deprive or (re)construct a migrant's identity and root them in their new home. She indicates that migrants compensate for the nutrition transition, and a loss of connection to their place of origin, by purchasing food from special vendors trading in 'food from home'. Research on acculturation, migration and belonging points to the maintenance of identity as a reason to continue eating traditional foods.

NAVIGATING LIVELIHOOD STRATEGIES IN A TRANSFORMING SPATIAL REALM

Both internal and external African migrants, who were the first to be incorporated forcibly into the colonial/capitalist wage economy, had to live lives of migration – between the marginal geographical areas to which they had been displaced and the urban areas/colonial territories where they provided labour in colonisers' mines, farms and industries. Drawing from Amin's analysis, the labour mobility of Africans who dwelt in rural peripheries was central to patterns of spatial development and accumulation established in South Africa. In turn, those patterns established a system in which Africans oscillated between mines in the urban centres where they were forced into cheap labour and so-called 'homelands'. That cycle of circular migration between rural dwellings and urban centres continues to this day, albeit under a democratic labour market regime.

Colonial and apartheid restrictions on wages, occupations and trades confined migrants to limited livelihood options. Relaxation of these restrictions in the post-apartheid era coincided with a gradual process of spatial economic transformation characterised by spatial inequality, urban decline and spatial mismatch; that is, a situation in which industries concentrate without creating sufficient jobs and settlement, including those with the right skills. Rakabe's chapter 10 illustrates that these spatial patterns not only limit livelihood options for migrants but also send incorrect migration signals, reproduce suboptimal spatial development patterns and create dilemmas for spatial remedial policies. Migrants continue to concentrate in areas with limited capacities to absorb job seekers and accommodate growing urban dwellers. Consequently, many migrants, both internal and external, seek refuge in the informal sector for jobs and housing as a survival option of last resort, which are discussed in chapters 6, 7, 8 and 9 respectively.

In chapter 6, Fadiran and Amusa reflect on the gendered dimension of migration and reject the notion that migrant women are overrepresented in the informal economy, despite the established body of literature locating migrant communities within the informal sector (Goyayi, 2022). Their findings reveal wage-induced migration patterns at a broader level and more nuanced ones at a gender level, linked to the quality of governance in countries of origin. The chapter accentuates the importance of distinct, gender-related drivers of migration such as evading gender-based violence or seeking improved prospects in care professions. It advocates for better conditions in destination nations, as mirroring discriminatory patterns of sending nations can exacerbate hardships for female migrants, especially where their socio-professional networks are already limited.

Kesselman explores the livelihood strategy of migrants from the perspective of a nutrition transition, shifting from traditional food consumed at home to new, foreign diets. In the process of balancing the need to reconnect with home food and adopting a new destination diet, migrants interact with three sub-economies: cross-border food traders and transporters; informal street traders; and large retail and fast-food chains. Ngoma and Ngcaweni see the concentration of large retail chains into spaces inhabited by local income earners as a threat to local and migrant livelihoods. When these large retailers enter the township market, they structure themselves in ways that have characteristics similar to informal traders, despite the retailers enjoying the benefits of dominant market power. For Ngoma and Ngcaweni, the solution lies in a regional integration approach, which would entail the Southern African Customs Union (SACU) most immediately, and SADC more broadly, formulating a synergistic macro strategy for the development of informal and township economies, as well as for micro and small enterprises.

INSTITUTIONALISED WEAPONS AGAINST MIGRATION

Migration in South Africa, as Moyo and Gumbi show in their chapters, mirrors the global trend of populism in which migrants are stigmatised as a threat to public order, national identity, labour market stability and economic security. Migration has been securitised and instrumentalised. The social construction of migration as a security concern results from powerful political and societal dynamics, which concretise migration as an undesirable social phenomenon. The chapters in this book highlight the populism and nationalist rhetoric engulfing the world and taking advantage of various forms of social deficit and resulting discontent for personal political ambitions. These incitements are not isolated to any specific region but tend to manifest as intra-regional and ethno-rivalry in ways that divide people who share a common heritage across regional borders. Chapter 2 offers an international articulation of populist ideals across America, Europe and Asia, and, more specifically, the stigmatisation of African mobility to Europe.

Borders are being securitised through contingents of border police and soldiers, thick and long walls, border surveillance systems and unethical sensors that can detect the heartbeat of a migrant from a distance. Upon entry into destination countries, migrants are constantly threatened with harassment and deportation. Many fall victim to neopatrimonialism with cross-border officials soliciting bribes from desperate cross-border actors, such as informal cross-border traders. South Africa is no different, as Gumbi's chapter demonstrates, offering a rich account of institutionalised securitisation. Yet, Moyo's chapter argues that migrants always find ways to breach borders no matter how securitised and militarised they are. This may be construed as the bravest form of migrant agency rather than an act of defiance. It is the precarity of enforcing thick borders against the human urge to survive. Duffield and Wiedel (2004: 4) eloquently capture this contrast between security and the longing for a better life in reference to migrants who set sail on perilous journeys across the Mediterranean to reach Europe:

It is specifically on the bare life of the abandoned boat that the two powerful grammars of 'political security' and 'human security' conflate. The boat as a space of exception is thus also a place of ambiguity, where bare life is managed both by the sovereign and the humanitarian. This contradiction is signified by security professionals, who manage both rescue and deportation. This is a biopolitical locus in the sense that the sovereign can actually foster life or disallow it to the point of death.

The tug of war between authorities seeking to securitise borders and cross-border actors attempting to circumvent these barriers is an endless one. Authorities fail to realise that the security of a nation-state is dependent on the security of other states at micro and macro levels. Moyo suggests that authorities should look to institutional liberalism for solutions rather than build additional thick border walls, recruit armies of border guards and tighten visa requirements. The fundamental tenet of institutional liberalism is that both domestic and foreign institutions must offer a platform for the advancement of human security and liberty. In the context of migration, such a platform would be a regional institution that controls borders and migration at the SADC regional level. As in relation to the politics of belonging, some chapters in this volume advocate for understanding the complexities of border control and migration rather than pandering to populist ideals. Miggiano (2009) points to an ongoing hiatus between laws and practice, which has allowed emergency measures, misaligned with national and international provisions on human rights and refugee protection, to take root. Nshimbi and Ngcaweni in the first chapter of this book argue that South Africa's White Paper on Citizenship, Immigration and Refugee Protection: Towards A Complete Overhaul of the Migration System in South Africa, which was introduced a few months before the publication of this book, falls somewhat into the category of emergency measures for stricter border controls and restrictions on 'belonging' to South African identity.

GOVERNANCE FOR SUSTAINABLE MIGRATION AND VESTED INTERESTS

There is a fine line between migration governance and border control that must be carefully trodden. Chapters in this volume show that South Africa continues to adopt and drive a legalistic approach to border control rather than one that embraces treaties, management and knowledge systems that facilitate the movement of people across borders. The world is increasingly moving towards the concept of sustainable migration, which, according to Faris (2001), should be the overriding goal for migration governance. Migration is sustainable if it has the democratic support of host nations, meets the long-term interests of all parties involved and is governed by basic human rights and ethical imperatives.

In their chapter, Rakabe, Ngcaweni and Lubale show that Africa was one of the first continents to introduce a legal regime for sustainable migration through the OAU Convention Governing the Specific Aspects of Refugee Problems in Africa. There are several other non-binding international agreements (e.g., United Nations 1951 Refugee Convention and its 1967 Protocol) that aim to promote sustainable migration practices in countries of origin, transit and destination. However, as Rakabe, Ngcaweni and Lubale note, the landscape governing migration is multi-layered and complex, and serves varied constituencies and interests. The ideals of a sustainable approach to migration fail to materialise due to conflicting stakeholder interests (politicians, citizens and business). Ultimately, effective migration governance in South Africa will require a long-term commitment from the government and other stakeholders to address the causes, consequences and dynamics of different migrations and to promote the integration of migrant workers and refugees in South African society in the interests of sustainable development.

CONCLUSION

Migration can be framed in the context of crime, unemployment and cruelty (securitisation) or equally in that of integration, cosmo-politanism and sustainable economic development. The contrast between these has played out in South Africa in the pre- and post-colonial eras in ways that denigrate and exploit migrants (including internal migrants) and reinforce capitalist and exclusive modes of economic development. As colonial patterns of development continue, South Africa finds itself having to navigate a historical legacy of a promised land (being a favourite migrant destination) and being home to 'native' South Africans who have been deprived of belonging by the apartheid regime and seek socioeconomic justice. The resulting tension expresses itself through constant struggles for nationhood, contestations for livelihood opportunities and clashes between border control authorities and those evading them. This book acknowledges the social, economic and political discord associated with migration and dispels the myths of migrant danger, unproductivity and widespread hostility between locals and migrants. At the same time, it calls for an understanding of the complexity of managing migration in a country with deep-rooted socioeconomic and identity divides. The complexity must be understood in this historical context as articulated by Neocosmos (2006: 23). He asks how many of the majority who deem themselves 'South Africans' were regarded as foreigners in their native land under the apartheid legislation that de-nationalised them.

REFERENCES

African Union (AU). 2018. 'Protocol to the Treaty Establishing the African Economic Community Relating to Free Movement of Persons, Right of Residence and Right of Establishment', https://au.int/en/treaties/protocol-treaty-establishing-african-economic-community-relating-free-movement-persons, accessed 10 November 2023.

Amin, S. 1972. 'Underdevelopment and dependence in black Africa: Origins and contemporary forms'. *The Journal of Modern African Studies*, 10(4), 503–524.

Faris, M. 2001. 'What is sustainable migration?'. Background Document No 11, Faces of Migration, https://gcap.global/wp-content/uploads/2021/04/BackGround-Document-n.-11-ENG-06.04.2021-1.pdf, accessed 15 December 2023.

Gashaw, T. 17 November 2017. 'Colonial borders in Africa: Improper design and its impact on African borderland communities'. *Africa Up Close,* https://www.wilsoncenter.org/blog-post/colonial-borders-in-africa-improper-design-and-its-impact-on-african-borderland-communities, accessed 1 December 2023.

Goyayi, M. 12 April 2022. 'Protecting the rights of migrant women entrepreneurs in the informal sector'. Democracy Development Program, https://ddp.org.za/blog/2022/04/12/protecting-the-rights-of-migrant-women-entrepreneurs-in-the-informal-sector/, accessed 1 December 2023.

Miggiano, L. 2009. 'States of exception: Securitisation and irregular migration in the Mediterranean', *Research Paper No. 177*, UNHCR, Policy Development and Evaluation Service.

Moyo, I. and Laine, J. 2021. 'Precarity of borders and migration regimes in the Southern African region', in Moyo, I., Laine, J. and Nshimbi, C. C. (eds), *Intra-Africa Migrations: Reimaging borders and migration management*. London: Routledge.

INDEX

A

Abahlali baseMjondolo 61

Abaluyia people 43

accumulation by dispossession 3, 31, 37, 38 (see also 'Marxist')

Afghanistan 72

Africa(n) 5, 7, 9–11, 14, 16–17, 27, 34–35, 37–48, 56–57, 63, 68–70, 79–80, 84–85, 87, 92, 112, 125–133, 135–136, 138, 142, 144–146, 152–153, 156, 158–159, 167, 171, 191, 193, 195, 197–198, 200, 210, 214, 226, 228–230, 243, 246, 251–252, 275, 281, 284, 287–289, 303–304, 327–331, 333, 335, 337

Africa of the labour reserves 37–38, 45–48, 328

African Commons Position on Migration and Development 8

African Development Bank (AfDB) 197–198

African diaspora 128

African National Congress (ANC) 13, 85–86, 92–93

African Transformation Movement (ATM) 61, 64

African Union (AU) 8, 191, 193

Agenda 2063 8, 198 (see also 'African Union (UN)')

agglomeration (dis)economies 241, 243–244, 247–249, 255–256, 266–267

Alexandra 171, 227

Algeria 70, 132

Aliens Act of 1937 276

Aliens Control Act of 1991 71

Angola 27, 46, 196, 226, 292

anti-immigrant 4, 69, 73, 87, 89, 91, 102, 155, 230, 330, 332

anti-migrant 59, 62, 64

apartheid 1, 16, 46, 56–57, 61, 63, 80–82, 85–87, 92, 95, 106, 110, 148, 219–222, 225–228, 231–232, 243, 250, 252–253, 259, 276, 283–284, 329, 331, 333, 337–338

apartheid spatial planning 251, 260, 264

asylum policies 68, 111

asylum seekers 6, 19, 57, 71, 85, 89, 105, 193–194, 225–226, 235–237, 281, 283–284, 286, 290–291, 313–318, 320–324

AU Protocol on Free Movement of Persons (2018) 329

autochthony 91, 95

B

Bangladesh 194, 331

Banking Association South Africa
(BASA) 321

Bantu Gusii people 40

Bantu Homelands Citizenship Act of
1970 227

Bantu speakers 40

Bantustans (aka 'homelands') 46, 227,
252, 254, 258–260, 264–265, 267,
333

Belgium 84, 319

belonging 79–82, 86, 89–92, 94–96,
168, 182, 327–333, 336–337

Berlin Conference of 1884 44

Bill of Rights 116, 284, 286

Boer 45

Border Management Authority
(BMA) 285, 289, 291, 298, 301,
307

Border Management Authority
(BMA) Act of 2020 298, 301

Border Management Authority
(BMA) Bill 72

Botswana 27, 45–47, 70, 105, 111, 292,
301, 305, 307

brain drain 130

Braverman, Suella 69

Brexit 69

British Broadcasting Corporation
(BBC) 69

Burundi 46, 70, 184

Business Act of 1991 236

Buthelezi, Mangosutho 86–87

C

Cameroon 40, 111

Canada 318

Cape Colony 84, 228, 305

Cape Town 181, 313

capital 35, 45–47, 241–242, 248, 331

capital accumulation 5, 253, 331

capital flight 229

capitalism 117

capitalist 35, 37–38, 44, 47–48, 208,
329–331, 333, 337

capitalist economy 44

Central Africa 127

Chad 70

China 194

Chris Hani Institute 109

Cities Support Programme 232–233,
265

Citizenship Act of 1995 13, 283, 285,
288

climate change 4, 134, 159, 194

climate disasters 135, 137

Cold War 58, 299

colonial 1, 5–6, 16, 34–35, 38–40,
44–48, 85, 94, 105, 117, 152, 182,
219, 226–228, 231–232, 253, 259,
278, 283, 328–329, 331, 333, 337

colonialism 5, 37, 39–40, 44, 47–48,
61, 95, 220, 228, 328

colonies 44, 84

colonisation 168

colonisers 37–39, 44, 47–48, 84, 333

Commission for Conciliation,
Mediation and Arbitration
(CCMA) 109

Commission for Employment Equity
(CEE) 66

common market 8

Comoros 27

Compensation for Occupational
Injuries and Diseases Act

(COIDA) of 1993 101–105, 109, 112, 114, 117
Comprehensive Rural Development Programme (CRDP) (2009) 265
Competition Commission 210, 212
Congo, Republic of 132
Congress of South African Trade Unions (COSATU) 109
Constitution of South Africa 102, 112–114, 117, 144, 235, 262, 267, 284, 288–289, 314, 322
Constitutional Court of South Africa 105, 115, 290, 314–315
constitutional rights 102, 106, 108, 114, 116–117, 317, 321
contract labour system 6, 85, 103, 106
Convention on the Elimination of All Forms of Discrimination against Women 281, 286–287
Convention on the Rights of the Child 281, 286–287, 314
Copenhagen School of Security Studies 12, 55, 58–60 (see also 'securitisation')
copper belt 45
Covid-19 109, 115, 196, 202, 313, 317–318
customs union 8
customs union theory 7

D
Dadaab refugee camp 70
De-agrianisation 198, 226
deindustrialisation 192, 198, 214, 243, 253
De Klerk, F.W. 86
democracy 55–56, 65, 115, 243, 251, 284

constitutional 112
democratic dispensation (aka 'democratic era') 63–64, 219–220, 225, 232, 252
Democratic Republic of the Congo (DRC) 27, 94, 110–111, 184
Department of Arts and Culture (DAC) 82, 90
Department of Employment and Labour (DEL) 290
Department of Home Affairs (DHA) 72, 86–87, 90, 283, 285, 290–291, 298, 313, 318, 320
Department of International Relations and Cooperation (DIRCO) 290
Department of Small Business Development (DSBD) 201, 202
Strategic Plan 2020–2025 202
Department of Trade, Industry and Competition (DTIC) 202, 213, 236
Derby, Idriss 70
development aid 105, 291
developmental state 196
diamond belt 45
dietary acculturation 168, 173, 181–182, 333
digital policy 15, 19, 214, 313–314, 322, 324
asylum 314–316, 323, 324
digital tools 313–314, 316–324
digitalisation 315, 317–318
District Development Model 265
Ditsela 109
diversity 81–83, 86, 171
Djibouti 132
domestic work(ers) 101–109, 112–117, 138, 330

double burden of malnutrition 165
   (see also 'under-nutrition' and
   'over-nutrition')
dual economy 32, 208–209
Durban 61, 181, 253, 313

E
East Africa 41, 126
eastern Africa 37–38
economic and monetary union 8
economic development 18
economic migrants 85
economic theory 7
economies of scale 7
Egypt 70
emigration 30, 34
entrepreneurship 205, 207, 209, 220
Equatorial Guinea 149
Eritrea 145
eSwatini 2, 6, 27, 46, 85, 105, 111, 115,
   131, 149, 196, 226, 292, 301, 305
Ethiopia 111, 224
ethnic group 3, 43, 93, 95, 322, 331
European Border and Coast Guard
   Agency (FRONTEX) 303
European Union (EU) 68, 197,
   303–304

F
financialisation 192, 214
First World 61
food insecurity 164, 168–169 (see also
   'nutrition insecurity')
food security 231, 233
foreign direct investment (FDI) 192,
   200, 212
foreign natives 93
France 84, 319

free trade 7, 192
free trade area (FTA) 8
Freedom Charter 92

G
Gabon 132
Gambia, The 132
gender-based violence (GBV) 109,
   116, 154, 334
Ghana 70, 111
global care economy 107, 117
global financial crisis of 2008 54
global food system 167
global governance 278
global North 69, 155, 168
global South 146, 155–156, 164–166,
   168, 230
globalisation 30, 68, 125, 128
Gqeberha 313
Gramsci, Antonio 101, 108–109,
   116–117 (see also 'hegemony,
   theory of')
gravity models 32, 133, 135–136, 152,
   155, 252, 256
Great Britain (see 'United Kingdom
   (UK)')
Greece 318–319
green economy zones 265
gross domestic product (GDP) 155,
   197–198, 201–202
gross regional domestic product
   (GRDP) 258–259
Group Areas Act of 1950 220, 251
growth management zones 265
Guinea 40, 41

H
Harris and Todaro Model 242

hegemony, theory of 101, 108, 117
  (see also 'Gramsci, Antonio')
homelands (see 'Bantustans')
homelessness 225
hostels 228
human capital 29
human rights 9, 17, 59, 101–104,
  106–108, 111–113, 115–117, 225,
  281, 284–286, 289, 291, 314–316,
  322, 324, 328, 330, 336–337
Human Sciences Research Council
  (HSRC) 64, 66
Hungary 69
hut tax 226

I
ILO Convention 143 (aka
  'International Convention on the
  Protection of the Rights of All
  Migrant Workers and Members of
  Their Families') 112
ILO Convention 189 109
ILO Convention 190 109
Imizamo Yethu informal settlement
  66
immigrants 5–6, 9–11, 16, 19, 54–57,
  60, 63, 66, 68–69, 71–72, 83–84,
  86–91, 105, 110–111, 130, 132,
  135, 142, 219, 221, 223–225, 227,
  229, 231, 235, 237
immigration 12–14, 17, 30, 34, 56–57,
  60, 68, 71–73, 85–86, 89, 128,
  131–139, 156, 158, 194, 225, 278,
  288, 291, 302, 307–308, 320–321
Immigration Act of 2002 13, 71, 89,
  106, 108, 285, 288, 290
immigration controls 2
immigration legislation 4, 14

immigration policies 68, 71, 88–89,
  128, 284
immigration status 6, 137
immigration system 5, 12
imperialism 37, 41
imperialist 84
India 194
industrial development zones (IDZs)
  263
industrialisation 8, 226–228, 248,
  262–263
informal cross-border traders
  (ICBTs) 306
informal economy 18, 137, 192, 201,
  205, 207–213, 232, 253, 330, 334
informal enterprise 193
informal sector 130–131, 137, 142,
  194, 202, 208–210, 212, 229–330,
  333–334
informal settlement 63, 220, 227–229,
  262, 264
infrastructure development 8
institutional liberalism 299–302, 336
Integrated Sustainable Rural
  Development Programme 264
Integrated System of External
  Surveillance (SIVE) 303
Integrated Urban Development
  Framework 265
International Convention on the
  Elimination of All Forms of
  Racial Discrimination 281, 314
International Convention on the
  Protection of the Rights of All
  Migrant Workers and Members
  of Their Families (ICRMW) 280,
  286–287
International Covenant on Civil and

Political Rights 281
International Covenant on Economic, Social and Cultural Rights (ICESCR) 113, 281, 314
International Human Rights Law (IHRL) 112
International Labour Organization (ILO) 105, 109, 144
International Labour Organization (ILO) Multilateral Framework on Labour Migration (MFLM) 283
international laws 225, 278, 288, 300, 319
International Monetary Fund (IMF) 62
International Organization for Migration (IOM) 125, 193, 277–280, 292
international relations 58
International Residual Mechanism for Criminal Tribunals 283
international security studies (ISS) 58
internationalisation 192
ISIS 67
Italy 84, 319
Ivory Coast (aka 'Côte d'Ivoire') 132

J
job intervention zones 265
Johannesburg 6, 17, 45, 62, 67, 71, 110, 164, 166, 169–170, 172–174, 177–183, 193, 220, 224, 227–232, 253, 262

K
Kenya 46, 70, 150
Kimberley 6, 45, 84, 193, 226, 305

L
labour laws 102, 108, 204
labour market 3, 17, 34, 91, 102–103, 129, 138, 142, 156, 158, 333–334
labour policies 128, 138
labour productivity 129, 138–141, 156, 158
labour reserves 45–46, 63, 219, 228
labour rights 17, 101–108, 116–117, 330
labour system 84, 251
Land Act of 1913 251
land reform 63
'Laws of Migration' 32
League Party 69 (see also 'Salvini, Matteo')
least-developed countries (LDCs) 127
Lesotho 2, 6, 27, 46, 85, 105, 111, 115, 131–132, 149, 196, 224, 226–276, 292, 301, 305
Liberia 148
local economy 4, 9, 193, 205, 213–214
low-income nation 70, 105, 230, 246–247
lower-middle-income nation 247
Luhya people 40
Luo people 40, 43
Luyia people 43

M
Mabusela, Faith 56, 67
Macro-Social Report 196
Madagascar 27, 132
Malawi 2, 6, 27, 46, 66, 105, 111, 115, 130, 149, 177, 224, 281–282, 292, 305
Mama, Amina 191
Mandela, Nelson (aka 'Madiba') 86, 284

Mapungubwe Institute for Strategic
Reflection (MISTRA) 83
*Nation Formation and Social
Cohesion in South Africa* 83
market economy 196, 197
Marxist 31, 35, 37–38, 108–110
Mauritania 150
Mauritius 27, 150
Mbeki, Thabo 208, 264
McKenzie, Gayton 65
middle-income nation 105, 230, 246
migrant labour 6, 13, 45, 85, 104–106,
108–110, 112, 115–117, 148, 169,
219, 227, 262, 283, 305, 328–330,
332, 337
migrant labour system 226, 228, 329
migrant-rights organisations (MROs)
110–111, 115–116
migrant tenant 221–224, 231, 233–235
migrant tenant–local landlord
relationship 222, 231, 237, 332
migrant women (see 'migration,
female')
migrant workers (see 'migrant
labour')
migrants 2–4, 6–7, 9–11, 13–18, 29–33,
44–47, 54–55, 57, 59–61, 63, 66–
68, 70–72, 79–82, 84–85, 87–96,
101–104, 106–108, 110–117, 126–
127, 129, 132, 134, 137–138, 150,
156, 164–174, 181, 183, 193–194,
203, 205, 207, 210, 214, 219–220,
222–227, 229–235, 237, 241–242,
247, 250, 252, 255–256, 267, 275,
278–279, 281, 287, 289, 291–292,
303, 307, 321, 327–335, 337–338
migration 1–13, 15–20, 25, 29, 31–33,
35, 38–39, 41–43, 47, 54–57, 59–

61, 68–73, 79–81, 84– 86, 88, 90,
95, 106, 110, 112, 123, 125–135,
145–148, 150, 152–154, 156–159,
168–169, 182, 191, 193–195, 207,
213, 219, 229–230, 241–250, 252,
255–256, 259–260, 262, 266–267,
276–280, 282–283, 287, 291–293,
297, 299, 301–303, 305, 307–308,
327–330, 332–338
circular 241, 262, 333
cross-border 114, 164, 166, 168,
171, 176, 183–184, 193, 256,
297, 302, 305, 308
economic 193–194
female 127–131, 133–138, 142–
145, 147–149, 152–159, 334
gendered 125, 128–130, 135,
137, 144–145, 147, 149–150,
152–154, 156–157, 333
global 130
internal 18, 45, 110, 114, 164, 166,
168, 171, 177, 182–183, 193,
230, 240, 242–243, 255
international 1, 2, 4–5, 15, 17, 20,
27–31, 34, 36–37, 39, 101–106,
108, 110, 112–113, 117, 125–
128, 145–146, 182, 193–194,
230, 240, 275, 278–279
irregular (aka 'illegal') 13–14,
28–29, 47, 56, 71, 87, 89,
106, 111, 137, 157, 193–194,
276–277, 291, 297–298, 302,
304–305, 307–308
labour 6, 17–18, 34, 45–47, 71,
84, 105, 135, 137, 193, 242,
246, 277–279
mixed 2, 13
pioneer 246

regional 19, 307–308

return 146

South–North 130, 144–145, 156

South–South 129–130, 144–145, 156–158

sustainable 336–337

transit 146, 147

Migration Act of 2002 57

migration crisis 14, 48

Migration Data Portal 292

migration governance 4, 15–16, 19, 27–28, 30–31, 34–35, 38–39, 46, 125, 129, 144–145, 153, 156, 158, 273, 275–280, 283–285, 289–293, 298, 304, 327–329, 336–337

Migration Governance Framework (MiGOF) 292

Migration Governance Indicators (MGI) 292–293

migration laws 64, 102, 106, 113, 116–117, 283

migration policies 6, 14, 34, 88, 106, 116, 157, 193–194, 196, 214, 276–279

Migration Policy Framework for Africa and Plan of Action (2018–2030) 8

migration system 13–14, 35, 45

migration theories 32, 330

migration–development nexus 4

migration-security nexus 55, 58, 61

Mineral Energy Complex 250

Mineral Revolution 219, 226, 250

monetary union 8

Morocco 70, 132

Motsoaledi, Dr Aaron 14, 283–288, 290–291

Mozambique 2, 6, 27, 46, 85, 105, 111, 130–131, 147, 149–150, 224, 226, 234, 281–282, 284, 297, 301–302, 305

multiculturalism 10

Multiple Deprivation Index 260

Museveni, President 112

Musina 313

N

Namibia 27, 66, 292, 307

Nandi people 43

(55th) National Conference of the African National Congress (ANC) 13

National Development Plan (NDP) 196, 205, 265

National Economic Development and Labour Council (Nedlac) 116, 287

National e-Government Strategy and Roadmap 316

National Health Act of 2003 (114)

National Health Insurance (NHI) 114

National Housing Code 235

National Housing Policy and Subsidy Programme 235

National Immigration Information System (NIIS) 320

National Intelligence Co-ordinating Committee (NICC) 284

national minimum wage 107

National Norms and Standards for School Funding (NNSSF) 262

National Spatial Development Framework (NSDF) 265

National Spatial Development Perspective (NSDP) 262

nationalism 34, 88, 92, 291, 328

nationalist 91, 93, 96, 115, 335

nation-building 10, 15–16, 79–83, 88–91, 94–95, 332

native foreigners 93

nativism 91

Neighbourhood Development Partnership Grant (NDPG) 264

neoclassical economic theory 29, 129, 135, 148

neocolonialism 37

neopatrimonialism 306–307, 309, 335

Netherlands 84, 318

new economics of labour migration (NELM) 4

New Regionalism Approach (NRA) 31, 36–37

Niger 148

Nigeria 2, 70, 111–112, 177

Nilotic Luo people 40 (see also 'Luo people')

non-communicable diseases (NCDs) 164–165, 167, 169

non-governmental organisation (NGO) 111, 170, 321

non-racialism 82

non-refoulement principle 281, 286, 316, 319, 321–322, 324

northern Africa 127

Northern Rhodesia (see 'Zambia')

Norway 318

nutrition insecurity 164 (see also 'food insecurity')

nutrition transition 17, 164–169, 174, 178–179, 181–182, 332, 334

Nxesi, Thulas 287

O

OAU Refugee Convention (see 'Organisation of African Unity (OAU) Convention Governing the Specific Aspects of Refugee Problems in Africa (1969)')

obesity 165–167, 169

occupational injuries and diseases 101, 103, 108, 114, 330

Operation Crackdown 88

Operation Dudula 231

Operation Fiela 88

Operation Passport 87

Orbán, Viktor 69

Organisation of African Unity (OAU) Convention Governing the Specific Aspects of Refugee Problems in Africa (1969) 112, 280, 284–285, 314, 337

Organisation for Economic Co-operation and Development (OECD) 248

organised labour 107

over-nutrition 165 (see also 'under-nutrition' and 'double burden of malnutrition')

P

Pakistan 111, 194, 331

pass laws 228, 251

Patriotic Alliance (PA) 65

patronage 108

political economy 18, 123, 192–194, 213

politics of belonging 10, 79–81, 84, 89, 94–95, 336

politics of fear 65

politics of identity 94

politics of othering 95
populism 4, 7, 20, 278, 328, 334–336
Portugal 84, 284
post-apartheid 1, 4, 6, 16, 55, 57, 79–
    80, 82–83, 85–88, 91–92, 94–95,
    105–106, 193–196, 198, 205, 213,
    220, 223, 228, 236, 252, 330–333
post-colonial 16, 46, 328, 337
post-democratic 259, 275–276
post-nationalist 83
pre-apartheid 94, 330
pre-colonial 1, 5–6, 34–35, 39–43, 250,
    337
primitive accumulation 37 (see also
    'Marxist')
Promotion of Access to Information
    Act (PAIA) of 2000 317
Promotion of Administrative Justice
    Act (PAJA) of 2000 288
Protection of Personal Information
    Act (POPI) of 2013 317
protectionism 69
Protocol on the Facilitation of
    Movement of Persons (2005) 8, 301
public employment programmes
    (PEPs) 242
public-interest law organisations
    (PILOs) 116
purposive sampling 223
push-pull factors 4, 7, 32–33, 35, 126,
    129, 158, 194, 246, 301
Put South Africa First 67

R
racism 61, 228
racist 40, 81, 85
rainbow nation 85, 92–94, 102, 329,
    331

RDP houses (aka 'RDPs') 221
realism 58
Reconstruction and Development
    Programme (RDP) 86, 220–221,
    263
redistribution 7, 18, 96, 240–241, 243,
    246–248, 260, 263, 266
refugee policies 111
Refugee Reception Office (RRO)
    313, 315–319, 321, 323–324
refugee status determination officer
    (RSDO) 288
refugees 6, 14, 57, 70–72, 85, 105,
    112, 114, 194, 225–226, 235–237,
    281–284, 286–291, 313–318,
    320–324, 337
Refugees Act of 1998 13, 57, 71, 89,
    114, 195, 285, 288, 314, 317
Refugees Amendment Bill of 2015 89
regional development 19, 297, 299,
    301–302, 309
regional economic community 27
regional economic integration (see
    'regional integration')
regional economy 4, 207, 212–214
Regional Infrastructure Development
    Master Plan (RIDMP) 2012–2027
    197
regional integration 7–8, 19, 36, 192,
    212–214, 299, 307, 334
regionalisation 36
regionalism 36–37
Rhodesia (see 'Zimbabwe')
Rosa Luxemburg Foundation 109
Rwanda 46, 285
Rwanda Act of 2024 291

S

SADC Declaration and Treaty 8

SADC Industrialisation Strategy and Roadmap (SISR) 2015–2063 197

SADC Regional Indicative Strategic Development Plan 8

Salvini, Matteo 69 (see also 'League Party')

School Infrastructure Backlog Grant (SIBG) 264

Sector Education and Training Authorities (SETAs) 316

securitisation of borders 297–299, 301, 303, 308–309, 335–336

securitisation of migration 4, 11–12, 15–16, 19–20, 54–56, 58–61, 68–73, 88, 102, 278, 290, 297, 327, 334 (see also 'Copenhagen School of Security Studies')

segregation 61, 228, 267

Senegal 150

separate development 63, 225, 229, 251

Seychelles 27

single currency 8

slave trade 41

small, medium and micro enterprises (SMMEs) 201, 204–205, 207–208, 210–213, 334

social capital 3

social cohesion 9–10, 15–16, 18, 25, 70, 72, 79–83, 85–92, 94–95, 220, 327–328, 330, 332

social grants 64, 232–233

social integration 72

social justice 11, 17, 101, 103, 115, 300

social security 105, 107, 113

social tension 10

social welfare 9

Solidarity Center 102, 109, 115

Somalia 94, 110–111, 224, 331

South Africa(n) 1–7, 9, 11–17, 19–20, 27, 30, 34, 39, 45–47, 54–57, 59–68, 70–71, 73, 79–95, 101–106, 108–116, 123, 125–126, 128–129, 131–132, 135–138, 144–148, 150, 152–153, 155, 157–159, 165, 167–171, 174, 181, 192–198, 200–203, 205, 207–214, 219–220, 222–223, 225–232, 234–236, 240, 243, 249–250, 253, 258–260, 267, 275–276, 278, 283–289, 291–293, 297–298, 301–302, 304–305, 307–309, 313–319, 322–323, 327–334, 336–338

South African Cities Network (SACN) 230

South African Domestic Service and Allied Workers Union (SADSAWU) 109, 116

South African Human Rights Commission 321

Position Paper on Access to Basic Education for Undocumented Learners in South Africa 321

South African Police Service (SAPS) 72, 86–87, 90, 290, 320–321

South African Schools Act of 1996 321

southern Africa(n) 1–7, 14–16, 18–19, 31, 37–39, 45–46, 48, 85, 106, 127, 130, 148–149, 165, 169, 192–193, 196, 198–200, 213, 219, 250, 297, 299, 304–305, 307, 327

Southern African Customs Union (SACU) 213, 334

Southern African Development
  Community (SADC) 6–8, 11, 13,
  15, 18–19, 27, 29–31, 35–37, 47,
  54, 72, 85, 192–194, 196–198, 200,
  207, 209, 212–213, 286, 292–293,
  297–298, 300–304, 306–307, 309,
  334, 336
Southern Rhodesia (see 'Zimbabwe')
Soviet Union 58, 68, 299
Soweto 18, 171, 219–234, 236–237,
  332
Spain 84, 319
spatial development 241, 249, 255,
  267, 333
spatial development initiatives (SDIs)
  262–263, 333
spatial disparities (aka 'mismatches')
  243, 246–248, 251, 253, 258–259,
  267, 333
spatial divisions 7, 18, 20, 232, 240–
  243, 249, 258–259, 263, 266–267
spatial (in)justice 63, 228, 264
spatial planning 225–226
Spatial Planning and Land Use
  Management Act (SPLUMA) of
  2013 264–265
spatial policies 260, 266, 333
spatial rebalancing 249
spatial transformation 9, 18, 241,
  243–247, 249–250, 253, 262–263,
  265–267, 332–333
spaza shops 18, 64 191–192, 202–203,
  206–207, 210–211, 222, 224,
  232–233, 331
special economic zones (SEZs) 263
Special Integrated Presidential
  Projects 263
Statistics South Africa Quarterly

Labour Force Survey 109
structural transformation 9, 18,
  212–214, 245, 248
sub-Saharan Africa (SSA) 127, 144,
  275
supermarketisation (aka 'supermarket
  revolution') 192, 203
survivalist business 2, 201, 203, 206
sustainable development 225, 337
Sustainable Development Goals
  (SDGs) 114, 198, 292
Sustainable Livelihoods Foundation
  (SLF) 232
Swaziland (see 'eSwatini')
Sweden Democrats 69

T
Tanzania 27, 46, 70, 196, 227
Tembisa 66
territorialisation 44
Third World 61
Todaro Paradox 242
township 10, 18, 63, 92, 171, 191–193,
  202–203, 205–206, 210, 212, 220–
  223, 228–229, 231–234, 236–237,
  252, 264, 331–332, 334
township economy 18, 64, 192,
  200–203, 212–213, 220, 230, 232,
  236, 334
trade 133, 137, 156–158, 193, 197, 207,
  212, 298, 329
trade liberalisation 166–167, 196
trade policies 157, 196
trade theory 7
trade unions 103, 107–110, 115–116,
  331
transhumance 41–42
Transition and Health during

Urbanisation of South Africans (THUSA) 167
Transkei, Bopthuthatswana, Venda and Ciskei (TBVC) states 284
transnationalism 15
Treaty Establishing the African Economic Community (1991) 8
Trump, Donald 69
Tshwane 313
Tutu, Archbishop Desmond 86

U
Uganda 46, 111–112, 281–282, 287
UN Convention Relating to the Status of Refugees (1951) 112, 225, 280–282, 284–287, 314, 337
UN Global Compact for Migration 283
UN Global Compact for Safe, Orderly and Regular Migration (GCM) 28, 292
UN Protocol Relating to the Status of Refugees (1967) 280–281, 314
UN Refugee Convention (see 'UN Convention Relating to the Status of Refugees (1951)')
under-nutrition 165 (see also 'over-nutrition' and 'double burden of malnutrition')
Unemployment Insurance Fund (UIF) 66
Union of South Africa 227–228
unions (see 'trade unions')
United Domestic Workers of South Africa (UDWOSA) 116
United Kingdom (UK) 69, 84, 291, 319
United Nations (UN) 28, 84, 130–131, 230, 281, 286–287
United Nations Department of Economic and Social Affairs (UNDESA) 127, 193
United Nations Development Programme (UNDP) 59, 64, 95
United Nations Food and Agriculture Organization 233
United Nations High Commissioner for Refugees (UNHCR) 14, 236
United Nations Office for the Coordination of Humanitarian Affairs (UNOCHA) 56, 71
United Nations Security Council (UNSC) 67
United States of America (USA) 299
Universal Declaration of Human Rights (UDHR) 281
University of KwaZulu-Natal 231
University of the Witwatersrand Human Research Ethics Committee 171
upper-middle-income nation 70
Urban Areas Act of 1923 228
Urban Renewal Programme 264
Urban Renewal Tax Incentive 264
Urban Settlements Development Grant (USDG) 264

V
value chain 200–201, 210–211, 250
venture capital 204

W
welfare state 10, 55
West Africa 54, 126
White Paper on Citizenship, Immigration and Refugee

Protection: Towards a Complete
Overhaul of the Migration System
in South Africa (2023) 13–14, 281,
283, 285–286, 288–289, 291, 336
White Paper on International
Migration (2017) 5, 13, 39, 71, 276,
291, 293
Witwatersrand 84, 226–227, 305
World Bank 30, 62–63, 105, 194, 209,
244, 246–247, 253
World Development Indicators
(WDI) 141

X
xenophobia 7, 9, 16, 54, 56–57, 62,

67, 89, 91, 110–111, 116–117, 207,
230–231, 235, 287, 328, 331–332

Z
Zambia 27, 45–47, 85, 105, 111, 177,
226, 292, 301, 305
Zimbabwe 2, 5–6, 27, 30, 34, 43,
45–47, 66, 85, 94, 105–106,
110–111, 115–116, 130–131, 138,
147, 149–150, 173, 177, 184, 196,
224, 235, 284–286, 292, 297, 302,
304–305, 332
Zimbabwe exemption permit (ZEP)
224, 276, 291
Zungula, Vuyo 55–56, 61, 64–66